P9-ANY-078

VULNERABLE INFANTS
A PSYCHOSOCIAL DILEMMA

VULNERABLE INFANTS

A PSYCHOSOCIAL DILEMMA

Edited by
Jane Linker Schwartz, R.N., M.N., M.S.W.

Lecturer, Division of Continuing Education
University of Washington, School of Nursing
University of Washington, School of Social Work

Lawrence H. Schwartz, M.D.

Clinical Associate Professor
Department of Psychiatry
University of Washington, School of Medicine

McGraw-HILL BOOK COMPANY
A Blakiston Publication

New York   St. Louis   San Francisco   Auckland   Bogotá   Düsseldorf
Johannesburg   London   Madrid   Mexico   Montreal   New Delhi
Panama   Paris   São Paulo   Singapore   Sydney   Tokyo   Toronto

RJ
250
.V84
R 1977
2 5
V 84

To Katherine J. Hoffman, who dedicated over 30 years to the education
of students at the University of Washington School of Nursing.

VULNERABLE INFANTS
A PSYCHOSOCIAL DILEMMA

Copyright © 1977 by McGraw-Hill, Inc. All rights reserved. Printed in
the United States of America. No part of this publication may be reproduced, stored in a retrieval system, or transmitted, in any form or by
any means, electronic, mechanical, photocopying, recording, or otherwise, without the prior written permission of the publisher.

1 2 3 4 5 6 7 8 9 0 D O D O 7 8 3 2 1 0 9 8 7

This book was set in Times Roman by National ShareGraphics, Inc.
The editors were Sally J. Barhydt and James R. Belser;
the cover was designed by John Hite;
the production supervisor was Thomas J. LoPinto.
R. R. Donnelley & Sons Company was printer and binder.

Library of Congress Cataloging in Publication Data
Main entry under title:
Vulnerable infants.

   "A Blakiston publication."
   Includes index.
   1.   Infants (Premature)—Addresses, essays, lectures. 2.   Pregnancy—
Psychological aspects—Addresses, essays, lectures. 3.   Maternal depriva-
tion—Addresses, essays, lectures. 4.   Maternal health services—Address-
es, essays, lectures. I.   Schwartz, Jane Linker.
II. Schwartz, Lawrence H.
RJ250.V84   618.3   76-16793
ISBN 0-07-055764-0

222 5056

Contents

List of Contributors   ix
Foreword   xiii
Preface   xvii
Acknowledgments   xxi

CHAPTER 1   Introduction   1

CHAPTER 2   Psychosocial Aspects of High-Risk Pregnancy   9

Commentary

Poverty as a Criterion of Risk   Howard J. Osofsky and
Norman Kendall   14

*Emotional Crises of School-Age Girls during Pregnancy
and Early Motherhood*   Maurine LaBarre   30

v

08866

WITHDRAWN
ST. CATHERINE LIBRARY

87 1931

A Study of the Relationship between Maternal Life-Change Events and Premature Delivery   Jane L. Schwartz   47

Psychosocial Assets, Life Crisis and the Prognosis of Pregnancy   Katherine B. Nuckolls, John Cassel, and Berton H. Kaplan   62

CHAPTER 3   The Crisis of Premature Birth   76

Commentary

Maternal Reactions to Premature Birth Viewed as an Acute Emotional Disorder   David M. Kaplan and Edward A. Mason   80

Four Studies of Crisis in Parents of Prematures   Gerald Caplan, Edward A. Mason, and David M. Kaplan   89

CHAPTER 4   Effects of Separation on Mother-Infant Bonding   108

Commentary

Mothers Separated from Their Newborn Infants   Marshall H. Klaus and John H. Kennell   113

The Effects of Denial of Early Mother-Infant Interaction on Maternal Self-Confidence   Marjorie J. Seashore, Aimee Dorr Leifer, Clifford R. Barnett, and P. Herbert Leiderman   136

The Critical Nature of the Post-Partum Period in the Human for the Establishment of the Mother-Infant Bond: A Controlled Study   Lee Salk   150

Development of Object Relations during the First Year of Life   Kenneth S. Robson   157

CHAPTER 5   Sequelae   178

Commentary

Reactions to the Threatened Loss of a Child: A Vulnerable Child Syndrome: Pediatric Management of the Dying Child, Part III   Morris Green and Albert J. Solnit   183

Psychologic Sequelae of Early Infancy Health Crises
William B. Carey   195

Failure to Thrive: A Retrospective Profile   Eleanor
Shaheen, Doris Alexander, Marie Truskowsky, and
Giulio J. Barbero   202

Studies of Child Abuse and Infant Accidents   Elizabeth
Elmer, Grace Gregg, Byron Wright, John B. Reinhart,
Thomas McHenry, Bertram Girdony, Paul Geisel, and
Clarissa Wittenberg   214

Improved Prognosis for Infants of Very Low Birthweight
Ann L. Stewart and E. O. R. Reynolds   243

*Communication Skills in Five-Year-Old Children with
High-Risk Neonatal Histories*   Carol H. Ehrlich,
Esther Shapiro, Bud D. Kimball, and Muriel Huttner   262

CHAPTER 6   Critical Issues in Comprehensive Care for
Mothers and Infants

270

Commentary

One Hundred Pregnant Adolescents: Treatment Approaches in a University Hospital   Helen O. Dickens,
Emily Hartshorne Mudd, Celso-Ramon Garcia, Karen
Tomar, and David Wright   273

Reducing Neonatal Mortality Rate with Nurse-Midwives
Barry S. Levy, Frederick S. Wilkinson, and William
M. Marine   288

*High-Risk Pregnancy, II: A Pattern of Comprehensive
Maternal and Child Care*   Howard N. Jacobson and
Duncan E. Reid   299

*Critical Issues in Newborn Intensive Care: A Conference
Report and Policy Proposal*   A. R. Jonsen, R. H.
Phibbs, W. H. Tooley, and M. J. Garland   312

*Involuntary Euthanasia of Defective Newborns: A Legal
Analysis*   John A. Robertson   335

INDEX   365

List of Contributors

Doris Alexander, M.S.W., A.C.S.W.
Children's Hospital of Philadelphia
Philadelphia, Pennsylvania

Giulio J. Barbero, M.D.
Professor and Chairman
Department of Child Health
University of Missouri School
   of Medicine
Columbia, Missouri

Clifford R. Barnett, Ph.D.
Department of Anthropology
Stanford University
Palo Alto, California

Gerald Caplan, M.D., D.P.M.
Clinical Professor of Psychiatry
Laboratory of Community
   Psychiatry
Harvard Medical School
Boston, Massachusetts

William Carey, M.D.
Department of Pediatrics
University of Pennsylvania Medical
   School at the Children's Hospital
   of Philadelphia
Philadelphia, Pennsylvania

John Cassel, M.D.
Department of Epidemiology
School of Public Health
University of North Carolina
Chapel Hill, North Carolina

Helen O. Dickens, M.D.
Associate Professor of Obstetrics
   and Gynecology
Department of Obstetrics and
   Gynecology
University of Pennsylvania School
   of Medicine
Philadelphia, Pennsylvania

Carol Ehrlich, Ph.D.
Director, Audiology and Speech
  Pathology and Adjunct Professor
University of Denver
The Children's Hospital
Denver, Colorado

Elizabeth Elmer, M.S.S.
Assistant Professor of Social Case
  Work
School of Medicine
University of Pittsburgh
Pittsburgh, Pennsylvania

Celso-Ramon Garcia, M.D.
Professor and Director
Division of Human Reproduction
Department of Obstetrics and
  Gynecology
University of Pennsylvania School
  of Medicine
Philadelphia, Pennsylvania

M. J. Garland, Ph.D.
Department of Pediatrics
University of California Medical
  Center
San Francisco, California

Bertram Girdony, M.D.
School of Medicine
University of Pittsburgh
Pittsburgh, Pennsylvania

Paul Geisel, Ph.D.
School of Medicine
University of Pittsburgh
Pittsburgh, Pennsylvania

Morris Green, M.D.
Professor and Chairman
Indiana University School
  of Medicine
Indianapolis, Indiana

Grace Gregg, M.D.
Associate Professor of Pediatrics
University of Pittsburgh School
  of Medicine
Director, Developmental Clinic
  of Children's Hospital
Pittsburgh, Pennsylvania

Muriel Huttner (deceased)
Formerly of Children's Hospital
Denver, Colorado

Howard N. Jacobson, M.D.
Professor, Department of Commu-
  nity Medicine
College of Medicine and Dentistry
  of New Jersey
Rutgers Medical School
University Heights
Piscataway, New Jersey

A. R. Jonsen, S.J. Ph.D.
Department of Pediatrics
University of California Medical
  Center
San Francisco, California

Berton H. Kaplan, Ph.D.
Professor of Epidemiology
School of Public Health
University of North Carolina
Chapel Hill, North Carolina

David M. Kaplan, Ph.D.
Associate Professor and Director
Division of Clinical Social Work
Stanford University School
  of Medicine
Palo Alto, California

Norman Kendall, M.D.
Department of Pediatrics
Temple University Health Sciences
  Center
Philadelphia, Pennsylvania

John H. Kennell, M.D.
Associate Professor of Pediatrics
Case Western Reserve University
School of Medicine and University
  Hospitals
Cleveland, Ohio

Bud D. Kimball, Ph.D.
Regional Audiologist
Southeast Alaska Communicative
  Disorders Program
State Health and Social Services
Public Health Service Hospital
Mt. Edgecumbe, Alaska

Marshall H. Klaus, M.D.
Professor of Pediatrics
Department of Pediatrics and
  Director of Neonatal Nurseries
Case Western Reserve University
  School of Medicine and Universi-
  ty Hospitals
Cleveland, Ohio

Maurine LaBarre, A.C.S.W.
Associate Professor of Psychiatric
  Social Work
Division of Child Psychiatry
Duke University Medical Center
Durham, North Carolina

P. Herbert Leiderman, M.D.
Professor of Psychiatry
Stanford University School
  of Medicine
Stanford, California

Aimee Dorr Leifer, Ph.D.
Assistant Professor
Harvard Graduate School
  of Education
Boston, Massachusetts

Barry S. Levy, M.D.
Acting State Epidemiologist
Minnesota Department of Health
  and Medical Epidemiologist
Bureau of Epidemiology
Center for Disease Control
Minneapolis, Minnesota

William M. Marine, M.D., M.P.H.
Department of Preventive Medicine
  and Community Health
Emory University School
  of Medicine
Atlanta, Georgia

Edward A. Mason, M.D.
Assistant Clinical Professor
  of Psychiatry
Laboratory of Community
  Psychiatry
Harvard Medical School
Boston, Massachusetts

Thomas McHenry, M.D.
School of Medicine
University of Pittsburgh
Pittsburgh, Pennsylvania

Emily Hartshorne Mudd, M.S.W., Ph.D.
Professor Emerita of Family Study
  in Psychiatry
Hospital, University of
  Pennsylvania
Philadelphia, Pennsylvania

Katherine B. Nuckolls, R.N., Ph.D.
Professor of Nursing
Yale University School of Nursing
New Haven, Connecticut

Howard J. Osofsky, M.D.
Professor, Department of Obstetrics
  and Gynecology
Temple University Health Sciences
  Center
Philadelphia, Pennsylvania

R. H. Phibbs, M.D.
Department of Pediatrics
University of California Medical
  Center
San Francisco, California

Duncan E. Reid, M.D. (deceased)
Formerly William Lambert
  Richardson Professor of Obstetrics,
  and Chairman of the Department
  of Obstetrics and Gynecology
Harvard Medical School
Boston, Massachusetts;
Chief-of-Staff, Boston Lying-In
  Hospital
Boston, Massachusetts

John B. Reinhart, M.D.
University of Pittsburgh School of
  Medicine
Pittsburgh, Pennsylvania

E. O. R. Reynolds, M.D., M.R.C.P.
Medical Research Council
Human Biochemical Genetics Unit
University College and
Department of Pediatrics

University College Hospital and
  Medical School
London, England

John A. Robertson, J.D.
Assistant Professor of Law
University of Wisconsin
Madison, Wisconsin

Kenneth S. Robson, M.D.
Associate Professor of Psychiatry
Director of Training in Child
  Psychiatry
New England Medical Center
  Hospital
Tufts University School of Medicine
Boston, Massachusetts

Lee Salk, Ph.D.
Clinical Professor
Director, Pediatric Psychology
New York Hospital—Cornell
  Medical Center
New York, New York

Marjorie J. Seashore, Ph.D.
Associate Professor and
  Chairperson
Department of Sociology
San Francisco State University
San Francisco, California

Eleanor Shaheen, M.D.
Staff Doctor
Child Health Department
University of Missouri
Columbia, Missouri

Esther Shapiro, Ph.D.
Child Psychologist
Children's Hospital Mental Health
  Center
Denver, Colorado

Albert J. Solnit, M.D.
Sterling Professor of Pediatrics and
  Psychiatry
Director, Yale University Child
  Study Center
New Haven, Connecticut

Ann L. Stewart, M.B., Ch.B.
Medical Research Council
Human Biochemical Genetics Unit
Galton Laboratory
University College London
London, England

Karen Tomar, M.S.W.
Division of Human Reproduction
Department of Obstetrics and
  Gynecology
University of Pennsylvania School
  of Medicine
Philadelphia, Pennsylvania

W. H. Tooley, M.D.
Department of Pediatrics
University of California Medical
  Center
San Francisco, California

Marie Truskowsky, R.N.
Children's Hospital of Philadelphia
Philadelphia, Pennsylvania

Frederick S. Wilkinson, M.D.
Staff, Permanentee Medical Group
Department of Emergency
  Medicine
Oakland, California

Clarissa Wittenberg
School of Medicine
University of Pittsburgh
Pittsburgh, Pennsylvania

Byron Wright, M.A.
University of Pittsburgh School
  of Medicine
Pittsburgh, Pennsylvania

David Wright, M.D.
Resident, Pathology
Hospital, University of
  Pennsylvania
Philadelphia, Pennsylvania

Foreword

This volume will be meaningful to all persons whose interests, either personally or professionally, relate to the outcome of pregnancy and/or the subsequent growth and development of children. For the last several decades the overriding concern has been to decrease maternal and infant mortality, and current statistics would indicate that in the United States we have achieved a reduction. This reduction has been accomplished through improved technology based on a scientific understanding of cause and effect with respect to the mortality issue. The level of maternal and infant mortality, however, is still moderate, and in fact, the picture of infant morbidity suggests a slight increase in rate. Particularly the current trends in infant morbidity, meaning problems in the subsequent growth and development of children, relate to the whole theme of quality of life once life has been established. This volume addresses essentially that point: the quality of life and the critical issues that relate to the outcome of pregnancy and the subsequent growth and development of children.

Jane and Larry Schwartz, whose professional backgrounds include nursing, social work, psychiatry, and psychoanalysis, have a unique perspective from which to offer this collection of readings providing a matrix of information, ideas, and charges directly related to basic preventive mental health issues. From their clinical background they have been able to draw together the best current and classical literature addressing our scientific understanding of the psychosocial influences on the quality of life of mothers and children. This volume stresses the need for increasing attention to the effects of environmental and psychosocial influences on basic life processes. It further suggests that improvements in the life of children can only come about by a commitment to the understanding and development of resources to alter the basic environmental conditions which greatly contribute to the poor quality of life associated with poverty and such specific childhood problems as prematurity, child abuse, and neglect. While most of the studies presented in this volume report dramatic cases in which poor outcome is evident, they represent only a small number of the children and families in our society who suffer conditions that do not allow optimal development or do not enhance the quality of their lives. We no longer need to wonder if the environment influences outcome. We have, as this volume attests, the proof that it does. We are now on the threshold of an exciting opportunity to further the development of our understanding of the specific events that make an individual child or family resistant or susceptible to health problems.

A major topic throughout this book is the particular problem of premature births of infants. The cause for prematurity is perhaps related to environmental stress, and the event itself causes further environmental stress for the family. Many issues in this one area alone desperately need to be explored. One such issue is the development of attachment or bonding on the part of the parent and infant and the influence of the separation which traditionally occurs when the infant is premature. We have strong reason to believe both from animal research and from human studies that there are sensitive periods in which the events that occur, such as the physical proximity or the separation of parents and infants, can have a direct effect on the attachment outcome. There are other ways in which the premature infant differs from the term infant. More study now going on suggests that one of the important roles the infant plays in influencing his caregiver's reaction to him is the type of feedback he gives to the caregiver and that the premature infant often gives less feedback, which again puts this parent-infant dyad into particular risk for attachment and bonding behavior. The work that is presented here in these areas represents the most pertinent literature that exists to explain some of the phenomena which have been studied and which suggest new areas of study and avenues of intervention.

The question which this volume raises and attempts to answer is whether our society can afford *not* to support programs which help identify and prevent maternal and infant mortality and morbidity. The waste of human potential resulting from situations of infant abuse, accidents, and failure to thrive indicates that from both a humanistic and an economic point of view, society as a whole, and particularly the professional community, must alter our present strong inclination to focus on pathology. Our orientation should be changed to include programs of screening and assessment which look for a proneness toward disability and which aim toward preventing as well as reducing disability.

It is possible to improve the quality of life of mothers and children. Certainly the final chapter in this book is illustrative of the exciting programs which are being implemented to identify and provide preventive approaches to reduce distress in our population. In contrast to our past preoccupation with technology, the issues raised by this volume suggest that our approach must be one based on a humanistic viewpoint and one which involves strengthening the network of human interaction in families, neighborhoods, communities, and society at large.

This volume reflects the fact that we are now at a crossroads in viewing the process of health and support during pregnancy and the early newborn period. We have gained a tremendous amount of information about the factors that support a healthy pregnancy and a healthy parent-child relationship. We have identified certain environmental variables which put parents and infants at risk for attachment and for subsequent emotional and cognitive development.

In my opinion this selection of readings and editorial comments is a primer which should be useful as a collection of basic knowledge to further our understanding and to suggest additional research related to high-risk pregnancy and the vulnerable newborn. This volume will be a contribution to directing more specific attention and research toward improving the quality of life for all mothers and their infants.

Kathryn Barnard, R.N., Ph.D.
Professor of Nursing
University of Washington School of Nursing

Preface

This volume represents the outgrowth of a study undertaken in 1972 at the University of Washington Graduate School of Nursing. My clinical specialty during that period was maternal-child health nursing. A long-time interest in preventive medicine and psychiatry had led me back to the study of the earliest infant-maternal relationships.

I was especially fortunate to have had the opportunity of carrying out my work under the supervision of Dr. Kathryn Barnard, a nurse-scientist, who had achieved prominence for her research related to premature infants. I was also privileged to have access to the neonatal intensive-care units of two medical centers where it was possible to observe the nursing staff as well as the infants and their families for approximately six months. Many infants were eventually able to leave the intensive-care units and join their families. Other children died, and I was sometimes able to talk with their bereaved parents.

As a graduate student I visited the homes of over twenty premature infants, some as long as three months after their birth. I interviewed at least thirty parents of premature infants, some at home and others while their babies were still in the unit. During the course of my study, an equal number of parents of full-term infants were interviewed. The masters thesis which resulted from my work, "A Study of the Relationship between Maternal Life Changes and Premature Delivery," is included (in part) in this book.

While visiting the homes of premature infants and especially those in the lower income groups, I became aware of the kinds of problems which beset many of the parents of these infants. There were mothers who lived alone and without significant help from family or friends, had the responsibility for a child who was small in size, unusually fragile, and whose infants sometimes had other physical problems or defects. It was clear that when a mother was poor and alone, the cumulative burden of infant care could at times become almost unbearable. One young mother had rescusitated her premature infant by mouth-to-mouth respiration when the baby temporarily suffered respiratory arrest. In this book we discuss respiratory problems as important occurrences in premature infants.

In another instance I visited a young mother who had premature twins. One twin died in the hospital. When I saw the mother, she was caring for her surviving twin and a six-year-old daughter living at home with a portable kidney machine. This mother was poor, limited in education, and with the minimal financial and emotional support to face this crisis.

It should come as no surprise to readers of this book that the poor, young, and single mothers have the greatest difficulties in managing high-risk infants and that these children later develop a disproportionate number of physical and mental sequelae. It is especially to this population that our efforts at improved comprehensive maternal-child care should be directed.

Since I began my career twenty-five years ago as an instructor of psychiatric nursing, that profession has changed significantly. The role of the psychiatric nurse has expanded to include preventive mental health as well as the integration of psychological concepts in patient care. Although my interest in psychiatry has remained, the focus has changed to the areas of prevention. When I worked in mental hospitals many years ago, I asked myself how the tragedies I saw might have been prevented. I believed then, as now, that early intervention is the key to the prevention of future pathology.

The coauthor of this volume, my husband, Lawrence Schwartz, has a background in psychiatry and psychoanalysis. Both of us have been influenced by a theoretical background which is psychoanalytic. The clinical information here presented, however, has more emphasis on psychosocial factors as they influence health. As a psychoanalyst, my husband's interest in this work is related to the contributions made by Margaret Mahler, Anna Freud, Rene Spitz, and John Bowlby.

This book represents a careful and often difficult selection from over 600 readings. The selections here include the work of eminent scientists with wide-ranging interests and humanistic orientation. In addition we have distilled from our own experience working with parents and professionals who are involved with these problems. We offer this book to encourage a fuller integration of the psychosocial aspects of high-risk pregnancy and prematurity with the physiological factors. We hope to present the state of our present knowledge in an attempt to explore how accumulated information can be applied wisely and effectively to help solve this major maternal and child health problem.

We then attempt to acquaint the reader with a variety of observations, studies, and opinions relating to high-risk pregnancy; the crisis surrounding delivery of premature and other high-risk infants; the impact of intensive infant care on the child and on the maternal child relationship; possible sequelae to high-risk infancy; and suggestions regarding prediction, prevention, and alleviation of these serious problems. We have also included further suggested readings and references.

Scientific findings and statistics in the readings within this volume were used to support specific opinions, but caution is always necessary in interpreting results, especially considering the small size of sample populations which is offered. Ideally, research projects are terminated when investigators believe they have collected sufficient data. It is hoped that any gaps will be filled by future researchers.

Since observations are difficult to condense and transmit to others, the articles are quoted in their entirety. We have attempted in our comments to coordinate the readings and add information from other sources.

This book is designed primarily for those people working with infants. It is our hope that nurses, physicians, social workers, and other caretakers will find new knowledge along with helpful organization of more familiar data.

In America, the poor have twice and sometimes three times the average number of high-risk premature infants. We can conclude, somewhat pessimistically, that there will continue to be a proliferation of these infants as a tragic reality of ghetto life unless significant social health changes occur.

Our intent throughout this book has been to offer psychosocial balance to the heavy emphasis heretofore placed on the technological aspects of perinatal care. We hope that this documentation will hasten the day when the social and psychological problems of high-risk infants and their families will be given the attention and care they need and deserve.

Jane Linker Schwartz
Lawrence H. Schwartz

Acknowledgments

Many colleagues and friends have assisted us during the development of this book, which began during graduate study at the University of Washington School of Nursing. Dr. Katherine Hoffman and Dean Madelaine Leininger offered support and encouragement from the beginning of this project.

We are especially grateful for the assistance of the maternal and child health nursing school faculty, especially Patricia Rose and Dr. Katherine Barnard. Dr. Thomas Holmes, of the Department of Psychiatry, University of Washington Medical School, was especially helpful during the initial phases of our work.

Murray McCord and other colleagues in the Social Service Department of the University of Washington Hospital offered valuable suggestions.

Dr. Edith Buxbaum provided psychoanalytic insights concerning both high-risk mothers and maternal-infant interactions. Dr. Marshall Klaus was not only one of the contributing authors to this volume, but also made a number of significant contributions based on his extensive experience in the field of perinatology.

We wish to thank our editor. Dr. Dorothy Bestor, for her suggestions regarding manuscript content and form, as well as for her assistance in the organization of the book.

Others to whom we wish to express our gratitude include Dr. Frances Abel, Robert Bennet, Dr. Roxy Berlin, Clella Cronshey, Helen Fraser, Gertrude McCord, and Alice Price.

We are indebted to the librarians of the University of Washington Health Service Library for assisting us through the use of the Medical Literature Analyst and Retrieval System, and in particular to Nancy Blaze and Doris Deschene. Katherine Barber, King County Medical Librarian, also lent assistance to our research efforts.

We wish to extend appreciation to our part-time student assistants from the University of Washington, particularly to Penelope Peterson, Lawrence Kreisman, and Dianna Dodson. To our secretary, Aletha Barnes, we wish to pay special tribute for preparation of this manuscript as well as for the years of association in working together.

Our warmest thanks are extended to the many authors listed as contributors to this volume. Their combined work has enabled us to develop our theme and to help document and understand the conditions relating to high-risk mothers and infants.

For permission to reprint the included articles, we wish to thank the publishers of the following journals: *American Journal of Epedemiology, American Journal of Obstetrics and Gynecology, American Journal of Orthopsychiatry, American Journal of Public Health, Clinical Obstetrics and Gynecology, Clinical Pediatrics, Community Mental Health Journal, Diseases of the Nervous System, Journal of the American Academy of Child Psychiatry, Journal of Personality and Social Psychology, Journal of Speech and Hearing Research, Mental Health Progress Reports, The New England Journal of Medicine, The Pediatric Clinics of North America, Pediatrics, Seminars in Psychiatry,* and *Stanford Law Review.*

In particular, we would like to thank those parents of premature infants whose cooperation provided us with personal experience and understanding about the subject matter of this book.

Finally, our deepest appreciation and thanks to Bhanu Goradia and our children, Karen, Joel, and David, for their patience, understanding, and support during the time this manuscript was in process.

Jane Linker Schwartz
Lawrence H. Schwartz

Chapter 1

Introduction

Major efforts have been made for at least half a century to bring to the attention of professionals and the public the plight of America's children. The White House Conference held at the beginning of this decade emphasized the seriousness of the problem with the following statement:

> America's families, and their children, are in trouble, trouble so deep and pervasive as to threaten the future of our nation. The source of the trouble is nothing less than a national neglect of children and those primarily engaged in their care—American parents.[1]

The broad comprehensive reports on American children indicate that vast sections of our population neglect their offspring. The "battered child" represents a portion of this group, and has finally received nationwide attention because the abuse is visible and undeniable. Children who suffer from neglect may be damaged in personality as well as in physical health.

[1] *Report to the President: White House Conference on Children,* U.S. Government Printing Office, Washington, 1971.

High-risk newborns constitute a significant percentage of those children and represent a group which is especially vulnerable to trauma. In spite of remarkable technical advances in the physical care of these infants, many of them die, while, all too frequently, the psychological and emotional needs of those who live are minimized or ignored. The largest number of children at high risk are newborns. Ironically, the greatest cost to the society is not from those infants who die but from those who survive, sustaining injuries or emotional trauma and often facing a lifetime with some disability.

Many of the children described in the articles that follow suffer from impaired intellectual function or behavioral disturbances, including hyperactivity, distractability, and low attention span, all factors contributing to intellectual retardation and problem behavior. The greatest impact is on the poorer segment of the population, especially nonwhites. This massive human damage results in enormous subsequent direct cost as well as in reduced productivity, lowered income, unemployability, and institutionalization.

These children represent a major public-health problem which is too often minimized and too little understood. The population with which this book is concerned is infants who weigh less than 5½ pounds, or 2,500 grams, at birth. They are our most vulnerable children in relation to disease and death. The latest clinical description for these children is "low birthweight." This category includes two groups of high-risk infants—the premature infants and the full-term infants who are "small for date." It is a generally accepted fact that the lower the birthweight of the infant, the higher the risk.

Our approach to understanding these infants and their mothers is from a psychological rather than a physiological view. Low-birthweight infants, whether premature or small for date, come most frequently from poor socioeconomic environments. To ignore the psychosocial factors in small, sick, high-risk infants is to deny the importance of epidemiological observations that poverty, malnutrition, overcrowding, and stress can influence the onset and course of disease.

When discussing low-birthweight infants, it is most helpful to have both the birth weight and the gestational age. Throughout most of the world, an infant weighing less than 5½ pounds is considered premature or immature. Because gestation dates are difficult to calculate, birthweight remains the single most important criterion in defining risk. Obstetricians, when possible, use the duration of pregnancy from the twenty-eighth week up to and including the end of the thirty-seventh week as an important criterion of prematurity.

In the United States, of every 100 expectant mothers who have carried a fetus more than twenty weeks, 3 will leave the hospital without a live baby. About 5 out of every 100 newborns, or at least 150,000 babies a year in the United States, are so ill or immature at birth that they require intensive care.

The increased survival rate among high-risk infants is largely the result of neonatal intensive care units, which are rapidly spreading throughout the United States. There are now dozens of these units, usually attached to medical centers, prepared to receive and treat critically ill newborns. Babies who would have died within hours or days, weeks, or months after birth are now being saved.

The dramatic technological advances in perinatal physical care and treatment have led to an increase in the number of low-birthweight infants who survive and eventually join their families. By the same token, ever smaller and less mature infants are successfully nurtured through the first critical crises of life. Thus, the improvements in perinatal physical care have made possible the survival of infants whose earliest physical and psychosocial environments are unavoidably deviant and may be potentially pathogenic.

In fact, the attempt to keep certain very high-risk, damaged babies alive by artificial means raises many complex ethical questions. For example, how much effort should be expended to save the life of a baby who is very likely to be brain-damaged or otherwise seriously handicapped? When should machines be turned off and life-support systems stopped, and who should be responsible for making such decisions?

The economic and emotional cost to the parents of these infants is sometimes staggering. The hospital stay for a sick premature infant may cost 15,000 to 25,000 dollars or more. Insurance may cover only a fraction or sometimes none of the cost beyond delivery of the baby. Because a high percentage of parents of prematures are young and poor, society eventually pays most of these expenses.

The moral, legal, and economic problems relating to these infants are only part of the greater dilemma which confronts us in our attempts to improve the long-range outlook for these children and their families.

The extraordinary circumstances of life in a neonatal intensive care unit not only necessitate separation of mother and infant but include numerous intrusive physical interventions required to maintain life. Procedures often used include gavage, intubation, intravenous feeding and medication, intramuscular and subcutaneous injections, and umbilical-vessel catheterization, plus the use of equipment such as incubators, monitors, respirators, etc. In no way can this environment be considered an "average expectable environment." Furthermore, the human contacts in the intensive-care unit are unavoidably inconsistent and often associated with discomfort or tension-producing stimuli resulting from the treatment measures, rather than the more usual cyclic tension-reducing and conforting ministrations given to the normal infant.

The mother, too, suffers from the separation from her infant. Added to

the shock and dismay which often accompanies the delivery of a tiny, underdeveloped, or otherwise defective infant, there is the apprehension about
the baby's possible death, fear of discovery of a birth defect, and concern
about the future physical health of the child. Often guilt and depression
from producing an "inadequate" child is burdensome and may lead to an
emotional rejection of the infant or a dangerous lowering of maternal self-
confidence. The normal positive maternal reactions to a newborn are thus
all too often inhibited or suppressed while the family waits anxiously for the
days to pass. When the infant finally joins its family, it is frequently tiny or
still underdeveloped and may require special care.

The statistics regarding the fate of high-risk infants are dramatic.
About two-thirds of infant deaths in the United States occur during the first
month of life. Most of these are associated with prematurity. Studies in the
United States on mortality and morbidity also disclose that a premature
infant is sixteen times more likely to die during the first month of life than
the infant whose birthweight is normal. The incidence of neurological and
psychological abnormalities occurring during the first year of life is four
times as high for smaller prematures as it is for full-term infants.

If the premature does survive, he is ten times more likely to be mentally retarded than the full-term infant. In addition to the high likelihood of
death, the premature infant also has a much greater risk of failure to thrive
and suffering from child abuse as well as succumbing to sudden infant
death. Since early death and predisposition to disease are closely associated
with prematurity, reduction of these outcomes should follow a decrease in
the rate of prematurity.

For over a half a century, investigators have noted that our highest-risk
maternal-child populations are among the most underprivileged socioeconomically. Ironically, the United States, the most affluent country in the
world, ranked eleventh in maternal mortality in 1967, thirteenth in perinatal
mortality in 1967, and thirteenth in infant mortality in 1968, among countries with a population of one million or more. Our national infant mortality in 1968 for children under one year was 21.7 deaths per 1,000 live births.
National birthweight data demonstrate that white deliveries of infants with
a birthweight of under 2,500 grams was 7.2 percent in 1965, and the corresponding figure for nonwhite infants was 13.8 percent. In situations where
adverse social factors exist, infant death rates are two to four times the
national figure.

The failure of our society to address itself to the problems of poor
children is especially critical in relation to black children, a disproportionate number of whom are born into poverty. Black children constitute about
15 percent of the nation's children but nearly 40 percent of the nation's
poor children. The infant mortality rate for black infants is more than twice
as high as that for the nation as a whole.[2]

---

[2] *Mortality Vital Statistics,* 1969.

The fact that nonwhite babies most frequently die or are handicapped from birth is due not to race but to socioeconomic status. The higher rate of prematurity among both the poor Caucasian and black populations was discussed nearly thirty years ago by Nicholson J. Eastman,[3] professor at the Department of Obstetrics, Johns Hopkins University. He reviewed the experience of the Johns Hopkins Hospital for a period of twenty years beginning in 1926, and he noted that the rate of prematurity rose sharply as one compared private patients with ward patients. The highest rate of prematurity was found among black patients. Socioeconomic status rather than race was the significant variable since Caucasians have as many prematures as blacks when they live at a poverty or near-poverty level.

Patrick Bouvier Kennedy, President Kennedy's youngest child, died as a premature infant, but by far the greatest number of premature infants enter their life in an environment of poverty. Premature infants from middle-class and upper-middle-class families usually have the advantage of better care as they are growing up. Their mothers are often better educated than those of the poor. The nonstimulating environments found in the ghettos contribute to slower physical and intellectual growth of high-risk infants.

This book attempts to acquaint the reader with a variety of observations, studies, and opinions relating to high-risk pregnancy; the crisis surrounding delivery of premature and other high-risk infants; the impact of intensive infant care on the child and on the maternal-child relationship; possible sequelae to high-risk infancy; and suggestions regarding prediction, prevention, and alleviation of these serious problems.

It may be useful for the reader to have a profile which reflects those mothers at high risk. First, we have mentioned that socioeconomic factors correlate highly with low-birthweight infants. Second, in the following chapters we shall look at the mother's age as another important variable. Teen-age women represent mothers at greatest risk for having prematures. If a young woman is unmarried, risk again statistically increases to endanger the life of her infant. The unmarried teen-ager often has the stress of an unwanted pregnancy as well as limited support systems available to see her through this crisis. Serious alcoholism, drug addiction, psychiatric disturbance, heavy smoking, and chronic physical illness are some other factors that put the young mother and her child "at risk," and are frequently seen in conjunction with low-birthweight infants.

Nutrition is also linked with high-risk infants. The poorly nourished mother is obviously less able to supply her child prenatally and postnatally with needed supplies of essential nutriments for its intellectual and physical growth and development.

First-born children are statistically most likely to be premature, but

[3] Nicholson J. Eastman, "Prematurity from the Viewpoint of the Obstetrician," *Am. Pract.*, vol. I, pp. 343–352 (1947).

mothers who have had premature infants are more apt to have other premature infants. It is for this reason that these mothers are instructed to take special care with subsequent pregnancies.

Infants born in rapid succession are more often premature. Perhaps repeated frequent pregnancies do not allow the mother sufficient recovery time to carry infants to term. Twins and other types of multiple pregnancies bring with them a higher percentage of prematures.

The most recent factor which seems to be important in decreasing the rate of high-risk infants relates to the liberalization of abortion laws. In New York state, the rate of premature infants has dropped since its abortion law became effective in 1970. Interpreting these findings relating to this controversial subject will undoubtedly be a serious undertaking during this decade.

Most of the reduction in the national infant mortality rate during the last half century has been due to a decrease in death after the first month of life. Principal causes of death in the neonatal period were infectious and gastrointestinal diseases. These are no longer as important as they once were in determining infant mortality. Improved sanitation, better nutrition, important discoveries in medicine, more adequate hospital care, and a wider distribution of health services have all contributed to this great saving of life. Unfortunately, these benefits have not extended equally to all parts of our population in the United States.

Following this introductory chapter, Chapter 2, "Psychosocial Aspects of High Risk Pregnancy," includes a discussion of the psychosocial aspects of high-risk pregnancy. Specific articles which relate poverty, teen-age pregnancy, psychosocial factors, stress, and life-change events are among the topics considered.

Chapter 3, "The Crisis of Premature Birth," contains articles documenting the types of critical events which may follow the birth of high-risk infants. Included are two classic articles which carefully identify the clinical problems presented by this type of crisis situation. The authors of these articles have studied the parents of premature infants for over a decade. This material can assist the reader to understand the value of crisis intervention for high-risk mothers at this time in their lives.

Chapter 4, "Effects of Separation on Mother-Infant Bonding," includes studies relating to the neonatal period in human and nonhuman mammals. The hypothesis is presented that close maternal-infant contact from the time of birth is probably of considerable importance to the development of a healthy mutual relationship. This chapter includes the work of psychiatrists, perinatologists, and psychologists to justify the extension of postpartum support and counseling in order to improve maternal care. Terms such as "bonding," "attachment," and "maternal-infant dyad" are explored in determining how separations impair the maternal-child relationship.

Hospital regulations for the care of high-risk infants often result in a prolonged separation of the mother from the baby. It is hypothesized that the limited visiting and minimal physical contact which result may interfere with the bonding which normally occurs when the mother and infant are in uninterrupted close contact.

Chapter 5, "Sequelae," describes the sequential development of high-risk infants. Infants of low birthweight often have slower or delayed development and are victims of failure to thrive, child abuse, sudden infant death, mental retardation, emotional disturbances, and learning disorders. Longitudinal studies have demonstrated striking incidence of physical and mental handicaps in children weighing three pounds or less at birth. Fortunately, with improved neonatal intensive care fewer impairments occur. The purpose of this chapter is to alert the reader to the physical, emotional, and intellectual sequelae relating to prematurity and early infant illness.

The failure to thrive is examined in relationship to vulnerability to further neglect and child abuse. Elizabeth Elmer, who has long studied this problem, documents an extensive study of the nature of these problems. These additional health hazards which interfere with child development are an extremely important area for further investigation.

Chapter 6, "Critical Issues in Comprehensive Care for Mothers and Infants," examines the most recent psychosocial challenges in providing extensive care for high-risk infants and mothers. The role of the nurse-midwife is discussed as one possibility in helping to lower the infant mortality rate. The first school of nurse-midwifery was started in New York City in 1931. Today, training is offered in ten medical colleges or nursing schools across the country. One article discusses the role of the nurse-midwife in a project in rural California.

A decade ago Dr. Howard Jacobson and Dr. Duncan Reid described a pattern for comprehensive maternal and child care. The proposal they submitted which is included in this chapter seems an excellent model which could be increasingly used.

The article, "Critical Issues in Newborn Intensive Care: A Conference Report and Policy Proposal," represents an interdisciplinary approach to ethical questions relating to the high risk-infant. The authors emphasize the urgent need for a coherent policy on questions of life or death for critically ill newborns. They attempt to set some guidelines for moral policy. Unprecedented scientific progress has brought with it increasing concern for ethical and social questions relating to recent discoveries. Crucial moral issues are often attached to the utilization of mechanical procedures for extending life. Our technical skills are transcending our sensibilities. We must explore the practical, human implications of tremendous advances in modern medicine.

In addition to documenting various aspects of a major public-health problem, we have raised issues in viewing some of the awesome questions which must be studied. Controversial subjects arise when one analyzes the world around the vulnerable newborn. These topics include abortion, birth control, sterilization, and life extension through the newest technology.

Diversity of opinions in a pluralistic society sometimes makes providing guidelines for the care of the high-risk infants very complex. As we come to grips with social, medical, and moral decisions regarding these children, we are establishing policies which may have far-reaching implications for the future of our society.

Psychosocial Aspects of High-Risk Pregnancy

Among the multiple factors which contribute to low birthweight, poverty stands out as a significant determinant. In the United States, studies for nearly half a century have amply demonstrated the high correlation between the rate of infant survival and socioeconomic class.

We have elected to discuss poverty and high-risk pregnancy as our first topic because the high incidence of infant morbidity and mortality in the United States can no longer be viewed primarily as a medical problem. Socioeconomic factors and their effects on pregnancy outcome are discussed by Howard J. Osofsky and Norman Kendall in the first reading, "Poverty as a Criterion of Risk." These physicians emphasize that low-income women are more likely to have early, frequent pregnancies and more often have premature deliveries with increased perinatal mortality. They conclude that preventive programs and services could and should be instituted which would substantially reduce risk for economically disadvantaged young mothers.

Ira Rosenwaike,[1] a biostatistician, studied the relationship between low birthweight and the educational level of the mother. This project demonstrated that better educated women have fewer low-birthweight infants. Poor education is most often seen with socioeconomic deprivation, diminished ability to use medical services, and increased maternal-infant risk. On the other hand, higher education bears a close relationship to higher social status, increased ability to seek and receive adequate medical care, and decreased maternal-infant risk.

In recent years, psychosomatic factors in a variety of health problems have received much attention. The work of Alexander,[2] Dunbar,[3] Grinker and Speigel,[4] Cannon,[5] Selye,[6] and Engel,[7] as well as others, has indicated that tension or stress occurring in one system of the body may have consequences in other systems as part of the human organism's total response to tension-producing stimuli. Thus, conscious and unconscious anxieties or fears generated by significant conflicts may be experienced not only through subjective feelings of dread or discomfort but also through significant alterations in body chemistry and physiological processes.

In discussing premature infants and habitual abortions, some obstetricians and psychiatrists have suggested a possible relationship between emotional factors and habitual abortions, but it has been very difficult to provide psychophysiological approaches to the study of this problem.

The significance of habitual abortion as it relates to prematurity has been studied by Mann,[8] Javert,[9] Dunbar,[10] and other investigators. Mann has noted important psychiatric factors which seem to indicate that stress is an important issue in certain women who tend to abort habitually. Treatment aimed at improving psychosocial circumstances may be indicated for patients in an unfavorable environment which seems to be related to habitual abortion. Workers in this field have documented cases of women with

---

[1] Ira Rosenwaike, "The Influence of Socioeconomic Status on Incidence of Low Birth Weight," *HSMHA Rept.* vol. 86, no. 7, pp. 641–649 (July 1971).

[2] Franz Alexander, *Psychosomatic Medicine: Its Principles and Applications,* W. W. Norton & Company, Inc., New York, 1950.

[3] H. F. Dunbar, *Emotions and Bodily Changes: A Survey of Literature on Psychosomatic Interrelationships,* Columbia University Press, New York 1954.

[4] Roy Grinker and John Speigel, *Men under Stress,* McGraw-Hill Book Company, New York, 1945.

[5] W. B. Cannon, *Bodily Changes in Pain, Hunger, Fear, and Rage,* Appleton-Century-Crofts, New York, 1920.

[6] Hans Selye, *The Stress of Life,* McGraw-Hill Book Company, New York, 1956.

[7] G. L. Engel, "A Life Setting Conducive to Illness: The Giving-up/Given-up Complex," *Ann. Intern. Med.,* vol. 69, pp. 293–300 (August, 1968); *Psychological Development in Healthy and Diseased Children,* W. B. Saunders Company, Philadelphia, 1962.

[8] Edward C. Mann, "Psychiatric Investigation of Habitual Abortion," *J. Am. Acad. Obstet. Gynecol.,* vol. 7, pp. 589–601 (June 1956).

[9] Carl T. Javert, "Repeated Abortion," *Obstet. Gynecol.,* vol. 3, pp. 420–434 (April 1954).

[10] H. F. Dunbar, *Emotions and Bodily Changes: A Survey of Literature on Psychosomatic Interrelationships,* Columbia University Press, New York, 1954.

habitual abortions who have been successfully treated psychotherapeutically. This, in addition to medical treatment, holds promise of helping these mothers carry pregnancy to term.

Berle and Javert [11] suggest through their studies that a combined regimen of medical care and psychotherapy may be of considerable benefit to these patients. The mechanisms by which stress produces uterine contractions, bleeding, and spontaneous abortion represent an area greatly in need of further study.

Javert, early in his study of habitual aborters, began to use psychotherapy as a form of treatment in conjunction with medical measures. His investigations increasingly pointed to emotional factors in the pathogenesis of habitual abortions. Other workers, such as Squier and Dunbar, [12] regard the "abortion habit" as being similar to the "accident habit" and feel that psychotherapy is indicated.

Helene Deutsch [13] described the psychoanalysis of a woman who had four premature infants. After analysis, she had a normal, full-term baby. While it has often been suggested that psychosomatic factors are associated with the incidence of abortion and premature labor, it remains difficult to delineate the effects emotions and life changes have on pregnancy. At present, it is almost impossible to show a positive correlation between specific psychosomatic factors and the outcome of pregnancy. More studies, properly designed, which include detailed psychological interviews as well as the Social Readjustment Rating Scale might be used to correlate the relationship between stress and the outcome of pregnancy.

Both the professional and popular literature recognize the relationship of life stress to the occurrence of repeated abortions. Folklore takes it for granted that acute anxiety, sorrow, or worry disturbs the fetus and causes physical harm. Javert notes that,

> For centuries, the Ancient Greeks believed that the womb was the seat of the emotions. Today, this view has been reversed, and the emotions are now regarded as affecting the uterus. [14]

Popular literature, such as the novels *Wuthering Heights*, [15] by Emily Bronte, and *The Wall*, [16] by John Hersey, include clinical examples of pregnant women delivering prematurely in circumstances of extreme stress.

Obstetric and midwifery texts in the late nineteenth and early twentieth

[11] Beatrice B. Berle and Carl T. Javert, "Stress and Habitual Abortion," *Obstet. Gynecol.,* vol. 3, pp. 298–306 (1954).

[12] R. Squier and F. Dunbar, "Emotional Factors in the Course of Pregnancy," *Psychosom. Med.,* vol. 8, pp. 161–175 (1946).

[13] H. Deutsch, *The Psychology of Women,* 2 vols., Grune & Stratton, Inc., New York, 1945.

[14] Carl T. Javert, "Repeated Abortion," *Obstet. Gynecol.,* vol. 3, p. 420 (April 1954).

[15] Emily Bronte, *Wuthering Heights,* Modern Library, New York, 1950.

[16] John Hersey, *The Wall,* Alfred A. Knopf, Inc., New York, 1950.

centuries record the observation that emotional outbursts in the form of excessive fear, joy, grief, or anger may be followed by abortion in predisposed women. One of the predisposing factors frequently mentioned by these authors is "the habit of abortion." Benedek notes that "extreme rage may lead to spontaneous abortion, especially during the first trimester of pregnancy." [17]

Abram Blau, in a preliminary report, found definite psychological and emotional differences between mothers of prematures and mothers of full-term infants.[18] The project included thirty subjects and thirty controls, which is rather a small sample. Since there are so few studies in this area, however, the article is an example of a relatively unexplored aspect of research into prematurity.

The second reading, "Emotional Crises of School-Age Girls during Pregnancy and Early Motherhood," is written by Maureen LaBarre, who, from her social-work experience, describes a pilot project designed to provide continuing education, health, and social services for high-risk teen-age mothers. It has been noted that pregnancy is one of the single most frequent physical conditions causing an adolescent to leave school. The high rate of interrupted education by pregnancy in teen-age groups corresponds to a need for additional services.

The author discusses the anxiety and emotional crisis which many of these young women experience during the early months when they are trying to cope with their pregnant state. In those cases where the young women chose to keep their babies, there appeared to be a high incidence of impaired maternal-infant attachment. Fortunately, many of these immature and ambivalent mothers seemed educable and motivated to develop their maternal competence with the help of the counseling provided by LaBarre and her group.

The many social and medical problems presented by this very high-risk population indicate that model programs such as the one described are of special importance in reducing the rate of maternal-infant disease and death.

The work of Holmes and Rahe has demonstrated that certain life-change events can also be important factors related to the onset of disease.[19] The third reading, "A Study of the Relationship between Maternal Life Change Events and Premature Delivery," is an attempt to determine wheth-

---

[17] Therese Benedek, "The Psychobiology of Pregnancy," in *Parenthood: Its Psychology and Psychopathology,* E. James Anthony and Therese Benedek (eds.), Little, Brown and Company, London, 1970, p. 144.

[18] Abram Blau, "The Psychogenic Etiology of Premature Births," *Psychoso. Med.,* vol. 25, no. 3, pp. 201–211 (1963).

[19] Thomas H. Holmes and Richard H. Rahe, "The Social Readjustment Rating Scale," *J.Psychosom. Res.,* vol. 11, pp. 213–218 (1967).

er life changes influence the outcome of pregnancy in relationship to prematurity. It was found in this study that mothers of premature infants, compared with mothers of full-term infants, showed a significantly higher number of life-change units, especially in the two years preceding their pregnancy and just before the pregnancy. It might further be surmised that these same mothers will continue to have an upswing in life change and stress after the birth of their babies.

The importance of psychosocial assets as well as life stresses in evaluating pregnancy outcome is the subject of "Psychosocial Assets, Life Crisis and the Prognosis of Pregnancy," by Katherine Nuckolls et al. Psychological investigations generally fail to consider the emotional or social strengths which may also be present. This article attempts to redress this balance.

Formidable methodological problems exist in determining social and psychological factors relating to prematurity. It is hoped that these articles will offer direction and suggestions for the reader.

Poverty as a Criterion of Risk

Howard J. Osofsky, MD
Professor, Department of Obstetrics and Gynecology, Temple University
Health Sciences Center

Norman Kendall, MD
Department of Pediatrics, Temple University Health Sciences Center

A concern for the health and well-being of all individuals in society is of fundamental importance to the medical profession. In the area of obstetrics, great pride has been taken in the figures which have demonstrated a marked decrease in both maternal and perinatal mortality during the past several decades. Maternal mortality in the United States has fallen from 60.8 per 10,000 live births in 1915 to 2.8 in 1967. Perinatal mortality has declined from 55.7 per 1,000 live births in 1935 (the first year for which rates were estimated) to 31.9 in 1968. Infant mortality has declined from 99.9 per 1,000 live births in 1915 to 20.7 in 1969 [43, 45–47]. However, although there is some reason to be encouraged there are also adequate reasons for dissatisfaction. From the mid-1950s to the mid-1960s there was relatively little progress in further improving the figures. Only since 1965 has there again been a moderate improvement in the figures.

International comparisons of mortality statistics are an important tool in evaluating national progress. It should be emphasized that great care must be taken in interpreting the data. For example, definitions of mortality and quality of data-collection vary among countries and many diverse factors enter into the individual national mortality rates [6]. However, within the limitations which are presented because of biasing and other factors, it is worth noting that the United States has fared relatively poorly. Although relative declines in rate of improvement also occurred in other countries between the mid-1950s and the mid-1960s, they were not as marked as in the United States. Among reporting countries with a population of one million or more, the available figures indicate that the United States ranked 11th in maternal mortality in 1967, 13th in perinatal mortality in 1967, and 14th in infant mortality in 1969 [45, 46]. In fact, between 1959–60 and 1963–64, the United States ranked only 30th among the 31 countries with adequate data [53].

In any attempt at understanding the multiple parameters which have contributed to adversely influencing the U.S. figures, the issue of poverty stands out as being of major importance. Therefore, it would seem pertinent to focus on the data concerning poverty in relationship to perinatal and infant mortality and in relationship to prognosis for surviving infants.

From *Clinical Obstetrics and Gynecology*, vol. 16, pp. 103–109 (March 1973).

POVERTY AND PREGNANCY OUTCOME

The Existent Conditions and Trends

The discrepancy in pregnancy outcome related to socioeconomic class becomes readily apparent when one analyzes the data which has accrued since 1935 on racial background. Marked differences in perinatal and infant mortality have occurred on the basis of racial background throughout this period, with nonwhites faring much worse than whites. In fact, the relative differential has actually risen during many of the approximately 30 years under study.

A divergence of the curves for whites and nonwhites can be noted readily in the data which has been reported for the years 1950–1964. Prior to 1950, the rate of decrease in mortality was somewhat parallel for the two groups. Between 1950 and 1964 a divergence on the basis of racial background was observed in almost all age subgroups studied. Although decreases in mortality during the first day of life occurred among white infants between 1935 and 1951, the decrease in the rate of loss during the first day of life among nonwhite infants stopped in 1943. From 1952–1964 an increase in mortality was reported for infants during the first day of life; the increase was proportionally greater among nonwhite than white infants. Among nonwhite infants during the 1950s, there were reasonable gains in reducing mortality only at 3 through 6 days, 7 through 13 days, and 6 through 11 months of life; during the early 1960s, even these trends were no longer existent [43]. Only since 1965 has there been a beginning trend for the disappearance of the divergence on the basis of racial background; the marked discrepancy itself continues to exist [46, 47].

The racially related differentials in mortality have also been noted beyond the first year of life. A marked decrease in childhood mortality was observed during the first half of the 20th century, with a considerably lessened decline reported since the mid-1950s. Throughout this period, nonwhite children have had considerably higher mortality rates than white children. Although the divergence observed in neonatal and infancy rates, on the basis of racial background, has not been noted among infants beyond the first year of life, racially related mortality rates have remained parallel, and there has been no closure of the gap. Nonwhite children of preschool age relatively consistently have had mortality rates approximately twice as high as white children; nonwhite school-age children have had rates approximately 50 per cent higher than white children. Deaths from almost all disease entities have occurred with greater frequency among the nonwhite childhood population. Even deaths from congenital anomalies, which until recently occurred with greater frequency among white children, have become relatively more common among nonwhite preschool children [43].

It should be stressed that much, if not all, of the racially related differentials in mortality are socioeconomically associated. Nationally and internationally, reports have demonstrated differentials on the basis of social class. British studies, which analyzed countrywide data from 1950 through 1958, revealed consistent differentials on the basis of socioeconomic class. Perinatal and infant mortality rates were higher among the poor and less well-educated, and were higher in the relatively less-affluent sections of the country [5]. Of some note, during the years under study, the British figures also tended to diverge on the basis of socioeconomic class [18, 19].

In the United States, studies have consistently demonstrated a strong relationship between perinatal and infant mortality rates and economic class. Densen [8], in reviewing neonatal mortality rates, and Yerby [54], in reviewing perinatal mortality rates in New York City between 1961 and 1963 have related the rates to race and occupation of the father. Although neonatal mortality rates among blacks tended to be somewhat higher than those noted among whites at almost all economic levels (one exception noted was that the rates were almost parallel among the highest risk group composed of out-of-wedlock deliveries), clear socioeconomic differentials were noted. There was a marked increase in mortality among both whites and blacks when socioeconomic class was lowered. Bedger [3], in a recent study in Chicago, found a strong relationship between social rank and infant death rates. As opposed to the Densen and Yerby data, his study was somewhat confounded by possible interaction of variables. Both infant mortality and racial background varied with social rank. However, the data indicated a relationship between economic class and mortality independent of race.

In a similar vein, Shapiro's 1955 through 1957 study of health-care delivery in New York City [42] suggested that racial differences could be considerably offset by improving quality of health care. Although a racial gradient existed, prepaid medical care strongly correlated with a decline in perinatal mortality among both racial groups. Further, as Shapiro has also noted, probably related to changing mobility and services with the United States, geographic differentials in perinatal mortality rates have largely disappeared among the white population; among the nonwhite population, where greater discrepancies in eocnomics, mobility, and quality of care exist, the differentials are still present to a considerable degree.

Factors Related to Economic Differentials

When one attempts to determine the factors which predispose low-income individuals to high perinatal and infant mortality rates, two sets of issues repeatedly appear to arise. The first is related to the general reproductive circumstances of the individuals, and the second to the specific pathology involved.

Birch has utilized the terminology "too young, too old, and too often" to describe the reproductive experience of low-income individuals [4]. Maternal age is known to be associated with perinatal mortality. Perinatal mortality follows a curve, and is high among the very young and the relatively old gravida. Similarly, the rank in number of the pregnancy is related to perinatal mortality. Perinatal mortality is relatively high among first pregnancies, drops with the second pregnancy, begins to rise thereafter, and is highest among fifth or more pregnancies. When age and parity are considered together, there is some variability due to the interaction, but the overall patterns strikingly and clearly reveal the excessive risk to the fetus and infant when the mother is at either extreme of age or parity. Both national and international data substantiate these trends [4, 26, 43, 47]. Similarly, and perhaps not unexpectedly, pregnancy prognosis appears to be affected adversely by too close spacing of gestations. It may be further worthy of note to observe that women with a history of prior perinatal loss have a markedly higher history of loss with current pregnancy. Infants born to mothers with a prior history of fetal death have twice the neonatal mortality rate of other children; where three or more prior fetal deaths have occurred, the incidence is almost 9 times as great [43].

Given these parameters which influence risk, it is important to look at patterns of reproduction among the poor. Low-income individuals tend to begin reproduction at an earlier age and end it at a later age than do women in the population at large [2, 4]. Although biasing factors, such as the availability of contraception and abortion, tend to confound the data for middle- and upper-class individuals, the reported information indicates that low-income women have a higher incidence of both marital and out-of-wedlock pregnancies at young ages. Similarly, not only does childbearing extend to a somewhat older age, but the prevalence of high parity increases with declining social class. This has been demonstrated in British and American studies [24, 37]. Education, economic level and racial background individually relate and interact in affecting family size. Further, as might be expected, whereas maternal age and birth order both relate to pregnancy outcome and economic status, there is an additive affect of economic status in prognosticating perinatal mortality. Women of low economic status have pregnancies which are at greater risk at each level of age and parity than do individuals of higher economic status [2, 4, 26].

When one approaches perinatal and infant mortality rates from the perspective of attempting to assess the medical etiologically contributing factors, the conclusions in respect to economic status remain somewhat similar. At present, prematurity and its complications represent the prime causative, or associative, factors related to perinatal mortality. The National Collaborative Perinatal Study has associated approximately 70 per cent of each component of perinatal mortality (antepartum stillbirth, intrapartum stillbirth and neonatal death) with low birthweight [27]. Premature birth in one pregnancy tends to prognosticate a higher incidence of prematurity in a subsequent pregnancy; the likelihood of prematurity of two previous pregnancies terminated prematurely, is 30 per cent. Further, both premature and small-for-dates infants are commonly associated with pregnancy problems such as abruptio placentae, placenta previa, "placental insufficiency," toxemia, and other problems which, by themselves, also predispose to perinatal mortality [14, 23, 32, 43, 49]. Such medical complications of pregnancy are more common among the poor [4, 18, 35, 43].

National birthweight data demonstrate that the median nonwhite birthweight is lower than that reported for whites. In 1967 there was a differential of 180 grams on the basis of race. This differential was greater than that which existed in 1950. Among white deliveries in the United States in 1965, 7.2 per cent of infants were born with a weight of under 2500 grams; the corresponding figure among nonwhite infants was 13.8 per cent [4]. That the differential is due not only to racial factors, but to economic factors as well, is borne out by numerous studies. Scott has demonstrated an increase in birthweights among black infants in a somewhat more favorable urban setting [40, 41]. Thomson has found a strong relationship between prematurity and social class within a relatively homogenous ethnic population in Scotland [44]. Rider has demonstrated a marked differential in prematurity in Baltimore on the basis of socieconomic class, and although the data is somewhat confounded by race, the economic differential persists quite clearly [36]. Crump, in Nashville, has demonstrated a marked increase in prematurity with descending socioeconomic class among black infants in Nashville [7].

What emerges in this area is not unexpected; it is comparable to the remainder of the data already cited. Low-income individuals, who are more likely to have early, frequent, and more numerous pregnancies extending into later life, are more likely to have premature deliveries with the increased risk of perinatal mortality, and are more likely to have the medical complications of pregnancy which predispose either to perinatal mortality directly or to premature and small-for-dates infants with their increased risk of mortality.

PREGNANCY PARAMETERS AND CHILD DEVELOPMENT

Somewhat similar to the effect of pregnancy patterns and complications upon perinatal mortality is the significance of these factors in prognosticating development of the surving infants. Individuals, whose handicap of poverty predisposes them to problems throughout the pregnancy and to high incidences of significant complications and death, are much more likely to have infants with significant developmental and neurological handicaps later in childhood. As has been reviewed by one of us, perhaps in part related to prematurity and complications of pregnancy, infants delivered to extremely young mothers have a high incidence of both developmental problems and neurological complications as childhood progresses [28]. Utilizing almost all developmental standards, this group represents one which is at extremely high risk. Similarly, at the other end of the scale, problems can be noted. Women having a fifth or greater pregnancy, and women having a pregnancy at age 40 and over, appear more likely to have infants with developmental handicaps. Russell's British study has demonstrated highly significant IQ differentials on the basis of such factors [38]. Further, Holley has recently presented information from the Collaborative Perinatal Project which suggests that conception within one year of a previous full-term pregnancy is significantly more likely to lead to lower Bayley scores at 8 months of age and lower scores on the revised Stanford-Binet form L–M at 4 years of age [17]. The IQ changes at 4 years of age could not be accounted for on the basis of diminished birthweight alone. As might be expected, IQ scores correlated with socioeconomic class within each maternal age, birth order, and birth spacing category, but both socieconomic class and the pregnancy parameters of maternal age, birth order, and birth spacing appear to have important effects.

When one approaches the complications-of-pregnancy data from the perspective of a spectrum of reproductive casualty, there also appears to be a continuum between pregnancy complications and subsequent infant difficulty. As has previously been noted, low-income individuals are considerably more predisposed to intercurrent illness and obstetrical complications during pregnancy. Pasamanick, Knobloch and co-workers have demonstrated a significant association between complications of pregnancy and birth and the incidences of childhood cerebral palsy, epilepsy, mental deficiency, behavioral disorders, reading disabilities, strabismus, hearing disorders and autism [22, 33, 34]. Recently-accumulated data from the Collaborative Perinatal Project have revealed relationships between medical complications, low Apgar scores, hypotonia and neurological abnormalities in the neonatal period and subsequent developmental abnormality [27]. Since Apgar scores and anoxia at birth have appeared to relate better to minimal neurological difficulty—especially of the fine motor variety—at 4 years of age, and less well to gross intellectual quotient changes [11], it seems worthwhile to at least note Windle's study of experimentally produced severe anoxia in the Rhesus monkey infant [52]. The marked neurological and behavioral deficits observed following such anoxia considerably diminished as development progressed; the outcome seemed analogous to that commonly reported at 4 years of age for infants, anoxic or otherwise depressed at birth. However, postmortem examination of the brains revealed considerable scarring related to primary focal lesions which had been caused by the asphyxia. There was no evidence of structural brain repair; if anything, the severity of the lesions appeared to worsen as the monkey grew older.

When one returns to the issue of prematurity, which is markedly elevated in incidence among the poor, it is possible to witness an apparently important relationship to subsequent altered developmental prognosis. In the United States, Pasamanick and Knobloch's group have related prematurity to severe neurological, mental, sensory, and behavioral deficits; cerebral palsy, epilepsy, mental retardation, blindness, autism, and other serious mental illness are among the problems which have been noted among the survivors [20, 21, 34]. Their studies have demonstrated that increasing the prematurity related to greater incidences of difficulty. Even children with birthweights between 1500 and 1999 grams scored on the average 5 points lower on the Stanford-Binet at ages 6 through 7, and 6.2 points lower on the WISC between ages 8 and 10 [20]. Similarly, recently released data from the Collaborative Perinatal Project is suggestive of increased developmental risk with increased prematurity among the infants followed up to 8 months and 4 years of age [27].

British results have been consistent with the American data. Douglas, in following up a group of premature infants from the British National Maternity Survey for 11 years, has noted highly significant differences between premature and mature infants on overall and specific subgroup measures of infant intelligence [9, 10]. Drillien similarly has reported marked difficulties related to prematurity on the basis of her extensive Scottish study [12]. Developmental quotients of children with birthweights of 3½ lbs or less averaged 82.5 at age 4; this was in contradistinction to quotients of 108.7 of infants with birthweights of 5½ lbs or more. In addition to the approximately 30 per cent who were unable to enter school, of the 72 children weighing 3 lbs or less at birth who passed school entrance examinations, 75 per cent had some congenital defect or mental retardation [13].

It should be noted that several of the studies have linked subsequent prognosis to socioeconomic class. With increasing class, there tends to be an increase in IQ noted between 4 and 10 years of age among premature infants, with eradication of much of the differential related to birthweight. However, although premature infants from higher socioeconomic classes may eventually obtain average IQ scores, within classes premature infants have tended to fare somewhat less well than mature infants and significant incidences of neurological deficits have been noted [12, 13, 16, 23, 25, 50, 51].

EXPERIENCE OF TEMPLE UNIVERSITY HEALTH SCIENCE CENTER

As an example of the medical risk which exists for low-income patients, the authors have elected to share their experience at Temple University Health Science Center. The center is situated within the largest low-income area in Philadelphia and serves predominantly economically poor individuals. Over a period of years, with population shifts within the community, the proportion of low-income and nonwhite patients has increased, and the proportion of traditionally private patients decreased. The experience of the Department of Obstetrics and Gynecology has reflected this trend. In 1971 between April 1 and December 31, 1,507 patients delivered at Temple University Hospital. Of this number, 1,038 attended the hospital out-patient clinic (396 of these qualified for the Maternal and Infant Care Program), 101 received care at an affiliated Maternal and Infant Care Program, 122 were registered at affiliated Neighborhood Health Center clinics, 110 were private patients, 30 had registered at another facility but arrived at the hospital for the first time when in labor and 106 were unregistered at any facility at the time of delivery. Further, 47.4 per cent of the patients were single, 37.3 per cent were married, the remainder being separated, widowed, or divorced, 15.7 per cent of the patients were 16 or younger, 24.4 per cent were 17–19, 56.1 per cent were 20–34 and the remainder were 35 or older. Of note, the number of mothers age 16 and younger increased both numerically and proportionally from 1970. In that year such young mothers counted for approximately 12 per cent of all deliveries; 22.8 per cent of the patients were white, 75.2 per cent were black, 14.7 per cent were Puerto Rican and the remainder were of other racial backgrounds. As may be apparent from the figures, almost all of the patients were poor; even among the private patients, a considerable number were of relatively low economic status.

Of the 1,371 patients who received prenatal care in a Temple University Hospital facility, 643, or 47.2 per cent, were found to be high risk by the departmental high-risk classification, which is similar to and in part based upon the classification cited in the article by Aubry and Pennington. The mothers were classified as non-high-risk delivered 658 infants who appeared normal and 75, or 10.2 per cent, which appeared to be high risk. The 643 high-risk patients delivered a much higher proportion of high-risk infants: 503 of these infants appeared normal, and 140, or 21.7 per cent, were considered high risk. The 30 mothers who had registered elsewhere, but who delivered at Temple University Hospital without prior prenatal care at the facility, delivered 10 infants who were considered high risk, and the 106 women, who were unregistered at any facility, delivered 41 high-risk infants.

Data concerning pregnancy outcome are presented in Tables 1–4. Although Pennsylvania law defines abortion as occurring only through the first 16 weeks of pregnancy, all tables will utilize the more medically and legally acceptable definition of abortion based upon fetal weight of less than 500 grams in determining fetal and perinatal mortality rates. Data are unavailable for fetal and perinatal mortality, as related to maternal parity, on the basis of the 500-gram definition of fetal mortality. It is therefore not being reported at this time. However, available information, based upon the Pennsylvania 16-week definition, is consistent with the national data already cited.

Over-all information dealing with pregnancy outcome is presented in Table 1. Two hundred twenty-five, or 15.4 per cent, of the live births weighed less than 2500 grams. This figure, although unacceptably high, is lower than the previous nine months incidence of 16.1 per cent. As would be expected, both fetal and neonatal mortality rates were considerably elevated when compared with national data.

Information related to pregnancy outcome, on the basis of maternal age, is presented in Table 2. As can be seen, females at the extremes of reproductive age experienced elevated incidences of both fetal and neonatal mortality. In spite of a special, if not completely satisfactory, program for young adolescents, their degree of pregnancy risk was exceeded only by females age 35 and older.

Table 3 describes information concerning the patient's race as related to pregnancy outcome. Again, consistent with the data already cited, the black population had the highest rates of low-birthweight infants and fetal and neonatal mortality. Puerto Rican women were in an intermediate position with a somewhat higher perinatal mortality rate than white patients. Much of the white, nonwhite differential in risk was related to the more favorable social class of the white patients; they comprised a disproportionate part of the private patient load. Studies are currently under way to better elucidate the parameters of difficulty.

Information concerning other types of pregnancy risk is presented in

Table 1 Overall Pregnancy Outcome

	Totals
Live births	1,459
Fetal deaths	24
Neonatal deaths	40
Live births < 500 grams	3
Live births < 1000 grams	18
Live births < 2500 grams	225
Fetal mortality rate	16.1
Neonatal mortality rate	27.4
Perinatal mortality rate	43.1
Low birthweight per cent	15.4

Table 2 Maternal Age vs Pregnancy Outcome

| | Maternal age | | | |
	<17	17-19	20-34	35+
Live births	232	356	818	53
Fetal deaths	4	5	12	3
Neonatal deaths	8	9	21	2
Live births <500 grams	0	0	3	0
Live births <1000 grams	3	5	9	1
Live births <2500 grams	37	48	129	11
Fetal mortality rate	16.9	13.8	14.4	53.5
Neonatal mortality rate	34.4	25.2	25.6	37.7
Perinatal mortality rate	50.8	38.7	39.7	89.2
Low birthweight per cent	15.9	13.4	15.7	20.7

Table 4. As would be expected, patients who were classified as being high risk during pregnancy, had higher incidences of low-birthweight infants and fetal and neonatal mortality. Their greater likelihood of adverse pregnancy outcome would be expected on the basis of data cited elsewhere in the volume. The information concerning patients who registered elsewhere but who delivered at Temple University Hospital without prior care, and the patients who received no prenatal care prior to delivery, would appear especially worthy of note. The women who received no prenatal care had approximately one chance in four of low-birthweight infants and one chance

Table 3 Maternal Race vs Pregnancy Outcome

| | Race | | | |
	White	Black	Puerto Rican	Other
Live births	118	1109	217	15
Fetal deaths	0	22	2	0
Neonatal deaths	2	31	6	1
Live births <500 grams	0	2	1	0
Live births <1000 grams	1	15	2	0
Live births <2500 grams	13	189	20	3
Fetal mortality rate	0	19.4	9.1	0
Neonatal mortality rate	16.9	27.9	27.6	6.0
Perinatal mortality rate	16.5	46.8	36.5	6.0
Low birthweight per cent	11.0	17.0	9.2	20.0

Table 4   Maternal Risk vs Pregnancy Outcome

	Maternal risk			
	Normal	High risk	Unregistered	Registered elsewhere
Live births	720	627	86	26
Fetal deaths	4	9	9	2
Neonatal deaths	11	23	6	0
Live births < 500 grams	1	2	0	0
Live births < 1000 grams	3	12	3	0
Live births < 2500 grams	75	123	21	6
Fetal mortality rate	5.5	14.1	94.7	71.4
Neonatal mortality rate	15.2	36.6	69.7	0
Perinatal mortality rate	20.7	50.3	157.8	71.4
Low birthweight per cent	10.4	19.6	24.4	23.0

in six of perinatal mortality. Although these individuals represented fewer than 6 per cent of all patients, they accounted for approximately 25 per cent of the hospital's perinatal mortality and represented the highest risk group of individuals. At present, an effort is being made both to reach out more effectively to individuals within the community who might be expected to remain unregistered during pregnancy and to gain a greater understanding of the factors which might be involved in the etiology of their disproportionate pregnancy risk.

SUMMARY AND CONCLUSIONS

From the studies cited as well as from our own data, it is obvious that the economically poor have a considerably elevated pregnancy risk. In almost all categories noted, pregnancy complications are increased and perinatal and infant mortality are elevated. The studies cited have also demonstrated that subsequent developmental prognosis for the surviving infants is reduced. If anything, during recent years the discrepancy between the poor and the affluent has actually increased.

Several sets of important issues appear to arise from the data presented. The first concerns additional scientific knowledge which is required to further understand the etiological factors involved in producing the increased risk on the basis of low socioeconomic class, and which is necessary in any attempt to prevent or decrease it. Better controlled data concerning the meaning of various aspects of environmental deprivation on pregnancy outcome and subsequent child development are needed. Information is required to better understand the reasons for the relationship between maternal age, parity, and spacing, and pregnancy outcome and developmental sequelae; the effects of multiple possible organic and environmental factors need elucidation.

Further investigations are needed concerning the relationship of poverty parameters—such as possible undernutrition, overcrowding, restricted physical surroundings, inadequate education, unemployment, anomie, etc—to pregnancy outcome and subsequent child development. The role of the adequacy, or inadequacy, of professional services requires more focus. Although Shapiro's previously cited data [42, 28, 30, 31] and some of the senior author's work with low-income pregnant teenagers have demonstrated improvement in morbidity and mortality when more adequate services are provided, the relative contributions of different aspects of medical care, under both optimal and suboptimal environmental situations, are still imperfectly understood. The effects, not only of intensive programs, but of selected aspects of different approaches, require further study. Given the current state of knowledge concerning the greater risk to low-income mothers and infants, it would appear worthwhile to gain additional information with some of the already available sophisticated biochemical and physiological assessments which may be of assistance in indicating risk and in leading to possible intervention aimed at prevention of difficulty; obviously, further investigation is needed in this area related both to the prevention of maternal and perinatal death and to the elucidation and possible prevention of subsequent developmental problems.

A second issue is both humane and scientific in scope. It concerns implementation of the knowledge which already exists. Much knowledge is currently available, and if a concerted effort were made, many of the problems discussed would be preventable. For example, although the effects of possible antenatal poverty nutritional deficit upon the mother and fetus still require further elucidation, it is likely from the data presented elsewhere in this volume that they are of considerable importance. Many of the complications of pregnancy may be related to the patient's inability to obtain adequate standards of nutrition, health, and overall living both before and during the pregnancy. A somewhat related area deals with the quality of medical care that is available when the patient becomes pregnant. The current situation in this country results in the highest quantity and quality of medical care being offered to the middle and upper socioeconomic classes, who are the lowest-risk members of the population. The poor, who are at highest risk, have least adequate care. Impersonal and fragmentary services, accompanied by long waits and inconveniences, are more common for this group. Their care frequently is provided by the least trained members of the medical profession. A number of approaches, both of a voluntary and of a governmental nature have been innovated, or at least proposed, in an attempt to improve the present situation. Although the answers are not available as to the best method, or methods, of insuring optimal baseline health and of providing higher caliber of care during pregnancy and after delivery, further efforts in these areas obviously must assume high priority.

Because of the statistics relating maternal age, parity, and the spacing of pregnancies to pregnancy outcome and subsequent child development, another area of major concern should be the availability of sex education and family planning. It is too often assumed that the poor begin their pregnancies at young ages, and have many closely spaced pregnancies, because of indifference or cultural patterns. Far too little attention has been paid to the provision of adequate education and birth-control services. Recent years have witnessed a decline in illegitimacy rates among individuals age 20 and over [29]; it is likely that some of this fall is related to the more adequate provision of family planning services to individuals within this age group. Reports are also beginning to demonstrate a considerable utilization of available contraceptive services by adolescents [1, 48]; the senior author and others have found a marked decline in the occurrence of repeat out-of-wedlock pregnancy among low-income teenagers provided with adequate educational and contraceptive services [15, 30, 31, 39]. Still better educational and family planning services are required as part of the effort to both increase optimal pregnancy outcome and decrease pregnancy risk.

Obviously, other issues could be raised. However, it can be stated in conclusion that the economically poor have greater difficulty in regard to pregnancy outcome and subsequent child development than do the more affluent members of society. Many factors are known to relate to their high-risk status. Still others need to be elucidated and better understood. With the current state of knowledge, improved services and options should be expected to result in a substantial lowering of the risk for low-income individuals. It is hoped that increased efforts will be made to obtain both the desired knowledge and services in the years to come.

REFERENCES

1   Arnold C. B., Cogswell B. E.: A condom distribution program for adolescents: The findings of a feasibility study. Amer J of Public Health 61:739, 1971
2   Baird D., Hytten F. E., Thomson A. M.: Age and human reproduction. J Obstet Gynaec Br Emp 65:865, 1958
3   Bedger J. E., Gelperin A., Jacobs E. E.: Socioeconomic characteristics in relation to maternal and child health. Public Health Rep 81:829, 1966
4   Birch H. G., Gussow J. D.: Disadvantaged children: health, nutrition and failure. Harcourt, Brace & World, Inc. New York 1970

5 Butler N. R., Alberman E. D.: Perinatal problems. The second report of the 1958 British perinatal survey. Edinburgh, E, Livingstone Ltd, 1969

6 Chase H. C.: The position of the United States in international comparisons of health status. Am J of Public Health 62:381, 1972

7 Crump E. P., Horton C. P., Masuoka, J., Ryan D.: Growth and development. I. Relation of birthweight in Negro infants to sex, maternal age, parity, prenatal care, and socioeconomic status. J Pediatr 51:678, 1957

8 Densen P. M.: Data cited on p 66 of Infant, perinatal, maternal, and childhood mortality in the United States, by S Shapiro, E. R. Schlesinger, R. E. L. Nesbitt, Jr., Harvard Univ Press, Cambridge 1968

9 Douglas J. W. B.: Mental ability and school achievement of premature children at 8 years of age. Br Med J 1:1210, 1956

10 Douglas J. W. B.: "Premature" children at primary schools. Br Med J 1:1008, 1960

11 Drage J., Berendes H. W., Fisher P. D.: The Apgar scores and four-year psychological examination performance. Perinatal Factors Affecting Human Development. Proceedings of the special session held during the Eighth Meeting of the PAHO Advisory Committee on Medical Research. June 1969, p 222

12 Drillien C. M.: The Growth and Development of the Prematurely Born Infant. Williams & Wilkins, Baltimore 1964, p 376

13 Drillien C. M.: Premature in school. Pediatric Digest, Sept. 1956 p 75

14 Eastman N. J.: Prematurity from the viewpoint of the obstetrician. Am Practitioner 1:343, 1947

15 Furstenberg Γ. F.: As cited in M.C.H. Exchange 1: No 4, 1971, p 5

16 Harper P. A., Weiner G.: Sequelae of low birthweight. Ann Rev Med 16:405, 1965

17 Holley W. L., Rosenbaum A. L., Churchill J. A.: Effect of rapid succession of pregnancy. Perinatal Factors Affecting Human Development. Proceedings of the special session held during the Eighth Meeting of the PAHO Advisory Committee on Medical Research. June, 1969, p 41

18 Illsley R.: The sociological study of reproduction and its outcome. Childbearing: Its Social and Psychological Aspects, edited by S. A. Richardson and A. F. Guttmacher. Williams & Wilkins. Baltimore 1967, p 75

19 Illsley R.: Data cited on p 17 of Disadvantaged Children: Health, Nutrition, and School Failure, by Birch H. G., Gussow J. D., Harcourt Brace & World, Inc. New York, 1970

20 Knobloch H., Pasamanick B., Harper P. A., Rider R.: The effect of prematurity of health and growth. Am J Public Health 49:1164, 1959

21 Knobloch H., Rider R., Harper P., Passamanick B.: Neuro-psychiatric sequelae of prematurity: A longitudinal study. JAMA 161:581, 1956

22 Lilienfeld A. M., Passamanick B.: The association of maternal and fetal factors with the development of cerebral palsy and epilepsy. Am J Obstet Gynecol 70:93, 1955

23 Lubchenco L. O., Horner F. A., Reed L. H., et al: Sequelae of premature birth. Am J Dis Child 106:101, 1963

24 Lunde A. S.: White-nonwhite fertility differentials in the United States. HEW Indicators 1965

25 McDonald A. D.: Intelligence in children of very low birthweight. Br J Prev Soc Med 18:59, 1964

26 Morrison S. L., Heady J. A., Morris J. N.: Social and biological factors in infant mortality. VIII. Mortality in the post-neonatal period. Arch Dis Child 34:101, 1959

27 Niswander K. R., Gordon M.: The Collaborative Perinatal Study of the National Institute of Neurological Diseases and Stroke—The Women and Their Pregnancies, W. B. Saunders, Philadelphia, 1972

28 Osofsky H. J.: The Pregnant Teenager: A Medical, Educational and Social Analysis. Charles C. Thomas, Springfield, Ill. 1968

29 Osofsky H. J.: Adolescent out-of-wedlock pregnancy: An overview. Clin Obstet Gynecol 14:442, 1971

30 Osofsky H. J., Osofsky J. D.: Adolescents as mothers. Results of a program for low-income pregnant teenagers with some emphasis upon infants' development. Am J Orthopsychiatry 40:825, 1970

31 Osofsky H. J., Rajan R., Wood P. W., DiFlorio R.: An interdisciplinary program for low-income pregnant schoolgirls: A progress report. J of Reprod Med 5:18, 1970

32 Page E. W.: Pathogenesis and prophylaxis of low birthweights. Clin Obstet Gynec 13:79, 1970

33 Pasamanick B., Knobloch H.: Brain damage and reproductive casualty. Amer J Orthopsychiat 30:298, 1960

34 Pasamanick B., Lilienfeld A. M.: Association of maternal and fetal factors with the development of mental deficiency. I. Abnormalities in the prenatal and paranatal periods. JAMA 159:155, 1955

35 Pasamanick B., Knobloch H., Lilienfeld A. M.: Socioeconomic status and some precursors of neuropsychiatric disorders. Am J Orthopsychiatry 26:594, 1956

36 Rider R. V., Tayback M., Knobloch H.: Associations between premature birth and socioeconomic status. Am J Public Health 45:1022, 1955

37 Russell J. K., Fairweather D. V. I., Millar D. G., et al: Maternity in Newcastle-upon-Tyne: A community study. Lancet 1a, 711, 1963

38 Russell J. K., Millar D. G.: Maternal factors and mental performance in children, Perinatal Factors Affecting Human Development. Proceedings of the special session held during the Eighth Meeting of the PAHO Advisory Committee on Medical Research. June 1969, p 41

39 Sarrel P.: Personal communication, 1970

40 Scott R. B., Cardoza W. W., deG Smith A., DeLilly M. R.: Growth and development of Negro infants. III. Growth during the first year of life as observed in private pediatric practice. J Pediatr 37:885, 1950

41 Scott R. B., Jenkins M. E., Crawford R. P.: Growth and development of Negro infants. I. Analysis of birthweights of 11,818 newly born infants. Pediatrics 6:425, 1950

42 Shapiro S., Jacobziner H., Densen P. M., Weiner L.: Further observations on prematurity and perinatal mortality in a general population and in the population of a prepaid group practice medical care plan. Am J Public Health 50:1 304, 1960

43 Shapiro S., Schlesinger E. R., Nesbitt Jr., R. E. L.: Infant, Perinatal, Maternal, and Childhood Mortality in the United States. Harvard Univ. Press. Cambridge, 1968

44 Thomson A. M.: Prematurity: Socioeconomic and nutritional factors. Bibl Paediatr 8:197, 1963

45 Vital and Health Statistics. Analytical studies, international comparison of perinatal and infant mortality: The United States and six West European countries. US Dept of Health, Education, and Welfare. Washington, DC, 1967

46 Vital and Health Statistics, US Dept of Health, Education, and Welfare. Washington, DC, 1972

47 Wallace H. M.: Factors associated with perinatal mortality and morbidity. Clin Obstet Gynecol 13:13, 1970

48 Wallace H. M.: As cited in M.C.H. Exchange 1:No 4, 1971, p 4

49 Weiss W., Jackson E. C.: Maternal factors affecting birthweight. Perinatal Factors Affecting Human Development. Proceedings of the special session held during the Eighth Meeting of the PAHO Advisory Committee on Medical Research. June 1969, p 54

50 Wiener G., Rider R. V., Oppel W. C., et al: Correlates of low birthweight: Psychological status at 6–7 years of age. Pediatrics 35:434, 1965

51 Wiener G., Rider R. V., Oppel W. C., Harper P. A.: Correlates of low birthweight: Psychological status at eight to ten years of age. Pediatr Res 2:110, 1968

52 Windle W. F.: Asphyxial brain damage at birth, with reference to the minimally affected child. Perinatal Factors Affecting Human Development. Proceedings of the special session held during the Eighth Meeting of the PAHO Advisory Committee on Medical Research. June 1969, p 215

53 World Health Organization. Epidemiological and Vital Statistics Report 19: 100, 1966

54 Yerby A. S.: The disadvantaged and health care. Am J Public Health 56:5, 1966

Emotional Crises of School-Age Girls during Pregnancy and Early Motherhood

Maurine LaBarre, A.C.S.W.

Associate Professor of Psychiatric Social Work, Division of Child Psychiatry, Duke University Medical Center

The theoretical concepts we have found most useful in studying and working with pregnant girls are those of "crisis." These young girls are experiencing concurrently a triple crisis of maturational or developmental phases of feminine life (Deutsch, 1941; LaBarre, 1968a). They have not yet completed adolescent development (Group for the Advancement of Psychiatry, 1968) when they are experiencing their first pregnancy (Bibring, 1959) and are struggling with adjustments to new roles as wives or unwed mothers-to-be (LaBarre and LaBarre, 1969; Benedek, 1959). In some cases the discovery of the pregnancy or other life events precipitates an acute crisis episode of shock, stress, and anxiety, disrupting the previous adjustment and requiring the reorganization or development of new coping methods to deal with the trauma (Caplan, 1959; Parad, 1965).

DATA ON WHICH THIS STUDY IS BASED

Experience in a program providing continuing education, health and social services for pregnant schoolgirls provided material for this documentary study. A pilot project, voluntarily supported by the community, was conducted in 1967–68. A 3-year grant, 1968–71, provided funds for conducting a small, separate junior-senior high school administered as part of the city schools system (Cooperative School Reports, 1969, 1970, 1971). Subsequently an appropriation from the County Commissioners to the city schools provided for continuance of a modified program. The Cooperative School followed the school system's policies of teacher certification, course credits, daily hours, and holiday schedules. A curriculum of basic subjects is offered. A "Special Home Economics Course," required of all students, is focused on life interests of the students, combining nutrition, budgeting, sewing, arts and crafts, infant care and development, health, and family life. A full-time public health nurse and three psychiatric social workers participated in the Home Economics course, provided individual and group counseling, and contributed research data.

Copyright, American Academy of Child Psychiatry, reprinted from the *Journal of the American Academy of Child Psychiatry*, vol. 11, pp. 537–557 (July 1972).

By written or unwritten policy in our community as in most other states, pregnant girls are required to withdraw from public schools when pregnancy becomes known or obvious. Many such girls grow discouraged and become permanent dropouts. In our program students were enrolled at any time during the year, continued homework assignments during the postpartum period, and returned to the program until they had completed a semester's work, when they were re-enrolled in their regular school or graduated. The students continued to live in their homes in the community, and nearly all planned to keep their babies. Of the 71 students enrolled the first year, 1 placed her baby for adoption, 2 left their babies in the care of relatives or friends, and all others continued to care for their babies in their homes with parents, relatives, or husbands. Both married and unmarried girls attend the school. Around 30 percent were married at intake during 1968–69; at the time of a follow-up study a year later, 55 percent were married or had definite plans for marriage in the near future. The ages of the students ranged from 13 to 19 years; 28 percent were 15 or younger; 25 percent were 16, and 47 percent were 17 or older. Eighty percent were senior high school students. Approximately 84 percent were black, 16 percent white. The majority of the students came from self-supporting working-class families, the incomes of most of which were near the poverty line. Around 24 percent came from families receiving public assistance and a smaller number from middle-class families.

Statistical data reported pertain to the 71 students enrolled the first year, 1968–69 with whom a follow-up study was conducted a year later. Social work counseling and health records provided case materials for this study, and staff discussions contributed to the analysis. Our knowledge was broadened by study of the literature and participation in workshops and conferences for multidiscipline programs for pregnant school-age girls, of which there are now nearly 200 in the United States, organized in a National Alliance Concerned with School-Age Parents (Holmes, 1970).

THE FIRST EMOTIONAL CRISIS: TELLING THE FAMILY

The first, most intense emotional crisis occurs when the pregnancy is suspected or confirmed and the girl must tell her family. Most girls vividly recalled this period as very upsetting to themselves and their parents. Some minimized or denied their own reactions, and only from their mothers did we learn how disturbed emotionally the girls had become. Many described a sense of shock, incredulity, bewilderment, embarrassment, dread and fear of telling their parents, grief and remorse for hurting and disappointing the family. The most striking, most often mentioned reaction was their own surprise, disbelief, and sense of shock when they found they were pregnant.

Even girls informed about sex and contraceptives had neglected using any safeguards (Von Der Ahe. 1969; Aug and Bright, 1970; Birdwhistell, 1968). "I just can't believe it yet." "I don't understand how it happened: of course I know in a way, but I can't figure it out." "I didn't think you could get pregnant at my age." "I never believed it could happen to me." "I sit and think and think—how did I get in this fix?" These spontaneous comments suggest fantasies of invulnerability, unrealistic expectations, rationalizations for yielding to impulse, defenses of denial so powerful that the girl felt genuinely "shocked" by the real consequences of her sexual behavior. Some persisted in this denial for months. Some reacted with passivity and helpless inability to plan or do anything. Others were overwhelmed by an intolerable burden of anxiety while trying to conceal their condition. Sometimes a teacher suspected a pregnancy before the girl "knew it" herself, "because she slept in class." In other cases, mothers grew concerned because the girl had become listless, withdrawn, unable to sleep or eat, "unlike herself," and took the girl to a doctor to find out if she was sick.

After describing their parents' reactions, many girls concluded, in tones of surprise and relief, that it had not been "as bad as I expected," or "they took it better than I thought they would." The intensity of apprehension the girls felt indicates that this crisis reactivated superego guilt and early childhood fears of overwhelming anger, reproach, punishment, or rejection by parents, in comparison with which the reality of their parents' reactions and behavior was mild. This exaggerated fear was reflected also in 4 cases in which the mother and daughter were extremely fearful of telling the girl's father, because of his explosive temper, and attempted to conceal the pregnancy for weeks, only to find him reasonably concerned and helpful.

Reactions among families varied. Most apparently experienced a period of a week or two with acute feelings of shock, grief, and consternation. Also described were frequent, prolonged storms of crying, feelings of hopelessness, repetitious worry, anger, reiterated questioning and reproaches, soul-searching for blame and responsibility. Discussions during this period were usually contained within the immediate family group. Then, as many parents expressed it, "We realized we had to accept it and do the best we could; she is our daughter and we still love her; anyone may be forgiven one mistake; we won't let it ruin her life; she needs our help and we will give her all the support we can." The parents could then begin to consider plans, to consult with relatives, minister, or teacher. Solicitude for the young girl who they felt was unaware of what was ahead of her, identification by mothers with daughters in this profound feminine experience, and protective feelings by fathers began to relieve tension and restore disturbed relationships.

REJECTION FROM SCHOOL AND THE EGO-SUPPORTIVE
VALUES OF A SPECIAL PROGRAM

The developmental tasks of adolescence have been delineated as the completion of biological maturation, the development of self identity, the determination of one's sexual identification and role and the development of the capacity for lasting relationships and for both tender and genital sexual love in a heterosexual relationship, the attainment of independence and separation from one's parents, the development of a personal value system, the choice of a vocation and commitment to work (Group for the Advancement of Psychiatry, 1968; Erikson, 1959; Calderone, 1966). In the crisis of adolescence, the multiple and fluctuating stresses of sexual and aggressive drives with biological and psychological changes, the resolution of oedipal and dependency relationships with parents, the search for values and self and sexual identity create anxiety and confusion. Old defenses and coping methods may be threatened and prove inadequate. New as well as former ego strengths are required for the reorganization and stabilization of the personality. In this adolescent crisis the potential ego-supportive functions of the school have been too little recognized or utilized. We offer some observations of the significance of school experience to pregnant girls.

A major concern of the girls and their families was the necessity of withdrawal from school. To many parents this was a bitter disappointment of their hopes for their daughters. In an earlier study, I observed that among white blue-collar working-class families there appeared to be a family or subcultural attitude which considered girls of 14 to 16 mature enough for marriage and motherhood (LaBarre, 1968a). Such girls usually left school before pregnancy and were not interested in further education. Among both black and white middle-class families the two most common patterns appear to be marriage as soon as possible after conception, or concealment of the pregnancy and placement of the baby for adoption. Among black working-class families, with few exceptions, we found a strong motivation for education, as parents realized their own work opportunities and income were limited by lack of education. A number of mothers were also concerned about the daughter being alone at home while mother worked, because they feared "she might do something" when she was depressed, or might be "molested," as unmarried pregnant girls are regarded as easy prey. As our School became more widely known, this opportunity provided a real answer to such family concerns (Howard, 1968a). To the girls our School offered a "way out" of a traumatic situation and a means of atonement and pleasing their parents.

The sudden loss of the major role and occupation of adolescents, that of student, constitutes a real rejection and punishment of the pregnant girl (Osofsky, 1968). To some students, withdrawal from school seemed an overwhelming frustration of hopes and plans and loss of their self-esteem. Others expressed fear of reproach, condemnation and rejection by school personnel, dread of other students "suspecting" or remarking on their condition. Some students defended themselves against painful feelings by denial and a façade of indifference, or by withdrawal or depressive reaction. In our first contact, many appeared very subdued, passive, and guarded, or blandly denied problems. Later the girls confided how apprehensive they had felt about coming to the new school, and their surprise when they were given a friendly welcome and a matter-of-fact acceptance of their pregnancy. Initially we invited both mother and daughter to come for an application interview, but soon found that the mothers dominated the discussion. Now we ask the girl to come alone for the first interview, and we make a home visit to the family later. This respect for the girl's own motivation and decision supports the independence strivings of adolescence. The step-by-step requirements of the intake process give the girl some concrete ego-oriented tasks and thereby help her cope with the emotional turmoil and feelings of helplessness and inadequacy which the pregnancy crisis evoked.

We believe some structure and requirements of the educational process are essential to and supportive of ego development in adolescence. The consistent daily tasks of school life provide a focus and framework for effort. The continuity, ongoing direction, challenge of, and opportunity for, goal-oriented activities, satisfaction in achievement and recognition provide a steadying and sustaining influence. Such experiences are especially constructive for girls whose inner balance of aggression, guilt, fear, and self-esteem has been disturbed by the precocious pregnancy experience. Occupation and engagement of self help combat mood swings, depressions, and absorption in fantasies or physical symptoms common among adolescents and especially among pregnant women. School experience is in marked contrast to the lonely, empty, depressing long period of waiting at home complained of by married pregnant girls who have dropped out of school (LaBarre, 1968a).

Our staff devoted much thought to the development of school policies to achieve a therapeutic milieu and attain a balance of flexibility and firmness with students. As in any other group of adolescents, after a few weeks of becoming comfortable in the new situation, students began testing our staff members, passively resisting or sometimes noisily protesting about homework, tests, lunches or some teacher's "unfairness" or student's "meanness." We found it very useful to have the authority figure of the principal for both teachers and students to consult about academic or discipline problems. Teachers share with social workers and nurse observations of tension or difficulties in classes or between students. The fears that haunt staffs of programs like ours are accidents at the school, open fights between students, and suicide. Hence we try to foresee and forestall incipient crises by counseling with the girls promptly and thereby dispelling tension before it peaks.

A wide range of individual differences in ability and maturity as well as in age and family background characterized the student body. We found, as has been observed in other programs (Howard, 1968b; Anonymous, 1970), that younger students presented special problems and challenges to the staff. As is characteristic of young adolescents (Blos, 1962), although there were variations, as a group the junior high school students were less motivated for regular classwork, more engrossed in peer relationships, ambivalent in relation to rules and authority figures, more needful of varied activities and specific assignments. Teachers experienced in work with this age group and some special program plans are necessary to meet the needs of this age group.

A major advantage of the special school situation is the opportunity to belong to a peer group, so important to adolescents. Small groups of girls who had known each other previously or who quickly developed friendships in this school helped establish their identity in the new setting. Most of these groups provided mutually satisfying and constructive relationships for all the girls involved. Occasionally a group showed a snobbish or rejecting attitude toward less fortunately situated or endowed students. One clique was definitely characterized as troublemakers, who made jeering comments about other students, contrived to push or joggle in the corridors or lunchroom, told tales from one girl to another about boyfriends. From time to time there emerged a "scapegoat" on whom other girls focused disapproval or ridicule, sometimes a slow, inept girl or an unusually deprived one. Discussions individually and in group sessions gave these adolescents a new awareness of their own attitudes, responsibility for their behavior, and experience in getting along in a group.

An interesting phenomenon noted in several instances was "the best friend" pair. There are suggestions that in such friendships the two girls share secrets about relationships with boyfriends and mutual concerns about sexual activity and pregnancy. When the second girl of such pairs came to the school, the one who had enrolled first "showed her about" and introduced her. Sometimes when one of the pair became involved with other students, her best friend became depressed and withdrawn. In one case the mutual identification was so strong that when one of the pair went into labor, the other experienced "false labor" symptoms. These intense friendships seemed to dwindle after the babies were born and the school year was over. We wonder whether this "best friend" phase, although normal in puberty, may complicate the development of self-identity and of heterosexual relationships (Deutsch, 1967).

The emotional import of belonging to a group of peers all of whom are involved in the same basic life experience, with whom they can identify, share, learn from and give to, is very significant for pregnant girls. Group identification was illustrated in many ways. One day word was received that a student's baby had been stillborn. Several girls burst into sobs, and throughout the day the pall of grief and mourning over all the student body was marked. One student became depressed as she went beyond her anticipated delivery date. When she heard that yet another friend had delivered, she began to cry, saying, "I'm all alone, they've all gone and left me." Pregnancy, I believe, provides the most profound sisterhood of mutual feeling and experience. Sharing this experience among white and black, married and unmarried, was salutary for all students. Participation in a program for girls who expect to keep their babies is a markedly different experience from that in maternity homes where girls are separated from their families and boyfriends and expect to give up their babies (Finck et al., 1965). Our program is geared to pregnancy *and* motherhood. All our staff members are married: all are mothers or in the process of becoming mothers. They provide good mother images with whom to identify, both in their maternal roles and in their feminine roles as workers in the helping vocations of teaching, nursing, and social work. In essays a number of girls expressed a new ambition to train for such occupations, "because they helped people and were kind."

DYNAMIC FACTORS AND THE DEVELOPMENT OF COPING METHODS DURING THE PREGNANCY CRISIS

The major crises which developed during pregnancy were related to situational-economic needs and conflicts in relationships with parents, boyfriends, or husbands. Vincent's study of unmarried mothers (1961) concluded that no single factor of age, religion, socioeconomic status, personality type, family structure, or relationships accounted for the occurrence of pregnancy out-of-wedlock. Instead, individual configurations of the various factors occurred and must be studied to understand the individual girl. Our case studies confirm this conclusion. Within the variety and complexity of adolescent pregnancy experiences, we did observe some clusterings which will be described.

Many girls were initially resistant to talking about problems. Their orientation to the program was to school. Like other adolescents, their moods fluctuated and they were wary of involvement with adults. Some were so unaccustomed to verbalizing feelings or discussing problems with anyone, even family members, that it required active reaching out and much encouragement to help them learn to communicate. Some seemed unaware or passively accepting of miserable circumstances or family griefs, and were surprised that anyone would be interested or believe they could do something about their situation. Often we found that absence from school, failure to keep clinic appointments or to complete class assignments occurred because of some crisis at home. Gradually, girls began to seek out the social worker or nurse when a crisis arose.

As we clarified our objective of ego-supportive counseling, the social workers focused their interviews on helping girls cope with crises by encouraging them to express feelings and ideas, to think about situations and their own behavior, to consider alternatives, make decisions, plan and carry out ideas around specific current situations. The girls found relief in talking it over, support from the social worker's interest, and some idea of how they might begin to deal with the situation. While frequently they did not carry through with continued discussion or sustained work on the problem, they returned when they again felt worried.

A few girls sought regular interviews to ventilate, examine their own feelings and relationships, and increase their self-awareness and interest in becoming more mature and independent. For girls with serious personality problems we used psychiatric consultation to assess the nature and severity of their problems, to formulate appropriate goals and methods of helping sustain them during the pregnancy, and work toward referral to special services in the community.

Although the majority of our students came from self-supporting families, many of them were living below or near the poverty line or were able to maintain somewhat more adequate standards only because both parents were employed. There were wide differences in the ability of families to cope (LaBarre, 1968b; Herzog, 1968). Some made great efforts to manage independently. Concrete help with financial needs for lunch, bus tickets, clothing, and special health expenses were available. Some students, however poor, had much pride and were reluctant to accept assistance. A donation enabled us to set up a loan fund which was more acceptable and tided them over emergencies. The uncomplaining attitude and passive endurance of some girls, their reticence in initiating requests for help, their lack of know-how and aggression in finding available resources, were marked. Helping such girls learn to take active steps in utilizing community resources was another way of developing coping methods.

We noted not only a variety but also a fluidity in family living arrangements. Twenty-nine of the 71 students lived with both parents; 24 with one parent; 13 had been raised partly or entirely by a grandmother, aunt, friend, or neighbor who assumed the rule of foster parent. Several moved repeatedly from one family setting to another, choosing this solution of adolescent-parental conflicts. A number of girls were caught in severe marital conflicts and felt the loss of one or another parent when separations occurred. Others felt rejected by a parent or suffered because a sibling was the preferred child in the family (Khlentzos and Pagliaro, 1965). We found several cases of inadequate parental care or pathological family situations, such as alcoholism, mental illness, neglect, and abuse of children (Konop-ka, 1966; Reiner, 1968; Joint Commission Report, 1969). Some girls decid-ed the only solution was to leave home and live with other relatives or friends, or establish separate domiciles when they could obtain employment or AFDC grants for themselves and their babies.

It is difficult to determine how much the pregnancy experience was affected by the life situation and how much the pregnancy complicated family relationships and the girl's adjustment. As far as we could ascertain, most of the students experienced little psychological stress reaction *to the pregnancy itself,* once the initial crisis had been resolved. In nearly all later crisis episodes we found indications that the girls who suffered emotionally were girls who had had conflictual relationships or inner conflicts *prior to the pregnancy* (Brenner, 1941; Heiman and Levitt, 1960; Young, 1954; Ko-nopka, 1966; Reiner, 1968).

As an illustration, Joyce, a 15-year-old 10th-grader, initially minimized her own and her family's feelings about her pregnancy. However, on the Mooney Problem Checklist, which is given all entering students, she report-ed feelings of self-condemnation, anxiety, and guilt over having become pregnant, thoughts of suicide, wishing she had never been born, and a strained relationship with parents. In a home visit, her mother revealed that the pregnancy had created a great deal of family turmoil, and Joyce had been very upset. Her mother described how carefully the girl had been supervised and that she had been "taken advantage of" by a soldier visiting a relative with whom the girl had spent the weekend. Her father was out-raged and very harsh toward mother and daughter. Psychiatric consultation was utilized to assess the girl's depression and to assist in planning. When the social worker initiated discussion, the girl tearfully acknowledged de-pressed feelings, but said they did not just start after her pregnancy. She had had similar feelings whenever she did not agree with her mother about something. She characteristically kept her feelings "inside" and was very unwilling to express openly any negative or angry feelings, feeling very guilty and fearing rejection. She considered herself and her family very religious and worried that God would punish her. With encouragement, the girl admitted her opposition to the family plan to raise the baby as the child of her parents, but was too apprehensive to communicate this to her par-ents. She accepted with relief the social worker's offer to discuss this with her mother. The mother eagerly entered into an alliance with the social worker to try to help the girl and to modify family attitudes. She planned with older siblings to help the father assume a more understanding and constructive attitude toward the girl's plans. The mother had been unaware of the girl's desire to be mother herself to the baby, and constructively encouraged the girl to take as much responsibility as she could for the baby's care. The girl seemed to gain assurance from her association with other students in similar circumstances, from the acceptance and interest given her as a person at the school, and with counseling developed some self-confidence and ability to communicate her feelings to her mother. Her growth was manifested when the putative father returned from service. He voluntarily assumed responsibility for medical expenses and support of the baby, and expressed interest in seeing the girl and baby. Joyce was able to acknowledge that she was pleased by his interest, and to point out to her mother that the family's negative attitude might discourage the man from continuing responsibility.

Crises in relationship to the putative father or husband, and crises with parents because of the boyfriend, constitute a major part of the pregnancy experience for most of our schoolgirls. Most studies of unmarried mothers have focused on those who placed their babies for adoption; these women rarely continued a relationship with the putative father. Some studies of very young ghetto girls report casual sexual encounters and discontinuance of the relationship after impregnation occurred (Barglow et al., 1968). Other studies of unmarried mothers who keep their babies report a sustained sexual love relationship with the baby's father, often eventuating in marriage (Sauber and Rubenstein, 1965). A few reports describe the young unwed father's reaction and concern about his responsibilities to the girl and the baby (Pannor et al., 1971; Robinson, 1969; LaBarre and LaBarre, 1969; Perkins and Grayson, 1968; David, 1970). Most of the students in our program had been "going steady" for several months or years. A few had known the boy for a short time or had had a more casual relationship; in a small number of cases, impregnation resulted from a single sexual experience. A larger number had been engaged or planned to marry, and sexual intimacy was part of their commitment to one another. Nearly all the girls who married did so after conception. To my knowledge, no studies in depth have been made of marital and parental relationships of teen-age couples (Burchinal, 1965). This subject is so important that, in view of the limitations of space, discussion is deferred.[1]

Although our data support the significance of the love relationship between the teen-age couple, in some instances the pregnancy clearly seemed to be related to dynamic factors in the girl's own personality and family relationships *irrespective* of her relationship to the young man. A number of studies have documented the conflictful mother-daughter relationship and related the pregnancy to acting-out rebellion, rivalry, or revenge against the mother, or search for nurturance which mother failed to provide (Barglow et al., 1968; Heiman and Levitt, 1960; Joint Commission

---

[1] "To Marry or Not to Marry: A Study of Marriage Decisions of Pregnant Girls and Young Fathers," by Maurine LaBarre, presented at the Annual Meeting of the American Orthopsychiatric Association, March 23, 1971.

Report, 1969; Konopka, 1966; Reiner, 1968; Robey et al., 1964). We also observed a few such cases. Our youngest applicant was a 13-year-old girl whose history of learning difficulties, despite superior intelligence, reflected a longstanding passive resistance to parental expectations. The girl had matured very early and related that her mother had always been very protective and fearful that she might get into trouble, as the boys flocked around her like bees around honey. The first time that she was alone in a car with a boy she became pregnant. "And now look what I've done," she said "just what my mother feared." Another girl concluded an account of her hostile relationship with an overstrict, punitive father, saying, "Now I've fixed it so he'll have something to argue with me about the rest of my life."

Other dynamic factors are suggested in 2 cases of girls whose pregnancy occurred soon after the death of the father with whom they had had a very close, dependent relationship (Gregory, 1965; Heiman and Levitt, 1960). In both cases the mother spontaneously expressed her feeling that the girl had become pregnant to try to replace this loss. Four girls, all under 15, expressed ambivalence about pregnancy, recognizing the difficulties entailed, but saying they were glad, as they had feared they never could become pregnant. They cited sisters or friends who had never been able to conceive, thereby projecting their fear that in some way they themselves were inadequate as women. In 4 cases there were strong indications that the mother was eager for the girl to bear a baby. One girl's mother had recently lost an infant of her own and wanted to adopt her daughter's baby. Another girl said she had expected her mother to be angry about her pregnancy, but instead her mother told her she was "proud." An older sister had lost a stillborn baby conceived out-of-wedlock and had placed a second illegitimate baby for adoption. The girl's mother mourned the loss of these babies and often questioned which one of her children would be the first one to give her a grandbaby whom she could keep.

In a few families there appeared to be a pattern of pregnancy out-of-wedlock and a more casual acceptance of the girl's pregnancy "as one of those things that happen," or, "it's nothing to be ashamed of." One mother herself continued to bear illegitimate children and could not understand why her daughter had not heeded her advice and taken the pills which she offered to share. A 15-year-old girl said her mother's only comment was that she "had done better than your sister who got pregnant when she was 12." In several families 2, 3, or more daughters in their teens had become pregnant out-of-wedlock (Ventura, 1969).

The examples of pathological family relationships should not overshadow the larger number of cases in which relatively stable, warm, supportive family relationships were evidenced before and during the pregnancy, and other instances in which the stimulus of this new crisis resulted in more active support and closer ties in the family (LaBarre, 1968b). The social workers were impressed by the many cases of good mother-daughter and family relationships. After the initial crisis, such parents were able to encourage and help the girl with her educational plans, leave her free to decide about marriage on the basis of her regard for the boy and his potentials as husband and father apart from the urgency of the baby's care, and to give a loving welcome to the baby when it arrived. The mothers welcomed the interest of the social worker and established a partnership to help the girl cope with the pregnancy experience and develop maternal responsibility.

HEALTH CRISES IN A HIGH-RISK GROUP

Teen-age girls are a high-risk group for complications of pregnancy and delivery, especially toxemia and prematurity (Herzog and Bernstein, 1964; Israel and Woutersz, 1963; Osofsky, 1968). Most of them have some degree of anemia, and many have problems of excessive weight gain and elevated blood pressure. We believe that a study in process of medical records of our students will confirm our impression that health conditions of our students and their babies are better than those reported in most obstetric studies (Sarrel, 1967). Our school program is structured around pregnancy. Students are required to attend prenatal clinics regularly, and special attention is given to medical recommendations. A morning snack and specially planned low-salt, low-fat, high-protein lunch are served to all students. Much instruction in health and home economics classes is focused on nutrition and weight control. Our full-time nurse is available for individual consultation about complaints or illness, and a sick bay and emergency transportation are available.

Health crises are met by students with various degrees of anxiety. Although medical advice usually relieved concern about a specific condition, sometimes anxieties persisted about other, related questions. For example, during pregnancy a girl with diabetes mellitus and essential hypertension gained a good understanding of her condition and adapted well to her medical regime. She confided she was more concerned about recurrent anxiety attacks and fears of dying. A student who became depressed and withdrawn while threatened with a spontaneous abortion revealed how much the baby had meant to her. Her chief concern was that her boyfriend might reject her when she was no longer pregnant. When she was reassured of his continuing love, she quickly regained her equilibrium. A girl who had a stillborn baby was overwhelmed with guilt because of her previous ambivalence about having a child. Another student reacted intensely to the discovery of her pregnancy, declaring she did not want a child and threatening suicide. She was hospitalized for treatment of hyperemia; psychiatric consultation was obtained and a therapeutic abortion recommended, which she refused. Both the girl and her mother, we learned, reacted hysterically to crises of various kinds: they identified with each other and mutually stimulated and tolerated dramatized reactions. Another student suffered numerous psychosomatic complaints throughout her pregnancy. Her mother had had several depressive episodes for which she was hospitalized. After years of marital conflict her parents had separated. Our student had developed migraine headaches before her pregnancy when she was worried about school marks. In classwork she was an able and model student, coping with some of her anxiety by intellectual effort, but setting overly high standards for herself and experiencing much tension. During the postpartum period, her anxieties turned to worries about the baby and her inadequacies as a mother.

For most health problems an opportunity to talk with social worker or nurse, with explanations, reassurance, and practical assistance, sufficed to help the girl proceed. An unanticipated anxiety came to light after a lecture by pharmacy students on the use and effects of hallucinogenic drugs. Many questions were asked by students about possible effects on the fetus. Subsequently several girls sought out the counselor to confide their concern because they suspected the putative father had been using drugs, were fearful about the effect on the baby, and concerned about real or anticipated personality changes in the young man.

The greatest fear about pregnancy for these girls, as indeed it is for most women of any age during their first pregnancy, is the unknown of labor and delivery (LaBarre, 1968a; Shereshefsky, 1969). The most popular girl at any time was the one who returned after delivery, when the other girls crowded around with questions about "what it was like." Much time was spent in classes discussing fears and expectations, folklore and old wives' tales, and in giving concrete, illustrated information, breathing exercises, visits to labor and delivery rooms at hospitals, etc. A grandfather who initially opposed his granddaughter attending the school later called to tell us that "when her time came, everyone was excited, but that young'un was the calmest one there, knew just where to go, what to do, what to expect. If you can teach that to a 15-year-old child, there isn't any praise too high for your school."

The nurse and social worker visit each girl in the hospital after delivery and at home. The girls look forward to these promised visits, are eager and proud to show their babies, and are full of questions about baby care. They inquire in detail about other students and send greetings. Homework assignments are given and arrangements made to return finished work and obtain additional lessons. The girls express interest and pleasure in having "something to do" during this interim period. We have noticed an almost complete lack of the proverbial "baby blues" among our students, and think it may be because students are enabled to maintain this tie to the school and anticipate resuming their student roles.

ADAPTATIONS TO THE MATERNAL ROLE

Numerous crises developed after delivery around the care of the baby. During the pregnancy, most girls were passively dependent on their mothers, accepted restrictions on their social activities, and found mother's solicitude and protectiveness gratifying and supportive. After the baby was born, we noted marked changes, and realized that some had suffered a mild depression throughout the pregnancy. Girls who had kept their coats on indoors, sat with their backs to the teacher, and were never able to raise their eyes to look directly at a staff member, now held their shoulders erect, looked one in the eyes, and smiled! The girls became more active, lively, blossomed out in clothing and makeup, were more communicative, and demonstrated new self-confidence and capability. A fresh assertion of independence, especially in relation to mother, became noticeable, and new or reactivated conflicts developed.

In family life classes as well as counseling, the girls became more aware of differences in family life styles and discussed their concerns about relationships with parents, struggles for independence, conflicts about dating, parental disapproval of the boyfriend, and pressures or resistances to the young couple's decision to marry. Now the girls began to voice complaints and dissatisfactions.

The unconscious rivalry which often emerges when the daughter becomes sexually mature and the mother faces the end of her reproductive period is well known. It is also demonstrated, we think, in the rivalry acted out between teen-age mothers and the grandmother over the maternal role, "whose baby" the child is, and who decides how the baby is to be cared for. Perhaps the mother's acceptance of her daughter's pregnancy and her willingness to provide care for the infant while the daughter completes her education is partially attributable to the still active maternal feelings of the grandmother, who identifies with the daughter during pregnancy and now has another baby to care for. Generational conflicts erupted when the girls insisted that the baby be cared for in terms of class instruction and books they had read, whereas grandmother or great-grandmother persisted in "old timey" customs. A common complaint of the girls was that relatives "spoiled the baby." However, most grandmothers wisely encouraged the girl to take as much responsibility as she could after school hours and weekends, stood by ready to help when asked, but wanted the girl to feel they were not usurping her role.

While the girls continued in school, their babies were cared for by the girl's mother in 24 cases; by the grandmother in 11; by other relatives—aunt, sister, or boyfriend's family—in 11; by hired sitters in 17 cases; by the girl herself in 4; and by foster home or adoption in 1. The greatest problems occurred when plans for baby care broke down, e.g., when a grandmother became ill or decided to take a job, or some other family crisis occurred. In a few cases, the girls were not able to make any acceptable plan for the baby's care, or concluded that they could not trust their baby to an unreliable or alcoholic mother or hired sitter, and withdrew from school to care for the baby themselves. Interestingly, the girls who experienced the most problems in living situations were the married girls, living in homes separate from their parents, who, in addition to schoolwork, housework, and medical care, had responsibilities for the feeding and care of husband, and then of baby, with no mother at hand to help. Three students in homes without mothers "drifted" into leaving their babies to the care of some other relative or family and retained little maternal responsibility, although only one girl decided on adoption.

All our staff members were impressed by numerous indications of the girls' desire "to learn to be a good mother" and their absorption in class discussions about child development, mother-infant relationships, and child care methods (Benedek, 1959; Jessner, 1959). Some were frank in expressing ambivalence about their new maternal role, saying, "I wanted to go out, but remembered I had to stay with the baby." "I get so tired of getting up every night, I don't know if I can stand it; I pretend I'm sound asleep when the baby cries and let my mother get up." In some cases anxious girls transferred their anxieties to the baby, fearing he was ill or not eating properly, and that they were inept or inadequate as mothers. Many of the students had had experience in helping care for younger siblings. Most of them demonstrated ease and competence in caring for the baby, and much warmth and interest. They assumed a good deal of responsibility for the care of their babies after school, on weekends, and during the summer.

Parenthood is a life task for which our traditional educational system provides almost no preparation. Special schools like ours offer an ego-developing program, the supportive help of good mother figures of the nurse and social worker, the experience of belonging to a peer group of other expectant teen-agers, and opportunities to "learn" the role of mothering. We believe these features enabled our students to mature, to develop coping abilities, and to assume maternal responsibility. Perhaps such gains cannot be demonstrated statistically, but they are incontrovertibly real to staff members working in programs like ours, and we offer our testimony of the potentiality of teen-age girls for responsible mothering. The widespread occurrence of parenthood in adolescence challenges us to help the young engage themselves thoughtfully in their own "thing" and their own emerging family life styles.

REFERENCES

Anonymous (1970). Pregnant teen-agers. *Today's Educ.,* 59:26–29, 89.

Anthony, E. J. (1969). The reactions of adults to adolescents and their behavior. In: *Adolescence: Psychosocial Perspectives,* ed. G. Caplan & S. Lebovici. New York: Basic Books, pp. 54–78.

Aug, R. G. & Bright, T. P. (1970). A study of wed and unwed motherhood in adolescents and young adults. *J. Amer. Acad. of Child Psychiatry,* 9:577–594.

Barglow, P., Bornstein, M., Exum, D. B., Wright, M. K., & Visotsky, H. M. (1968). Some psychiatric aspects of illegitimate pregnancy in early adolescence. *Amer. J. Orthopsychiat.,* 38:672–687.

Benedek, T. (1959). Parenthood as a developmental phase. *J. Amer. Psychoanal. Assn.,* 7:389–117.

Bebring, G. L. (1959). Some considerations of the psychological processes in pregnancy. *The Psychoanalytic Study of the Child,* 14:113–121. New York: International Universities Press.

Birdwhistell, M. (1968). Adolescents and the pill culture. *Family Coordinator,* 17:27–32.

Blos, P. (1962). *On Adolescence: A Psychoanalytic Interpretation.* New York: Free Press of Glencoe.

Brenner, R. F. (1941). Case work service for unmarried mothers. *The Family, J. Soc. Case Wk.,* 22:211–219.

Burchinal, L. G. (1965). Trends and prospectives for young marriages in the United States, *J. Marr. & Fam.,* 27:243–254.

Calderone, M. S. (1966). Sex and the adolescent. *Clin. Pediat.,* 5:171–174.

Caplan, G. (1959). *Concepts of Mental Health and Consultation.* Washington, D.C.: Children's Bureau.

Cooperative School for Pregnant Girls, *Reports* (1969, 1970, 1971). Durham, N.C.

David, L. (1970). The secret wish of unwed fathers. *Seventeen,* 29:128–129, 190, 192.

Deutsch, H. (1944). *The Psychology of Women.* New York: Grune & Stratton.

—— (1957). *Selected Problems of Adolescence.* New York: International Universities Press.

Erikson, E. H. (1959). *Identity and the Life Cycle [Psychological Issues,* Monogr. 1]. New York: International Universities Press.

Finck, G. H. et al., (1965). Group counseling with unmarried mothers. *J. Marr. & Fam.,* 27:224–229.

Gregory, I. (1965). Anterospective data following childhood loss of a parent: I. Delinquency and high school dropout. *Arch. Gen. Psychiat.,* 13:99–109.

Group for the Advancement of Psychiatry (1968). *Normal Adolescence: Its Dynamics and Impact* (Report No. 68), New York: Scribner's.

Heiman, M. & Levitt, E. G. (1960). The role of separation and depression in out-of-wedlock pregnancy. *Amer. J. Orthopsychiat.,* 30:166–174.

Herzog, E. (1968). Social and economic characteristics of high-risk mothers. In: *Mothers-at-Risk,* ed. F. Haselkorn, Washington, D.C.: Children's Bureau, pp. 26–47.

—— & Bernstein, R. (1964), *Health Services for Unmarried Mothers,* Washington, D.C.: Children's Bureau.

Holmes, M. (1970). Parenthood in adolescence. *Sharing Supplement.* Washington: Cyesis Programs Consortium.

Howard, M. (1968a). Comprehensive services programs for school-age pregnant girls. *Children,* 15:193–197.

—— (1968b). School continues for pregnant teenagers. *Amer. Educ.,* 5:5–7.

Israel, S. L. & Woutersz, T. B. (1963). Teen-age obstetrics: a cooperative study. *Amer. J. Obstet. Gynec.,* 85:659–668.

Jessner, L. (1959). The role of the mother in the family. In: *Emotional Forces in the Family,* ed. S. Liebman, Philadelphia: Lippincott, pp. 19–36.

Joint Commission on Mental Health of Children, Report of (1969). *Crisis in Child Mental Health: Challenge for the 1970's.* New York: Harper & Row.

Khlentzos, M. T. & Pagliaro, M. A. (1965). Observations from psychotherapy with unwed mothers. *Amer. J. Orthopsychiat.,* 35:779–786.

Konopka, G. (1966). *The Adolescent Girl in Conflict.* Englewood Cliffs, N.J.: Prentice-Hall.

LaBarre, M. (1968a). Pregnancy experiences among married adolescents. *Amer. J. Orthopsychiat.,* 38:47–55.

—— (1968b). The strengths of the self-supporting poor. *Soc. Casewk.,* 49:459–466.

—— & LaBarre, W. (1969). The triple crisis: adolescence, early marriage and parenthood. Part I, motherhood: Part II, fatherhood. In: *The Double Jeopardy: The Triple Crisis—Illegitimacy Today.* New York: National Council on Illegitimacy.

Osofsky, H. J. (1968). *The Pregnant Teen-ager.* Springfield, Ill.: Thomas.

Pannor, R., Masserik, F., & Evans, B. (1971). *The Unmarried Father: New Approaches for Helping Unmarried Young Parents.* New York: Springer.

Parad, H. J., ed. (1965). *Crisis Intervention: Selected Readings.* New York: Family Service Assn. of America.

Perkins, R. F. & Grayson, E. S. (1968). The juvenile unwed father. In: *Effective Services for Unmarried Parents and Their Children.* New York: National Council on Illegitimacy.

Reiner, B. S. (1968). The real world of the teenage Negro mother. *Child Welf.,* 47:391–396.

Robey, A., Rosenwald, R. J., Snell, J. E. & Lee, R. E. (1964). The runaway girl: a reaction to family stress. *Amer. J. Orthopsychiat.,* 34:762–767.

Robinson, D. (1969). Our surprisingly moral unwed fathers. *Ladies Home J.,* 86(8):48–50.

Sarrel, P. M. (1967). The university hospital and the teenage unwed mother. *Amer. J. Publ. Hlth.,* 57:1308–1313.

Sauber, M. & Rubinstein, E. (1965). *Experiences of the Unwed Mother as a Parent: A Longitudinal Study of Unmarried Mothers Who Keep Their First-Born.* New York: Community Council of Greater New York.

Shereshefsky, P. M. (1969). The childbearing experience: is anatomy destiny? *J. Otto Rank Assn.,* 4:88–116.

Ventura, S. J. (1969). Recent trends and differentials in illegitimacy. *J. Marr. & Fam.,* 31:446–450.

Vincent, C. E. (1961). *Unmarried Mothers.* New York: Free Press of Glencoe.

Von Der Ahe, G. V. (1969). The unwed teen-age mother. *Amer. J. Obstet. Gynec.,* 104:279–287.
Young, L. (1954). *Out-of-Wedlock.* New York: McGraw-Hill.

A Study of the Relationship between Maternal Life-Change Events and Premature Delivery

Jane Linker Schwartz, R.N., M.N., M.S.W.

I. INTRODUCTION

Social Readjustment Rating Scale

This study is based on the Social Readjustment Rating Scale (SRRS), developed in 1949 at the University of Washington School of Medicine, Department of Psychiatry, by Dr. Thomas H. Holmes and Dr. Richard H. Rahe. Since the early 1950s, this test has been administered to more than 5,000 persons from a variety of sociocultural backgrounds. It has been repeatedly demonstrated by these investigators, as well as by researchers elsewhere, that specific kinds of life events and changes frequently precede the onset of disease.

Holmes and Rahe used the term "disease" to apply to a change in health status which relates to a broad spectrum of medical, surgical, and psychiatric disorders. Diseases were classified into seven categories: infectious and parasitic, allergic, musculoskeletal, psychosomatic, psychiatric, physical trauma, and miscellaneous.

The original scale included a weighted assessment of forty-three life events which require individual adaptation and adjustment. Each item on the scale had been quantified in proportion to its relative relationship to an individual's life change. It was noted that the magnitude of certain life events had a meaningful connection not only with the onset but also with the severity of illness. For example, death of a spouse was classified as the most serious life change and was rated as having 100 life-change units (LCU) to 11 life-change units (LCU) for receiving a traffic violation [25, 36].

A quantitative amount of life change was listed for each item in any given year. Holmes and Rahe identified subjects with a yearly total of less than 150 LCU per year as having little or no life change. Subjects with a yearly total of 150 to 199 LCU were identified as having mild life crises. Subjects with yearly totals from 200 to 299 were defined as having moderate life changes. Subjects with 300 or more LCU were regarded as having major life changes [18, 7]. Table 1 lists the mean value of life changes for each item on the scale.

Holmes and Rahe further documented that diseases influenced by significant life changes appeared within a two-year period following moderate or major environmental alterations. They also noted that approximately 20 percent of cases with major life changes (300 LCU or more) continued to have good health for the succeeding two years. They recommended that this population be studied intensively in order to determine the nature of their resistance to disease [20, 37].

It seems desirable to study life events as they relate to the similarities and differences between mothers of premature and full-term infants. If there is a relationship between high life-stress scores and prematurity, it would indicate that this scale might provide a helpful means of identifying high-risk patients during the prenatal period as well as afterward.

Statement of the Purpose

The purpose of the current investigation was to conduct a pilot study to explore similarities and differences in the life changes experienced by mothers of premature and full-term infants during the two years immediately preceding the pregnancy and the three trimesters of the pregnancy itself.

The SRRS (Table 1) was used as the tool for identifying life changes. Demographic information was collected through the use of a parental screening interview (Table 2) in which material relating to the mother's age, marital status, nationality, education, previous pregnancies, and health related to previous as well as present pregnancies was recorded. The data was tabulated to describe the relevant social and health characteristics of the group completing the SRRS.

Hypothesis to Be Tested

There has been limited research to support the view that mothers of premature infants may have undergone more life change and possibly more stress than mothers of full-term infants. In this study, the early onset of labor was viewed as an "illness" in order to determine whether certain psychosocial factors might influence the progress or disruption of the pregnancy.

It was hypothesized that mothers of premature infants would have higher SRRS preceding and during the pregnancy than mothers who would deliver full-term infants.

II. METHOD OF STUDY

Population Studied

Fifty subjects for the study were selected from a large medical-center facility. Twenty-five of the mothers were patients on the obstetrical unit of the

Table 1 Social Readjustment Rating Scale

Rank	Life event	Mean Value
1	Death of spouse	100
2	Divorce	73
3	Marital separation	65
4	Jail term	63
5	Death of close family member	63
6	Personal injury or illness	53
7	Marriage	50
8	Fired at work	47
9	Marital reconciliation	45
10	Retirement	45
11	Change in health of family member	44
12	Pregnancy	40
13	Sex difficulties	39
14	Gain of new family member	39
15	Business readjustment	39
16	Change in financial state	38
17	Death of close friend	37
18	Change to different line of work	36
19	Change in number of arguments with spouse	35
20	Mortgage over $10,000	31
21	Foreclosure of mortgage or loan	30
22	Change in responsibilities at work	29
23	Son or daughter leaving home	29
24	Trouble with in-laws	29
25	Outstanding personal achievement	28
26	Wife begins or stops work	26
27	Begins or ends school	26
28	Change in living conditions	25
29	Revision of personal habits	24
30	Trouble with boss	23
31	Change in work hours or conditions	20
32	Change in residence	20
33	Change in schools	20
34	Change in recreation	19
35	Change in church activities	19
36	Change in social activities	18
37	Mortgage or loan less than $10,000	17
38	Change in sleeping habits	16
39	Change in number of family get-togethers	15
40	Change in eating habits	15
41	Vacation	13
42*	Christmas	12
43	Minor violations of the law	11

*Holmes and Rahe have recently deleted item 42 from the Rating Scale, it was not used in this study.

hospital and had given birth to full-term infants. They all were interviewed in the hospital within three days following delivery during a time span of one to two weeks. The other twenty-five mothers interviewed had given birth to premature infants between January and April 1973. Their infants were in the neonatal intensive care unit of the same hospital. Some of the mothers were interviewed at home and the remainder in the hospital.

The only criterion used in the selection of full-term mothers was that they had given birth to infants during the last two weeks of April 1973 and were in the hospital in the obstetrical unit at the time the study was being conducted.

The mothers of the premature group were not all interviewed in the hospital because of an insufficient number of infants hospitalized in the neonatal intensive-care unit during the last two weeks of April. The unit log was used as a method of selecting babies who had either been in the unit recently or were currently hospitalized. Geographical and time limitations meant that only mothers who lived within the environs of Seattle and, for the most part, those who could be reached by telephone for appointments were studied. Lack of a telephone was noted as a limitation in this study since this may imply an isolating factor as well as a possible socioeconomic problem.

Procedure

The purpose of the study was explained to all mothers meeting the criteria of having delivered either a full-term (thirty-seven to forty weeks) or premature (less than thirty-seven weeks) infant. Their permission to participate in the study was obtained before administration of the SRRS and the parental screening interview.

The SRRS was then self-administered by mothers in each group. When the mother had questions, the investigator was available to clarify wording and assist her if necessary. The interviewer then asked the questions from the parental screening interview.

Participation in this study was voluntary, and subjects were allowed to withdraw at any time. There was one refusal by a mother of a full-term infant and one by a mother of a premature infant.

Limitations

The size of the sample population was limited to fifty mothers. A larger, heterogenous population with a greater mixture of minority groups and socioeconomic classes would probably have revealed more information. The highest-risk population, which is the young, the poor, the black, and the unmarried, was not sufficiently studied in this sample population. The geographical area studied was small, and the sampling was restricted to one hospital.

Furthermore, since the sample population was drawn from a large metropolitan medical center with primary emphasis on a high-risk premature infant population, it does not represent the full variety of types of premature infants but focuses on those needing intensive care. It should be taken into consideration that the findings of this study may apply only to such a population.

Differences are present in the time and setting of the interviews with the two groups of mothers. The mothers of the full-term infants were interviewed within the first two to four days after the birth of their babies. The birth dates of all of these babies were within two weeks of each other. Some mothers of premature infants were interviewed within the hospital setting while their infants were in the intensive care unit, others were interviewed at home within three months of the birth of their infants. This was necessary due to the small census of the neonatal intensive care unit, the time limitations in collecting data, and the fact that many parents of premature infants lived out of the city.

One significant limitation seems to be that mothers of prematures were often under much stress: under such circumstances their memories may have emphasized certain events less easily recalled by the mothers of full-term infants. The general mood of the latter group was one of cheerfulness and relief since they were seen shortly after the birth of their babies, which tended to overshadow earlier life changes.

The characteristics of the group of infants were also different. There was a broad range of gestation ages and weights in the premature infants but less difference in the full-term infants.

Another limitation of the study was that prematures are born somewhere between the seventh and ninth months, so that life-change units on the SRRS could not be as accurately determined during the last trimester.

The SRRS questionnaire was set up with responses for each trimester (Table 5). In order to tabulate the responses in proper relationship to previous time intervals, such as during 1971 and 1972, it seemed best to add together the scores of the three trimesters so that they would more closely approximate the previous yearly scores. In doing so, any repetitive responses by mothers during the three trimesters were scored as a single answer, which is referred to in all tables as "1972–1973" (after subject knew she was pregnant).

Analysis of the Data

The data collected for this study consisted of the classification of fifty mothers (twenty-five mothers of full-term infants and twenty-five mothers of premature infants), demographic information on these fifty mothers by interview, and SRRS scores for a three-year period including the trimesters of the pregnancy for all fifty mothers. The data for the last year, or during the trimesters, were collapsed as described in the section on limitations.

The data were analyzed with the use of certain descriptive and parametric statistics. The Mann-Whitney U Test was used to examine the differences in the two groups of mothers on the Holmes SRRS. The Mann-Whitney U Test is similar to the Wilcoxon Rank Sum Test with the advantage that it does not require matched subjects [31]. The main purpose of using this test was to identify whether or not the two groups studied were similar or different as they related to the life changes listed in the Holmes scale.

If the two groups were similar, the sum of the ranks would be approximately equal. Conversely, if there was a difference in the groups, the sum of the ranks would differ "significantly." This particular test was used because of doubt about the validity of the normality assumption for the totals of each group. This nonparametric test does not assume underlying normal distributions.

III. RESULTS

Introduction

A high level of cooperation was demonstrated by the mothers in both groups. An appreciable difference was clinically apparent in the mood of the two sets of mothers. Many of the mothers of premature infants who were still hospitalized seemed especially concerned about their infants. The mothers of the full-term infants, on the other hand, were in most instances elated and expressed few concerns relating to their babies. They also showed greater ease in completing the SRRS and needed very little assistance from the interviewer.

The results of this study were based on information related to the demographic material in the parental screening interview as well as to the responses of these women to the SRRS.

Parental Screening Interview

The parental screening interview was an attempt to describe demographic characteristics relating to the mother's age, marital status, nationality, education, other pregnancies, and health in previous as well as present pregnancies. These data were tabulated to obtain a descriptive profile of the women participating in the study.

From examination of the frequency distribution presented in Table 2, the two populations showed similar characteristics in age, marital status, race, education, number of previous pregnancies, live births, and medical complications during present pregnancy. No further analysis of the mentioned variables was done since, from visual inspection of the data, it was apparent that the populations were highly similar. The one variable that appeared to show differences was the number of previous abortions and

Table 2 Description of Population Studied on Relevant Social and Medical Variables

Selected characteristics	Number	
	Premature	Full term
Total	**25**	**25**
Age		
Under 16	2	2
16–19	2	3
20–34	18	17
35 and over	3	3
Marital status		
Married	19	17
Single	3	6
Separated	2	2
Divorced	1	0
Race		
Caucasian	20	16
Negro	3	7
American Indian	0	0
Oriental	2	2
Chicano	0	0
Education		
Beyond high school	8	9
High school graduate	11	10
Less than high school	6	6
Number of previous pregnancies		
0	7	9
1 or more	18	16
Number of live births		
1	8	9
2	10	9
3	4	3
4 or more	3	4
Abortions and/or miscarriages		
0	12	20
1	8	3
2	3	1
3 or more	2	1
Medical complications during pregnancy		
0	4	3
1	8	8
2	9	8
3 or more	3	6

Table 3 Results of Comparison between the Number of Previous Abortions in Mothers Whose Present Pregnancy Resulted in a Premature Infant and Mothers Who Had a Full-Term Infant, Using the Mann-Whitney *U* Test for Significance

Rank sum score	Mann-Whitney *U*	*Z* -score	Level of significance
523	198	3.93	.0001

miscarriages. The mothers who delivered premature infants had had significantly more previous abortions. A Mann-Whitney *U* test was performed. Table 3 presents a summary of these data, indicating that this difference was significant at the .0001 level.

Social Readjustment Rating Scale

The data from the SRRS were analyzed in several ways. First, Table 4 gives the total sum of responses on the SRRS for the two groups of mothers over all the time periods. This included the 2½ years before becoming pregnant and the period of the pregnancy itself. The total number of responses for the mothers of premature infants exceeded those of the full-term mothers. The values attached to the life-change events in this investigation were the same as used in all studies by Holmes.

From inspection of a chart of the comparative distribution of life-change events for mothers of full-term and premature infants it was apparent that the group had similar life events to report; however, the mothers of premature infants had reported more life events. The premature group reported considerably more occurrences of the following events:

1 Personal injury or illness
2 Change in financial state
3 Trouble with in-laws
4 Change in recreation
5 Change in church activities
6 Change in social activities
7 Mortgage of less than $10,000
8 Change in eating habits

On only seven of the items did the full-term group of mothers report more occurrences in life change, and then only slightly. The greatest difference on any one item was trouble with in-laws, with eight times the frequency shown in the premature group compared with the full-term mothers.

Table 4 Responses to Social Readjustment Rating Scale

Value	Life-change event	Pre-mature	Full term
Total responses		**490**	**312**
100	Death of spouse	0	2
73	Divorce	3	0
65	Marital separation	10	6
63	Jail term	7	5
63	Death of close family member	10	8
53	Personal injury or illness	18	7
50	Marriage	11	9
47	Fired at work	0	2
45	Marital reconciliation	3	0
45	Retirement	10	8
44	Change in health of family member	20	17
40	Pregnancy	16	7
39	Sex difficulties	3	2
39	Gain of new family member	18	9
39	Business readjustment	2	2
38	Change in financial state	25	11
37	Death of close friend	3	4
36	Change to different line of work	10	4
35	Change in number of arguments	12	8
31	Mortgage over $10,000	5	2
30	Foreclosure	2	1
29	Change in responsibilities	7	4
29	Son/daughter leaves home	1	2
29	Trouble with in-laws	25	3
28	Outstanding personal achievement	1	2
26	Wife begins/stops work	13	9
26	Begins or ends schooling	9	10
25	Change in living conditions	15	10
24	Revision of personal habits	22	17
23	Trouble with boss	6	3
20	Changes working hours	13	7
20	Change in residence	40	40
20	Change in schools	4	7
19	Change in recreation	17	4
19	Change in church activities	12	3
18	Change in social activities	27	9
17	Mortgage less than $10,000	19	9
16	Change in sleeping habits	16	18
15	Change in number of family gatherings	11	12
15	Change in eating habits	24	12
13	Vacation	16	15
11	Minor violations of law	4	2

Table 5   Frequency of Life-Change Events in Mothers of Full-Term Infants and Mothers of Premature Infants

Life change	1970	1971	1972[a]	1972–1973[b]
Mothers of premature infants				
Little or none[c]	16	15	13	11
Mild[d]	4	3	4	5
Moderate[e]	4	5	6	6
Major[f]	1	2	2	3
Mothers of full-term infants				
Little or None[c]	20	22	20	17
Mild[d]	2	2	3	4
Moderate[e]	2	1	1	3
Major[f]	1	0	1	1

[a]Before a subject knew she was pregnant.
[b]After subject knew she was pregnant.
[c]Less than 150 LCU = little or no life change.
[d]150–199 LCU = mild life change.
[e]200–299 LCU = moderate life change.
[f]300 or more LCU = major life change.

One way of analyzing the scores was to use the Holmes' classification of little or no, mild, moderate, or major life change. Table 5 presents these data. It is evident that in the two years before the pregnancy and during the pregnancy, the women who delivered premature infants had more moderate and major life changes than the women who had full-term infants. In fact, the majority (80 percent) of women delivering full-term infants reported little life change before or during pregnancy, while 36 percent, or a difference of 16 percent in the two groups, of the women delivering premature infants reported mild to major life events.

Another way of looking at the scores was to calculate the means for each group. Table 6 demonstrates mean scores and standard deviations of the rating on the SRRS in the periods preceding and during the pregnancies for mothers of full-term and mothers of premature infants. A continued increase in life-change scores persisted in both groups throughout the two-year period before and during the pregnancy. The mothers of premature infants consistently had a higher score throughout the intervals studied. Mothers of premature infants had a shorter gestation period than the mothers of full-term infants but still had higher scores in regard to life change.

It was of interest to note results from the Mann-Whitney Test, which indicated that the greatest difference was in the year before becoming pregnant ($p = >$ .00001). These data are presented in Table 7. During all peri-

Table 6   Mean Scores and Standard Deviations of the Social Readjustment Rating Scale for Mothers of Full-Term Infants and Mothers of Premature Infants

	Premature		Full-term	
Time	Mean	Standard deviation	Mean	Standard deviation
1970	114.00	98.62	75.16	110.40
1971	146.12	116.56	77.80	66.64
1972*	157.52	107.27	95.32	92.83
1972–1973†	170.64	112.10	123.00	85.74

*Before subject knew she was pregnant.
†After subject knew she was pregnant.

ods before the pregnancy, the differences in the two groups were beyond the .01 level of significance. During the pregnancy, the significance of the difference dropped ($p = <.05$); the unequal time representation may account for this, since the mothers of premature infants were reporting on approximately seven months of pregnancy versus the full-term period.

Summary of Findings

Within recent times, increasing attention has been given to improving prenatal care for high-risk mothers. Commentary in the professional literature has advocated more emphasis on finding these high-risk patients sooner and providing them with better prenatal care. This study was an attempt to explore the use of the SRRS as a variable in predicting mothers who are at risk for premature delivery. This project was designed to determine whether there were significant differences between the mothers of full-term infants and those of premature infants in relation to life-change units. The investi-

Table 7   Summary of Differences between the Two Groups on the Social Readjustment Rating Scale Using the Mann-Whitney U Test

	Rank sum score	Mann-Whitney		Level of
Time	T	U	Z-score	significance
1970	748.5	201.5	2.20	.0139
1971	825.5	124.5	3.66	.0001
1972*	760.0	190.0	2.38	.0087
1972–1973†	710.0	240.0	1.41	.0793

*Before subject knew she was pregnant.
†After subject knew she was pregnant.

gator studied specific life changes which took place before or during the pregnancy of mothers in both groups.

From a demographic point of view, the two groups were similarly matched. The largest group of mothers studied included the ages of twenty to thirty-four. As noted in the literature, this is not the highest-risk population as far as problems relating to prematurity go. The same is true in the other categories, since there was a predominance of married, Caucasian mothers who had had previous pregnancies. Abortions and/or miscarriages, as reported by the mothers, showed that the mothers of premature infants appeared to be a high-risk group in that over half reported one or more abortions and/or miscarriages.

The SRRS, however, indicated that there were statistically significant differences in life changes between the two groups. The mothers of premature infants demonstrated more personal injury or illness, marital separation, gaining of new family members, change in financial state, change in number of arguments, trouble with in-laws, change in social activities, and change in eating habits.

IV. IMPLICATIONS OF THE STUDY AND RECOMMENDATIONS

Summary of Findings

The data from the SRRS support the hypothesis predicting that mothers of premature infants would have more life changes than mothers of full-term infants.

Mothers of premature infants, as compared with mothers of full-term infants, indeed, showed a significantly higher number of life-change units, especially in the years preceding their pregnancy and just before the pregnancy. A graph illustrating the mean scores on the SRRS for both groups of mothers made it possible to visualize the upswing in life-change units as these mothers approached pregnancy. Furthermore, it demonstrated that the mothers of premature infants consistently had higher scores in life-change units preceding and during pregnancy. It might further be surmised that these same mothers would continue to have an upswing in life change and stress after the birth of their babies.

Implications of This Study

The SRRS can be used as part of a process of early intervention to assist in identifying those mothers who show many life changes preceding and during pregnancy. If crisis intervention is to be useful, there are implications in this study of a need for increased personnel to support the psychological needs of the mother as well as to respond to the physical and emotional needs of the infant.

It would appear, from this study, that high-risk patients can be identified through the use of the SRRS. From the review of the literature, there are many indications that there is an important need to respond to the problems of patients in the high-risk category. While maternal and infant programs have been established to work with high-risk patients, there is every indication that these must be expanded in order to diminish the mortality and morbidity rates in our infant population significantly.

Recommendations for Further Study

The results of this study suggest that further investigation with the use of the SRRS may help clarify how the pregnant woman can be made aware that life changes can influence the course of her pregnancy.

The multiple needs of mothers delivering premature infants were impressive and have led this investigator to further concern for the high-risk mother. Several recommendations can be made:

1 A replication of this study could be conducted under circumstances which allow examination of a larger and more representative population.

2 More follow-up and detailed interviews could be used to study the long-term effects on parents who have a premature infant.

3 Fathers of premature infants could be given the SRRS to determine the relationship of their life-change scores to those of their wives.

4 Assessments could be made regarding types of health services which could be extended to meet the immediate and long-term needs of this group of parents and their infants.

5 It is obvious from the results of this study, as well as others, that prematurity represents a psychosocial as well as a medical problem. For this reason, the investigator suggests that any large-scale study be conducted using a multidiscipline approach.

BIBLIOGRAPHY

1 Amiel-Tison, Claudine: "Neurological Evaluation of the Maturity of Newborn Infants," *Arch. Dis. Child.,* vol. 43, pp. 89–93 (1968).

2 Battaglia, F. C., and L. O. Lubchenco: "A Practical Classification of Newborn Infants by Weight and Gestational Age," *J. Pediatr.,* vol. 71, no. 2, pp. 159–163 (1967).

3 Benedek, Therese: "The Psychobiology of Pregnancy," in E. James Anthony and Therese Benedek (eds.) *Parenthood: Its Psychology and Psychopathology,* Little, Brown and Company, London, 1970.

4 Bergman, Abraham B., C. George Ray, Margaret A. Pomeroy, Patricia W. Wohl, and J. Bruce Beckwith: "Studies of the Sudden Infant Death Syndrome in King County, Washington: III. Epidemiology," *Pediatrics,* vol. 49, no. 1, pp. 860–870 (June 1972).

5 Berle, Beatrice B., and Carl T. Javert: "Stress and Habitual Abortion," *Obstet. Gynecol.,* vol. 3, pp. 298–306 (1954).

6 Bibring, G. L., T. F. Dwyer, D. S. Huntington, and A. F. Valenstein: "A Study of the Psychological Processes in Pregnancy and of the Earliest Mother-Child Relationship: I. Some Propositions and Comments," *Psychoanal. Study Child,* vol. 4, pp. 9–92 (1961).

7 Bishop, Edward H.: "Prevention of Premature Labor," *Proc. Natl. Conf. Prev. Ment. Retardation Improved Matern. Care,* New York Medical College, U.S. Department of Health, Education, and Welfare, Children's Bureau, Social and Rehabilitation Service, Washington, D.C., March 27–29, 1968, pp. 115–124.

8 Bronte, Emily: *Wuthering Heights,* Modern Library, Inc., New York, 1950.

9 Caplan, Gerald: "Patterns of Parental Response to the Crisis of Premature Birth," *Psychiatry,* vol. 23, pp. 365–374 (1960).

10 Deutsch, Helena: *The Psychology of Women,* 2 vols. Grune & Stratton, Inc., New York, 1945.

11 Droegemueller, W., C. Jackson, E. L. Makowski, and F. C. Battaglia: "Amniotic Fluid Examination as an Aid to the Assessment of Gestational Age," *Am. Obstet. Gynecol.,* vol. 105, pp. 424–428 (1969).

12 Dubowitz, T. M. S., V. Dubowitz, and C. Goldberg: "Clinical Assessment of Gestational Age in the Newborn Infant," *J. Pediatr.,* vol. 77, no. 1, pp. 1–10 (1970).

13 Eastman, Nicholson J.: "Prematurity from the Viewpoint of the Obstetrician," *Am. Prac.,* vol. 1, pp. 343–352 (1947).

14 Elmer, Elizabeth: "Studies of Child Abuse and Infant Accidents," in Julius Segal (ed.), *Mental Health Program Rept., no. 5,* Department of Health, Education, and Welfare, National Institute of Mental Health, Rockville, Md., December 1971, pp. 58–89.

15 Guttmacher, Alan F.: "Prematurity: The Obstetric Viewpoint," *N.Y. State J. Med.,* vol. 53, pp. 2781–2784 (1953).

16 Harmon, D. K., Minoru Masuda, and T. H. Holmes: "The Social Readjustment Rating Scale: A Cross Cultural Study of Western Europeans and Americans," *J. Psychosoma. Res.,* vol. 14, pp. 391–400 (1970).

17 Hersey, John: *The Wall,* Alfred A. Knopf, Inc., New York, 1950.

18 Holmes, T. H., and Minoru Masuda: "Life Change and Illness Susceptibility," University of Washington School of Medicine, Department of Psychiatry, Seattle, 1972 (mimeographed).

19 Holmes, T. H., and R. H. Rahe: "The Social Readjustment Rating Scale," *J. Psychosom. Res.,* vol. 11, pp. 213–218 (1967).

20 Holmes, T. Stephenson, and T. H. Holmes: "Short-Term Intrusions into the Life Style Routine," *J. Psychosoma. Res.,* vol. 14, pp. 121–132 (1970).

21 Javert, Carl T.: "Repeated Abortion," *Obstet. Gynecol.,* vol. 3, pp. 420–434 (April 1954).

22 Komaroff, Anthony L., Minoru Masuda, and T. H. Holmes. "The Social Readjustment Rating Scale: A Comparative Study of Negro, Mexican, and White Americans," *J. Psychoso. Res.,* vol. 12, pp. 121–128 (1968).

23 Levy, Barry S., Frederick S. Wilkinson, and William M. Marine: "Reducing

Neonatal Mortality Rate with Nurse-Midwives," *Am. J. Obstet. Gynecol.*, vol. 7, pp. 589–601 (June 1956).

24 Mann, Edward C.: "Psychiatric Investigation of Habitual Abortion," *J. Am. Acad. Obstet. Gynecol.*, vol. 7, pp. 589–601 (June 1956).

25 Masuda, Minoru, and Thomas H. Holmes: "Magnitude Estimations of Social Readjustments," *J. Psychosom. Res.*, vol. 11, pp. 219–225 (1967).

26 Masuda, Minoru, and Thomas H. Holmes: "The Social Readjustment Rating Scale: A Cross Cultural Study of Japanese and Americans," *J. Psychosom. Res.*, vol. 11, p. 227 (1967).

27 Rahe, R. H.: "Life-Change Measurement as a Predictor of Illness," *Proc. R. Soc. Med.*, vol. 61, pp. 1124–1126 (1968).

28 Rahe, R. H.: "Multi-cultural Correlations of Life Change Scaling: America, Japan, Denmark, and Sweden," *J. Psychosom. Res.*, vol. 13, pp. 191–195 (1969).

29 Robinson, R. J.: "Assessment of Gestational Age by Neurological Examination," *Arch. Dis. Child.*, vol. 41, pp. 437–447 (1966).

30 *The Seattle Times*, July 11, 1973, p. A6, col. 1.

31 Siegel, S.: *Non-parametric Methods for the Behavioral Sciences (March–April Psychosom. Res.*, vol. 14, pp. 59–64.

32 Siegel, S.: *Non-parametric Methods for the Behavioral Sciences*, McGraw-Hill Book Company, New York, 1956.

33 Squier, Raymond, and Flanders Dunbar: "Emotional Factors in the Course of Pregnancy," *Psychosoma. Med.*, vol. 8, pp. 161–175 (1946).

34 Terris, Milton, and E. M. Gold: "An Epidemiologic Study of Prematurity: II. Relation to Prenatal Care, Birth Interval, Residential History, and Outcome of Previous Pregnancies," *Am. J. Obstet. Gynecol.*, vol. 103, pp. 371–379 (1969).

35 White House Conference on Children: *Profiles of Children*. U.S. Government Printing Office, Washington, 1970.

36 Wolff, Harold George: *Stress and Disease*, 2d ed. Charles C Thomas, Publisher, Springfield, Ill., 1968.

37 Wyler, Allen R., Minoru Masuda, and Thomas H. Holmes: "Magnitude of Life Events and Seriousness of Illness," *Psychosom. Med.*, vol. 33, no. 2, pp. 115–121 (March–April 1971).

38 Wyler, Allen R., Minoru Masuda, and Thomas H. Holmes: "The Seriousness of Illness Rating Scale: Reproducibility," *J. Psychosom. Res.*, vol. 14, pp. 59–64 (1970).

39 Wylie, Burdett: "The Challenge of Infant Mortality," *Bull. Cleveland Acad. Med.*, June 1965.

Psychosocial Assets, Life Crisis and the Prognosis of Pregnancy

Katherine B. Nuckolls, R.N., Ph.D.
Professor of Nursing, Yale University School of Nursing

John Cassel, M.D.
Department of Epidemiology, School of Public Health, University of North Carolina

Berton H. Kaplan, Ph.D.
Professor of Epidemiology, School of Public Health, University of North Carolina

Attempts to document the role of psychosocial factors in the genesis of human disease and, in particular, in the disorders of pregnancy have yielded intriguing but often confusing or conflicting results. Despite the plethora of anecdotal and case study reports, the findings of carefully conducted epidemiologic or clinical investigations have tended to be ambiguous. This is in sharp contrast to the dramatic results which have been obtained with animal experiments [1–10]. To some extent, this may be due to the methodological difficulties inherent in such studies, but to a larger extent it is probably a function of inadequacies in the current theoretical framework. A recent review of some of these theoretical issues [11] has identified one of the central problems to be the nature of the model of causation subscribed to (often implicitly) by the majority of such investigators. Conditioned by the model provided by the germ theory, we have become accustomed to thinking in mono-etiologic terms. Accordingly, much of the work concerned with social or psychological antecedents to disease has attempted to identify a particular situational set (usually labelled "stress" or "a stressor") as having a specific causal relationship to some clinical entity, following a model analogous to the relationship between the typhoid bacillus and typhoid fever. Furthermore, it is assumed that the only factors influencing this relationship will be the strength and duration of exposure to this source of "stress". Such a formulation would appear to be clearly at variance with some of the known evidence. The animal studies particularly would seem to indicate that variations in the social milieu (with all other factors—genetic stock, diet, temperature and sanitation—held constant) will lead to numerous pathologic conditions, including, for example, an increase in maternal and infant mortality rates, a reduced resistance to a wide variety of insults such as toxins, x-rays and microorganisms, an increase in the incidence of

From the *American Journal of Epidermiology*, vol. 95, no. 5, pp. 431–441 (May, 1972).

arteriosclerosis and of hypertension, and an increased susceptibility to various forms of neoplasia. Thus, rather than searching for a specific relationship between social factors and a particular disease or pathologic outcome, it might be more profitable to regard the role of such factors as enhancing susceptibility to disease in general. With that formulation, the specific manifestations of such increased susceptibility may not be a function of the particular social process under study but rather a function of the genetic constitutions of the exposed individuals and the nature of the physicochemical or microbiological insults encountered.

In addition, both animal and human studies indicate that the pathologic effects of any social process can be markedly modified by the availability of various sources of support [12–14]. Therefore, to determine the harmful consequences of any postulated "stressful" situation, it would not be sufficient to attempt to measure only the strength and duration of the "stress"; rather the balance between the stressful situation and the nature and strength of the supportive or protective elements would need to be assessed.

Only a limited number of investigators have addressed themselves to conceptualizing and attempting to identify both deleterious and protective psychosocial processes. An approach that we have found useful is one developed by Holmes and his associates [15]. Their approach to identifying "stressful" situations has been through the concept of the magnitude and importance of life changes.

Beginning in 1949, this research group began to study systematically the quality and quantity of life events observed to cluster at the time of illness onset. These events include changes in the family structure, marriage, occupations, friendship groups and other significant areas which are usually associated with some adaptive or coping behavior on the part of the individual. The term "life crisis" was coined to represent the occurrence of an extraordinary number of these changes in life adjustment clustered into one or two years. Through the use of a constant referent technique, a magnitude of significance was assigned to each of 43 life events. The resultant scale reflected the magnitude of change required in the ongoing life adjustment by each event, and the values were defined as life change units (LCU). An individual's total LCU score was calculated from his experience as reported on the Schedule of Recent Experiences (SRE), and it was found that the higher the quantitative estimate of life crisis, the greater the probability of an associated major health change occurring within the succeeding two years. Subsequent prospective studies [16] have borne out the initial findings showing illnesses to be preceded by clustering of life changes.

In an attempt to quantify the protective elements available to individuals, which they termed "psycho-social assets", Berle et al. [17] developed a guide to prognosis in stress diseases which Holmes and associates later used successfully as a prognostic instrument in a follow-up study of patients with tuberculosis [18].

The study here reported is an attempt to explore the degree to which psychosocial assets are protective, as well as the degree to which multiple life changes are detrimental to health. Thus, we have examined the relationship of an index of psychosocial assets to various health parameters of pregnancy and the puerperium, a life change score to these same conditions and, perhaps most importantly, the relationship of psychosocial assets to these health states in the presence and absence of high life change scores. By this latter type of analysis, we hoped to come closer to the formulation of the "balance" between the protective and the deleterious processes and the relationship of this balance to health status.

Outcome of pregnancy was chosen as the dependent variable partly for pragmatic reasons such as sample size, temporal predictability, and ease of data collection, and partly because of other advantages which it offers. Although not an illness per se, pregnancy is a health change which clearly challenges the adaptive capacity physiologically, psychologically and socially. It carries with it risks for a defined body of pathologic conditions, some of which may be considered as maladaptive responses. There is, in addition, a need for further research into the psychosocial variables which contribute to the prognosis of pregnancy. This is evidenced by the comparatively high infant mortality rate in this country and by the persistent incidence of certain complications of pregnancy which fail to yield to improvements in obstetrical skill. Although gross social factors are unquestionably the major contributors to the excess infant mortality in the United States, it seems reasonable to believe that other psychosocial factors may also affect the outcome of pregnancy.

Other researchers who have investigated the relationships of psychosocial factors to pregnancy have focused on either discrete complications like hyperemesis, toxemia or prematurity, or on a total "complication score" for the whole child-bearing episode. McDonald [19] in a review of the role of emotional factors in obstetrical complications summarizes these findings with the comment that "self-report of anxiety is to date the most discriminating behavioral measure for presaging complications." A number of retrospective studies have related stressful occurrences during pregnancy to difficult labor or untoward outcomes [20–25]. Abramson [26] in a prospective study in Durban, South Africa, found a significant association between a woman's own report of stress during pregnancy and the development of her infant. Because we had no theoretical reason to believe that psychosocial assets or stress are specific to any one complication of pregnancy, it was decided to define the dependent variable "complications" as any untoward condition or outcome of pregnancy not related to an anatomical or other known maternal defect.

METHOD

The Instruments

In keeping with the general approach of Berle et al. [17] and Holmes et al. [18], psychosocial assets were defined as any psychological or social factors which contribute to a woman's ability to adapt to her first pregnancy. We decided to measure them with a questionnaire from which a single index score could be derived representing the adaptive potential for pregnancy (TAPPS).

Details of the development of this instrument and the methods used to score it are available elsewhere [27]. In summary, the score was derived from responses to questions designed to measure the subject's feelings or perceptions concerning herself, her pregnancy and her overall life situation including her relationships with her husband, her extended family and the community. Table 1 shows the factors tapped in each category of assets.

Questions were classified into one or another of these categories as the questionnaire was developed. In scoring, the raw scores for each item were transformed to standard scores to equalize the variances and means. The standard scores were then summed to give category scores. The total score, TAPPS, is the sum of the category scores equally weighted.

The instrument was self-administered. In general, the format was such that responses could be checked on a 20-point scale, which unlike the conventional multiple choice test, does not limit the subject to a few prestructured categories but allows answers to be placed along a broad continuum.

Table 1 Factors Tapped in Each Category of Assets

Self	Ego strength, loneliness, adaptability, trust, hostility, self esteem, crying, perception of health
Marriage	Duration of marriage, marital happiness, concordance of age, religion
Extended family	Relationship of subject with own parents, siblings, and in-laws. Confidence in emotional or economic support, if needed
Social resources	Adjustment to community. Friendship patterns and support
Definition of pregnancy	1 Extent to which pregnancy was desired and planned
	2 Feelings about pregnancy and childbirth, confidence in physician, fear of labor
	3 Anticipation of baby; confidence in outcome

Such a format has been used successfully by Jenkins and others [28, 29] to measure attitudes and beliefs about disease.

Life crisis was measured by the life change score (LCS) which was calculated from the Schedule of Recent Experience as developed by Holmes and Rahe [15]. The form of the instrument used in this research provides for a summed score of the life changes which occurred in the two years before pregnancy, and a second score for more recent changes which occurred during pregnancy. The weights used to score the separate events were the same as those used in the work cited.

Scoring complications

Since any single complication of pregnancy is a relatively rare event, a prospective study requires a large sample in order to assure that the "desired" complication will appear with sufficient frequency. This is particularly true if the study population is not an exceptionally high risk group. Attempts to solve this problem usually result in the decision to use some measure of "all complications," conceptualizing them as derivatives of a common process [19, 30–33]. Such measures do serve to optimize the variance of the dependent variable, but they present a difficult problem in scoring because there is a high degree of variability in the number, nature and severity of complications occurring in any single pregnancy.

In order to determine if there exist regular patterns of clustering of complications which could be ranked for severity by expert judges, we obtained data from the Collaborative Study by the Perinatal Research Branch, National Institute of Neurological Disease and Blindness, on all complications for 1000 white primigravidas.[1] Review of these data convinced us that apart from known syndromes, such as toxemia, identifiable cluster patterns do not occur, and that the reliability of a ranking procedure would be questionable. It was therefore decided to categorize the total course and outcome of each pregnancy as either "normal" or "complicated." Medical records were reviewed following delivery and all abnormal findings for each mother and infant were recorded using previously established criteria derived from a standard obstetrical text [34].

Since obstetrical care for the entire sample was provided by a limited number of physicians using the same standards for care and standardized record forms, the actual medical records were more reliable than would usually be found. A research assistant spot-checked 10 of the records for

[1] The authors thank Dr. Zekin A. Shakhashiri, Assistant to the Chief, Perinatal Research Branch, National Institute of Neurological Disease and Blindness, for providing these data from that agency's continuing Collaborative Study on Cerebral Palsy, Mental Retardation and Other Neurological and Sensory Disorders of Infancy and Childhood.

the reliability of our coding. No errors were found for those 10 patients. Patients were classified as "complicated" if they had one or more of the following conditions:

A systolic blood pressure during pregnancy of over 139 mm or a diastolic blood pressure of over 89 mm or a systolic elevation of more than 30 mm, any one of these in combination with proteinuria.

Admission to the hospital for preeclampsia.

Threatened abortion.

Admission to the hospital for hyperemesis.

Premature rupture of the membranes for more than 24 hours before delivery in the absence of cephalo-pelvic disproportion.

Prolonged labor. First stage longer than 20 hours or the second stage longer than 150 minutes in the absence of cephalo-pelvic disproportion.

Apgar rating of infant less than 7, or reported infant respiratory distress in the absence of cephalo-pelvic disproportion.

A systolic blood pressure of over 139 mm and/or a diastolic blood pressure of over 89 mm during both the labor and post-partum periods.

Birthweight of less than 2500 grams.

Abortion, stillbirth or neonatal death within the first three days.

With this definition, 96 or 47.1 per cent of the 204 patients were classified as "complicated." (The base for these figures includes 34 patients who were not included in the final analysis because their life change scores were not completed.) Of the 96 patients, only eight had single complications and only one was classified as "complicated" solely on the basis of blood pressure. This complication rate is comparable with the rate of 50.2 per cent found for the Collaborative Study sample using the foregoing criteria.

At first glance, these figures seem high but similar rates have been found in other studies. Heinstein [33] reports that in a sample of 156 gravidas, only 20 per cent were classified as having had no physical complications, either mild or severe, while 47 per cent were judged to have had mild complications and 33 per cent were thought to be serious. In other studies using similar classification schemes, Grim [32] categorized 122 out of 227 patients as "abnormal" and in McDonald's sample of 107 patients, 89 were classified as abnormal [19].

The Sample

This study was conducted at a large military hospital. The subjects were white primigravidas, married to enlisted men, registered for obstetrical care prior to the 24th week of pregnancy. At the time of prenatal registration, the TAPPS questionnaire was administrered to all women who met these criteria. The intake sample size was 340 . . .

Table 2   Distribution of Subjects by Age at Clinic Admission

Subjects	<18	18-19	20-24	25-29	>29	Total
No.	16	111	181	16	1	325
%	4.9	33.9	55.9	4.8	0.3	100.0

The Schedule of Recent Experience was mailed to subjects during the 32nd week of their pregnancies and the medical records were reviewed following delivery and hospital discharge. Complete records were obtained for 170 subjects who delivered in the military hospital.

Attempts were made to follow-up all patients who were transferred before delivery by obtaining permanent addresses at the time of intake, maintaining a careful check on the clinic discharge book and, when a subject was transferred, sending a letter requesting the name of the physician who would deliver her. Modified data forms were mailed to these physicians. Responses from 88 per cent of the doctors contacted resulted in an additional 67 completed records. These were analyzed separately due to the possibility of varying criteria for complications and are not included in this discussion. In all, military transfer or discharge, coupled with failure on the part of either the physician or the subject to provide follow-up data, accounted for the loss of 85 subjects. An additional 18 were dropped from the sample. . . . [2]

As can be seen from tables 2, 3, 4 and 5 the original sample was quite homogeneous in terms of age, social class, educational level, and duration

---

[2] Reasons for dropping from sample: twins, 5; not pregnant, 3; incomplete records, 4; previous illness, 1; previous miscarriage, 5.

Table 3   Distribution of Subjects by Social Class as Determined by Occupation and Education of Head of Household of Subject's Family Orientation

	Social class*					
Subjects	I	II	III	IV	V	Total
No.	4	13	53	164	91	325
%	1.2	4.0	16.3	50.4	28.0	100.0

*Hollingshead's Two Factor Index of Social Class [35].

Table 4 Distribution of Subjects by Educational Attainment

Subjects	No. of Years or Type of Schooling						
	<10	10–11	12	Tech-nical	Some college	Bachelor degree or +	Total
No.	9	45	165	47	51	8	325
%	2.7	13.9	50.7	14.5	15.7	2.5	100.0

of pregnancy. In order to determine whether or not there were any significant differences between those who were excluded from this analysis and those included, chi square tests for homogeneity for these characteristics were performed. No significant differences were found. In addition, as seen in table 6 (the mean and standard deviation of life change scores) and table 7 (the mean and standard deviation of TAPP scores), no significant differences were found between the two groups for the major independent variables. We are therefore reasonably sure that those subjects included in this analysis did not differ in any important respect from those lost or omitted.

Since no correlations between complications and age ($r = -.02$) and social class ($r = -.003$) occurred in this homogeneous sample, these factors were not controlled for in the final analyses (table 8). (Social class was scored for head of household of the woman's family of origin using Hollingshead's Two Factor Index of Social Class [35].)

RESULTS

Table 9 shows the correlations between the life change scores, both before and during pregnancy, and complications of pregnancy, and the correlation between the TAPPS (psychosocial asset score) and complications. As can

Table 5 Distribution of Subjects by Duration of Pregnancy at Clinic Admission

Subjects	Week of pregnancy				
	12	12–15	16–19	20–24	Total
No.	47	118	108	52	325
%	14.4	36.3	33.2	16.1	100.0

Table 6   Range, Mean and Standard Deviations of Life Change Scores

Life change scores	Delivered on military base, N = 170	Delivered by private M.D., N = 67	p
Before pregnancy			
Range	0–741	0–642	N.S.*
Mean	187.24	165.89	
S.D.	148.53	144.7	
During pregnancy			
Range	0–714	0–526	N.S.
Mean	188.78	204.75	
S.D.	114.39	109.82	
Total			
Range	70–1349	59–1091	N.S.
Mean	375.51	370.6	
S.D.	199.80	186.79	

*N.S. = not significant.

be seen from the table, none of the correlations attained even borderline significance. Similarly, figures 2 and 3 show no significant difference in the percentage of patients with complications given either high and low life change or high and low TAPPS scores. (Life change scores and TAPPS scores were divided at the means for the entire sample giving subsets with "high" and "low" scores for each variable.) Thus it is evident that, if considered separately, neither multiple life changes nor variations in psychosocial assets were related in this study to complications of pregnancy.

To test the extent to which the effect of multiple life changes might be modified by psychosocial assets, a contingency table was set up [which showed] that in the presence of mounting life change (life change scores high both before and during pregnancy), women with high psychosocial assets had only one-third the complication rate of women whose psychoso-

Table 7   Mean and Standard Deviation of the Adaptive Potential for Pregnancy Score

Sample	N	$\bar{X}$	S.D	p
Delivered on military base	170	45.07	3.75	N.S.*
Delivered by private physician	67	44.41	3.60	N.S.

*Not significant.

Table 8 Correlation of Age and Social Class* with Complications (N = 204†)

Variable	r
Age	
	−.02
Social class	
	−.003

*Scored for head of household of woman's family of origin using Hollingshead Two Factor Index of Social Class [35].

†This correlation included 34 subjects for whom there were complete delivery records but no interim data.

cial assets were low. In the absence of such life changes, particularly for the period before pregnancy, the level of psychosocial assets was irrelevant, there being essentially no difference in the complication rate between those having high and low TAPPS scores.

DISCUSSION

These findings, if replicated, could help to explain some of the discrepant results in the current literature. Taken alone, neither exposure to socially stressful situations nor the availability of multiple psychosocial assets will be consistently related to poor health states. Instead, the balance between these two processes will need to be assessed for an explanation of enhanced disease susceptibility. It should be emphasized further that we are not pro-

Table 9 Correlation of Life Change Scores (LCS*) and TAPPS† with complications

	r
LCS before pregnancy	.003
LCS during pregnancy	.07
Total LCS	.05
TAPPS	−.07

*N = 170.

†N = 204. Included 34 patients for whom there were no interim data.

posing this combination of high psychosocial stressors and low assets as the cause, or even *a* cause for any specific clinical entity, but rather propose that it may enhance susceptibility to a variety of environmental insults. As illustrated by the somewhat heterogeneous list of conditions we have included as complications, we suggest that the manifestations of such enhanced susceptibility will depend upon the nature of these environmental insults plus presumably the genetic constitution of the exposed subjects. Such a concept of generalized susceptibility would be consistent with the situation in the United States where it has recently been demonstrated that those regions of the country which have the highest death rates from cardiovascular disease (age, race, sex specific) also have higher than expected death rates from all causes, including cancer and infectious diseases [36]. This illustration, of course, does not necessarily document that social processes are responsible for such an increased susceptibility, but does lend credence to the view that variations in generalized susceptibility may be a useful concept. Somewhat more direct evidence is provided by Christenson and Hinkle [37] whose data show that managers in an industrial company who, by virtue of their family background and educational experiences were least well prepared for the demands and expectations of executive industrial life, had the highest rate of all diseases—major as well as minor, physical as well as mental, long-term as well as short-term. It would also be consistent with the finding that widowed and divorced men, particularly of young ages, have from 3 to 5 times the death rate of married men of the same age from *every* cause of death [38].

As indicated earlier, this notion then casts serious doubt on the utility of specificity (as far as current clinical syndromes are concerned) in research concerned with psychosocial factors in disease etiology. Similar psychosocial factors may be related to different disease syndromes (depending upon the prevalent environmental factors and genetic make-up of the populations), and attempts to document and quantify the relevance of such factors will of necessity have to take this into account in the research design. Perhaps a more elegant and satisfactory approach to attempting to measure all disease manifestations in populations exposed to these psychosocial forces would be to standardize for the "manifestational" agents. To select populations all of whom have been exposed to the tuberele bacillus, for example, and determine whether the postulated psychosocial factors discriminate between those who develop and do not develop clinical disease. Alternatively, population at high risk of developing myocardial infarction, by virtue of their "risk" factors, could be selected and a similar strategy employed.

Should such approaches be successful, the implications for intervention could be of considerable importance. By strengthening the psychosocial assets (a task which surely is not beyond human ingenuity), presumably we could reduce the incidence of illness and improve the quality of life.

REFERENCES

1   Ader R, Hahn E. W.: Effects of social environment on mortality to whole body x-irradiation in the rat. Psychol. Rep. 13: 214–215, 1963.
2   Ader R., Kreutner A., Jacobs H. L.: Social environment emotionality and alloxan diabetes in the rat. Psychosom. Med. 25: 60–68, 1963.
3   Andervont H. B.: Influence of environment on mammary cancer in mice. J. Natl. Cancer Inst. 4: 579–581, 1944.
4   Calhoun J. B.: Population density and social pathology. Sci. Am. 206: 139, 1962.
5   Christian J. J., Williamson H. O.: Effect of crowding on experimental granuloma formation in mice. Proc. Soc. Exp. Biol. Med. 99: 385–387, 1958.
6   Davis D. E., Read C. P.: Effect of behavior on development of resistance in trichinosis. Proc. Soc. Exp. Biol. Med. 99: 269–272, 1958.
7   Henry J. P.: Systematic arterial pressure as a measure of stressful social interaction. (Manuscript).
8   King J. T., Lee Y. C. P., Visscher M. B.: Single versus multiple cage occupancy and convulsion frequency in C.H mice. Proc. Soc. Exp. Biol. Med. 88: 661–663, 1955.
9   Ratcliffe H. L., Cronin M. T. I.: Changing frequency of arteriosclerosis in mammals and birds at the Philadelphia Zoological Garden. Circulation 18: 41–52, 1959.
10 Swinyard E. A., Clark L. D., Miyahara J. T., et al: Studies on the mechanism of amphetamine toxicity in aggregated mice. J. Pharmacol. Exp. Ther. 132: 97–102, 1961.
11 Symes S. L., Reeder L. G. (editors): Proceedings of the National Workshop Conference on Socioenvironmental Stress and Cardiovascular Diseases—Phoenix, Arizona, Feb 14–16, 1966. Milbank Mem. Fund O. 55: No. 2, 1967.
12 Bogdanoff M. D., Klein R., Estes E. H., et al: The Psysiologic response to conformity pressure in man. Ann. Inter. Med. 57: 389–397, 1962.
13 Conger J. J., Lawrey W. L., Turrell E. S.: The role of social experience in the production of gastric ulcers in hooded rats placed in a conflict situation. J. Abnorm. Soc. Psychol. 57: 214–220, 1958.
14 Henry J. P., Mechand J. P., Stephens P. M.: The use of psychosocial stimuli to induce prolonged hypertension in mice. Psychosom. Med. 29: 408–432, 1967.
15 Holmes T., Rahe R.: Life crisis and disease onset, Parts I, II, III. Unpublished research reports. Seattle, Washington: Department of Psychiatry, University of Washington School of Medicine, 1966.
16 Rahe R. H., Meyer M., Smith M., et al: Social stress and illness onset. J. Psychosom. Res. S.: 35–44, 1964.

17 Berle B. B., Pinsky R. H., Wolf S., et al: A Clinical Guide to Prognosis in Stress Diseases. JAMA 149: 1624–1627, 1952.

18 Holmes T. H., Joffe J. R., Ketcham J. W. et al: Experimental study of prognosis. J. Psychosom. Res. 5: 235–252, 1961.

19 McDonald R. L.: The role of emotional factors in obstetric complications, a review. Psychosom. Med. 30: 222–237, 1968.

20 Brandon M. W. G.: An epidemiological study of maladjustment in childhood. M.D. Thesis, University of Durham, 1960. *In* Childbearing. Edited by E. Gruenberg. Baltimore, Williams and Wilkins, 1961.

21 Gunter L. M.: Psychopathology and stress in the life experience of mothers of premature infants. Am. J. Obstet. Gynecol. 86: 333, 1963.

22 Hetzel B. S., Bruer B., Poidevin L. O. S.: A survey of the relation between certain common antenatal complications in primiparae and stressful life situations during pregnancy. J. Psychosom. Res. 5: 175–182, 1961.

23 Scott E. M., Thomson A. M.: A psychological investigation of primigravidae. J. Obstet. Gynecol. 63: 1956.

24 Stott D. H.: Physical and mental handicaps following a disturbed pregnancy. Lancet 1: 1006–1011, 1957.

25 Stott D. H.: Some psychosomatic aspects of casualty in reproduction. J. Psychosom. Res. 3: 42, 1958.

26 Abramson J. H., Singh A. R., Moambo V.: Antenatal stress and the baby's development. Arch. Dis. Child 36: 42–49, 1961.

27 Nuckolls K. B.: Psychosocial Assets, Life Crisis and the Prognosis of Pregnancy, Ph.D. Dissertation, University of North Carolina at Chapel Hill, 1967.

28 Jenkins D. B.: The semantic differential for health: A technique for mass beliefs about diseases. Public Health Rep. 81: 549–558, 1966.

29 Rosenstock I. M., Hochbaum G. M., Kegeles S. S.: Determinants of Health Behavior. Presented at Golden White House Conference on Children and Youth, 1961.

30 Erikson M. T.: Relationship between psychological attitudes during pregnancy and complications of pregnancy, labor, and delivery. Proc. Am. Psychological Assoc. 1: 213–214, 1965.

31 Werner E., Simonian K., Bierman J. M., et al: Cumulative effect of perinatal complications and deprived environment on physical, intellectual, and social development of preschool children. Pediatrics 39: 490–505, 1967.

32 Grim E., Venet W. R.: The relationship of emotional attitudes to the course and outcome of pregnancy. Psychosom. Med. 28: 34, 1966.

33 Heinstein M. I.: Expressed attitudes and feelings of pregnant women and their relations to physical complications of pregnancy. Merrill-Palmer Q 13: 217–236, 1967.

34 Eastman N., Hellman L.: Williams Obstetrics. (13th rev. ed.) New York, Appleton-Century-Crofts, 1966.

35 Hollingshead A. B., Redlich F. C.: Social Class and Mental Illness. New York, John Wiley and Sons, 1958.

36   Syme S. L.: Personal communication, 1968.
37   Christenson W. N., Hinkle L. E. Jr.: Differences in illness and prognostic signs in two groups of young men. JAMA 177: 247–253, 1961.
38   Kraus A., Lilienfeld A.: Some epidemiologic aspects of the high mortality rate in the young widowed group. J. Chronic. Dis. 10: 207–217, 1959.

Chapter 3

The Crisis of Premature Birth

The unexpected onset of early labor and the delivery of a premature infant represent critical events in the lives of all concerned. For the infant, the crisis is frequently life-threatening and leads to active and vigorous medical intervention. For the mother, the crisis is both a physiological and psychological one. The physiological aspects, thanks to our advanced technology, are more quickly resolved, but the emotional and psychosocial ramifications are more complex and far-reaching.

In recent years, the mothers of premature infants have been studied from the standpoint of their psychological reactions to having a high-risk baby. It has been informative to study patterns of mothers of prematures during the early postpartum period to help clarify these issues.[1]

The nature of the crisis of pregnancy varies with each woman, according to her personality structure, degree of psychological adjustment, and her life setting. The likelihood of a favorable resolution of this conflict

---

[1] Nora Smith, et al., "Mothers' Psychological Reactions to Premature and Full-Size Newborns," *Arch. Gen. Psychiat.* vol. 21, pp. 177–181 (August 1969).

increases when pregnancy induces feelings of enjoyment and enhances the mother's sense of well-being.

Bibring,[2] Benedek,[3] Deutsch,[4] and other psychoanalytic researchers, have written extensively regarding the psychological processes of pregnancy and the psychosexual functioning of women. Bibring[5] describes pregnancy as a maturational crisis and considers pregnancy, puberty, and menopause as periods of stress involving emotional as well as biological changes.

During the last weeks of the normal gestation period, the mother has the opportunity to master feelings about the anticipated stress of labor and delivery and to prepare psychologically for her new baby. Premature delivery interrupts and interferes with this important process. Futhermore, the appearance and tenuous physical condition of many premature infants arouse feelings of fear, guilt, disappointment, and grief in the mother.

Initially, our focus on premature infants stemmed from a concern for the survival of these babies. These unusually small infants are not only less likely to survive but are more apt to show neurological or intellectual impairment.

An increased incidence of "mothering disorders" seems to occur related to high-risk infants.[6] Early identification of these mothers and infants may be useful in helping us to concentrate our limited resources on women and babies with special needs.

Pregnant mothers frequently have fantasies concerning their unborn children. These include the desire for a perfect child, as well as the fear of bearing a damaged one. Solnit and Stark[7] describe the process which takes place in mothers of premature children as a mourning reaction to the loss of the fantasied child and a simultaneous need to adapt to the existing baby.

The father, also, may undergo conflicts which affect his initial acceptance of the infant, especially since fathers now participate more actively in the care of their infants. He may experience guilt feelings for his involvement in the child's prematurity, and, further, may be fearful that the circumstances of the premature delivery may reflect upon his own masculinity. The necessarily close relationship between the mother and infant, with a consequent diminishing of her attentions towards the father, may cause him

[2] G. L. Bibring, T. F. Dwyer, D. S. Huntingdon, and A. F. Valenstein, "A Study of the Psychological Processes in Pregnancy, and of the Earliest Mother-Child Relationship: I. Some Propositions & Comments," *Psychoanal. Study Child*, vol. 16, pp. 9–92 (1961).

[3] T. Benedek, "The Psychobiology of Pregnancy," in *Parenthood: Its Psychology and Psychopathology*, London 1970.

[4] H. Deutsch, *The Psychology of Women*, 2 vols., Grune & Stratton, Inc., New York, 1945.

[5] Op. cit.

[6] D. Levy, *Maternal Overprotection*, W. W. Norton & Company, Inc. New York, 1956.

[7] A. J. Solnit, and M. H. Stark, "Mourning and the Birth of a Defective Child," *Psychoanal. Study Child*, vol. 16, pp. 523–537 (1961).

to feel jealous of the high-risk infant. The resulting dissatisfaction, according to Dane Prugh, tends to undermine any support which the father, under normal circumstances, might be able to offer both mother and child.[8]

Crisis intervention in such a situation is based on the premise that at the time of stress an individual, family, or other human group is thrown into a state of emotional or social disequilibrium. In the individual, this refers to an acute or unusual disorganization of the psychological mechanisms relating to personality functioning. During the period of crisis, the person may regress and resort to maladaptive responses. During this disequilibrium, crisis intervention attempts to suggest new and more adaptive modes of functioning which may then persist because of the more successful results of the ensuing behavior.

There has recently been much emphasis on crisis theory, especially since the Second World War. The need for individual, group, and family crisis intervention has been delineated by many experts. Investigations have suggested that early detection and intervention at the time of stress provide an important factor in the prevention of later emotional illnesses.

In the first article, "Maternal Reactions to Premature Birth Viewed as an Acute Emotional Disorder," David Kaplan, a social worker, and Edward Mason, a physician, describe their research project relating to mothers of premature infants. They indicate the psychological tasks for the mother which are posed by prematurity, and attempt to delineate normal and pathological modes of coping with these tasks.

In the second article, "Four Studies of Crisis in Parents of Prematures," by Gerald Caplan, Edward Mason, and David Kaplan, their study includes the responses of eighty-six families to the birth of a premature baby. These responses have been investigated in four linked studies in order to refine the concept and understanding of crisis. Patterns of grappling behavior during the crisis were identified, making accurate predictions of the short-term mental-health outcome possible. Psychological tasks presented by the stress of premature delivery were also documented. The adequacy with which these tasks were accomplished is predictive of the patterns of early maternal care and mother-child relationships. Results indicate that this type of study is relevant to studies of the causation of mental health and mental illness, as well as to preventive intervention.

Certain implications for research and methodology are derived from these studies, pointing to further research effort which is now practical and desirable. The best summary relating to the crisis of premature birth seems to be included in Helen Wortis's discussion. She comments:

---

[8] D. G. Prugh, "Emotional Problems of the Premature Infant's Parents," *Nurs. Outlook,* vol. 1, no. 8 pp. 461–464 (August 1953).

Perhaps we may say that the premature delivery is the result of a broad spectrum of causes which have a physiologic end result although they may be socioeconomic or psychological in origin. We will then regard the small baby as actually the product of a stressful life situation, and we will not be surprised if, when she delivers, the mother whose experience is associated with stress continues to act like a stressful person.[9]

[9] Helen Wortis, Discussion of "Maternal Reactions to Premature Birth Viewed as an Acute Emotional Disorder," by David M. Kaplan and Edward A. Mason, *Am. J. Orthopsychiat.,* vol. 30, p. 539 (1960), p. 551.

Maternal Reactions to Premature Birth Viewed as an Acute Emotional Disorder

David M. Kaplan, Ph.D.
Associate Professor and Director, Division of Clinical Social Work, Stanford University School of Medicine

Edward A. Mason, M.D.
Assistant Clinical Professor of Psychiatry, Harvard Medical School

Traditionally, psychiatric theory, in referring to acute problems, conceives them as primarily stemming from previously existing chronic conditions. Thus a combat fatigue reaction is viewed as an exacerbation of an existing neurosis and an acute psychotic episode is seen as arising out of a previously quiescent schizophrenia. In our paper, we propose to focus on a specific stress[1] situation, namely, the one occasioned by a premature birth, and to show that the maternal reactions to this event can usefully be described as acute emotional disorders. There are many parallels between these reactions and those in an acute infectious process. For example, the range of severity of reaction to a psychologically stressful event is a broad one ranging from the mild and generally self-correcting type to the severe, in which the likelihood of adverse sequelae is high.

The expanded idea of acute emotional disorder has been developed from the theory of traumatic neurosis [4, 5, 6, 8], from "crisis" theory [2], from the study of bereavement by Lindemann [9], and from the model of the acute infectious diseases [7] by one of the authors (D.M.K.). We believe the occurrence of an acute disorder does not depend upon the prior existence of an established chronic process; rather it results from the individual's attempt to cope with a threatening event for which he is not sufficiently psychologically prepared.

This concept of illness does not preclude the fact that the reactions to a stressful event will be heavily conditioned by previously existing personality factors. However, even where such chronic conditions exist, they alone do not necessarily determine outcome. There are current situational forces which have an important bearing on outcome, such as hospital practices, the behavior of the father, and the role of health agencies.

The most important advantage of this concept of acute emotional disorders is that it helps direct attention to the significant mental health prob-

From *American Journal of Orthopsychiatry*, vol. 30, no. 3 pp. 539–552 (July, 1960).

[1] "Stress" is defined here as a state of psychological upset or disequilibrium in an individual. This disequilibrium is of relatively brief duration and is generally self-limiting. It is a reaction to a specific event which is commonly perceived by those who experience it as an unexpected threat or loss. Examples of such events are: death, retirement, serious illness, birth, loss of job, loss of income, or a surgical operation. These events may have positive elements as well as threatening ones.

he more "normal" group in the population. It also makes possible
clin   eatment of this relatively healthy group which is affected, as
          unavoidably are affected, by a variety of stressful events.
We believe the successful resolution of stress can avert chronic conditions
which might otherwise result. This approach illustrates the preventive orientation in the field of community mental health.

STUDY DATA

The present study of the maternal reaction to premature birth is one of
several approaches to the analysis of our data on the responses of family
members to stress. These studies are being carried out in the Harvard
School of Public Health Family Guidance Center [1]. To date, 60 families
have been interviewed during the period following the premature birth and
continuing until the baby has been home for two months. Examination of
the clinical material from these interviews indicates that there is a typical
psychological experience for the mother of the premature baby which can
be distinguished from the experience following full-term delivery.

The maternal stress accompanying premature birth begins with the
onset of labor, and the experience she must face should be seen in contrast
to what most women expect in a normal delivery [3]. At term the woman is
impatient both to see the baby and to discharge her burden. Whether she
comes to delivery anxious or calm, the atmosphere encourages her to feel
that she will produce a normal child. The setting is geared to her needs and
she manages the discomforts of labor because they are seen as temporary.
When the events follow the expected pattern, the mother more readily feels
a pride in her achievement and she receives rewards and recognition on the
part of the doctor, hospital staff, husband, family and friends. She is encouraged to feel happy and proud, and after a brief period of rest begins to
share this with her baby as she holds and feeds it. This closeness and the
feeling of success serve to encourage the continuation and heightening of
the relationship to the child. The baby's presence can be openly acknowledged and plans and expectations can continue on the basis of its established normality. Having accomplished her first major maternal task successfully, the mother moves from one step to the next on the basis of
success, and she is carried along in spite of any anxiety she may feel by the
immediacy of the needs of the infant.

Premature Labor and Delivery

In contrast to the normal pregnancy there are distinct differences in the
experience of the mother of a premature. In spite of her anxieties about
possible pregnancy failure, the average pregnant woman does not seem to
be concerned about premature delivery. Rather, she has the notion that a

baby born before term is nonviable or deformed. Even during pregnancies where there has been bleeding, amniotic fluid loss, or pain, the expectant mother's primary concern is to "hold on" until term, with the alternative, miscarriage. As a result, premature labor comes as a shock and the woman, even though intellectually aware of the possibility, is emotionally unprepared when it happens to her. The import of earlier signs of difficulty is frequently ignored, denied, or minimized. These women often misinterpret the onset of labor and describe the experience later as "unreal," as though clinging to the wish that delivery would not be early.

The hospital atmosphere is more characteristic of an emergency than of a normal labor; there is more than usual listening for the fetal heart, there is general apprehensiveness, and the woman is informed that for the protection of the baby there will be no anesthesia. These experiences confirm the woman's feelings that this is a dangerous situation for the baby, but there is often, even at this late point, a disbelief that delivery will follow.

> Mrs. A said she was admitted for a "virus infection" and she considered delivery "impossible." She had bleeding during her first 4½ months and was "wet continually" in her sixth month, and many times had thought that miscarriage or delivery was imminent and the child would be abnormal if it lived. Her doctor had warned her not to expect a live birth and she was admitted for observation at 6 months. An attempt to induce labor was unsuccessful, and several hours later she had a "shaking chill" which she believed was "appendicitis." There followed a period when first the students and then "a procession of doctors" tried to find the fetal heart and could not. When labor finally began three doctors tried to start intravenous feeding. She was told she would have no anesthesia whereas she had wished for a deep anesthesia; she remembered no "real labor."

A mother of a premature as opposed to a full-term baby has a *heightened* concern after delivery about whether the baby is alive and will live, and later whether there is any abnormality. She sees the baby briefly before it is hurried into an incubator and taken off to a separate nursery or even a different hospital. Her most vivid recollections are about the baby's small size; its unusual color and unattractive appearance add further to the shock.

The mother frequently returns to a ward with other women who have lost their babies, and typically feels "lonely" and "lost." Mrs. T wandered about the ward, eating and, sleeping poorly, missed her baby and her husband, and only went to look at her baby once in the four days she was there. Many a mother expects at any moment to hear news of her baby's death. Mrs. K described herself as upset and feeling like crying, but unable to *do* anything; it was the "worst time" in her life because of the lonesomeness and separation. She felt the ward was full of "worthless souls" and "no one" talked to her until the baby was better.

Usually the physician talks to the mother in guarded words, or else avoids contact with her for a few days. In general, there seems to be no prompt and frank discussion about the prognosis or cause of prematurity, and a state of suspense is encouraged. The hospital staff finds it difficult to know how to respond; the mother needs support, but it is hard to give without confirming her feeling of failure or futilely raising her hopes. A mother expecting to hear at any moment that her baby has died is apprehensive and prone to pick up the anxieties of other mothers or of the staff.

> Mrs. K was unable to get in touch with the pediatrician, who deliberately talked instead with Mr. K and encouraged him not to "worry" his wife. The nurse told Mrs. K, "We don't want you to feel the baby is better or worse so that you won't pin too much hope on what we say." She therefore didn't know how serious the situation was until three days after the birth when she went to have her first look at the baby.

The premature nursery frustrates most mothers in their desire to see the baby. The nursery is often on a different floor. The incubator obscures a good view, and often must remain on the other side of the room from the window in order to have oxygen immediately available. When mothers do visit, their babies' appearance is frightening. Mrs. A commented that to her it felt like visiting a "zoo" with many "strange creatures" behind the glass. Mrs. K said her baby "looked awful" and his "terrible color was more of a shock than his size." Mrs. T said her baby reminded her of a "turtle without a shell," a "frog" or a "chicken." Most frequent is the comment that it is so tiny and weak. It is hardly a baby to inspire pride, and if anyone visits at all there is no cause for the normal congratulations. Visitors usually speak with sympahty and caution, and generally cards, cigars and christenings are delayed at least several weeks. Mothers feel helpless and useless, separated from the baby, and frequently remark that they don't even deserve to be in the hospital. They may avoid visiting the nursery altogether or else be drawn to look at the baby in spite of the baby's reminding them of their failure.

There are some notable exceptions [2] to the pattern as generally described above, and comment should be made here on the group of women who experience minimal shock, failure and grief. These are a portion of those women who have already experienced premature delivery or who have had previous pregnancy failure. They are often pleased to have any baby, no matter how small, and they feel a sense of achievement as long as it is a baby that may live.

[2] Very few of the mothers in our study had private obstetrical and pediatric care. Probably such care alters the experience but it does not eliminate the stress.

Mrs. G. had several miscarriages and previous premature deliveries, and although she was anxious and upset she showed no preoccupation with failure. She wanted the baby and was happy that it might live—she was ready to accept it because she had managed her feelings about the failure to deliver a normal baby in earlier pregnancies.

The Mother's Homecoming without Her Baby

When the mother leaves the baby in the premature nursery and returns home empty-handed she experiences a reinforcement in her feelings of disappointment, failure, and deprivation [10].

There is wide variation in the amount of contact she maintains. Some mothers go daily to see their baby even though hospital regulations allow them only a few minutes' look through the nursery window. There is little noticeable change from day to day in the beginning. Others never visit, feeling it is a "waste of time." There is also variation in the use of telephone contact to learn about the baby's weight. The universal concern focused on weight change results from the mother's using weight gain as evidence of progress and the hospital's using a weight criterion for determining readiness for discharge. Some hospitals do not give out weight reports on the telephone; some insist that the mother visit the nursery or ask the private physician for information. A rare mother maintains a more personal contact by the considerable effort of pumping her breasts and sending the milk to the hospital.

After the Baby Is Home

Although mothers anticipate the time when the baby can be brought home, they are frequently anxious when the moment comes. Their worry focuses on the smallness of the baby. They feel that it is fragile and they worry about their competence in adequately handling a child who has needed such expert care and who has been so inaccessible to them. Typically, the mother finds herself more anxious at first. In others there is often a persistent eagerness for weight gain and a focus of concern on food intake [11]. Some mothers begin to give the baby cereal before it is recommended by the physician. There are continuing concerns in some about congenital abnormalities which might show up later, and there is a variable amount of anxiety or curiosity about when the baby will "catch up" with the full-term infant.

THE PSYCHOLOGICAL TASKS POSED BY PREMATURITY

Having thus far described the typical experience of the mother of a premature baby, we now turn to a discussion of the special ways in which such a mother copes with the stress. We have found that she has four psychological tasks which appear to be essential both to successful mastery of the situation and to a sound basis for a future healthy mother-child relationship.

The *first* of these tasks should take place at the time of delivery. It is the preparation for a possible loss of the child whose life is in jeopardy. This "anticipatory grief" [9] involves a withdrawal from the relationship already established to the coming child so that she still hopes the baby will survive but simultaneously prepares for its death. In a *second* task she must face and acknowledge her maternal failure to deliver a normal full-term baby. The anticipatory grief and depression which can be observed are signs of the fact that she is struggling with these tasks. These reactions are healthy responses and usually last until the baby's chances for survival seem secure.

The baby may remain in the hospital from two to ten weeks. During this period the third and fourth tasks need to be performed. The *third* is the resumption of the process of relating to the baby which had been previously interrupted. The mother has lost the opportunity which full-term delivery would have provided for the development of readiness for the mothering role. She has previously prepared herself for a loss, but as the baby improves she must now respond with hope and anticipation to this change. The baby's improvement symbolizes to the mother the possibility of retrieving, from what had been a total disappointment, a good measure of her hopes during the pregnancy.

Characteristically, there is a point at which the mother really begins to believe that the baby will survive. The event which serves to stir her may be the baby's regular gain in weight, a change in feeding pattern or method, a change in the nurses' manner, the baby's filling out, or its becoming more active. She then begins to prepare herself, gathers the layette, watches closely and seeks information on the care of a premature. After a period of increased anticipation she finally knows when the baby will be coming home and is ready, though anxious.

> Mrs. A. went almost daily with her husband and began gradually to respond with expectation as the baby "filled out," became more active, and his eyes opened. They read Spock and pamphlets they obtained about prematurity, hesitantly at first, and more openly after they felt more hope by his change to bottle feedings, his "amazing strength" in turning around, banging his head, and crying lustily. The A's saw the baby fed once (against the usual rules) and at this time felt it was fun to visit, became certain the baby would come home, and longed for him. Mrs. A. was making preparations at home, and gathering information about care—it was as though she used the time to catch up and finish the preparation for maternity interrupted by premature delivery.

In the *fourth* task the mother must come to understand how a premature baby differs from a normal baby in terms of its special needs and growth patterns. This is in preparation for her imminent job of caring for the infant, and takes place while she is visiting the nursery, talking with nurse or doctor, reading baby care books, or discussing baby care with other mothers of prematures. In order to provide the extra amount of care and protection, the mother must see the baby as a premature with special needs and characteristics. But it is equally important for her to see that these needs are temporary and will yield in time to more normal patterns. Generally she is advised to be careful about infections, and given special feeding advice. Her task is to take satisfactory precautions without depriving herself and the child of enjoyable interactions.

> Mrs. B. had a "sinking feeling" before she brought her twins home, was nervous and developed a gastrointestinal upset, but within a few days the schedule seemed to be more settled. The B's became more confident and realized "the babies won't break"; they were concerned about such things as overfeeding and temperature regulations of the room, but not so much about infection. They thought of the babies less as prematures than as twins and foresaw a normal development.

In those cases which appear to have a good outcome, the mother has accomplished the four tasks: anticipatory grief; acknowledgment of failure; resumption of active relating to the baby; seeing its special needs as a premature and prematurity as a temporary state yielding to normality. Thus far in the evaluation of outcome, we have used clinical impressions of the early mother-child relationship. A good outcome has been considered one in which the mother sees the baby as potentially normal, gives it realistic care, and takes pride and satisfaction in that care.

PATHOLOGICAL DEVIATIONS

On the other hand, deviations from the typical pattern appear to be associated with poor outcome of the stress situation. Some mothers handle the real threat to the baby and their own maternal failure to carry to term by denying either the threat or the failure, or both. When denial is used as a defense there are certain observable changes in the mother. While an early depression may be evident following delivery, this may too rapidly give way to a more cheerful appearance. Such mothers eat and sleep well and do not appear to have difficulty in talking with other mothers about their babies or in seeing mothers with normal babies in the same room or ward in the hospital.

> Mrs. V. was subject to acute depersonalization episodes after her baby came home. In discussing these attacks, which are referred to as "headaches," she said that she did not cry in the beginning, but felt that she let her feelings build up. She thought this was the reason for her "headaches." In the hospital she slept and ate well. She remembers missing the baby, but she was not aware of

a feeling of sadness. She recalled that when the baby was moved to another hospital (for special premature care) she pretended that she visited the baby and imagined what he was like. The other mothers, particularly the one she roomed with, were quite free to tell about their babies because Mrs. V. did not seem to be upset about not having hers with her. She thought she had not been upset by the baby's difficulties because she had had a lot of experience with illness, which she had learned to take calmly. She didn't become weepy until she came home.

Where the mother fails to respond with hope to the indications of survival and development of the infant, we have another pathological deviation. A number of factors may underline this failure to respond to the infant's progress. For example, the infant may continue to symbolize her failure despite its progress and thereby impede the task of relating to the baby. This may be reflected in her inability to discuss the experience retrospectively with the interviewer.

In one family, although the interviewer made a number of attempts to discuss the baby, the parents avoided discussion except for brief perfunctory comments. Instead they talked at length about themselves and their extended families. At the end of the interview the father smiled and commented that "every time we get together to talk about the baby it seems that we don't do this, but switch to talk about other things in the family!" In this family the adjustment to the baby was unusually difficult, with poor outcome for mother-child relationship.

If the mother sees the baby as continuing to represent the threat of death or abnormality, or of unusual difficulties and care, such perceptions can seriously impede the tasks of relating to and caring for the infant.

Mrs. Q.'s mother is a patient in a state mental hospital. In a number of interviews Mrs. Q. talked at length about mental health and her concern about transmitting illness hereditarily. Although the medical evaluation of her premature was quite good, she remained preoccupied with his "mental development." She began to refer to him as a "nervous baby," expressing concern about the noise her older children made, which she thought contributed to the baby's nervousness.

Mrs. B. expressed concern soon after the birth of her premature baby that he might have heart trouble. She has a functional heart murmur. Although he progressed well, gaining weight and developing normally, she continued to express concern about the baby's heart, asking the doctor at each examination if he could detect heart trouble, although each time she was assured that nothing showed in these examinations.

The following also illustrates the unsuccessful resolution of the necessary psychological tasks we have described:

In discussing their immediate reactions to having such a small baby, a father described himself as "shocked." He "almost keeled over" when she lost weight, dropping from 4–6 to 3–12. The mother, in contrast, said she "wasn't worried about it" and expected a loss of weight. Her first reaction to seeing the baby was that the baby was so tiny. "The pediatrician said she was beautiful. I couldn't see anything beautiful about her. I was worried in the beginning but the doctor and nurse reassured me." The mother had no previous experience with prematures.

During the period when the baby was in the hospital nursery, there was little visiting by the mother. She said there was not too much advantage in going to see the baby, "You can't tell much by looking at her."

In anticipation of the baby's homecoming the mother compared the premature to her previous full-term baby and didn't think "any extra care would be needed," since it would only weigh a half pound less than the previous normal baby at homecoming. When the premature came home, the early adjustment was good; the mother seemed loving and able to handle the baby. The situation quickly deteriorated when the full impact of the difference between the babies became apparent. The baby's cry was weak, the parents said she did not have a good pair of lungs, and they were afraid they would not hear her.

They became increasingly fearful of handling her, of bathing her—they bagan to treat her as if she were very fragile. The mother later commented that one pound certainly made a lot of difference. She became progressively negative to the baby and overwhelmed by the need to care for the children and keep up housecleaning at the same time.

We believe the mother must accomplish each task in the appropriate period in order to deal successfully with the stress of premature birth. For example, the inability to face and accept the failure connoted by premature birth makes it difficult for the mother to use the opportunity to visit with the baby in a psychologically productive way. In turn, the failure to visit and observe the baby in the nursery makes the adjustment to the baby at home a more difficult one. In the case just cited, the mother so quickly and completely denied her concern about danger to the child that she found herself grossly unprepared for meeting its needs and became burdened and resentful. Although such a woman may appear to the hospital staff to have adjusted promptly to the stress, the signs of potential difficulty are present. When these signs can be used by all health workers to screen women who deliver prematurely, it will be possible to direct preventive intervention to those more likely to have a poor outcome.

Future plans for this study include the testing of the ideas concerning reaction to premature birth by objective measurement and an exploration of intervention techniques appropriate to this stress.

REFERENCES

1   Caplan, G. *An Approach to the Study of Family Mental Health*. Pub. Hlth Rep., 71:1027–1030, 1956.

2   ———. *Concepts of Mental Health and Consultation.* Washington: Children's Bureau, 1959.

3   Deutsch, H. *The Psychology of Women: Motherhood.* New York: Grune & Stratton, 1945.

4   Fenichel, O. *The Psychoanalytic Theory of Neurosis.* New York: Norton, 1945.

5   Freud, S. *Beyond the Pleasure Principle.* London: Hogarth Press, 1920.

6   ———. "Mourning and Melancholia." *Collected Papers,* IV: 152–170. London: Hogarth Press, 1925.

7   Halliday, J. L. *Principles of Aetiology.* Brit J. Med. Psychol., 19:367–380, 1943.

8   Kardiner, A. *The Traumatic Neuroses of War.* Washington: National Research Council, 1941.

9   Lindemann, Erich. *Symptomatology and Management of Acute Grief.* Am. J. Psychiatry, 101:141–148, 1944.

10   Prugh, D. *Emotional Problems of the Premature Infant's Parents.* Nurs. Outlook, 1:461–464, 1953.

11   Spock, B. *Avoiding Behavior Problems.* J. Pediat., 27:363–382, 1945,

Four Studies of Crisis in Parents of Prematures

Gerald Caplan, M.D., D.P.M.,
Clinical Professor of Psychiatry, Laboratory of Community Psychiatry,
Harvard Medical School

Edward A. Mason, M.D.,
Assistant Clinical Professor of Psychiatry, Laboratory of Community
Psychiatry, Harvard Medical School

David M. Kaplan, Ph.D.
Associate Professor and Director, Division of Clinical Social Work, Stanford
University of Medicine

The concept of crisis has received increasing attention in mental health investigations because it offers hope for better understanding of the etiology and prevention of mental disorders. This article will review a series of crisis studies to illustrate the theoretical and methodological issues, and problems in crisis research. Some of these studies have been reported elsewhere, but this overview will show how they are interrelated and present their implications for further crisis research.

Our interest in acute crises derives from the assumption that these relatively short periods of psychological disequilibrium, which occur in everyone's life in response to developmental transitions or to situational hazards and challenges, are potential turning points which may lead to mental health disorder. Retrospective studies such as by Levy (1945) sug-

From *Community Mental Health Journal*, vol. 1, no. 2 pp. 149–161 (Summer 1965).

gest that sudden changes in vulnerability to mental disorder occur during such periods. We have become interested in studying the grappling with the problem which takes place during the period of disequilibrium; we wish to identify characteristic patterns and correlate these with types of mental health outcome. Our hope is that we may learn to identify persons whose behavior in specific crisis situations predicts a mentally unhealthy outcome. Subsequently, we hope to show that it is possible to intervene at that time and influence these persons to change their behavior so that they achieve a healthier result. The latter hope is related to our conviction that during the upset of a crisis a person usually has an increased desire to be helped and that he is more susceptible to influence then than during periods of relatively stable functioning (Caplan, 1964).

The early work of Lindemann (1944; 1956) on bereavement is a landmark for studies of specific crisis, although attention had been drawn to this subject as early as 1926 (Becker, 1926: Eliot, 1929). Lindemann described various aspects of mourning, indicating that certain of these were associated with a healthy outcome and others with a continuation of dependence on the dead person; among the latter also were a variety of psychosomatic disorders and difficulties in relating to others.

In other significant crisis research, Janis (1958) has described the patterns of reaction of adult patients in a general surgical ward; reports on psychological responses to the stress of severe burns have been made by Hamburg, Hamburg, and deGoza (1953), and on coping behavior of patients with polio by Visotsky, Hamburg, Goss, and Lebovits (1961). Tyhurst (1951) has studied reactions to natural disasters. Hill (1949) and Koos (1946) studied wartime separations and people with "troubles." Silber, Hamburg, Coelho, Murphey, Rosenberg, and Pearlin (1961) have investigated the patterns of behavior of high school students during crises precipitated by the transition from school to college. Murphy (1962) has investigated the variety of coping responses of young children facing the ordinary experiences of life for the first time. Rosenberg and Fuller (1957) have studied the responses of nursing students during the crises related to the succession of stresses which are part of their training. Caplan (1951), Bibring (1961), and others have investigated the range of responses of women during the course of pregnancy.

Some of these studies have been restricted to a description and classification of the way different people behave. Categories of behavior have sometimes been evaluated as desirable or undesirable, adaptive or maladaptive, on the basis of *a priori* value judgments. A few of the studies have attempted to correlate such value judgments with eventual outcome. Several of the studies have tried to elucidate the reasons why different subjects behaved as they did during the crisis and to disentangle pre-existing personality factors from situational influences during the period of the crisis. Rarely has the research attempted to test predictions regarding eventual outcome based upon judgments of current crisis behavior.

In studying these researches, we have been impressed by the following points:

1   Behavior during a crisis appears to be determined by the interaction of at least four factors, including influences of the situation itself, the pre-existing personality, cultural factors, and the interactions with significant others. Although major emphasis in the past has been on pre-crisis personality, it is no longer possible to consider this factor as the exclusive determinant of crisis behavior. We will discuss this further below.

2   The varieties of behavior of persons in crisis are classifiable into a relatively small number of patterns.

3   All crises resemble each other in certain fundamental particulars. Crises are time-limited periods of disequilibrium, or behavioral and subjective upset, which are precipitated by an inescapable demand or burden to which the person is temporarily unable to respond adequately. During this period of tension, the person grapples with the problem and develops novel resources, both by calling upon internal reserves and by making use of the help of others. Those resources are then used to handle the precipitating factor, and the person achieves once more a steady state.

4   Crises also differ from one another along certain specifiable dimensions: the type of precipitating factors, e.g., whether "developmental" or "accidental" (Caplan, 1964); and the type of challenge or hazard, e.g., death of a loved one, change of occupational role, personal injury, or relocation of domicile. In any subcategory of crises, there appear to be certain regularly occurring psychological and environmental tasks (Caplan, 1961), and different persons accomplish the tasks with a greater or lesser degree of adequacy (Rapoport, 1963).

In line with these considerations, our research on the crisis of prematurity developed along two main related paths: a study of the patterns of the behavior of parents grappling with the problems of a premature birth and a study of the psychological tasks presented by this situation and of the adequacy with which these tasks are accomplished. Each of the studies has consisted of two phased substudies. The first substudy has explored the process of the crisis in order to develop hypotheses on the connection between patterns of grappling or task accomplishment with mental health outcomes. The second substudy represents a preliminary test of these hypotheses on a new sample of parents: data were collected during crisis on the basis of which a prediction of mental health outcome was made, and this was compared with what was actually found by independent observers after the termination of the crisis period.

PARENTAL REACTIONS TO PREMATURE BIRTH AS AN EXAMPLE OF CRISIS

After preliminary explorations with token cases in several common crisis situations while establishing collaborative relationships with public health workers (Hamovitch, Caplan, Hare, & Owens, 1959), we eventually chose the birth of a premature baby as a suitable example because: (a) it occurred in sufficient numbers (8 per cent of live births) to provide an adequate supply of research subjects; (b) all cases of prematurity in the area were routinely referred by the maternity hospitals to the health department, and each family was visited in its home by a public health nurse before the baby was discharged from the hospital; (c) access to the case was therefore possible relatively early in the crisis; (d) the total list of cases could be sampled; (e) the onset of the crisis was easily definable by the onset of premature labor; (f) the severity of the crisis was likely to be graduated by the danger to the life expectancy of the baby and the degree of unpreparedness of the parents, thus making it feasible to study the same crisis in increasing degrees of severity; and (g) although prematurity occurs more frequently in lower socioeconomic class mothers, a randomly selected sample of study cases would probably include the range of socioeconomic classes and ethnic and social groups found in that area of Boston.

We realized that prematurity had certain obvious disadvantages as a crisis study topic. First, it was usually not a very disrupting crisis as measured by the degree of disequilibrium, and its outcome, whether bad or good, was not likely to be as dramatic as some other crises. Moreover, except in most unusual circumstances, the outcome would be observable in terms of changes in mental health rather than as actual mental disorder, and its value as a focus for crisis research which might lead to the prevention of mental disorder was based on assumptions which would need separate research verification. We felt that we could work out some valid measures of mental health changes based upon our previous studies on disorders in mother-child relationships (Caplan, 1951). We also hoped that our understanding of this crisis would be enriched by our previous studies on normal pregnancy and birth, which would form a baseline of comparable reactions of lesser intensity. The unlikelihood of outcomes in the form of mental disorder did not at this stage seem a serious drawback because our primary interest was focused upon the *process* of the crisis. Any differences in outcome, even if in the middle range of healthiness, could become the basis for identifying significantly different patterns of coping and of crisis task accomplishment.

GENERAL METHOD OF DATA COLLECTION

The two exploratory hypothesis-developing studies represent different analyses of the same body of data. This set of study records represents our accumulated data on 86 cases of premature birth in intact families in our study area. There was no systematic selection of the cases. The homes of listed premature births were visited within 7 to 10 days after the birth.

Introduced by the public health nurse, we attempted to arouse the motivation of the family to collaborate with us in "a study of how families deal with prematurity, so that we can find out how to improve our public health services" (Mason, 1958a). We used a variety of interviewers in these studies: psychiatrists, psychologists, social workers, mental health nurses, sociologists, and anthropologists. In our early work we sent two interviewers into the home at the same time, one to interview and the other to observe. We occasionally made tape recordings of the interviews for purposes of developing interviewing skills, but the data were chiefly assembled in process records dictated by the interviewer within 4 hours. The mother and the father were seen separately and together, as well as with their children, relatives, and friends when they happened to be present. Some interviews were carried out in our offices, and a few parents were seen there for psychological testing or for specialized psychiatric examinations to elucidate idiosyncratic elements in the case (Parad & Caplan, 1960).

By fitting into the already existing and well-developed nursing service, the interviewers were, at first, thought likely to be able to gain entry to the cases without having to "pay" for their subjects' cooperation by themselves providing help in the crisis. Subsequently, the researchers realized that some flexibility in being helpful did not alter the crisis situation and, in fact, increased the cooperation of the families.

As far as possible, we attempted to see the family members about once a week while the baby was in hospital, and at regular weekly or fortnightly intervals for 2 to 3 months after the baby's discharge from hospital. There was an average of 11 interviews with each family.

Although ideally the relationships between a crisis and its long-term outcome should be investigated, our research never planned to include this. We believed that strategically it would be wise first to demonstrate a correlation with short-term outcome since this would at least be one of the factors determining ultimate mental health outcome. We therefore planned that each case be studied until there appeared to be a stabilization of responses. From our experience in the early cases, this seemed to have occurred by the time the baby had been home for two months. Actually, there may be at least two peaks of upset involved in premature delivery: the more dramatic around the birth and hospital stay, and a briefer upset on the baby's homecoming. Essentially uniform, however, was the expected duration of the crisis, in spite of the variation in degree of upset and patterns of grappling.

Early in the project we tried to obtain data on the response of each individual to the crisis, as well as the interpersonal happenings in the family as a group, in the present crisis as well as in previous hazardous situations. In order to limit the volume of data, we finally decided to focus on the grappling behavior, the time sequence, the associated psychological tasks, and the picture of current and past family functioning. A more orderly collection and recording of data was possible after Interview Guides were developed (Mason, 1958b).

Regretfully we eventually decided to bow to the inevitability imposed by our current lack of knowledge of the family as an operating social system, to restrict our focus to the reactions of the mother in her crisis struggles, and to study the behavior of other family members only insofar as they affected her and her relationship with her baby. This restriction involved our losing sight of some of the potentially most interesting phenomena of crisis, but we felt that it was all we could handle adequately at that time. However, since the mother usually appeared to be the family member most intensely involved in the crisis of premature birth, apart of course from the baby, our interest in exploring the significance of crisis processes was reasonably well served by concentrating upon her.

For a variety of reasons many of the records, especially those accumulated in the early period of the study, were not satisfactory. There were inevitable gaps in the data as a result of variations in family motivation, interviewer skills, and the types of concurrent situations. Many families found themselves in multiple crises, some of which were unrelated to prematurity. When the time came for the data analysis, it was decided that only records providing consistently full data continuously until the baby had been home from hospital for 6 to 8 weeks would be acceptable. These cases cannot be considered representative of any particular population, but by chance they turned out to be about equally divided among whites and Negroes, and to include families both of low and of middle socioeconomic classes. There was also a representative spread as regards birth weight. Although generalizations may not be possible to a larger population, the cases do illustrate the variety of responses to crisis likely to occur in various subgroups and serve as models for further investigation.

DEVELOPMENT OF HYPOTHESES ON THE RELATIONSHIP OF GRAPPLING PATTERNS AND MENTAL HEALTH OUTCOME

This study (Caplan, 1960) analyzed the records of ten cases in which two psychiatrist judges could agree on the rating of mental health outcome. A Healthy Outcome was defined as being characterized by unambiguous and positive evidence that all dyadic relationships among family members two months after the baby came home were at least as "healthy" as they had been in the months prior to the premature birth. An Unhealthy Outcome represented a situation in which at least one dyadic relationship was worse after the crisis.

The records were divided into the two contrasting groups and each psychiatrist independently appraised the grappling by parents with their crisis problems. Consensus was obtained in respect to the following three relatively distinct categories of grappling:

Cognitive Grasp of the Crisis Situation

In the Healthy Outcome cases, the parents continually surveyed the situation and actively gathered as much information as possible about the baby and the causes and manifestations of prematurity. The assessment of the situation was maintained in consciousness most of the time, and perceptions were reality-based and minimally distorted by irrational fantasies.

In the Unhealthy Outcome cases, there was little active searching for evidence upon which a current assessment of the situation and a judgment about outcome or plans for handling it could be made. Thoughts about danger or burden were suppressed, avoided, or denied, and outcome was considered in terms of a global belief that all would be well or that luck would be bad, both of which appeared dependent more upon inner fantasies than appraisal of external reality.

Handling Feelings

In the Healthy Outcome cases, the parents showed a continuous awareness of negative feelings throughout the crisis, and there was free verbal and nonverbal expression of these feelings in interaction with others. Occasionally at peak periods of stress there was a temporary utilization of the defenses of denial, suppression, and avoidance; but anxiety, anger, depression, and frustration were soon readmitted to awareness and a conscious attempt was made to master them, both alone and with the help of others.

In the Unhealthy Outcome cases there was little or no verbal admission of negative feelings, and the parents pretended to be cheerful and denied discomfort. The only negative feeling which was permitted open and continuous expression was blaming others.

Obtaining Help

In the Healthy Outcome cases, the parents actively sought help from within the family or the community in relation to the tasks associated with the care of the premature baby, and assistance in dealing with their negative feelings. Emotional assistance included nonspecific support, and specific attention to reassure and share anxieties, relieve guilt, and assuage deprivation. The helping process characteristically included counteracting occasional maladjustive coping patterns.

In the Unhealthy Outcome cases, there was a reluctance or inability to seek help or to accept it when offered. The parents did not help each other in any consistent way, and when they did, they often supported each other in maladaptive grappling, such as urging denial and avoidance of difficulties, stimulating blaming oneself or others for the prematurity, and engaging in bickering as a means of nonspecific tension release.

Discussion

Based upon the above analysis and in collaboration with other staff efforts, a series of hypotheses was developed linking the contrasting patterns of cognitive and affective handling of the crisis situation, and patterns of obtaining help, to the two extreme types of outcome. At that stage of the research, it was not felt possible to distinguish the relative weight of the various details of the grappling patterns, and the hypotheses had to be couched in global terms. Parents who actively sought information about the premature baby and used this to plan for its future, who expressed negative feelings which were consonant with their perceptions of threat to the baby, and who sought and benefited from the assistance of readily available helping persons, would tend to have a healthier mental health outcome than parents who avoided information, denied feelings, and did not seek or accept help. No causal relationship could be hypothesized between the antecedent grappling patterns and the subsequent outcome rating, and it was felt to be sufficient at the present stage to maintain that a particular grappling pattern was predictive of the likelihood of a healthy or unhealthy mental health outcome. It was recognized that both the grappling pattern and the signs of outcome might be manifestations of the underlying personality of the parents, and might be related because of this rather than because of the dynamics of the crisis and its pattern of resolution. Certainly, aspects of all three categories seemed of an enduring nature related to personality. But the category "Obtaining Help" seemed in addition to include not only interpersonal and cultural elements but also factors related to the social network in which the parents were involved.

A PREDICTIVE STUDY TO TEST HYPOTHESES RELATING GRAPPLING PATTERNS AND MENTAL HEALTH OUTCOME

The data for this study (Mason, 1963) of twenty-eight randomly selected mothers who were admitted to a lying-in hospital in premature labor consisted of interviews during the first five days following the birth of the baby. Information concerning the mother's cognitive and affective response to the crisis was collected as well as about her relationships with available helping persons, including husband, friends, relatives, and caregiving professionals. Judgments about her maternal qualities were made according to the way she talked about her real and fantasied relationships with babies, and note was made of the nature of her previous experience, if any, with prematurity.

Based upon the data from the interviews and upon the hypotheses of the previous study, a prediction was made in each case of the quality of mother-child relationship to be found six weeks after the baby would be home from the hospital. The prediction took the form of a global rating of the relationship as Good or Poor in regard to the mother's attitudes toward the baby and her effectiveness in taking care of it.

After her discharge, each mother was interviewed in her home by a social worker. Observations of the cognitive and affective response of individual family members to the situation and to the course of events, and of the handling of the practical and psychological tasks were recorded. Particular attention was paid to evidence of the mother's relationship with the new baby.

The social workers who collected this information were not given any details of the earlier interviews and did not know what predictions had been made. The reports for the end of the study period (between six and ten weeks after the baby came home) were rated in regard to the quality of outcome by a clinical psychologist who was also ignorant of the predictions. The judgment on outcome focused upon the mother-child relationship and was forced into either a "good" or "poor" category, based on the mother's acceptance and care of the child, as well as the latter's progress.

Of the 19 mothers in which both prediction and outcome ratings could be made, 11 were predicted to have a Good outcome and 8 were predicted to have a Poor outcome. The outcome ratings agreed in 10 of the Good and 7 of the Poor predictions.

Discussion

This is clearly a rough clinical study involving global judgments both of prediction and outcome categories. There are many overlapping and potentially contaminating factors. However, the findings lend additional support to the implications of the first study that a meaningful categorization of individuals undergoing a hazardous situation can be made along these di-

Table 1 Hospital Prediction of Early Mother-Child Relationship

| | Outcome | |
Prediction	Good	Poor
Good	10	1
Poor	1	7

p < .01 (Fisher Exact Test).

mensions. It should be noted that no correlation was observed between outcome and socioeconomic status, cultural group, or pre-crisis personality. However, no standardized rating of these was attempted. Although the numbers are small, they are statistically significant, and the study does indicate that predictions of the mental health outcome on the basis of be-havior *during* the crisis of prematurity are feasible.

AN EXPLORATORY STUDY TO DETERMINE THE PSYCHOLOGICAL TASKS FACING THE MOTHERS OF PREMATURE BABIES, AND THE RELATIONSHIP OF TASK ACCOMPLISHMENT TO MENTAL HEALTH OUTCOME

This study (Kaplan & Mason, 1960) took the form of a qualitative analysis of the records of cases collected by the research team in its initial explora-tions. The analysis focused upon the mother's experience of the prematurity crisis, and upon the successive problems with which she was confronted. The researchers isolated four major psychological tasks which appear to be a characteristic of this experience for most mothers, and the adequate ac-complishment of which seems to be essential both for successful mastery of the crisis situation and for providing a sound basis for a future healthy mother-child relationship.

The following were postulated as being the four tasks:

1   The first task confronts the mother at the time of delivery. It is the preparation for a possible loss of the baby whose life is in jeopardy. This "anticipatory grief" (Lindemann, 1944) involves a withdrawal from the re-lationship already being established during pregnancy with the expected child. The mother hopes the baby will survive, but simultaneously prepares for its death.

2   At about the same time the mother must face and acknowledge her feelings of failure due to not delivering a normal full-term baby. The moth-er struggles with both these tasks until the baby's chances for survival seem secure. According to its weight and physical condition, the baby may con-tinue to remain in hospital for a further two to ten weeks, and during this period the third and fourth tasks need to be performed.

3   The third task is the resumption of the process of relating to the baby which previously had been interrupted. The mother has lost the usual opportunity provided by a full-term pregnancy for the development of readiness for the mothering role. Characteristically, there is a point at which the mother really begins to believe that the baby will survive. The event which stimulates activity on her third task may be the baby's gain in weight, a change in feeding pattern, a change in its activity or appearance, or a change in the nurses' manner.

4   The fourth task faces the mother with the challenge of under-standing how a premature baby differs from a normal baby in terms of its special needs and growth patterns. In order to provide the baby with the necessary extra care and protection, the mother must see him as a premature with special needs and characteristics. But it is equally important for her to see that these special needs are temporary and will yield in time to more normal patterns. Her task is to take satisfactory precautions without depriving herself and the child of enjoyable interactions.

In this study no attempt was made to separate the cases into contrasting outcome groups. Instead, the records were inspected in order to identify typical patterns of mothers who apparently accomplished the four tasks and a contrasting group of cases in which the four tasks were not accomplished in whole or in part. In the first group the outcome seemed good, in that the mother developed a healthy relationship to the baby by the time it was two months old. She gave it realistic care in relation to its needs, she took pride and satisfaction in handling it, and she saw the baby as potentially normal.

The cases also included mothers who did not follow the above pattern. Some mothers handled the hazard to the life of the baby and their own maternal failure by denial. Some mothers failed to respond with hope to the indications of the survival and satisfactory development of the infant. In some such cases it appeared that the baby continued to symbolize the mother's failure despite its progress and she continued to preceive it in a fixed distorted way as a case of impending death or abnormality. This perception seriously impeded her sensitivity to the baby's real needs. Other mothers either took insufficient precautions in sheltering the baby from excessive stimulation, prematurely treated it "like a normal infant", or else they continued to coddle and overprotect it after such special care was no longer realistically necessary. They overfed or underfed the baby. There were a variety of signs of tension in the mother-child relationships.

Discussion

Beyond showing an association between task accomplishment and outcome, this study suggests that certain tasks are specific for certain stages in the crisis and, further, that any interruption in the sequence of these tasks leads to increased difficulty in achieving a healthy outcome. It is important to note that any crisis is usually made up of a number of smaller peaks of upset, sometimes overlapping and sometimes consecutive. Of course, there are frequently chance occurrences and other crises which may be indirectly related and which add to the stress to which the family must adjust. Occasionally in our families, along with the premature delivery, a husband lost his job or the family moved to a new home and this colored the family's crisis behavior. Some writers (Wortis, 1960) believe that the premature delivery is the *result* of another crisis and therefore that such other crises as we found might be caused or at least codetermined by some other common agent. In these studies no attempt was made to determine the "cause" of the premature delivery. In regard to psychogenic factors or chronic physical stresses, etc., no pattern of relationship was apparent in examining the data. Although it is true that our sample represented a group more apt to be at a disadvantage both financially and physically, what was important was that *within* such a group distinguishing characteristics about grappling behavior could be identified. Thus, regardless of cultural, socioeconomic, or personality factors, it is believed that there are tasks which are universal.

A STUDY TO TEST THE HYPOTHESES RELATING TASK ACCOMPLISHMENT TO MENTAL HEALTH OUTCOME

Data on 30 cases of prematurity were collected (Kaplan, 1961) in a form which allowed the prediction of the healthy or unhealthy quality of maternal care on the basis of the mother's handling of the tasks imposed by the crisis of premature delivery. The data collection was carried out by social workers who interviewed the mothers in their homes. Process records of their interviews were kept and observations were made on 11 items which the researcher had derived from the hypotheses on task accomplishment developed in the previous study. The case records were independently coded and rated by other workers so that there would be a minimum of contamination in the composite prediction assessment.

The cases were followed by social workers who were given no information about the mothers' statements or behavior during the period when the babies were in hospital, and were not told the outcome predictions. The outcome data consisted of interview and observation material about maternal behavior. Twelve items were defined to cover the outcome area, and independent judges, who had not seen the earlier parts of the record, coded and rated each of these.

The prediction and outcome categories were then compared in each case in order to test the hypotheses; and a variety of correlations with outcome were also analyzed in order to investigate the relations to outcome of other apparently significant factors, such as birth weight of the babies, parity of the mothers, prior experience with prematurity, visiting patterns while the babies were in hospital, etc.

Prediction Assessment

The early parts of each record were coded and rated to cover the eleven items assessing the accomplishment of the third and fourth tasks. These included the mother's pattern of visiting the premature nursery, her preoccupations with the infant, her report on her own observations of the infant, the content of her references to the infant which indicated hopes or concerns elicited by changes in his appearance and behavior, her expression of feelings of deprivation in being separated from the infant, her concern with premature traits in the infant, her discussion of actual or potential defects in her infant without medical basis, and her estimate of the infant's care requirements after discharge from hospital. Each item was scored as either present or absent, an appropriate numerical rating was assigned, and these scores were added to form a composite prediction score. The distribution of these total scores made it apparent that three categories of prediction were warranted: Good, Poor, and Very Poor.

Outcome Assessment

The records dealing with the behavior and attitudes of the mothers toward their children at the end of the study were rated for items such as evidence of maternal pride, satisfaction in handling and talking about the baby, apprehension about defects in the infant not observed by the doctors, marked indifference to the infant including neglect, overfeeding, and "pushing" to have the infant develop too quickly beyond its premature state.

As with the prediction assessment, the total score of the outcome assessment was obtained by adding together the scores on all the items. The group was then divided into three bands: Good, Poor, and Very Poor outcome.

Table 2 shows the association of these prediction and outcome ratings. Of the 30 cases, 18 were judged to have a Good outcome and of these, 13 were accurately predicted; 10 were rated Poor in outcome, of which 9 had been predicted; and the 2 cases of Very Poor outcome were correctly predicted. The predictions were 80 percent successful.

One finding among the results of item analysis which is of special interest is the high correlation of the rating of the mothers' visiting pattern with the final overall outcome rating. A good visiting pattern means that

Table 2 Task Accomplishment as a Prediction of Maternal Care

	Outcome		
Prediction	Good	Poor	Very poor
Good	13	1	0
Poor	5	9	0
Very Poor	0	0	2

p < .01 (Chi Squared Test).

the mother visited the baby in hospital at least once a week during the last two weeks of his stay, or that she visited more frequently during this period than in previous weeks. Table 3 indicates that from the visiting pattern alone a better prediction of outcome can be made than from all the other prediction items.

This finding means that in our study population the visiting pattern is apparently an excellent index of the whole area of task accomplishment. If it holds up under further study as a simple indicator of outcome it would be most valuable in practice. Unfortunately, any such discrete indicator is subject to considerable overuse or misinterpretation, and might be invalidated by administrative or policy changes in regard to mothers' visiting.

Discussion

The chief contribution of this study is the further evidence that maternal grappling patterns are predictive of maternal care patterns. Again the hypothesis is supported which suggests that there are certain tasks which pertain to this crisis situation whose accomplishment is correlated with successful outcome.

CONCLUDING DISCUSSION

Our studies have shown that there is some merit to studying the reactions of parents to the premature birth of a baby as an example of a crisis. We did not choose prematurity because we believed that it represented a serious threat to the mental health of the family members and would be likely to be associated with a significantly increased risk of mental illness such as might be found in other crises precipitated by stresses like bereavement or serious physical illness. On the other hand, a study of prematurity has some meaning in its own right from the mental health point of view. Earlier clinical experience had given us the impression that the stress of prematurity might

Table 3   Visiting Pattern and Outcome

	Outcome	
Visiting pattern	Good	Poor
Good	17	2
Poor	1	10

$p < .02$ (Chi Squared Test).

color the behavior and attitudes of a mother to her premature infant through many years of childhood (Prugh, 1953; Spock, 1945). A mother who delivers before term frequently has been observed to urge the baby to eat and grow as if to reassure herself about her ability as a mother. If this emphasis on satisfaction of the mother's own needs outweighs her concern for the needs of the infant, a mother-child relationship may be established which will interfere with healthy personality development in the child (Caplan, 1959; Caplan, 1961).

Although in our four studies we did not conduct follow-up investigations to trace the effects on the children, the not inconsiderable number of mothers whose relationships with their children were rated as "unhealthy" 6 to 8 weeks after the baby's discharge from hospital has confirmed our clinical impression that prematurity may be associated with emotional difficulties. It is, of course, possible that the disturbance of the mother-child relationship which we identified in certain cases was not influenced by the mother's pattern of grappling with the crisis of premature birth, and we will discuss this point later on. But at the very least, our studies do seem to indicate that such disordered relationships can be predicted or identified from the behavior of the mother shortly after the birth of her baby, and it is a plausible assumption that the disorder in mother-child relationships is likely to be of some significance for the future personality development of the premature baby.

Apart from their relevance for the study of factors influencing mental disorder or mental health, our studies of the crisis of prematurity have made some significant contributions to crisis research in general. We have come to believe, particularly in connection with the Family Studies under Rhona Rapoport (1963), that in a study of the processes involved in reacting to a crisis it is meaningful to differentiate both general grappling patterns and also crisis task accomplishment. We have shown that these factors can be defined, that data relating to them can be systematically collected, recorded, and reliably rated, and that some regularity can be found in the association of different patterns of each of these factors and a mental health outcome variable.

In the absence of a clear indication of changes in respect to mental disorder, we have shown that it is possible to define as an outcome variable certain aspects of the interpersonal relationships of persons who have undergone crisis; also we have shown that it is possible to collect data in a consistent manner and report these details in such a way that they can be reliably rated by independent judges and assessments made which will differentiate the outcome in one case from that in another. We have shown that there is a sufficient spread both in the ratings of the antecedent and consequent variables defined in this way so that meaningful associations between the two sets of variables can be documented. Our studies have also shown one approach to the problem of controlling for the investigator's bias in favor of his own hypotheses by using separate sets of workers to collect the data for the antecedent and consequent factors in our equation. In utilizing the services of part-time social workers to collect clinical data by means of structured interviews, we have followed the example of Freeman and Simmons (1963). Our studies have also demonstrated that it is feasible to obtain the cooperation of a high proportion of a randomly selected group of persons in one type of crisis in carrying out research of this type, and we have learned something about the problems of arousing the motivation of research subjects.

In addition to the above, our studies have provided support for our original assumption that it is possible to hypothesize particular patterns of crisis grappling and of accomplishment of crisis tasks which are associated with good and bad outcome. Despite the small size of our samples, our results have supported our assumption that we can make reliable predictions about mental health outcome from a judgment based upon an appraisal both of patterns of grappling and also of task accomplishment. If future studies on the crisis of prematurity with larger samples confirm our findings, we will be in the position of being able to communicate to clinical workers a series of clear-cut behavioral items which they can observe among mothers shortly after premature delivery that will allow them to predict a subgroup likely to have disordered relationships with their children at a crucial period of the latter's development. Whatever other factors are involved in the development of these children, it is plausible to assume that it would be useful to separate out this group for special attention by the doctors, nurses, and social workers who will intervene preventively in order to try to ameliorate the predicted disorder of mother-child relationship or to safeguard the child from its ill effects.

Our studies have not been designed to show a causal relationship between patterns of grappling and task accomplishment and the nature of the mental health outcome; but if such a causative relationship is eventually demonstrated by subsequent studies, our research points the way to a possible rationale for this preventive intervention. Assuming that poor coping and task accomplishment influence the mother in the direction of an unhealthy relationship with her baby, the prevention of a bad outcome might consist of identifying the poor grapplers and influencing them to grapple more adequately and to accomplish their crisis tasks in the appropriate sequence.

Our studies have been inadequate on two counts. The smallness of our sample has prevented us from differentiating possible differences in crisis grappling and task accomplishment among persons of different socioeconomic classes, educational levels, and cultural backgrounds. Future studies with larger representative samples will reveal whether or not there is one fundamental "good" or "bad" pattern of dealing with crisis or whether there is a variety of patterns of each category which are associated with cultural and social structure differences in a population.

The more significant drawback in our studies has already been mentioned. In this preliminary work, we restricted ourselves to trying to demonstrate an *association* between types of crisis grappling and task accomplishment and varieties of mental health outcome. This association may represent a causal relationship, which would be highly significant for preventive psychiatry, or it may represent two sets of factors each of which is the resultant of an antecedent set of conditions. It may be, for instance, that women with healthy personalities cope adequately with the crisis of prematurity and also develop healthy relationships with their premature babies. Also, it may be that women with unhealthy personalities will manifest undesirable problem solving during the crisis of prematurity and will also have disorders in their relationships with their babies. Not only pre-existing personality factors but also perhaps particular constellations of sociocultural factors which antedate the onset of the crisis may predetermine a mother's behavior during the crisis and even the nature of her relationship to her infant.

The investigation of this problem is particularly difficult. An effective study would demand access to the sample prior to the onset of crisis in order to assess adequately the pre-crisis personality of the mother. In the case of the crisis of prematurity, it is difficult to determine where to draw the base line. The studies of Caplan (1951) and of Bibring (1961) have shown that pregnancy itself leads to significant changes in the manifestations of a woman's personality functioning. Even apart from this difficulty, the only way to study the personalities of women before premature delivery would be to obtain access to a total population of pregnant women with the expectation that a certain proportion of them would deliver prematurely. Since prematurity occurs in only 8 per cent of live births, this would be a formidable task (though we might make it a little easier by drawing our sample from the lower socioeconomic class population, in which prematurity is more common). Other examples of crisis might lend themselves more to a design of this type. For instance, the crises associated with certain military stresses such as going into battle for the first time, or predictable crises such as termination of employment in an industry which is in the process of being automated, would present us with a situation in which a researcher might gain access to a population which he can study before, during, and after a crisis.

One research approach does offer some hope of solving the problem of causality. If future researches confirm a consistent contrast in mental health outcome between groups of people who behave differently during crisis in relation to grappling pattern and task accomplishment, it should be possible to isolate a group of poor grapplers who can reliably be predicted to have a poor mental health outcome. If this group is then divided into two, and one subgroup is exposed to preventive intervention so that their grappling is steered in a positive direction while the other subgroup is used as a control, an amelioration in the mental health outcome of the experimental group would favor the hypothesis that the pattern of grappling and task accomplishment was causally related to mental health outcome rather than merely being associated with it because of some antecedent set of factors. We believe that this avenue is well worth exploring.

REFERENCES

Becker, H. A social psychological study of bereavement. Masters Thesis, Northwestern University, 1926.

Bibring, G. L., Dwyer, T. F., Huntington, D. S., & Valenstein, A. F. A study of the psychological processes in pregnancy and of the earliest mother-child relationship. *Psychoanal. Stud. Child*, 1961, 16, 9–27.

Caplan, G. A public health approach to child psychiatry—an introductory account of an experiment. *Ment. Hyg., N.Y.*, 1951, 35, 235–249. (a)

Caplan, G. Mental hygiene work with expectant mothers, *Ment. Hyg., N.Y.*, 1951, 35, 41–50. (b)

Caplan, G. *Concepts of mental health and consultation.* Washington: Children's Bureau, 1959.

Caplan, G. Patterns of parental response to the crisis of premature birth. *Psychiat.*, 1960, 23, 365–374.

Caplan, G. *An approach to community mental health.* New York: Grune and Stratton, 1961.

Caplan, G. *Principles of preventive psychiatry.* New York: Basic Books, 1964.

Eliot, T. D. The adjustive behavior of bereaved families: A new field for research. *Soc. Forces*, 1929, 8, 543–549.

Freeman, H. E., & Simmons, O. G. *The mental patient comes home.* New York: John Wiley, 1963.

Hamburg, D. A., Hamburg, B., & deGoza, S. Adaptive problems and mechanisms in severely burned patients. *Psychiat.*, 1953, 16, 1–20.

Hamovitch, M. D., Caplan, G., Hare, P., & Owens, C. Establishment and maintenance of a mental health unit—a case history and general principles. *Ment. Hyg., N.Y.*, 1959, 43, 412–421.

Hill, R. *Families under stress.* New York: Harper, 1949.

Janis, I. L. *Psychological stress.* New York: John Wiley, 1958.

Kaplan, D., & Mason, E. A. Maternal reactions to premature birth viewed as an acute emotional disorder. *Amer. J. Orthopsychiat.*, 1960, 30, 539–547.

Kaplan, D. Predicting outcome from situational stress on the basis of individual problem-solving patterns. Unpublished Ph.D. Thesis, University of Minnesota, 1961.

Koos, E. L., *Families in trouble,* New York: Kings Crown Press, 1946.

Levy, D. M. Psychic trauma of operations in children. *Amer. J. Dis. Children,* 1945, 69, 7–25.

Lindemann, E. Symptomatology and management of acute grief. *Amer. J. Psychiat.,* 1944, 101, 141–148.

Lindemann, E. The meaning of crisis in individuals and family living. *Teachers Coll. Rec.,* 1956, 57, 310–315.

Mason, E. A. Family study method. In *Family Guidance Center Report to the Commonwealth Fund,* 1958. Chapter 3.(a)

Mason. E. A. Interview guides. In *Family Guidance Center Report to the Commonwealth Fund,* 1958, Appendix 3.(b)

Mason, E. A. A method of predicting crisis outcome for mothers of premature babies. *Publ. Hlth. Rep.,* 1963, 78, 1031–1035.

Murphy, L. B. et al. *The widening world of childhood—paths toward mastery.* New York: Basic Books, 1962.

Parad, H. J., & Caplan, G. A framework for studying families in crisis. *Soc. Wk.,* 1960, 5, 3–15.

Prugh, D. Emotional problems of the premature infant's parents. *Nurs. Outlook,* 1953, 1, 461–464.

Rapoport, R. Normal crises, family structure and mental health. *Fam. Process,* 1963, 2, 68–80.

Rosenberg, P. P., & Fuller, M. L. Dynamic analysis of the student nurse. *Group Psychother.,* 1957, 10, 22–37.

Silber, E., Hamburg, D. A., Coelho, G. V., Murphey, E. B., Rosenberg, M., & Pearling, L. I. Adaptive behavior in competent adolescents. *Arch. Gen. Psychiat.,* 1961, 5, 354–365.

Spock, B. Avoiding behavior problems. *J. Pediatrics,* 1945, 27, 363–382.

Tyhurst, J. S. Individual reactions to community disaster. *Amer. J. Psychiat.,* 1951, 107, 764–769.

Visotsky, H. M., Hamburg, D. A., Goss, M. E., & Lebovits, B. Z. Coping behavior under extreme stress. *Arch. gen. Psychiat.,* 1961, 5, 423–448.

Wortis, H. Discussion. *Amer. J. Orthopsychiat.,* 1960, 30, 547–552.

Effects of Separation on Mother-Infant Bonding

The importance of the earliest mother-infant contacts is the subject of this chapter. During the past two decades, there has been a marked increase in interest and research pertaining to the earliest days and weeks of life. Although the newborn infant may be in a "prepsychological" state for several weeks following birth, the vital maternal-infant attachment begins to develop immediately postpartum. It is within the context of this attachment, or bonding, that the infant's social and psychological potential unfolds. If the bonding is delayed or impaired, the likelihood of later disorders in the child increases. It is for this reason that these authors have studied the mother-infant dyad and report their conclusions and suggestions in the following articles.

Marshall H. Klaus and John H. Kennell, in "Mothers Separated from Their Newborn Infants," summarize ethological studies pertaining to the neonatal period in nonhuman mammals in order to make cautious analogies. They then report in detail on their observations and experiences with various patterns of practice in premature nurseries. They emphasize the likelihood that close maternal-infant contact from the time of birth is probably of considerable importance to the development of a healthy mother-infant relationship and that separation can have a deleterious effect.

These authors, as well as other perinatologists, have encouraged more contact between mothers and their premature infants during the time their babies are in incubators. They allow mothers to enter the nurseries, place their hands in the isolettes, and carry out simple caretaking tasks for their babies. This supports the concept that close contact between the mother and infant during the early days and weeks of life may facilitate positive mothering behavior.

Marjorie J. Seashore et al. have studied "The Effects of Denial of Early Mother-Infant Interaction on Maternal Self-Confidence" and report their findings and the statistical methods used in the study. The results of their research indicate that denial of early mother-infant relationships has a negative effect on maternal self-confidence. This supports studies of maternal behavior in other species which suggest that restriction of interaction between mother and infant during early postpartum time diminishes subsequent maternal performance.

In "The Critical Nature of the Post-Partum Period in the Human for the Establishment of the Mother-Infant Bond: A Controlled Study," Lee Salk, a pediatric psychiatrist, has carefully examined the position in which the baby is held. He emphasizes the importance of the "natural" mother-infant reaction which takes place during the first twenty-four hours postpartum and strongly suggests that the period immediately postpartum is critical for the establishment of a positive mother-infant response. He also found that prolonged postpartum separation has a detrimental effect on the mother's response to her offspring.

The final article, "Development of Object Relations during the First Year of Life," by Kenneth S. Robson, offers the reader information from the fields of ethology, developmental psychology, learning theory, and psychoanalysis. As a psychiatrist, Dr. Robson's clinical observations correlate with the earlier findings noted by such psychoanalytic researchers as Bibring, Benedek, Deutsch, Spitz, and Mahler. In addition to providing information from a variety of sources, Dr. Robson has studied eye-to-eye contact between the mother and her baby and believes that the visual system occupies a central place in human social interactions.

The purpose in including these articles is to give the reader an introduction to the importance of the earliest maturational processes during the first year of the child's development.

Terms such as "bonding," "attachment," "symbiosis," "maternal-infant dyad," etc., have been applied to the earliest mother-infant interactions. It is certain that a powerful, significant mother-infant relationship begins to be established at birth and—from the mother's point of view—

even before hirth, since the mother has already established a fantasied relationship with her unborn baby. The precursors of ego development and of the capacity for object relations, that is, relations with other persons, begin to be laid down at the time of the first maternal-infant interactions. Any prolonged separation inevitably delays or impairs the establishment of a nurturing mother-child dyadic relationship and may contribute to a disturbance in personality development.

Psychoanalysts and developmental psychologists have attempted to determine when psychological life begins following birth. Margaret Mahler[1] considers the first few weeks of life to be a period of "normal autism." This is, in effect, a prepsychological period during which the infant exists only as a physiological organism without any psychological functioning. In Mahler's developmental sequence, at about three weeks of age the period of symbiosis begins, during which the infant gradually becomes vaguely aware of inner experiences of tension and satisfaction, as these are rhythmically experienced in relationship to the mother person. By the age of four to five months, symbiosis is well established, and the mothering person has begun to emerge as the need-satisfying object, although still not differentiated, that is, separated distinctly, from the infant's self-awareness. Thus it is that during the early weeks and months of life the infant's psychological world consists of global experiences combining the caretaking functions of the mothering person with its own inner states of tension and satisfaction. The mothering person does not become clearly identified as a separate person until several months later, when the infant is about eight or nine months of age. The completion of the separation-individuation process (with its four subphases) occurs between 24 and 36 months of age.

The child by this time (about 36 months of age) has achieved a sense of individuality and at least a degree of object constancy. This implies that, even in the absence of the mother (or "love object"), the child can maintain a mental image of her. In addition, it suggests that the earlier tendency to divide the mother into a "good" and a "bad" mother gives way to a more unified image of her as possessing both good and bad qualities. This is the early phase of what will later be extended to include mature relationships.

Mahler writes that all aspects of psychic development participate in the eventual establishment of object constancy. Thus an early separation and defective "bonding" could interfere with normal symbiosis and ultimately affect adversely the development of object constancy.

Rene Spitz[2] discusses the environmental and inborn conditions which enable the newborn to progress normally from a condition at birth of hav-

---

[1] Margaret Mahler, *The Psychological Birth of the Human Infant.* Basic Books, Inc., New York, 1975, pp. 41–120.
[2] Rene A. Spitz, *The First Year of Life,* International Universities Press, Inc., New York, 1965, pp. 41–42.

ing "no world image at all, no stimuli from any sensory modality that he can recognize as signals," to the time, many months later, when a stimulus can become a "signal, to which other signals are added step-by-step to build up the coherent image of the child's world." The conditions for accomplishing this development include, first, the existence of the stimulus barrier, an inborn protective psychophysiological screening mechanism which protects the infant from the great majority of stimuli to which he ordinarily is exposed. This barrier includes neurological immaturity, so that the receptor organs are not functioning fully at birth. Second, most of the infant's day is spent in sleep or dozing. Finally, there is only a gradual development of the capacity to process the incoming stimuli mentally.

Spitz characterizes the unique neonatal environment as "a world in itself, with which the mother surrounds the infant and which the mother extends into many directions. To begin with, the mother actually protects the infant physically from the overload of stimuli of any kind. Much of our child-rearing practices—the crib, the cot, the warmth, the clothing, etc.— serve to shield him from stimuli coming from the outside."[3] He adds that the mother assists in dealing with stimuli and helps to afford the infant discharge by feeding him when hungry, diapering him when wet, covering him when cold, etc. Spitz emphasizes, however, that "by far, the most important factor in enabling the child to build gradually a coherent ideation image of his world derives from the reciprocity between mother and child."[4] He refers to this part of human relations as the "dialogue." He writes, "The dialogue is a sequential action-reaction-action cycle within the framework of mother-child relations. This very special form of interaction creates for the baby a unique world of his own with his specific emotional climate."[5] These quotations from Spitz highlight the difference between the experience of the normal newborn from that of the premature, who is in an intensive-care unit undergoing active treatment to assure its survival. In almost every respect, there is a marked deviation from the conditions which Spitz feels are essential for orderly and normal psychological growth.

Other students of human development believe that as early as one week following birth, the infant shows some signs of "seeking" behavior. This strongly suggests some psychological life even at that early age. In any event, many premature infants are still in the intensive-care nursery during the time when psychological functioning is presumed to begin (one to four weeks) and therefore when the mothering person becomes increasingly significant to the normal development of the child.

The establishment of a satisfactory symbiotic phase requires that

[3] Ibid., p. 42.
[4] Ibid., p. 42.
[5] Ibid, p.42–43.

mothering person and infant be attuned to each other—all of which is part of the usual human environment into which most infants are born. Interference with the establishment of a satisfactory symbiosis may lead to defects in early ego development, which, in turn, can lay the foundation for personality problems, mood disorders, learning difficulties, or even psychotic regressions in later life.

Mothers Separated from Their Newborn Infants

Marshall H. Klaus, M.D.
Professor of Pediatrics and Director of Neonatal Nurseries, Case Western
Reserve School of Medicine and University Hospitals

John H. Kennell, M.D.
Associate Professor of Pediatrics, Case Western Reserve University School
of Medicine and University Hospitals

Mothers separated from their young soon lost all interest in those whom they were unable to nurse or cherish.—P. Budin

Multiple observations suggest that a human mother's care of her baby derives from a complex mixture made up of her endowment or genetics, the way the baby responds to her, a long history of interpersonal relations within her own family, past experiences with this or previous pregnancies, and absorption of the values and practices of her culture [5, 11, 13, 42, 67, 69]. Recently, attention has been directed toward another significant factor—the events of the early postpartum days. Behavioral studies in a large range of animal species as well as preliminary studies of human maternal behavior suggest that what happens in the period immediately following delivery may be critical to later maternal behavior [4, 35, 57]. Observations in humans have proceeded far enough to allow us to infer that a woman's physical relationship with her infant in the early days and months after delivery require thorough investigation.

This report will review these studies in animals and humans as well as a number of situations noted in women following the birth of premature or high-risk infants, and suggest their clinical relevance. To understand the human mother's current position in the high-risk and newborn nurseries, it is necessary for us to begin with a review of how she has been treated historically.

HISTORY

During the past 90 years, the role and responsibilities of the mother in the hospital nursery have varied. In the American hospital of the 1880's, rooming-in (still an accepted mode in Europe) was prevalent. The Johns Hopkins Hospital, built without a separate nursery, continued rooming-in as standard procedure until 1890; the Nursery and Children's Hospital did so until after 1896, and the New York Hospital until after 1898 [47].

In the premature nurseries of Pierre Budin [14] (1895), the most famous

From *The Pediatric Clinics of North America*, vol. 17, no. 4 pp. 1015–1037 (November 1970).

of the early neonatologists, the mother's participation in the care of her baby was welcomed. Although most of the milk for the small premature babies was supplied by wet nurses, mothers were encouraged to breast feed their premature infants, because as Budin noted, "Unfortunately . . . a certain number of mothers abandon the babies whose needs they have not had to meet, and in whom they have lost all interest. The life of the little one has been saved, it is true, but at the cost of the mother." Because of the increased survival rate of infants who were discharged feeding from their mothers' breasts, Budin gave special instructions to keep up the milk supply and suggested that the mothers of small premature babies also nurse full-term infants to stimulate milk production.

The first change in the mother's role occurred as a result of Budin's desire to gain approval for his methods of premature infant care. A young Alsatian student, Martin Cooney, was sent to the Berlin Exposition of 1896 to display the survival of premature infants brought to his *Kinderbrutanstalt* ("child hatchery"). He became both a clinical and commercial success [44]. Cooney subsequently traveled as an exhibitor to fairs in England and the United States. He finally settled on Coney Island where during the next 39 years, he raised over 5000 premature infants. . . . In most respects, Cooney's handling of the infants was similar to that of Budin; however, mothers did not participate in the care of the infants in the exhibits, but were allowed to attend with free passes. It is significant that Cooney sometimes had difficulty inducing parents to take the children back. Despite Cooney's commercialism, many of his methods were adopted in the first premature nurseries in hospitals in the United States.

By the early 1900's, the high mortality and morbidity of infants (usually resulting from epidemic diarrhea, respiratory infection, and inadequate equipment) [12, 17] led to stricter isolation techniques and to the development of separate wards for all patients who were free from infection. At this time, small premature infants were housed either in the regular nursery or on the infant ward. Hospitalization was avoided whenever possible; special rules were adopted to prohibit visiting by relatives and friends; handling of the infant was reduced to a minimum [21, 23, 48]. Rigid measures to prevent infection, and the example set by Cooney's exhibits, thus completely removed the mother from the hospital nursery.

The first hospital premature infant center was started at the Sarah Morris Hospital in Chicago in 1923 by Hess. He also used wet nurses as a source of milk, although the infants in the hospital were not usually nursed at the breast. Like Budin, Hess made every attempt to continue breast milk feeding [29]. He encouraged the mother to produce milk for her own infant and bring it to the hospital daily, and to continue breast feeding after discharge. As soon as the infant's condition warranted, the mother was instructed in his hospital care and was permitted to nurse him at the breast.

Premature units which developed after the Sarah Morris Nursery had similar rules and regulations: babies were kept in separate units of the hospital; careful and minimal handling by everyone, including physicians, was recommended; strict isolation techniques were used; mothers were categorically excluded, except in some nurseries when just before discharge they were permitted to nurse or bottle feed their infants; and early discharge was suggested to prevent infection.

Recommendations for the hospital care of full-term and premature infants written by Ethel Dunham and Marian Crane [18] for the Children's Bureau in 1943 outlined special measures to protect the infant from infection and specified that visitors should be excluded from the nursery, limiting the mother to viewing her premature infant through the glass windows. Standard textbooks on newborn care from 1945 to 1960 by Parmelee [56], Crosse [15], and Hess [30], as well as the newborn manual of the American Academy of Pediatrics, continued to recommend minimal handling, strict isolation, and the exclusion of all visitors from the nursery. It is significant that a survey of children's wards in 1954 revealed that for over 50 percent of the beds, visiting hours were limited to 1 to 2 hours once a week [43]. About this time, renewed interest in rooming-in for the mother of a full-term infant was stimulated by the work of Edith Jackson [31].

During this later period, two other different approaches to premature care were begun. In Miller's studies of home nursing of premature babies at Newcastle-on-Tyne [49] mortality was, surprisingly, only moderately greater than in a comparable group of infants nursed in the hospital. Miller believed that care at home gave the infant a good start and "is far better than if he were taken away to hospital and returned a month or 6 weeks later, an unknown infant, feared and strange." Another system of care originated because of a shortage of skilled nurses. At the Baragwanath Hospital in Johannesburg, South Africa, Kahn arranged for mothers to remain in the hospital, and, with supervision, care for their premature infants. [32, 33].

Mothers are still excluded from the majority of premature nurseries in the United States; however, at present several nurseries have begun to admit mothers on a trial basis [4, 35, 64].

ANIMAL STUDIES

As in other areas of neonatology, it has been useful to study mothers and infants of many species during the neonatal period. Although certain aspects of behavior differ from species to species, there are some over-all patterns and trends which can be discerned. Despite the reluctance of many investigators to accept the concept that these patterns may apply to humans, the possibility of their extension to the human should not be neglected when they are found in a large number of species.

First, in goats, sheep, and cattle, when a mother is separated from her young in the first hour or the first few hours after delivery and then the two are reunited, the mother will show disturbances of mothering behavior, such as failure to care for her young, butting her own offspring away, and feeding her own and other babies indiscriminately [27, 40, 50]. In contrast, if the mother and infant are kept together for the first 4 days and are separated on the fifth day for an equal period of time, the mother quickly returns to the maternal behavior characteristic of her species when the pair is reunited. It thus appears that there is a sensitive period immediately after delivery; if the animal mother is separated from her young during this interval, deviant maternal behavior may result. (It is important to note that not all mothers are equally affected by these early separations and that the disturbed mothering performance can be modified by special handling.) Surprisingly, in spite of this sensitive period, adoptions can be arranged. Hersher, Richmond, and Moore induced sheep and goats to adopt strange lambs and kids—between as well as within species [28]. This required delicate arrangements of timing to prevent the mother from destroying the strange infant. In other species, such as mice and rats, when mother and young are separated in the first few hours following delivery and then brought together again the rodent mother will care for the young, but not as skillfully [60]. Thus the effects of early separation on later maternal behavior vary with the species. Harlow studied rhesus monkey mothers deprived of tactile contact but allowed to see and hear their infants [25]. After 2 weeks without any tactile contact these mothers rapidly decreased the amount of time they spent viewing their infants. This indicated that viewing alone is not enough stimulus to maintain maternal interest. The results of similar studies in humans will be considered later.

Secondly, clear-cut species-specific maternal behavior patterns such as nesting, retrieving, grooming, and exploring have been observed in non-human mammalian mothers immediately after delivery. For example, in the cat during labor and just before delivery the mother licks the genital region; then, following delivery, the mother licks the kitten completely, eats the membranes and placenta, and remains in close, almost constant physical contact through the first 3 to 4 days. This perinatal behavior may be severely distorted if the mother herself has received abnormal care as an infant [8, 24] or if the normal sequence of behavior is altered, as shown in Birch's experiments with rats. Noting the increased amount of self-licking (especially in the anogenital region) in the pregnant rat and hypothesizing that this self-licking might extend to the pups after delivery, Birch fashioned high collars which were placed on the necks of pregnant rats to prevent self-licking [8]. The collars were removed shortly before birth. These rats subsequently exhibited abnormal maternal behavior; waiting a long interval before initial licking of the pups, consuming them once licking began, and in the instance of pups surviving the licking period, refusing to allow them to suckle; no offspring survived the nursing period. Control mothers and mothers wearing collars similar to those described but notched to permit self-licking did not exhibit this aberrant behavior.

Thirdly, for some period after delivery, usually weeks or even months, animal mothers have characteristic patterns of behavior and orders of behavior. For example, the rhesus monkey mother grooms her infant more at 1 month than at other times. Initially she spends little time retrieving, whereas at 1½ months retrieving is maximum [25]. Recurring patterns of maternal behavior within a species can be distinguished in a large number of animal species. Careful observations by Ainsworth in Uganda suggest that repeating sequences are also found in human mothers [1].

HUMAN MATERNAL BEHAVIOR IN OTHER CULTURES

Dr. Clifford Barnett [3], an anthropologist, has searched for variations in human maternal behavior following delivery in the Human Relations File which lists 220 cultures. He found that every society exhibited some regularized manner of dealing with the entry of a new member into that society. In most cultures, during the 3 to 7 days while the navel heals the mother and infant are secluded together. The mother has little or no responsibilities other than the infant. This is true even in Israel, where infant houses separate from those of the parents have been established (in the socialistic communities known as kibbutzim). In the early days after delivery the mother-infant pair are kept together part of the day; separation does not occur until after the fifth day and then usually for only part of each 24 hours [66]. In Russia, mothers are not separated from their infants in the early weeks of life [45].

It is therefore of special interest that routine complete separation of mother and infant in the first days after delivery exists only in the high-risk and premature nurseries of the Western world.

MATERNAL BEHAVIOR OF THE HUMAN MOTHER

Preliminary data on the behavior of the human mother following separation from her infant have been brought together from a number of different sources: (1) long-term, extensive in-depth interviews of a small number of mothers, primarily by psychoanalysts: (2) clinical observations during medical care procedures; (3) naturalistic observations of mothering; (4) structured interviews or observations; and (5) preliminary results from a small number of controlled studies of the mothers of premature infants [5, 51–53].

From these diverse observations it is possible to begin to piece together how affectional bonds between human mothers and their infants are built, and to determine what alters or distorts this process temporarily or permanently. Because the human infant is wholly dependent upon his mother or caretaker for all his physical and emotional needs, the strength of these attachment ties may well determine whether he will survive and develop optimally. The actual process by which attachment bonds are formed between mother and child is unknown; however, the time-periods which are probably crucial in this process are listed in Table 1.

Pregnancy

Bibring [7], Deutsch [16], and Benedeck [6] have described in detail the behavioral changes that occur during pregnancy. Bibring outlines the first phase for a mother in the early weeks of pregnancy as the acceptance of the growing fetus as an "integral part of herself." When fetal movement becomes perceptible the developing baby begins to be considered as a separate individual, and the woman gradually prepares psychologically for delivery and anatomic separation. Interview data covering this time-period often describes marked changes in attitude toward the unborn infant. Once fetal movement begins, infants who are unplanned and unwanted by the mother often become more accepted. Any medical problem which threatens the health or survival of the fetus or the mother during this period may delay the mother's planning for the infant and retard the process of bonding.

Delivery

Surprisingly, specific data for this period are scanty. Newton and Newton [34] noted that the mothers who were most likely to be accepting and pleased with their infants on first sight were those who stayed calm and relaxed in labor, cooperated with their attendants, received more solicitous care, and had good rapport with their attendants. These observations are in agreement with veterinary experience that dams and sows are more easily induced to accept their offspring if their surroundings during delivery are quiet, peaceful, and private. Although unconsciousness during delivery in certain animals results in the rejection of offspring, no such effects have been noted in humans [55]. Using the degree of mourning as a measure of affectional bonding, Kennell, Slyter, and Klaus [36] noted affectional ties to be present after delivery even before tactile contact was made. In a study of

Table 1   Steps in Attachment

Planning the pregnancy
Confirming the pregnancy
Fetal movement
Birth
Seeing the baby
Touching the baby
Caretaking

20 mothers they observed that clearly identifiable mourning was present in each woman whose infant had died. The mother grieved whether the infant lived for 1 hour or 12 days, whether he weighed 3000 gm. or a nonviable 580 gm., and whether or not the pregnancy was planned.

First Weeks after Delivery

As in other animal species, the human mother demonstrates an orderly progression of behavior after she gives birth. Using filmed observations, Klaus, Kennell, Plumb, and Zuehlke [38] observed that when nude full-term infants were brought to their mothers shortly after birth the mothers started a routine pattern of behavior which began with fingertip touching of the infant's extremities and proceeded in 4 to 8 minutes to massaging and encompassing palm contact on the trunk . . . In the first 3 minutes, the extent of fingertip contact was 52 per cent, 28 per cent being palm contact. In the last 3 minutes of observation, fingertip contact had markedly decreased. Rubin [62] observed a similar sequence but at a much slower rate (3 days). Mothers of normal premature infants who were permitted early contact followed a similar sequence of touching but at a slower rate. Perhaps this is an example of species-specific behavior.

Both groups of mothers expressed strong interest in eye-to-eye contact. Robson [58] suggests that eye-to-eye contact is one of the innate releasers of maternal caretaking responses. The mother's marked concentration on the eyes of the infant is of interest when considered in conjunction with the early functional development of the human infant's visual pathways. His ability to attend and follow, especially during the first hours, coincides with his mother's interest in his eyes.

Though the process of affectional bonding is well underway prior to delivery, the clinical observations of Rose [59], and Kennell and Rolnick [37] suggest that the affectional ties can be disturbed easily and may be altered permanently. Relatively minor illnesses in the immediate newborn period appeared to alter the relationship between mother and infant. Some of these minor problems included slight elevations of bilirubin, slow feeding, and the need for incubator care in the first 24 hours for mild respiratory distress secondary to meconium aspiration. Even though the infant's problem had been resolved completely prior to discharge, the behavior of his mother was often disturbed for the first year of his life or longer.

Support for the concept that close continual contact between mother and infant during the first days of life may facilitate mothering behavior came from observations in Duke Hospital when rooming-in was made compulsory. After this change was effected, McBryde [47] noted that the incidence of breast feeding rose from 35 to 58.5 per cent, while phone calls from anxious mothers during the first weeks after discharge decreased by 90 per cent.

Barnett et al. [4, 41] from Stanford and the authors from Case Western

Reserve University [35, 36, 38] are engaged in a long-term study to evaluate the effects of the early mother-infant separation which is now a standard aspect of care in most premature nurseries. Mothers in one of the study groups are permitted to enter the nursery, place their hands in the isolettes, and even carry out simple caretaking tasks, beginning in the first 5 days after delivery and continuing throughout the hospitalization (Early Contact). Those in the second group have only visual contact with their infants in the glass-enclosed nursery and are unable to touch, smell, or hear them until after the first 20 days (Late Contact 1). In a third group, handling is delayed until the infants are 30 to 40 days of age (Late Contact 2). A control group of mothers of full-term infants from similar socioeconomic backgrounds is also being studied. The hypothesis is that if human mothers are affected by this period of separation, then one might expect to see altered maternal attachment during the first weeks or months of life, and, as a result, to find that differences in infant development were produced and would become evident as the infant grows. To date, these studies have shown no increase in infection when mothers and fathers are permitted to visit and no disruption in the care of the infant. (It has been a consistent observation that mothers wash their hands longer and more thoroughly than most physicians!)

Though both projects are still in progress, two separate studies of maternal behavior after different periods of separation have been reported.

The first study [41] compared two sets of mothers, Early Contact and Late Contact 2. Observations of the mother and infant were made on three occasions: (1) on the mother's fifth visit to her infant in the discharge nursery, (2) in the home one week after discharge, and (3) in the pediatric clinic one month after discharge. Mothers allowed early physical contact with their infants were more skillful in caretaking only during the first observation. Attachment behavior (looking at the infant, smiling at the infant, the closeness with which the infant is held, and caressing the infant) of the non-separated mothers was greater than that of the separated mothers at each of the three observations; it was significantly greater only at the third observation.

In the second study [35] observations were recorded using time-lapse photography and were analyzed for the first 10 minutes of each feeding. The behavior of mothers who had been separated from their infants for 20 days (Late Contact 1) was studied at a feeding just before discharge and was compared with the discharge feeding of the group of mothers who were permitted physical contact within the first 5 days of life (Early Contact). Feeding was chosen as a measure of maternal performance because of its universality and its central position in the mother-infant relationship [13]. Twenty-five activities were recorded for each mother, including her caretaking skills (such as the position of the bottle and the presence of milk in the tip of the nipple) as well as measurements of maternal affection (such as the contact of the mother's chest or abdomen with the infant's trunk, which was termed "cuddling"). Figure 1* shows a posed mother on the left with her eyes on the baby in the "en face" position (defined as the mother's face in such a position that her eyes and those of the infant meet fully in the same vertical plane of rotation). Figure 2 is a Picasso drawing which appears to illustrate both en face and close contact or cuddling. In Figure 1 note that on the right the mother's eyes are on the baby but she is not in the en face position. On the left the mother's abdomen touches the infant's trunk (cuddling). The bottle is perpendicular to the baby's mouth and milk

*Figure numbers have been changed here to reflect the deletion of two figures.—*ed.*

A B

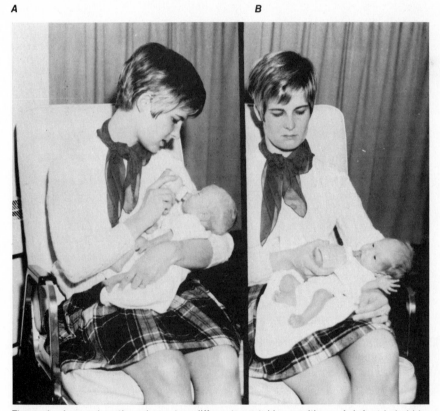

Figure 1 A posed mother shows two different caretaking positions. *A,* Infant is held in close contact (cuddling), mother is looking at infant en face, and milk is in the tip of the nipple. *B,* Infant's trunk is held away from mother, mother is looking at infant but not en face, and there is no milk in the tip of the nipple.

Figure 2 A Picasso line drawing illustrating en face position and cuddling. *(Courtesy of the Fogg Art Museum, Harvard University. Bequest of Meta and Paul J. Sachs.)*

is in the tip of the nipple. On the right the mother is holding the baby but not cuddling. The bottle is not perpendicular and milk is not in the nipple. . . . Cuddling was a universal component of infant-feeding before this century when almost all infants were breast-fed. When mothers in one group show an increased tendency to hold their babies away from their bodies during feeding, we can question whether this unusual behavior may reflect incomplete attachment or diminished maternal affection. In the monkey maternal affection appears to wane progressively as the frequency of close ventral contacts between mother and infant decreases [25].

One month after discharge, after almost 200 feedings at home, the mothers were filmed again during a feeding. The Late Contact mothers held their babies differently, changed position less, burped less, and were not as skillful in feeding as mothers in the Early Contact group. These differences in mothers are of interest when taken in light of the observations of Judith Rubenstein [61] who has shown that early maternal attentiveness facilitates later exploratory behavior in infants. Thus stimulation may have a decisive influence on the infant's later development.

DISCUSSION

If the procedures for the care of mother and baby in the hospital today were to be based on what is known of other cultures and what has been learned from studies and observations of both animal and human behavior, it would not be unreasonable to change many of our existing rules and regulations. However, no widespread change should take place until there is strong evidence that what we are doing today is damaging, and that a change would be desirable. In the past it has been the custom of the health professions to make major changes affecting behavior and environment in order to promote what appeared to be a beneficial innovation in medical care without prior critical study of all the side effects. In this century both birth and death, the two most important events in the life of the individual have been moved into the hospital and away from the family and centuries of traditions and cultural patterns of behavior. Practices surrounding both events appear to have been almost wholly determined by the psychological needs, the convenience, the limited perspective and the bias of the dominant members of the hospital culture (nurse, physician, and administrator).

With these historical perspectives in mind, we think it is important that the needs of the human mother be thoroughly investigated before radical changes are recommended. The experience with rooming-in provides one example. This naturalistic arrangement may be of immense value for the mother and child. Yet it has not been and never will be widely adopted in the Western world until more data clearly support its advantages.

It is our impression that massive alterations may be required once information about the behavioral requirements of mothers is collected. For example, if we adopt the standards or levels of deprivation suggested by Barnett [4] (Table 2) it is apparent that most normal deliveries in this country are associated with several days of deprivation for the mother (Table 3). The mother who delivers a premature suffers complete deprivation from the first day and severe deprivation from then until the eighth week (if she can

Table 2   Levels of Interactional Deprivation and Component Variables*

Levels of deprivation	Duration of deprivation	Sensory modalities of interaction	Caretaking nature of interaction
I. no deprivation	Full time	All senses	Complete
II. partial deprivation	Part time	All senses	Partial
III. moderate deprivation	Part time	All senses	None
IV. severe deprivation	Part time	Visual only	None
V. complete deprivation	None	None	None

*From Barnett, C., et al.: Pediatrics, 45:199, 1970. Reproduced by permission.

only see her infant through a glass wall). Only mothers who deliver at home or room-in with their infants experience no deprivation.

Kaplan and Mason and others [34, 35, 65, 71] have viewed the maternal reactions to the birth of a premature as an acute emotional crisis and note four psychological tasks which the mother must complete: (1) prepare for possible loss (anticipatory grief); (2) acknowledge and face maternal failure to deliver a full-term infant; (3) resume the process of relating to the infant; and (4) learn how the premature differs from a full-term infant and understand his special needs. These tasks may relate in part to what a physician says and to whether or not the mother and infant are separated.

The mothering behavior of each mother, her ability to tolerate adverse stresses, and her need for special attention differ greatly and depend on a multitude of factors. . . . At the time the infant is born some of these determinants are ingrained and unchangeable, such as the mother's own mothering, the practices of her culture, her endowment, and her relations with her family and husband. Other determinants (framed with a dotted line) can be altered: the attitudes, statements, and practices of the doctor in the hospital; whether or not there is separation from the infant in the first days of life; and the nature of the infant himself—his temperament as well as whether he is healthy, sick, or malformed. One of the most easily manipulated variables in this scheme is the separation of an infant from his mother during the first hours and days after birth.

On the schematic diagram are a series of disorders of mothering which range from mild (such as persisting concerns about a baby following a minor abnormality which has been completely resolved in the nursery) to the most severe manifestation, the battered child syndrome. It is our hypothesis that this entire range of problems may be, in part, the end result of

Table 3 Deprivation Levels over Time, Related to Birth Situation*

Birth Situation	Deprivation Level, Days and Weeks Postpartum						
	Day 0	Day 1	Day 3	Day 7	Week 8	Week 9
Home, full term	II, partial deprivation	I, no deprivation	I, no deprivation	I, no deprivation	I, no deprivation	I, no deprivation
Hospital, full term, rooming-in	III, moderate deprivation	I, no deprivation	I, no deprivation	I, no deprivation	I, no deprivation	I, no deprivation
Hospital, full term, regular care	III, moderate deprivation	II, partial deprivation	II, partial deprivation	I, no deprivation	I, no deprivation	I, no deprivation
Premature, mother allowed in nursery	V, complete deprivation	IV, severe deprivation	III, moderate deprivation	II, partial deprivation	II, partial deprivation (discharge nursery)	I, no deprivation
Premature regular care (separated)	V, complete deprivation	IV, severe deprivation	IV, severe deprivation	IV, severe deprivation	II, partial deprivation (discharge nursery)	I, no deprivation
Unwed mother, refuses contact	V, complete deprivation	V, complete deprivation	V, complete deprivation	V, complete deprivation	V, complete deprivation	V, complete deprivation

*From Barnett, C., et al.: Pediatrics, 45:200, 1970. Reproduced by permission.

separation in the early newborn period. This concept is supported by the high incidence of premature infants who return to the hospital because of failure to thrive. In studies of failure-to-thrive infants [2, 63], 15 to 30 per cent had no organic disease; of this group, 25 to 41 per cent were premature. In their report on the vulnerable child syndrome (children who are expected by their parents to die prematurely and who develop severe emotional disturbances). Green and Solnit [22] observed that 44 per cent of these infants were either premature or severely ill and separated from their mothers in the first weeks of life.

It is the present custom in this country for adoptions to take place at 3 to 6 weeks of age or later. Would the behavioral problems of the adopted child be as great if adoptions occurred at 1 day or 1 hour of life? In many societies where there is a high maternal mortality rate, a substitute mother is close at hand and ready to take over immediately following the death of a mother.

The battered child syndrome provides the most dramatic evidence of a disorder of mothering. We have searched the literature to determine the incidence of separation following delivery in these mother-infant dyads, but the authors usually fail to record this information. The incidence of either prematurity or serious illness was 39 per cent, combining two series (totaling 44 patients) reporting birth weight or gestational age [19, 70]. During the period in which this project has been underway, the authors have been told about a number of clinical examples in which battering occurred after discharge of normal healthy premature infants who had been small and seriously ill shortly after birth so that they had been separated from their parents for prolonged periods [39]. Although multiple factors contribute to this problem (such as the mother's own rearing), early separation may be a significant factor [26]. The formation of close affectional ties may remain permanently incomplete if extended separation occurs and anticipatory grief becomes too far advanced.

PRACTICAL CONSIDERATIONS

Over-all nursery practices should remain basically the same until more definitive studies are completed. Until that time each physician must make certain arbitrary decisions about his management of mothers and infants. The following section is a combination of our present impressions which could be titled "Clinical Hints."

We have found it useful to pick out in advance the mother who is most likely to have special difficulties in relating to her infant. Blau [9] noted that mothers who deliver premature infants have more negative attitudes toward their pregnancies, greater emotional immaturity, and more body narcissism.

In our own experience mothers who have a high incidence of severe mothering difficulties often have one of the following characteristics: (1) the previous loss of a newborn infant, including miscarriage and induced abortion; (2) a fertility problem, with no living children; (3) a previous seriously ill newborn infant; (4) Primiparity if younger than 17 or older than 38 years; (5) a medical problem with which the infant may be affected, such as Rh disease, toxemia, or diabetes.

Clinically, we have been impressed and disturbed by the devastating and lasting untoward effects on the mothering capacity of women who have been frightened by the physician's pessimistic outlook about the chance of survival and normal development of an infant. For example, when the newborn infant is a 3 lb. premature baby who is doing well, but the mother is told by a physician that there is a reasonable chance that the baby may not survive, the mother will often show evidence of mourning (as if the baby were already dead) and reluctance to "become attached" to her baby. We have repeatedly observed that such mothers may refuse to visit or will show great hesitation about any physical contact. When discussing such a situation with a physician who has spoken pessimistically with the mother, we have often been told that it is important to share all worries with a mother so that she will be prepared in case of a bad outcome. If there is a close and firm bond between the mother and infant (which occurs when an infant has been home for several months) there is no reason for the physician to withhold his concern. However, while the bonds of affection are still forming, they can be easily retarded, altered, or permanently damaged. It is not easy to keep from sharing all the problems with a mother, but with the evidence available at present, it is our conviction that both the obstetrician and the pediatrician should do their best to hold back. This does not mean that they should be untruthful, because parents will quickly sense the physician's true feelings. They must base their statements on today's situation (infant mortality rates in low birth weight nurseries have decreased steadily year by year), not yesterdays' high mortality figures of the period during which they were being trained. Today the vast majority of these infants will live.

During the past several years we have made many changes in the physical arrangements for mothers and our approach to them. We find it best to describe what the infant looks like to us and how the infant will appear physically to the mother. We do not talk about chances or survival rates or percentages but stress that most babies survive in spite of early and often worrisome problems. We do not emphasize problems which may occur in the future. We do try to anticipate common developments (e.g., the need for bilirubin lights for jaundice in small premature infants). The following guidelines may be helpful:

1 A mother's room arrangements should be adjusted to her needs. Mothers are often best able to express themselves and work out their problems when they are alone.

2 If at all possible, mother and infant should be kept near each other in the same hospital, ideally on the same floor.

3 It is useful to talk with the parents together whenever possible. When this is not possible, it is often wise to talk with one parent on the phone in the presence of the other.

4 At least once a day we discuss how the child is doing with the parents; we talk with them at least twice a day if the child is critically ill.

5 It is necessary to find out what the mother believes is going to happen or what she has read about the problem. We move at her pace during any discussion.

6 The physician should not relieve his anxiety by adding his worries to those of the parents. If there is a possibility, for example, that the child has Turner's syndrome, it is not necessary to share this with the parents while the infant is still acutely ill with other problems and while affectional bonds are still weak. If the physician is worried about a slightly high bilirubin, it is not necessary to discuss kernicterus. Once mentioned, the possibility of death or brain damage can never be completely erased.

7 Before the mother comes to the neonatal unit the physician should describe in detail what the baby and the equipment will look like.

8 The nurse should go into detail in describing all the equipment surrounding the infant. She should be near so that she may answer questions and give support during the difficult period when the mother is first seeing her infant.

9 When a woman comes to see her infant who is under bilirubin lights it is important to remove the eye patches so that she can see his eyes.

10 Extended visting for the mother of a normal full-term infant when the mother is able to handle and completely care for the infant from 1 PM. to 7 PM., has been a useful practice. Rooming-in is still preferred.

11 The nursery should keep a record of all phone calls and visits by parents. Our preliminary data suggests that when there are fewer than two phone calls or visits per week, there is a high incidence of subsequent severe mothering disorders [2].

12 The nurses should feel at ease in reporting any worries or problems they have about a mother's behavior. To accomplish this, there must be a good working relationship between the physician and nurses. Meetings with the nursery staff in the intensive care unit should be held every 2 weeks. This provides an opportunity for them to express their concerns and problems.

CASE PROBLEMS

The clinical relevance of this subject can best be appreciated by the following case example and the questions it raises.

Mrs. H. was happily married, had had a previous miscarriage, and had planned on having a baby for the past 3 years. She delivered a 3 lbs., 2 oz. male infant following a normal pregnancy. The infant cried immediately but then developed moderate respiratory distress, requiring arterial catheterization and a plastic hood over his head for administration of oxygen. At 36 hours of age in an environment of 70 per cent oxygen the pH was 7.31, the Pco_2 60 mm. Hg, and the Po_2 73 mm. Hg.

The following questions must be answered when caring for this mother-infant dyad:

1 Should the mother be permitted to go into the nursery?

2 Should she be in a separate room on the maternity division?

3 What is the best method of communicating with both parents?

4 How should advice be given when first discussing the situation with the parents? What should they be told about their infant and his chances for survival?

5 Can the nurses help the mother adapt to the premature infant?

6 Should the mother go home before the respiratory distress syndrome has subsided?

7 If the infant dies, how can the mother be helped and how long will she grieve?

8 If the infant survives, what problems will the mother face and how can she be helped?

Answers to these questions follow. We encourage the reader to think out his own answers first.

Answers to Case Problems

1 The mother should be permitted to enter the nursery if she wants to. With current therapy the outlook for this baby is good. There is no evidence that the mother will have an unduly upsetting reaction if he does die; on the contrary, having already had a miscarriage, she will probably be relieved to see for herself that the baby is well-formed.

2 The mother should be alone in a separate room on the maternity division if she so desires, and as far away as possible from the sights and sounds of normal babies and more fortunate mothers whose healthy infants *come to them* every 4 hours.

3 The best method of communicating with both parents is to have both sitting down together with you in a quiet, private room. You will be most effective if you can listen to the parents. Let them express their worries and feelings; then give simple, realistically optimistic explanations.

4 When first discussing the situation with the parents, advice should be given promptly, simply, and optimistically. As soon as possible after the birth, the mother can be told that the baby is small but well-formed, that you will be doing routine tests and giving the usual treatment for a premature infant, and that you will report back to her when you have had time to complete more tests and observations.

When it is clear that the baby has respiratory distress and arterial catheterization is necessary, you can explain to the mother that the child has a common problem of premature infants ("breathing difficulty") owing to the complex adjustments he must make from life in utero to life outside. Further, it should be stated that because it is common you know how best to treat it; that this treatment will involve putting a tube in the blood vessel through which she fed the baby while he was inside her, and that you will use this tube to obtain tiny amounts of blood on frequent occasions to guide your therapy; that the baby will be transferred to a nursery for small babies; that prior to his transfer her husband can see the baby and the baby will be brought to her in a special transport incubator for her to see; that babies sometimes get worse before they improve, but the outlook is good for complete recovery after several days; that you will keep her and her husband posted on the baby's progress and will tell them if problems arise; that you would like them to call at other times if they have questions; and that you would like her to come to the nursery to visit and see the baby.

At 36 hours you have a firmer basis for an optimistic report, which should be kept simple but should include an explanation of the hood, apnea monitor, and other visible aspects of therapy. You might say, for example, "I'm pleased with your son's progress. He has responded well to our treatment, and his outlook is excellent. If you haven't been over to see him yet, I'd like to encourage you to do this today, because you will be pleased with his progress."

5   The nurses can help the mother adapt to the premature infant by standing close to the mother and explaining about the equipment being used for him; by welcoming the mother by name and with personalized comments at each visit, and encouraging her to come back soon; by carefully considering the mother's concerns and feelings; by explaining to her that the baby will benefit from her visits; and by showing her how she can gradually assume more of the baby's care and do the mothering better than the nurses. An example of the nurses' encouragement to mothers to continue visits later on in the patient's course is the type of note our nurses put on a baby's crib: "My mother is coming to feed me at 1:30. Boy! Will I be happy to see her!—David."

6   If mother is confident that the infant will live, she should go home before the respiratory distress has subsided. Staying in a maternity unit and only visitng her baby one or two times a day is not tolerated very long by many mothers unless they can actively care for their babies or provide breast milk. It is particularly difficult for a woman if she has young children at home. Most mothers can return daily to visit the baby from home.

If she lives far away, is unlikely to return for many days, and is greatly concerned the baby will die, the mother should not go home before the respiratory distress syndrome has subsided. It is best to reach a point where both you and the mother are confident about the baby's survival.

7   If the baby dies, at the time of death it would be wise to tell the parents about the usual reactions to the loss of a newborn infant (crying, sadness, loss of appetite, inability to sleep, increased irritability, preoccupation with the lost infant, inability to return to normal activities, and feelings of guilt about the early delivery, the illness, and death of the baby). It will be beneficial if you can indicate to the parents that it is best for them to talk freely with each other about their feelings. Many couples who have communicated well with each other prior to a loss will keep their feelings to themselves, and this lack of full communication will often intensify the distress of both. When you meet with them again one or two days after the death and go over the same suggestions, you will find that many of your suggestions have been missed or misunderstood owing to the emotional shock of the baby's death. Another interview is important 3 or 4 months after the death to inquire about their activities and mood as an indication of how they are working through their grief, to discuss the autopsy findings and to

answer any further questions. These three discussions are of value to all parents who lose a child. The normal grief reaction will last approximately 6 months, with brief episodes of sadness on occasion after that time.

8 When the infant survives, in spite of all the steps that have been recommended this mother may have withdrawn some of her attachment to the baby through anticipatory grief. Under the best of circumstances she will have had much less contact with her baby than a normal mother. Therefore, affectional bonds will not be as well developed as with a healthy full-term infant and she will have done relatively little caretaking. The continuation of support to the mother, so that she will visit, touch, and provide increasing care for the baby (holding, feeding, bathing, and diapering) is important during the hospital period. Detailed preparation for the care of the baby at home, the availability of support by telephone during the hospital stay, and continuing support after the baby returns home are indicated, especially during the first months at home. Through the early years of the infant's life the pediatrician should be alert to evidence that the baby is being handled differently than other children (delay in weaning, over-protection, excessive permissiveness, or excessively regimented management). A discussion at this time with the mother about her early experiences, and her feelings and worries about the baby may be advisable. When specific questions have been answered it may be best, if appropriate, to reassure the mother that the baby's early problems are over and will not recur, that the baby was small in the beginning but is now normal in size and development, and that for his ultimate well-being he should be handled as normally as possible.

SUMMARY

Changes in medical practices during the past 50 years have remarkably altered maternal care practices that have evolved over centuries.

Detailed observations of a wide range of mammalian mothers and babies have shown that each species exhibits recurring sequences of maternal behavior around the time of delivery and during the first days and months of life. Interference with these behavior patterns may result in undesirable, even catastrophic, effects on the young. The knowledge that there is a sensitive period shortly after birth during which brief periods of partial or complete separation may drastically distort a mother animal's feeding and care of her infant would lead a caretaker or naturalist to be extremely cautious about any intervention in the period after birth.

Observations in human mothers suggest that affectional bonds are forming before delivery, but that they are fragile and may be easily altered in the first days of life. A preliminary inspection of fragments of available data suggests that maternal behavior may be altered in some women by a period of separation, just as infant behavior is affected by isolation from the mother [10].

The studies of maternal behavior in animals, a survey of maternal practices in other cultures, and preliminary observations in human mothers after periods of early separation from their infants force a thorough review and evaluation of our present perinatal care practices. Before any major changes should be made again, the following unknowns must be answered:

1 Is there a critical or sensitive period in the human mother as there is in the animal mother?

2 What are the needs of most mothers with normal full-term infants in the first hours after delivery and during the first week?

3 Has the hospital culture, which has taken over both birth and death, produced disorders of mothering which last a lifetime?

4 Are the diseases of failure-to-thrive, the battered child syndrome, and the vulnerable child syndrome in part related to hospital care practices?

5 How should the minor problems as well as the major problems which the infant develops or is born with be handled with mothers of different backgrounds, cultures, and requirements?

6 Should the adopting mother receive her infant in the first hour of life? Are the problems of the adopted child a result of adoption practices and early separation? What are the needs of the biological mother who gives the baby up for adoption?

REFERENCES

1 Ainsworth, M.: Infancy in Uganda. Baltimore, The Johns Hopkins Press, 1967.

2 Ambuel, J., and Harris, B.: Failure to thrive: a study of failure to grow in height or weight. Ohio Med. J., 59:997, 1963.

3 Barnett, C.: Personal communication.

4 Barnett, C., Leiderman, P., Grobstein, R., and Klaus, M.: Neonatal separation: the maternal side of interactional deprivation. Pediatrics, 45:197, 1970.

5 Bell, R: A re-interpretation of the direction of effects in studies of socialization. Psychol. Rev., 75:81, 1968.

6 Benedek, T.: Studies in Psychosomatic Medicine: The Psycho-Sexual Function in Women. New York, Ronald Press Co., 1952.

7 Bibring, G.: Some considerations of the psychological processes in pregnancy. Psychoanal. Study Child., 14:113, 1959.

8 Birch, H.: Sources of order in the maternal behavior of animals. Amer. J. Orthopsychiat., 26:279, 1956.

9 Blau, A., Slaff, B., Easton, K., Welkowitz, J., Springarn, J., and Cohen, J.: The psychogenic etiology of premature births: a preliminary report. Psychosomat. Med., 25:201, 1963.

10 Bowlby, J., Ainsworth, M., Boston, M., and Rosenbluth, D.,: The effects of mother-child separation: a follow-up study. Brit. J. Med. Psychol., 29:211, 1956.

11 Bowlby, J.: Attachment and Loss, New York, Basic Books, Inc., Vol I, 1969.

12 Brenneman, J.: The infant ward. Amer. J. Dis. Child, 43:577, 1932.

13 Brody, S.: Patterns of Mothering. New York. International Universities Press, Inc., 1956.

14 Budin, P.: The Nursling. London, Caxton Publishing Co., 1907.

15 Crosse, M.: The Premature Baby. Boston, Little, Brown, 2nd ed., 1957.

16 Deutsch, H.: The Psychology of Women: A Psychoanalytic Interpretation. Vol. II, Motherhood. New York, Grune & Stratton, 1945.

17 Dunham, E., and McAlleney, P., Jr.: Study of 244 prematurely-born infants. J. Pediat., 9:717, 1936.

18 Dunham, E., and Crane, M.: Standards and Recommendations for Hospital Care of Newborn Infants, Full-Term and Premature. U.S. Children's Bureau, Washington, Bureau of Publications, No. 242, 1943.

19 Elmer, E., and Gregg, G.: Developmental characteristics of abused children. Pediatrics, 40:596, 1967.

20 Fanaroff, A.: Personal communication.

21 Gleich, M.: The premature infant: Parts III and IV. Arch. Pediat., 59:157, 1942.

22 Green, M., and Solnit, A.: Reactions to the threatened loss of a child: a vulnerable child syndrome. Pediatrics, 34:58, 1964.

23 Gyllensward, C.: Anticatarrhal vaccination in homes for children under school age. Acta Paed., 17 (Suppl.):78, 1935.

24 Harlow, H., and Harlow, M.: The effect of rearing conditions on behavior. Bull. Menninger Clin., 26:213, 1962.

25 Harlow, H., Harlow, M., and Hansen, E.: The maternal affectional system of rhesus monkeys. In Rheingold, H., ed.: Maternal Behavior in Mammals. New York, John Wiley and Sons, 1963.

26 Helfer, R., and Kempe, C., eds.: The Battered Child. Chicago, University of Chicago Press, 1968.

27 Hersher, L., Richmond, J., and Moore, A.: Maternal behavior in sheep and goats. In Rheingold, H., ed.: Maternal Behavior in Mammals. New York, John Wiley and Sons, 1963.

28 Hersher, L., Richmond, J., and Moore, A.: Modifiability of the critical period for the development of maternal behavior in sheep and goats. Behaviour, 20: 311, 1963.

29 Hess, J., and Lundeen E.: Premature infants, a report of 761 consecutive cases. Penn. Med. J., 33:429, 1930.

30 Hess, J., and Lundeen, E.: The Premature Infant: Medical and Nursing Care. Philadelphia, J. P. Lippincott Co., 2nd ed., 1949.

31 Jackson, E., Olmstead, R., Foord, A., Thomas, H., and Hyder, K.: Hospital rooming-in unit for 4 newborn infants and their mothers: descriptive account of background, development, and procedures with few preliminary observations. Pediatrics, 1:23, 1948.

32 Kahn, E., Wayburne, S., and Fouche, M.: The Baragwanath premature baby unit—an analysis of the case records of 1,000 consecutive admissions. South African Med. J., 28:453, 1954.

33 Kahn, E.: Pediatrics in industrialized part of Africa. J. Pediat., 58:277, 1961.

34 Kaplan, D., and Mason, E.: Maternal reactions to premature birth viewed as an acute emotional disorder. Amer. J. Orthopsychiat., 30:539, 1960.

35 Kennell, J., Gordon, D., and Klaus, M.: The effects of early mother-infant

separation on later maternal performance. Ped. Res. (accepted for publication, 1970).

36 Kennell, J., Slyter, H., and Klaus, M.: The mourning response of parents to the death of a newborn. New Eng. J. Med., 283:344, 1970.

37 Kennell, J., and Rolnick, A.: Discussing problems in newborn babies with their parents. Pediatrics, 26:832, 1960.

38 Klaus, M., Kennell, J., Plumb, N., and Zuehlke, S.: Human maternal behavior at the first contact with her young. In Pediatrics, 46:187, 1970.

39 Klein, M.: Personal communication.

40 Klopfer, P., Adams, D., and Klopfer, M.: Maternal "imprinting" in goats. Proc. Nat. Acad. Sci., 52:911, 1964.

41 Leifer, A., Leiderman, P., and Barnett, C.: Mother-infant separation: effects on later maternal behavior. Child Develop., 1970 (in press).

42 Levy, D.: Behavioral Analysis. Springfield, Illinois, Charles C Thomas, 1958.

43 Liberal Visiting Policies for Child in Hospital. Report by Citizens' Committee on Children of New York City, J. Pediat., 46:710, 1955.

44 Liebling, A.: Profiles: Patron of the preemies. New Yorker Magazine, June 3, 1939, pp. 20–24.

45 Mason, E.: A method of predicting crisis outcome for mothers of premature babies. Public Health Report, 78:1031, 1963.

46 Maternal and Child Care. Report of the Medical Exhcange Mission to the U.S.S.R. Department of Health, Education and Welfare, Publication No. 954, 1960.

47 McBryde, A.: Compulsory rooming-in in the ward and private newborn service at Duke Hospital, J.A.M.A., 145:625, 1951

48 McKhann, C., Steiger, A., and Long, A.: Hospital infections. Amer. J. Dis. Child, 55:579, 1938.

49 Miller, F.: Home nursing of premature babies in Newcastle-on-Tyne. Lancet, 2:703, 1948.

50 Moore, A.: Effects of modified care in the sheep and goat. *In* Newton, G., and Levine, S., eds.: Early Experience and Behavior. Springfield, Charles C. Thomas, 1968, pp. 481–529.

51 Morris, M.: Psychological miscarriage: An end to mother love. *Trans*-actions, January, 1966.

52 Moss, H.: Methodological issues in studying mother-infant interaction. Amer. J. Orthopsychiat., 35:482, 1965.

53 Moss, H.: Sex, age and state as determinants of mother-infant interaction. Merrill-Palmer Quart. Behav. Develop., 13:19, 1967.

54 Newton, N., and Newton, M.: Mothers' reactions to their newborn babies. J.A.M.A., 181:206, 1962.

55 Newton, N., Peeler, D., and Rawlins, C.: Effects of lactation on maternal behavior in mice with comparative data on humans. Lying-In: J. Reproduc. Med., 1:257, 1968.

56 Parmelee, A.: Management of the Newborn. Chicago, Yearbook Publishers, Inc., 2nd ed., 1959.

57   Rheingold, H., ed.: Maternal Behavior in Mammals. New York, John Wiley and Sons, 1963.

58   Robson, K.: The role of eye-to-eye contact in maternal-infant attachment. J. Child Psychol. Psychiat., 8:13, 1967.

59   Rose, J., Boggs, T., Jr., Alderstein, A., et al.: The evidence for a syndrome of "Mothering Disability" consequent to threats to the survival of neonates: a design for hypothesis testing including prevention in a prospective study. Amer. J. Dis. Child. 100:776, 1960.

60   Rosenblatt, J., and Lehrman, D.: Maternal behavior of the laboratory rat. *In* Rheingold, H., ed.: Maternal Behavior in Mammals, New York, John Wiley and Sons, 1963, pp. 8–57.

61   Rubenstein, J.: Maternal attentiveness and subsequent exploratory behavior in the infant. Child Develop., 38:1089, 1967.

62   Rubin, R.: Maternal touch. Nurs. Outlook, 11:828, 1963.

63   Shaheen, E., Alexander, D., Truskowsky, M., and Barbero, G.: Failure to thrive—a retrospective profile. Clin. Pediat., 7:255, 1968.

64   Smith, N., Schwartz, J., Mandell, W., Silberstein, R., Dalack, G., and Sacks, S.: Mothers' psychological reactions to premature and full-size newborns. Arch. Gen. Psychiat., 21:177, 1969.

65   Solnit, A., and Stark, M.: Mourning and the birth of a defective child. Psychoanal. Study Child, 16:653, 1961.

66   Spiro, M.: Children of the Kibbutz. Cambridge, Mass., Harvard University Press, 1958.

67   Spitz, R.: The First Year of Life. New York, International Universities Press, Inc., 1965.

68   Standards and Recommendations of Hospital Care of Newborn Infants. Committee on Fetus and Newborn: W. A. Silverman, Chariman, Evanston, Illinois, Amer. Acad. Pediatrics, 1964.

69   Steele, B., and Pollock, C.: A psychiatric study of parents who abuse infants and small children. *In* Helfer, R., and Kempe, C., eds,: The Battered Child. Chicago, Illinois, University of Chicago Press, 1968, pp. 103–147.

70   Weston, J.: The pathology of child abuse. *In* Helfer, R., and Kempe, C., eds.: The Battered Child. Chicago, Illinois, University of Chicago Press, 1968, pp. 77–100.

71   Wortis, H.: Review of Kaplan, D., and Mason, E.: Maternal reactions to premature birth viewed as an acute emotional disorder. Amer. J. Orthopsychiat., 30:549, 1960.

The Effects of Denial of Early Mother-Infant Interaction on Maternal Self-Confidence

Marjorie J. Seashore, Ph.D.
Associate Professor and Chairperson, Department of Sociology, San Francisco State University

Aimee Dorr Leifer, Ph.D.
Assistant Professor, Harvard Graduate School of Education

Clifford R. Barnett, Ph.D.
Department of Anthropology, Stanford University

P. Herbert Leiderman, M.D.
Professor of Psychiatry, Stanford University School of Medicine

Studies of maternal behavior in nonhuman mammals suggest that restriction of interaction between mother and infant in the early postpartum period influences subsequent maternal performance and may, in fact, produce clearly incompetent mothering (Harlow, Harlow, & Hansen, 1963; Klopfer, Adams, & Klopfer, 1964; Moore, 1968; Noirot, 1964; Rosenblatt & Lehrman, 1963). In the past, studies of mother-infant separation in humans have concentrated on the detrimental effects of long-term maternal separation on the infant's development (Ainsworth, 1962; Bowlby, Ainsworth, Boston, & Rosenbluth, 1956; Spitz, 1954), leaving largely unanswered the question of how the human mother is affected by separation from her infant.

In this article, which is part of a more comprehensive study of the influence on mothers and their infants of early separation during the first weeks following birth, we focus on one aspect of this question: the psychological effects of such separation on a mother's confidence in her ability to care for her infant. Based on clinical impressions of mothers of premature infants, some of whom had experienced early prolonged separation from their infants (Barnett, Leiderman, Grobstein, & Klaus, 1970), we hypothesized that if mothers are denied early contact and caretaking experience with their infants, they will have lower self-confidence than if they are permitted such contact. In addition to presenting the evidence for this hypothesis, we present our findings on the consistency of a mother's attitude about her ability with objective observations of her actual skill in caretaking.

In human societies, prolonged separation of mother and infant in the early postpartum period is a relatively rare occurrence. Typically, the new mother assumes responsibility for her infant's care shortly after birth. In the case of the mother of a premature infant, however, the traditional hospital

From *Journal of Personality and Social Psychology*, vol. 26, no. 3, pp. 369–378 (1973).

practice has been to separate the mother and infant immediately after birth for a period generally lasting 3–12 weeks until the infant measures up to certain health and weight criteria. Since the mother is generally not permitted either to care for or have tactile contact with her infant during this time, she cannot test her perceptions of her ability against her actual performance. Even more important, she is denied the opportunity to learn and practice caretaking skills and to receive feedback on her infant's response to her care.

In considering the effects of separation on human mothers, we must take into account not only the physical separation of mother and infant per se but also the mother's interpretation of the conditions attending separation. For mothers of premature infants, the typical hospital care procedures may themselves induce feelings of inadequacy in the mother. By placing the infant in an intensive care unit in which he is cared for by trained medical personnel rather than by the mother, the hospital is not only increasing the physical distance between mother and infant but is communicating to the mother that her infant requires care that she is not able to provide. The mother may internalize the hospital's assessment of her ability or at least her perception of that assessment and reflect this in low self-confidence.

Once the baby is ready for discharge, the hospital's evaluation of the mother's ability to care for the infant implicitly changes, but her self-evaluation may not change as readily. Having been an outsider in the care and mothering of her infant, the mother may well feel that by this time the pediatric nurses know her infant better than she does.

For mothers of premature infants, prematurity itself may influence maternal self-confidence. By not successfully carrying her baby to term, the mother of a premature has failed to fulfill one of her primary initial functions as a mother (Kaplan & Mason, 1960). To the extent that she feels responsible for this failure, these feelings of inadequacy may generalize to her confidence in her ability to provide for the postpartum needs of her infant.

Related to her presumed biological failure is the perceived or actual physical condition of the premature infant at birth. Even if otherwise healthy, the infant is not a normal baby in the sense that he was not born at full term. Moreover, he visibly differs from a normal, full-term baby, appearing even at best noticeably smaller and more fragile. He requires intensive nursing and medical care after birth, and for the first 72 hours, there is often some question as to whether the baby will even survive. If a mother's self-confidence is at all vulnerable, the initial appearance and condition of her infant give her little reassurance that everything will go smoothly.

Feelings of biological incompetence or the abnormal appearance or condition of her infant may either directly lessen a mother's self-confidence or only make her more vulnerable to the situational effects of separation. In either case, the subsequent separation tends to reinforce any initial doubts the mother may have as to her ability to provide for the needs of her infant.

We would expect both the impact of the separation experience and the tendency toward a feeling of biological incompetence to vary according to the parity of the mother. A mother who has previously cared for an infant of her own has had direct experience in developing and testing her maternal caretaking ability. Having previously carried an infant to full term, she may also be less susceptible to doubt about her biological competence as a mother. Since the primiparous mother does not have recourse to these past experiences to bolster her confidence, we would expect her self-confidence to be more seriously affected by the separation than that of a multiparous mother.

METHOD

In order to assess the effects of denial of interaction on maternal self-confidence, two groups of mothers of premature infants were followed from the time of the infant's birth until 21 months after the infant had been discharged from the hospital. In this article, we are reporting the data through 1 month postdischarge. This covers the period during which we would expect self-confidence to be directly affected by separation. (See Table 1 for the schedule of testings and observations.)

Mothers and infants included in the study met the following criteria: (a) The mother had no previous history of premature or low-weight births; (b) the infant weighed 890–1,899 grams (2.0–4.2 pounds) at birth, was free from obvious congenital abnormalities, and was not a multiple birth; and (c) there was a father present in the home. Mothers and infants meeting these criteria were randomly assigned to one of two treatment groups, each of which included primiparous and multiparous mothers and male and female infants. The first group of 21 mothers (separation group) were able to view their infants from the nursery window during the 3–12 weeks while the infant was in the intensive care nursery but had no other contact with their infants during this time. The 22 mothers in the second group (contact group) were permitted to enter the intensive care nursery and were able to interact directly with their infants—handling them, diapering them, and feeding them when the infant was able to suck from a bottle.

When an infant reached a weight of 2,100 grams (4.6 pounds), he was taken out of the incubator in the intensive care nursery and transferred to a discharge nursery where he remained for 7 to 10 days until his weight reached 2,500 grams (5.5 pounds). During these 7 to 10 days, mothers in both groups were permitted to come in and care for their infants, initially under the supervision of a nurse and later independently. When the infant reached 2,500 grams, he was discharged to the mother's care at home.

The separation and contact phases of the study were alternated in blocks of 3 to 6 months so that at any given point in time all mothers with infants in the nursery had the same experience (separation or contact). Mothers knew that they and their infants were participating in a study of families of premature infants but did not know that our specific interest was in the impact of separation.

As may be seen in Table 1, measures of a mother's confidence in her ability to care for her baby were obtained at three points in time during the infant's stay in the hospital: (*a*) Testing 1, after the mother first saw her baby in the nursery (24–48 hours after birth) but before a mother in the contact group knew she would be allowed into the intensive care nursery; (*b*) Testing 2, after the mother first visited and cared for her infant in the discharge nursery 7–10 days before discharge; and (*c*) Testing 3, the day before the infant was discharged from the hospital. A fourth rating was obtained 1 month after the infant's discharge from the hospital (Testing 4). At each of these times, the mother filled out a paired comparison questionnaire comparing herself and five other possible caretakers: father, grandmother, experienced mother, pediatric nurse, and doctor. Comparisons were made for each of six caretaking tasks. For purposes of analysis these tasks were classified as being either social or instrumental. Calming the baby, understanding what the baby wants, and showing affection to the

Table 1   Testing and Observation Schedule for All Mothers

Average length of time between-contacts	Testing time	Observation time
	1 Mother first sees baby in intensive care nursery	
36 days		
	2 Mother's first visit to discharge nursery	
6 days		
		A Mother's fifth visit to discharge nursery
4 days		
	3 1 day before infant's discharge	
8 days		
		B 1 week postdischarge
21 days		
	4 1 month postdischarge	C 1 month postdischarge

baby were classified as social tasks, while diapering, feeding, and bathing the baby were classified as instrumental. There were several reasons for maintaining the analytic distinction between self-confidence on social and on instrumental tasks. Conceptually, it is quite different to believe that other persons are better at what may be considered mechanical skills such as diapering or feeding than to believe that others are better at relating to your infant by showing affection, etc. Although correlations between the two measures within separation-contact experience and parity divisions were generally as high as +.50, a few dropped to near zero. Results of analyses of variance were similar using either measure, but in regression analyses the two were differentially related to observed skill as discussed later in this article.

From her responses to the questionnaire, we calculated the percentage of instances in which, given a choice between herself and another caretaker as more able, a mother chose herself. In the interest of simplicity only the percentage analysis will be presented in this article although a paired comparison analysis was also done substantiating the results.

Additional evaluations of mothers' self-confidence were made on the basis of interviews with each mother at Testings 1 through 4. For each interview, a mother was rated on her expressed evaluation of her ability to care for her infant. The ratings were done by coders who were blind to the purposes of the study and to the identity of mothers in the study. These ratings were made on a 5-point scale ranging from high (anticipating or having no problems caring for the infant) to low (unsure of herself, worried about baby's response to her).

In addition to gathering data on a mother's confidence in her caretaking ability, each mother was observed caring for her infant (Leifer, 1970; Leifer, Leiderman, Barnett, & Williams, 1972). These observations were made by an independent observer during the mother's fifth visit to the discharge nursery (Observation A), at home 1 week after the infant had been discharged (Observation B), and in the pediatrics clinic 1 month after discharge (Observation C). A point-sampling technique with 15-second intervals was used. Mother and infant were observed for approximately the first 5 seconds of each interval. During the remaining 10 seconds, the observer used a check list to record the relevant maternal and infant behaviors that had occurred. Measures of the relative frequency of many behaviors were obtained. Those measures that had high inter-observer reliability were subjected to further analysis. Caretaking skill was represented by the sum of the following percentage measures: (a) the percentage of intervals during the total observation that the infant was not crying, (b) the percentage of intervals during which the infant was not sucking that the mother stimulated the infant to suck, (c) the percentage of intervals during which the bottle was in the infant's mouth that the infant was sucking, and (*d*) the percentage of intervals during which the mother was feeding the infant that she did not remove the bottle without burping the infant.

RESULTS

Self-Confidence

Paired Comparison Questionnaire The mean percentages of self-choices for primiparous and multiparous mothers in each treatment group at each of the four testing times are presented in Table 2 and graphed in Figures 1 and 2. In order to correct for the nonnormality of the distributions, an arcsine transformation was applied to the data. Using the transformed scores, a two-way analysis of variance was performed to assess the effects of parity and separation individually and in interaction. The results of the analyses of variance are summarized in Table 3. The variability over time in the number of cases is due to the fact that three mothers missed one testing each but were included in analyses for the other testings so as to use as much information as possible. Excluding them from the data does not alter the direction nor significance of the results.

From the data presented in Tables 2 and 3, it is apparent that although the separation experience had little if any effect on the multiparous mothers' self-confidence, it substantially altered the self-confidence of the primiparous mothers. At the initial testing, before any mothers were allowed contact with their infants or knew it was possible, neither separation nor parity had a significant effect, although the primiparous mothers had somewhat lower self-confidence than the multiparous mothers in both the separation and contact groups.

At the second testing, immediately after mothers had first cared for their infants in the discharge nursery, the interaction of parity and separation was significant for both social tasks ($F = 7.62, df = 1/39, p < .01$) and instrumental tasks ($F = 5.48, df = 1/39, p < .025$). The primiparous mothers in the separation group were significantly less self-confident than other mothers using the Scheffé test of multiple comparisons. This was true for both social tasks ($F = 4.76, df = 3/39, p < .01$) and instrumental tasks ($F = 5.51, df = 3/39, p < .01$). Note that while both groups of multiparous mothers and the contact group of primiparous mothers had gained self-confidence by the second testing, the separation group of primiparous mothers had even less self-confidence than they had initially. . . .

At the third testing, just prior to the infant's discharge, interaction effects were still significant for social tasks ($F = 8.44, df = 1/39, p < .01$) and for instrumental tasks ($F = 6.40, df = 1/39, p < .025$). Although the self-confidence of the primiparous mothers in the separation group had

Table 2   Mean Percentage of Choices of Self over Other Caretakers

| | | Treatment group | | | |
| | | Social tasks | | Instrumental tasks | |
Time of testing	Parity*	Separation	Contact	Separation	Contact
1 First see baby in nursery	Primip				
	M	86.7	86.2	74.0	79.6
	SD	18.1	17.8	22.2	26.6
	n	10	12	10	12
	Multip				
	M	98.0	91.7	91.3	86.8
	SD	4.3	10.7	16.1	12.8
	n	10	9	10	9
2 First enter discharge nursery	Primip				
	M	76.5	92.0	64.6	85.8
	SD	18.6	14.0	22.4	17.1
	n	11	13	11	13
	Multip				
	M	98.7	92.2	94.0	89.8
	SD	2.7	10.4	8.1	12.4
	n	10	9	10	9
3 Day before discharge	Primip				
	M	82.3	98.0	73.5	94.9
	SD	17.3	4.0	23.2	8.7
	n	11	13	11	13
	Multip				
	M	98.7	96.9	95.3	94.1
	SD	2.7	4.7	7.3	8.6
	n	10	9	10	9
4 1 month postdischarge	Primip				
	M	93.3	94.4	87.6	99.4
	SD	9.4	13.0	18.1	1.8
	n	11	13	11	12
	Multip				
	M	98.5	94.8	94.8	97.8
	SD	2.8	8.8	12.5	6.3
	n	9	9	9	9

*primip = primiparous, multip = multiparous.

increased from the second testing, these mothers continued to be significantly lower on self-confidence for both sets of tasks. (For social tasks, $F = 6.72$, $df = 3/39$, $p < .01$; for instrumental tasks, $F = 5.81$, $df = 3/39$, $p < .01$.)

By 1 month postdischarge, the self-confidence of primiparous mothers

Table 3 Summary of the Analysis of Variance at Each Testing

Source	Social tasks			Instrumental tasks		
	MS	df	F	MS	df	F
Testing 1: First see baby in nursery						
Treatment (A)	.11	1	<1	.00	1	<1
Parity (B)	.55	1	3.25	.96	1	3.18
A × B	.08	1	<1	.33	1	1.11
Error	.17	37		.30	37	
Testing 2: First visit discharge nursery						
Treatment (A)	.23	1	1.60	.65	1	3.14
Parity (B)	.97	1	6.80*	1.87	1	9.07†
A × B	1.09	1	7.62‡	1.31	1	5.48*
Error	.14	39		.21	39	
Testing 3: Day before discharge						
Treatment (A)	.49	1	6.02	.93	1	6.05*
Parity (B)	.48	1	5.88*	.77	1	5.04*
A × B	.69	1	8.44†	.98	1	6.40*
Error	.08	39		.15	39	
Testing 4: One month postdischarge						
Treatment (A)	.00	1	<1	.52	1	4.62‡
Parity (B)	.06	1	<1	.06	1	<1
A × B	.08	1	<1	.17	1	1.54
Error	.09	38		.11	37	

Note. Analyses of variance performed on arc sine transformed scopes.
‡$p < .025$.
†$p < .01$.
*$p < .05$.

in the separation group had increased to a level comparable to that of other mothers for social tasks and was no longer significantly lower for instrumental tasks. Even at 1 month, however, the overall effect of separation was significant for instrumental tasks ($F = 4.62$, $df = 1/37$, $p < .05$).

A further analysis was done comparing the effects of separation on (a) mothers who were initially high in self-confidence, defined as choosing themselves over other caretakers 100% of the time and (b) mothers initially low in self-confidence (less than 100% self-choices). As may be seen in

Table 4 for both social and instrumental tasks, those mothers who had high self-confidence at the initial testing were still high at the third testing, when the baby was ready for discharge, regardless of separation experience or parity. Those mothers who were initially low, however, were more likely to have high self-confidence by the time the infant was ready to go home if they had been allowed to interact with their infants in the intensive care nursery.

These findings hold for both social and instrumental tasks. A statistical comparison between the separation and contact groups (disregarding parity) of the number of persons moving from low to high as opposed to staying low indicated that significantly more mothers moved from low to high in the contact group than in the separation group. Chisquare, using the Fisher exact probability test, was significant at $p = .02$ for social tasks and at $p = .01$ for instrumental tasks. Parity differences were not significant. Substantially the same results were found when comparisons were made between the first and second testings.

Table 4 Patterns of Changes in Self-Confidence Over Time

		Number of subjects			
		Separation		Contact	
Level of confidence		Primip*	Multip*	Primip*	Multip*
Social tasks					
Testing 1	**Testing 3**				
High	High	4	8	5	5
High	Low	1	0	0	0
Low	High	0	0	5	1
Low	Low	5	2	2	3
Total		10	10	12	9
Instrumental tasks					
Testing 1	**Testing 3**				
High	High	1	7	6	1
High	Low	0	0	0	1
Low	High	1	0	3	5
Low	Low	8	3	3	2
Total		10	10	12	9

*primip = primiparous, multip = multiparous.

The data were also analyzed to assess the effect of sex of the infant on maternal self-confidence. No differences in self-confidence were found between mothers of males and mothers of females either overall or within separation-contact groups.

Interviews   The results of analyses of interview data are consistent with those of the paired comparison questionnaire using the Mann-Whitney U one-tailed test. Primiparous mothers in the separation group were consistently rated lower as a group than primiparous mothers in the contact group at each testing, this difference being significant at the second testing after the first visit to the discharge nursery ($U = 34, p < .025$). Multiparous mothers in the separation group were rated lower than multiparous mothers in the contact group for the first three testings, significantly so at the third testing ($U = 30, p < .05$). At 1 month postdischarge, however, there was no difference between ratings of multiparous mothers in the two groups.

Within each of the two treatment groups, primiparous mothers were rated lower as a group than multiparous mothers at each contact. The parity difference was significant for the separation group at the second testing ($U = 27, p < .05$) and at the fourth testing 1 month after discharge ($U = 20, p < .01$). For the contact group, primiparous mothers were rated significantly lower than multiparous mothers at the third testing just prior to discharge ($U = 33, p < .05$).

Skill Behavior

Although maternal self-confidence is the focus of this article, we are also interested in whether or not a mother's confidence in her caretaking ability is consistent with her observable skill in caretaking. Analyzing skill behavior alone, two-way analyses of variance at each of the three observations showed no significant differences in observed skill by separation-contact experience or parity although mothers in the contact group tended to be more skillful than the separation group of mothers at the first observation ($F = 4.05, df = 1/36, p < .10$) regardless of parity (see Table 5).

Additional analyses of variance indicated no overall differences in skill attributable to sex of the infant. At Observation A in the discharge nursery, however, there was a significant interaction between separation-contact experience and sex of the infant ($F = 5.42, df = 1/36, p < .05$), mothers of females in the contact group being the most skillful. Separation had no effect on mothers of males, but mothers of females in the separation group were significantly less skillful than mothers of females in the contact group using the Scheffé test ($F = 3.75, df = 3/36, p < .05$). Since male infants tend to be more demanding than female infants (Moss, 1967), the effects of separation on mothers of males may be masked by the male's demands for her attention.

Table 5 Mean Summary Scores for Observed Skill in Caretaking

Time of observation	Parity*	Treatment group	
		Separation	Contact
A Fifth visit to discharge nursery†	Primip		
	M	263.9	280.9
	SD	17.3	24.8
	n	10	13
	Multip		
	M	268.5	274.9
	SD	12.0	13.4
	n	8	9
B 1 week postdischarge	Primip		
	M	283.7	288.0
	SD	23.2	24.3
	n	10	11
	Multip		
	M	270.2	280.8
	SD	28.3	29.6
	n	8	8
C 1 month postdischarge	Primip		
	M	291.8	279.3
	SD	24.8	28.9
	n	11	10
	Multip		
	M	266.0	279.7
	SD	20.6	30.1
	n	6	8

*primip = primiparous, multip = multiparous.
†At observation A, F(separation) = 4.05, $df = 1/36$, $p < .10$.

There were no differences between mothers of males and mothers of females in the separation group. Within the contact group, however, mothers of females had significantly higher skill scores than mothers of males ($F = 2.93$, $df = 3/36$, $p < .05$). The sex differences in the contact group were consistent with those found by Moss (1967) on two measures (crying and stimulating to feed) included in the skill summary score used in the present study.

As noted before, although primiparous mothers in the separation group felt significantly less self-confident than did other mothers, they were only slightly less skillful. In order to assess more directly what, if any, relationship exists between a mother's attitudes about her skill and the skillfulness of her behavior, two sets of multiple regression analyses were performed (*a*) using a prior measure of skill as a predictor of subsequent self-confidence and (*b*) using a prior measure of self-confidence as a predictor of subsequent skill. These two sets of regression analyses differ not only in which variable is treated as dependent but also in the times of measurement included. Except for the analysis at 1 month after discharge, when measures of both self-confidence and skill were obtained on the same day, the measure of the dependent variable included in each analysis was obtained at a later point in time than the predictor variable of principal interest (i.e., skill or self-confidence) included in the same analysis. We also included the following as independent variables in each analysis: separation-contact experience, parity, sex of infant, and time of observation in relation to discharge.

When controlling for these variables (separation-contact experience, etc.), skill never predicted self-confidence for either social or instrumental tasks. Thus, observed skill in the discharge nursery (Observation A) did not predict self-confidence just prior to discharge (Testing 2), skill 1 week after discharge (Observation B) did not predict self-confidence at 1 month after discharge (Testing 3), and skill at 1 month after discharge (Observation C) did not predict self-confidence at 1 month after discharge (Testing 3). Even though a mother may be observed to be skillful in caring for her infant relative to other mothers, she does not necessarily then become confident of her own ability.

Analyzing the influence of level of self-confidence on subsequent skill behavior, however, we found some relationship between the two variables, again controlling for separation-contact experience, parity, sex, and time. Self-confidence for instrumental tasks just prior to discharge (Testing 3) did predict skill 1 week after discharge (Observation B) ($F = 4.73$, $df = 1/30$, $p < .05$). Similarly, self-confidence for social tasks just prior to discharge slightly predicted skill 1 week after discharge ($F = 3.46$, $df = 1/30$, $p < .10$). These findings indicate that during the 1-week period following discharge, a mother's degree of self-confidence does have some bearing on her skill in caring for her infant. Self-confidence soon after entry into the discharge nursery (Testing 2), however, did not predict skill just prior to discharge (Observation A) nor did self-confidence 1 month after discharge (Testing 4) predict skill at 1 month after discharge (Observation C).

Other Measures

In addition to parity, initial level of confidence, and skill, we tested the relationship between self-confidence and the following variables that we thought might affect self-confidence: sex of the infant, infant's birth weight, infant's physical condition during hospitalization, mother's initial desire to have an infant (reaction to learning she was pregnant), and an index of neuroticism obtained from the Cornell Medical Index. None of these variables were found to correlate significantly with level of self-confidence.

DISCUSSION

The results of this study indicate that denial of early mother-infant interaction has a negative effect on maternal self-confidence. Primiparous mothers and mothers who do not initially have high self-confidence are most vulnerable to these effects. For primiparous mothers, the data support our specific hypothesis that mothers of premature infants who have been denied early contact and caretaking experience with their infants have lower self-confidence than do mothers of premature infants who have been permitted such contact. The data for multiparous mothers suggest that overall the separation experience has little effect on their self-confidence. Even for multiparous mothers, however, separation has a negative effect on those who are initially low in self-confidence.

Considering psychological, social, and physiological variables, there are several dimensions to an explanation for these findings. It may be that in the immediate postpartum period, the mother is both physiologically and psychologically primed to assume the maternal role. As the lapse between giving birth and having physical contact with the child increases, this readiness may decline. Physiologically, contact with the infant may be an important stimulus to maintaining or enhancing certain, as yet undetermined, hormonal states that might heighten maternal feelings. Psychologically, the mother has certain normative expectations of interacting directly with her infant—that her role as a mother is to provide care for her newborn infant. The mother who is initially uncertain of her ability to fulfill this role adequately may need the reinforcement and learning experience that she is denied when kept separate from her infant. A mother who lacks confidence in her ability to care for her infant may, as Kaplan and Mason (1960) have suggested, feel biologically incompetent because she has given birth prematurely. The feeling of biological incompetence alone, however, cannot account for later low self-confidence. Although all mothers in this study had given birth prematurely, those who were permitted early contact with their infants increased in self-confidence whereas mothers who were denied interaction decreased in self-confidence during the same period.

Although mothers in either group were not the primary caretakers for their infants during the infant's hospitalization, the mother who entered the intensive care nursery was included in the social matrix of persons caring for her infant whereas the mother who remained outside the nursery was at most a peripheral member of the group providing care. Inclusion as part of the caretaking team provided social support for those mothers already high in self-esteem and was a positive reinforcement for those with lower self-esteem.

The data further suggest that modifications in attitudes prior to discharge were associated with subsequent behavior at 1 week post-discharge. This would suggest the prepotency of a social attitude in directing or organizing one of the specific skills. While the findings are not conclusive, they do suggest that the modification in attitudes that we have found in this study should not be discounted.

What are the possible limitations of this study? First, the study was done on a group of mothers of premature infants. Generalization to population groups substantially different from ours probably would be unwarranted. Particularly, full-term mothers should be examined independent of this study although the effects of mother-infant separation for this group are commonly complicated by the fact that the infant is kept separate because he is not healthy.

Second, it is important to note that the special characteristics of the study population tended to militate against producing vulnerability to the separation experience. All of the mothers in the study came from intact families so that the social, economic, and maternal commitment problems common to the unwed mother were not involved. This selection variable also gave us a population that was considerably higher in social class than is to be expected from the normal population of mothers of premature infants. Further, frequent interview contacts with mothers in both groups provided a great deal of psychological support to the families during a period of crisis. The fact that separation produced any changes within the first 2 to 3 months of the infant's birth under these conditions emphasizes the need to examine the effects of separation on families in less optimal conditions.

REFERENCES

Ainsworth, M. D. The effects of maternal deprivation: A review of findings and controversy in the context of research strategy. In *Deprivation of maternal care: A reassessment of its effects.* Public Health Paper No. 14. Geneva: World Health Organization, 1962.

Barnett, C. R., Leiderman, P. H., Grobstein, R., & Klaus, M. Neonatal separation: The maternal side of interactional deprivation. *Pediatrics*, 1970, 45, 197–205.

Bowlby, J., Ainsworth, M. D., Boston, M., & Rosenbluth, D. The effects of mother-child separation: A follow-up study. *British Journal of Medical Psychology*, 1956, 29, 211–247.

Harlow, H. F., Harlow, M. K., & Hansen, E. W. The maternal affectional system of rhesus monkeys. In H. L. Rheingold (Ed.), *Maternal behavior in mammals.* New York: Wiley, 1963.

Kaplan, D. M., & Mason, E. A. Maternal reactions to premature birth viewed as an acute emotional disorder. *American Journal of Orthopsychiatry,* 1960, 30, 539–552.

Klopfer, P. H., Adams, D. K., & Klopfer, M. S. Maternal "imprinting" in goats. *Proceedings of the National Academy of Sciences,* 1964, 52, 911–914.

Leifer, A. D. *Effects of early, temporary mother-infant separation on later maternal behavior in humans.* (Doctoral dissertation, Stanford University) Ann Arbor, Mich.: University Microfilms, 1970, No. 71–2792.

Leifer, A. D., Leiderman, P. H., Barnett, C. R., & Williams, J. A. Effects of mother-infant separation on maternal attachment behavior. *Child Development,* 1972, 43, 1203–1218.

Moore, A. U. Effects of modified maternal care in the sheep and goat. In G. Newton & S. Levine (Eds.), *Early experience and behavior.* Springfield, Ill.: Charles C. Thomas, 1968.

Moss, H. A. Sex, age, and state as determinants of mother-infant interaction. *Merrill-Palmer Quarterly,* 1967, 13, 19–36.

Noirot, E. Changes in responsiveness to young in the adult mouse: The effect of external stimuli. *Journal of Comparative Physiological Psychology,* 1964, 57, 97–99.

Rosenblatt, J. S., & Lehrman, D. S. Maternal behavior of the laboratory rat. In H. Rheingold (Ed.), *Maternal behavior in mammals.* New York: Wiley, 1963.

Spitz, R. A. Unhappy and fatal outcomes of emotional deprivation and stress in infancy. In I. Galdston (Ed.). *Beyond the germ theory.* New York: Health Education Council, 1954.

The Critical Nature of the Post-partum Period in the Human for the Establishment of the Mother-Infant Bond: A Controlled Study

Lee Salk, Ph.D.
Clinical Professor, Director, Pediatric Psychology, New York Hospital–Cornell Medical Center

About twelve years ago I was spirited by some of my random observations to pursue what might be an unlikely question for someone in the behavioral sciences. Having knowledge that the hypothalamus had a rightful place in the expression of emotions I was constantly impressed by the fact that poets, lyricists, and other creative writers from all periods in history and from all parts of the world chose a different part of the anatomy, the heart, as the site from which some deep feelings originate. I tried to combine my

Nervous System, vol. 31, no. 11, pp. 110–115 (November 1970).

knowledge with their style. It just did not work when I tried to say "I love you from the bottom of my hypothalamus," or "My hypothalamus longs for you".

I quickly abandoned my attempts to alter literary style but was still left with many unanswered questions about this anatomical paradox.

As my observations increased, so did my respect for the creative writers.

I had noticed in the Central Park Zoo that a mother rhesus monkey in fact held her newborn baby closer to her heart than to her hypothalamus. In 42 random observations, of the same mother, I had noticed also that she held her newborn on the left side 40 times and only twice on the right side. Could it be that "close to mother's heart" is more than a literary expression? Perhaps it is a literary expression that has a counterpart in behavior and represents a psychobiological process. A careful survey of the scientific literature revealed no reports of any studies concerned with this problem. I was left with the question: "What do human mothers do when presented with their newborn infants?"

To answer this question a study was planned, carried out, and reported in the literature by this author in 1960. [19] From the results of that study (Table I), we see that the large majority of 287 mothers were noted, in observations made during the first four days post-partum, to hold their newborn babies on the left side of the chest or the left shoulder, regardless of the mother's handedness. All these mothers had access to their infants shortly after birth and were considered to have had normal newborns.

Observations of women in well-baby clinics holding their own infants [24] confirmed these findings: a significantly larger proportion held their infants to the left of the midline over the precordial area, regardless of the handedness of the mother.

In a relatively unsystematic fashion it was observed [20, 21] that of 466 paintings and pieces of sculpture created in the past few hundred years, where a child is held by an adult, 373 images or 80 percent were constructed

Table I Side of Body against Which the Mother Holds Her Child

	Left side	Right side
Right handed mothers (N = 255)	83.1%	16.9%
Left handed mothers (N = 32)	78.1%	21.9%

so that the child was on the left side of the adult and 20 percent with the child on the right side.

In a more systematic study, not previously reported, of numerous photographs and artistic reproductions of infants and children held by adults, we see again that the same significantly large number of children are held on the left side. These pictures are in the books noted in Table II.

It seems clear, on the basis of all these data, that there is a significantly large tendency on the part of mothers to hold their offspring on the left side of the body. Moreover, there seems to be a similar tendency for artists in their sculpture and paintings to depict the child on the left side of the adult.

For years, when asked what all these observations mean, I have been hard put to claim anything more than a series of naturalistic observations not previously reported in the scientific literature.

This was the case until recently, when I began to notice maternal behavior that seemed at variance with all the data presented thus far among mothers who brought their children for monthly visits to the follow-up clinic for premature infants at The New York Hospital–Cornell Medical Center. It seemed that an unusually large number of mothers attending this clinic held their babies on the right side.

This observation led to a number of speculations about the possible factors that might cause mothers of premature babies to behave differently towards their offspring from mothers of full-term infants. Weighing heavily, as an explanation for any differences between these two groups, is the fact that a period of prolonged post-partum separation between mother and

Table II   Side of Body against Which Baby Is Held

Source (title and author)	Pictures in which a child is held	Percentage	
		Left	Right
Growth and Culture Margaret Mead	N = 131	85.5	14.5
The Christ Child in devotional images (14th Century Italian) Dorothy Shorr	N = 436	84.6	15.4
Madonnen Herbert Lemperle	N = 29	75.8	24.2
Mother and Child Henry Moore	N = 22	68.6	31.4

newborn follows the birth of a premature infant while little or no separation follows the birth of a full-term infant.

On the basis of this reasoning it seemed appropriate to raise the following question: "Does prolonged post-partum separation of the human mother from her newborn infant have any effect on the mother's response to her offspring?"

Since the question arose from the general observation that mothers of premature babies seemed to show some departure from the "natural" tendency to hold them on the left side, it appeared that a logical index of the mother's response would be the side on which she holds her child.

To investigate this question, a series of observations of how mothers held their babies was made on two groups of mothers.

One group, the experimental group, consisted of 115 mothers who had experienced prolonged post-partum separation from the child they were observed holding. Prolonged post-partum separation was designated to mean that the mother did not hold her infant at all during the first 24 hours following delivery. The second group, the control group, consisted of 286 mothers from a comparable population who had experienced no prolonged post-partum separation from the child they were holding. These mothers all held and handled their infants sometime during the first 24 hours and continued to care for them thereafter. The observations of both these groups were conducted during the same time period and at The New York Hospital–Cornell Medical Center.

The experimental group consisted largely of mothers of premature infants, since prolonged post-partum separation occurred most frequently following premature birth. The observations were made when the mothers brought their babies to the premature follow-up clinic for regular medical care. In some instances the observations were made in the premature nursery when the mother visited to feed or to be with her baby. Some infants in the experimental group were full-term but experienced prolonged post-partum separation because the mother may have been diabetic or the infant needed intensive care. (An infant was considered premature if the gestation period was less than 38 weeks.) The control group consisted solely of mothers selected at random who were observed in the Well-Baby Clinic when they came for regular well-baby medical care.

For all subjects in this study, the following procedure was employed in obtaining the neccessary data:

The experimenter approached each mother while she sat in the waiting room prior to her visit with the physician and ushered her with her baby into an examining room or cubicle, explaining that we were interested in seeing how she held her child and in asking her some questions for a survey. The baby was taken by the examiner and presented directly to the midline of the mother who was asked to stand for his observation. The mother was asked to show which side of her body she felt was most comfortable for holding her baby. The experimenter noted on which side she held the baby and then asked the following questions:

1 How long was it from the time the baby was born until you first got to hold him and take care of him?

2 Did you give birth to any other children before this one, and, if so, how long after birth was it before you held and cared for each of them?

3 Which hand do you write with?

4 When was the baby born?

5 How much did he weigh?

6 For prematures—what was the expected date of birth?

These last three answers were checked against the patient's chart to determine reliability of the mother's report. . . .

It appears that the control group which experienced no post-partum separation showed a marked preference for holding their babies on the left side (77 per cent on the left side and 23 percent on the right side) in striking similarity with the earlier data obtained ten years ago. This is in contrast to the behavior of mothers who experienced prolonged post-partum separation and who showed no particular side preference (53 percent on the left side and 47 percent on the right side) which is a significant departure from the control group.

From these results it appears, in fact, that prolonged post-partum separation *does* alter the response of the human mother to her offspring. Moreover, these results suggest that the time immediately post-partum is a critical period during which the stimulus of holding the infant releases a certain maternal response. This process may have some resemblance to the phenomenon of imprinting.

If this is true, we would expect to find among mothers who experienced prolonged post-partum separation a difference in response between those who had not had any children previously and those who had had at least one child from whom they had not had prolonged post-partum separation.

By dichotomizing both the control group and the experimental group according to those who had had no previous children and those who had had previous children from whom they were not separated during the post-partum period we can see if this occurs.

. . . Post-partum separation results in a considerable alteration in the mother's response to her newborn. However, if she had had a previous infant with whom there was early contact during the post-partum period, the mother had established a reaction to her newborn similar to that of mothers who had not experienced post-partum separation. It is interesting that this established response seems to persist even when there is prolonged post-partum separation following subsequent childbirth experiences.

In short, these data strongly suggest that, for the human, the period immediately post-partum is a critical period for the establishment of the mother-infant response, and that prolonged post-partum separation has a significant effect on the mother's response to her offspring.

Since prolonged separation, post-partum, in this study was considered to be 24 hours or longer before the mother handled and cared for her newborn, one may question whether various amounts of separation have varying degrees of effect on the mother's response.

To determine if, in fact, this is true, the population studied was broken down into those subjects who experienced one to seven days of separation and their responses were compared with those who experienced more than seven days of separation. . . . These data indicate that there appears to be as much alteration in maternal response following short periods of separation as there is following longer periods of separation.

It seems evident, therefore, that the critical period for the establishment of the "natural" mother-infant reaction takes place during the first 24 hours, post-partum.

Although the majority of the subjects in the experimental group were mothers of premature infants; some mothers who experienced prolonged post-partum separation had had full-term babies. By examining the responses of these two different groups to their babies we can determine if prematurity of birth played any role in determining the mother's response to her offspring. These data . . . show that both sub-groups manifest the same tendencies and seem to reaffirm the fact that prolonged post-partum separation causes a significant alteration in the mother's response to her offspring and that the period immediately post-partum represents a critical period for the establishment of the "natural" mother-infant response.

Now that I have taken you through the sequences of my various thoughts and recent explorations which originated 12 years ago from my attempts to bring the world of art and the world of science together, what does all this mean in the context of biological development?

To begin with, these findings represent a method of quantifying human maternal behavior in relatively objective terms and demonstrate a previously unreported phenomenon in the human that is consistent with the behavior observed in infra-human species [1–18, 22–23, 27, 28]. Furthermore, theoretical formulations about maternal behavior in both humans and animals have described processes that are consistent with the empirical findings described in this study.

Finally, these data emphasize that consideration must be given to a possible biochemical mechanism which places the mother in a state of increased sensitivity to the development of a maternal response for a given period shortly after childbirth. This response perhaps is stimulated by contact with her newborn and has a significant impact on the establishment of a bond between the human mother and her child.

REFERENCES

1   Blauvelt, H.: Dynamics of Mother-Newborn Relationship in Goats, in Schaffner and Bertram: *Group Processes,* Transactions of the First Conference, 1954. Josiah Macy Jr. Foundation in New York, 1955.

2   Cairns, Robert B.: Attachment behavior of mammals. *Psychological Review,* 1966, Vol. 73, No. 5, 409–426.

3   Collias, N. E.: Some Factors in Maternal Rejection of Sheep and Goats, *Bull, Ecological Soc. Amer.* 34: 78, 1953.

4   Collias, N. E. and Collias, Elsie C.: Some Mechanisms of Family Integration in Ducks. *Auk,* 1956, 73: 378–400.

5   Hersher, L., Richmond, J. B. & Moore, A. U. (1957). Critical periods in the development of maternal care patterns in the domestic goat. *Am. Psychol.,* 12, 398 (abstract).

6   Hersher, L., Moore, A. U. & Richmond, J. B. (1958). Effect of post partum separation of mother and kid on maternal care in the domestic goat. *Science,* 128, 1342–1343.

7   Hersher, L., Richmond, J. B. & Moore, A. U. (1963a). Modifiability of the critical period for the development of maternal behaviour in sheep and goats. *Behaviour,* 20, 311–320.

8   Hersher, L., Richmond, J. B. & Moore, A. U. (1963b). Maternal behaviour in sheep and goats. *Maternal Behaviour in Mammals* (Ed. by H. L. Rheingold,) chap. 6. New York: Wiley.

9   Hess, E. H.: Imprinting. *Science,* 1959, Vol. 130, No. 3368, 133, 141.

10 Klopfer, P. H., Adams, D. K. & Klopfer, M. S. (1964). Maternal 'imprinting' in goats. *Proc. Nat'l. Acad. Sci.,* U.S.A., 52, 911–914.

11 Levine, S.: Maternal and Environmental Influences in the Adrenocortical Response to Stress in Weanling Rats. *Science.* April 14, 1967. Vol. 156, No. 3772, 258–260.

12 Moltz, H.: Imprinting: Empirical Basis and Theoretical Significance. *Psychological Bulletin,* 1960, Vol. 57, No. 4, 291–314.

13 Moltz, H., Robbins, D., & Parks, M.: Caesarean delivery and the maternal behavior of primiparous and multiparous rats. *Journal of Comparative and Physiological Psychology,* 1966, 61, 455–460.

14 Moltz, H. & Weiner, E.: Effects of ovariectomy on maternal behavior of primiparous and multiparous rats. *Journal of Comparative and Physiological Psychology,* 1966, 62, 382–387.

15 Moltz, H., Levin, R., and Leon, M.: Differential Effects of Progesterone on the Maternal Behavior of Primiparous and Multiparous Rats. *Journal of Comparative and Physiological Psychology,* 1969, Vol. 67, No 1, 36–40.

16 Moore, A. U. & Moore, F. (1960). Studies in the formation of mother-neonate bond in sheep and goats. *Am. Psychol.,* 15, 413.

17 Newton, N., & Newton M.: Mothers' reactions to their newborn babies. *J.A.M.A.,* July 21, 1962, Vol. 181, 206–210.

18 Richards, M. P. M.: Maternal behavior in rodents and lagomorphs: A review. In A. McLaren (Ed.), *Advances in reproductive physiology.* Vol. 2. New York: Academic Press, 1967.

19 Salk, L.: The Effects of the Normal Heartbeat Sound on the Behavior of the

Newborn Infant: Implications for Mental Health. *World Mental Health,* 1960, Vol. 12, No. 4, 168–175.

20 Salk, L.: The Importance of the Heartbeat Rhythm to Human Nature: Theoretical, Clinical, and Experimental Observations. *Proceedings of the Third World Congress of Psychiatry,* University of Toronto Press, 1961, 740–746.

21 Salk, L.: Mothers' Heartbeat as an Imprinting Stimulus. *Transactions of the New York Academy of Sciences,* May, 1962. Ser. II, Vol. 24, No. 7, 753–763.

22 Salk, L.: Thoughts on the Concept of Imprinting and Its Place in Early Human Development. *Canadian Psychiatric Association Journal,* Volume 11, Special Supplement, 1966. S295–S305.

23 Smith, F. V., Van-Toller, C., & Boyes, T.: The 'critical period' in the attachment of lambs and ewes. *Anim. Behav.,* 1966, 14, 120–125.

24 Smith F. V. (1965). Instinct and learning in the attachment of lamb and ewe. *Anim. Behav.,* 13, 84–86.

25 Thompson, W. R.: Early Environmental Influences on Behavioral Development. *American Journal of Orthopsychiatry,* 1960, 30: 306–314.

26 Weiland, I. H.: Heartbeat Rhythm and Maternal Behavior. *Journal of the American Academy of Child Psychiatry,* January, 1964, Vol. 3, No. 1, 161–164.

27 Weisner, B. P. & Sheard, N. M.: *Maternal behavior in the rat.* Edinburgh: Oliver & Boyd, 1933.

28 Zarrow, M. X., Sawin, P. B., Ross S., Denenberg, V. H., Crary, D., Wilson, E. D., and Faroog, A. (1961). Maternal behavior in the rabbit: Evidence for an endocrine basis of maternal nest building and additional data on maternal nest building in the Dutch-belted race. *J. Repro & Fertil.* 2: 152–162.

Development of Object Relations during the First Year of Life

Kenneth S. Robson, M.D.
Associate Professor of Psychiatry, Director of Training in Child Psychiatry, New England Medical Center Hospital, Tufts University School of Medicine

Psychoanalysts who have rightly emphasized the significance of instinctual experience . . . have failed to state with comparable clearness or conviction the tremendous intensity of these nonclimactic experiences that are called playing. We now see that it is not instinctual satisfaction that makes a baby begin to be, to feel that life is real, to find life worth living . . . here is a part of the ego that is not a body-ego . . . but that is founded on body experiences . . . [that] . . . belong to object-relating of a nonorgiastic kind, or to what can be called ego-relatedness. . . .

D. W. Winnicott
International Journal of Psychoanalysis, vol. 48, p. 368 (1966).

Reprinted by permission of Grune & Stratton, Inc., and Dr. Kenneth S. Robson from *Seminars in Psychiatry,* vol. 4, no. 4, pp. 301–316 (November 1972).

The past decade has evidenced a remarkably fruitful increase in both experimental and theoretical approaches to the first year of life. In general, research studies have taken two distinct but complementary directions. Laboratory investigations designed to explore perceptual and cognitive skills in young babies have revealed the presence of previously unimagined capacities. Simultaneously, naturalistic observations of mother-infant interaction are beginning to document the nature of the infant's earliest social experiences within which he puts these perceptual capacities to use. The theoretical backdrop for much of this research stems from three primary sources: ethology, the systematic study of animal behavior; the developmental psychology of Jean Piaget; and learning theory.

From the clinical point of view, past considerations of infancy borrowed heavily from the formulations of Freud, the "ego psychologists," and Erik Erikson. Within these latter models relatively few direct observations of infant behavior were carried out. The advent of psychoanalytic object relations theory, however, has contributed to the development of a clinical language that seems more compatible with the data of hard-core research. Hence, the present era of infancy studies is one of convergence and integration of what were once quite disparate shcools of thought and methodologies.

My purposes in this article are, after summarizing current theoretical models, to review investigations of both normative and deviant development during the first year of life and to offer speculations, based on clinical material, regarding some adult derivatives of these experiences. Since a review of this nature is subject to omissions and bias, I have provided sufficient references for the interested reader to form his own critical judgments.

CURRENT THEORETICAL MODELS

Psychoanalytic Object Relations Theory

Because it offers a point of view most closely akin to the events and experiences that are observable during the first year of life, this theoretical position deserves far more attention that it has received in the clinical literature. In my opinion, the contributions of W. R. Fairbairn, D. W. Winnicott, and Harry Guntrip are particularly important. An excellent and readable review of the object relations school is now available [26]. Classical psychoanalytic theory has tended to view the human infant as an unintegrated organism dominated by powerful drives (aggression and primitive sensuality) and appetites (hunger). Both his ties to his parents and his social being— ego or, introspectively, sense of self—are viewed as *secondary* elaborations that evolve from the interplay between these drives and appetites and their modulation by his caretakers. Love is born, so to speak, out of the hand that feeds him, and life, at least in its earliest months, alternates between orgiastic instinctual experiences and their blissful relief. In general, this model is unidirectional in that the infant is shaped by his parents' behaviors but does relatively little shaping of theirs.

The object relations theorists, however, give *primacy* to *social motivations* that are present in the infant at birth. Fairbairn [26], for example, speaks of the baby as "object seeking." Unlike the more classical model, instinctual drives are viewed as object-related and as located within a fragile but already intact ego, whose mode of interaction with its primary objects is both interpersonal and *nonorgiastic*. Winnicott, given his dual identity as pediatrician and psychoanalyst, was attuned to the critical nature of what he referred to as experiences of "ego-relatedness" [63, 64]. The casual play between mother and baby that occurs, for example, during or after a feeding becomes more significant for subsequent development than the feeding itself. Object relations theory focuses from the clinical perspective on the precise behaviors that are pertinent to more academic approaches to developmental theory and research. Of such approaches, the discipline of ethology has exerted substantial influence.

Ethology

The systematic study of animal behavior in its natural habitat has provided useful concepts and methodologies for the exploration of human infancy. Hess [31] has summarized the essentials of ethologic principles and techniques, while Hinde [32] and Eibl-Eibesfldt [17] provide more comprehensive surveys. Tinbergen's [60] monograph on social behavior is especially pertinent to this review. The esthetics of ethologic research have been eloquently captured in Goodall's observations of free-ranging chimpanzees [25], and Schaller's study of the mountain gorilla [55].

Although known for their interest in instinctual behavior, an interest that should ally them with the classical psychoanalytic orientation, the ethologists have much in common with object relations theorists. Their focus is on observable behavioral sequences in intact animals. Behavior is viewed in its evolutionary context as subject to the pressures of natural selection. Hence, survival value for the species is a major criterion of a particular behavior's retention in the animal's repertoire.

Freud and Konrad Lorenz [38], the great Austrian ethologist, share relatively common views on motivation. Both conceive of a "hydraulic" system wherein a reservoir of instinctual energy accumulates to the point of overflow (i.e., discharge of the particular behavior in question). More recent ethologic conceptions of motivation [32] stress the complex interplay between internal factors (hormones, neurophysiologic mechanisms) and external releasing or terminating stimuli. These stimuli are species-specific and play a critical role in regulating social behavior between members of the same species. As in object relations theory, the ethologists pay careful attention to *interactive processes* and the forces that control them.

The work of John Bowlby has provided the major link between object relations theory and ethology. Bowlby, a psychoanalyst with a long-standing interest in early object relations, has devoted himself to the problem of attachment, the process of focal bonding between mother[1] and infant. Bowlby's own studies, and his theoretical formulations, have been catalytic in fostering developmental studies by students of both human and animal behavior. His contributions have been summarized in his book on attachment [10]. Attachment is viewed as developing out of the interaction between a series of innate infant behaviors—crying, sucking, smiling, clinging, and following—and the parental responses that they release. The origins of this bond, and the proximity-seeking or maintaining behaviors that mediate it, lie in its survival value of defending the infant against predators by insuring the protective closeness of the mother. Bowlby, like the object relations theorists, stresses the relational aims of instinctual behaviors in infancy.

One aspect of Bowlby's theory that is gaining increasing support from research studies is that the infant's behaviors influence and shape those of his parents. In studying this problem of the *direction of effects* in parent-infant interaction, it has become clear that many variables—such as the infant's age, sex, biologic state etc.—exert control over caretaker behavior [5, 9, 40]. Recognition of these bidirectional processes in infancy require that we alter our views of "who is doing what to whom," which for so long have left the burden of influence to the parents.

It appears that the phenomenon of attachment is emerging as the *fundamental process of the first year of life*. The behavioral interactive sequences that determine the nature of this attachment are the data from which we are coming to understand its nature. Before turning to a more detailed discussion of normative and deviant development, I would like to review briefly the models of Jean Piaget and learning theory insofar as they shed light on these sequences.

The Developmental Psychology of Jean Piaget

For a more exhaustive account of Piaget's work, which has become a discipline in its own right, I would recommend the summaries of Baldwin [4],

---

[1] The term *mother* in this review is used interchangeably with parent(s), caretakers, and primary objects. Investigations of father participation in infancy [43] suggest an important role, and other studies [53] document the significance of other adults (or siblings) as objects of attachment.

Flavell [20], and Wolff [65]. Piaget's major interest has been in mapping the development of the structure and function of cognitive processes. Both because of his neglect of the emotional life and the complexity of his writings, his theories, until recently, met with considerable resistance from clinicians. Nevertheless, his elegant observations of his own children place him in the forefront of infant research.

Piaget's position shares some common ground with object relations theory and ethology. He views development as both interactive and intrinsically motivated from birth. His basic behavioral unit is the *schema,* an innate almost reflexive behavior of which sucking, clinging and looking are examples.[2] The exercise of these schemata is self-motivating; their discharge and expansion to incorporate increasingly complex aspects of the externally perceived world are their own reward. Piaget's emphases are on the motivating power of mastery, and on *"the infant's delight in being a cause."* A baby's capacity to shape his world in a predictable manner is central to the development of an intact and meaningful sense of self [47, 62]. And in Piaget's theories the infant's expectancies in relation to external events are always salient.

This theme of an infant's *response expectancies* has, I believe, great clinical relevance to both normal and pathologic development during the first year of life. It is particularly pertinent to the Piagetian concept of *object conservation* (object constancy in clinical parlance), which refers to the infant's ability to perceive the outside world as stable and expectable by means of internal representations of it that are not subject to the vagaries of space, or the object's actual presence. An infant's ability to conceive of his mother as having permanence in this way is obviously important to the quality of his attachment to her. Selma Fraiberg [21] and Silvia Bell [6] have written thoughtful papers on this subject. The marriage of Piaget's formulations with object-relational research holds great promise.

Learning Theory

In relation to Piaget's examination of the manner in which infants learn about their world through repetitive behavioral sequences, the learning theorists have stressed another dimension. Students of this point of view, such as Jacob Gewirtz [24], pay keen attention to the *contingencies* of behavioral interaction between mother and infant. Gewirtz suggests that attachment is a learned phenomenon, and he stresses that the degree to which maternal responses are contingent upon the baby's signals, such as crying and smiling, leads to effective learning. For example, a highly responsive mother

---

[2] The *schema* is similar in structure and function to the basic behavioral unit in ethology, the fixed action pattern. As yet, however, the two disciplines have operated in isolation from one another.

Parent see's these often can better suit the needs of the child

whose behavior is unrelated *in time* to her infant's cues, may contribute to his experiencing psychologic poverty in the midst of plenty [47].

To me, this viewpoint seems compatible with Piaget, ethology, and object relations theory. Once again, the nature of response chains, expectancies, and the variables controlling them are central to an understanding of the quality of the infant's earliest relationships. Later in this report, I shall speculate on the role played by the infant's *response expectancies* and his parents' *response failure* as they relate to his experiences of "ego-relatedness." With these various theoretical persuasions in mind, and with our focus on the task of attachment, I can now examine some aspects of normal development in the first year of life.

NORMATIVE STUDIES OF DEVELOPMENT

Visual Interaction and the Gaze System

My own research efforts over the past several years have been devoted to observational studies of mother-infant social interaction. The paradigm that I have used involves the reciprocal interchange of mutual gazing or eye-to-eye contact between a mother and her baby [47]. The visual system occupies a central position in human social interchange. In infancy, the visual mode is highly developed at birth, and it provides a major channel through which the external world is taken in. Eye contact is a powerful releaser of the infant's social smile. Furthermore, language development seems to be intimately linked to reciprocal gazing. Generally speaking, mothers and infants vocalize to one another mainly during gaze interchanges, and deviant language capacities and gaze behavior accompany all of the major behavior disorders that occur in infancy.

Another aspect of the gaze system that makes it a fascinating context within which to study early object relations is its evolutionary history. In subhuman species, face-to-face looking is employed mainly to assess danger or to convey threat. In part, this is also the case in human interaction. Lorenz [58] has suggested that the smiling response, which is intimately linked to and released by eye contact, is a ritualized appeasement gesture. Gaze aversion itself may indicate submission. Nevertheless, the role of eye contact in mediating *social approach* behavior in humans seems to be unique to our species. Hence, the gaze system can express both ego-relating and "orgiastic" (instinctual) styles of interaction. The viscissitudes of this system during the first year of life can index the experiences of both mother and infant in one another's presence.

Maternal Aspects of Early Attachment

Assumptions about the beneficence of human mother love have been subjected only recently to scientific investigation. My colleague Howard Moss and I conducted one study of this problem as part of a longitudinal research project of mother-infant interaction over the first 3 mo of life [49]. A group of 54 primiparous mothers were interviewed when their infants were 3 mo old. The mothers were asked to describe their feelings toward their infants during this period of time. We had already learned from interviews held during the last trimester of pregnancy that most of these mothers experienced a minimal sense of love or attachment to their infants prenatally. We were interested in learning about changes in this state of mind following birth.

The majority of mothers reported a little sense of relatedness to their babies at first contact; the infants were described in vague and impersonal terms. The absense of such feelings tended to persist through the first 4–6 wk of life. One of our subjects, in describing this perception of her infant, said: ". . . at times I felt that she was completely unconnected to me in any way, flesh or otherwise, (and) that she was just a little thing that had come into my life and brought all this trouble. . . ." Another mother noted in the early weeks of life: ". . . I don't think there is an interaction . . . they are like in a little cage surrounded by glass and you are acting all around them but there is no real interaction. . . ." These remarks suggest a phase of interpersonal estrangement in which the maternal desire for relatedness is frustrated by the infant's unresponsiveness.

Recent observational studies by Marshall Klaus and his colleagues [35–37] have documented an orderly and predictable pattern of exploration of the newborn during first contact with his mother. Tactile manipulation was followed by intense interest in eye contact that increased rapidly over the first 5 min of the first visit. Increasing the frequency of maternal contacts during the hospital stay led to increased maternal soothing, fondling, and eye contact 1 mo later. In another study [41], Moss and I found that a mother's interest in establishing contact with her infant, rated during pregnancy, was positively related to the amount of face-to-face gazing between her and her infant at both 1 and 3 mo of age. Klaus suggests that there may be a "maternal sensitive period," as seen in subhuman species, where separation of mother and infant at birth may impair bond formation. At present, the evidence for such critical or sensitive periods in humans is minimal, but it seems clear that maternal needs to establish relatedness in general, and through gaze interaction in particular, are an important anlage for subsequent parenthood.

Around 4–6 wk, the age when true eye contact and social smiling begin to emerge, the modal mother in our study felt an increasing sense of pleasure in and affection for her baby. In part, this shift was accounted for by adaptation to the infant's rhythms (sleep cycling, feeding). But the infant's "responses" (a term that implies reciprocation) were stressed as a source of acknowledgment of the mother's presence. Smiling, being looked at, and visual fixation and following dominated the responses mentioned, while feeding and holding were reported far less frequently.

At least for our sample it appeared that the infant's ability to engage in reciprocal social interchange with his mother was an important aspect of her developing attachment to him. There is evidence, too, that an infant's inability to provide these responses, as in congenital blindness [22] or brain damage [44], may interfere with maternal attachment and release aggressive impulses in mothers. It may be that infant social responsiveness (smiling, gaze interaction, and, I suspect, vocalization) are specific inhibitors of parental aggression in infancy [49]. In this sense, I agree with Tinbergen's comments about parental behavior in birds [60]: "Instead of being astonished when abnormal parents desert their chicks we should be astonished that most parents do not, and manage to bring this very difficult and complicated task to an end."

In any event, by 3 mo the modal mother in our sample felt strongly attached to her infant and perceived him as recognizing her as an individual. These first 3 mo seem to represent a critical phase of bond formation, and it is after this point in time that infant susceptibility to separation increases markedly [66]. To understand this developing mutuality we must turn now to the baby's contributions to the attachment process.

Infant Object Relating during the First 3 Mo

One of the more dramatic discoveries of the past decade is that infant perceptual and integrative abilities, notably in the visual mode, are highly developed at birth. Since the pioneering observations of Robert Fantz [19] on pattern vision in newborns, a number of fascinating studies of social visual behaviors in early infancy have appeared in the literature. It is important to keep in mind that visually-perceived mother during the first year of life is primarily *mother's face;* and the eye area of that face seems especially important [47]. There is convincing evidence that, in the first week of life, infants show a preference for facial configurations. Marshall Haith developed a technique for mapping the infant's visual scanning of faces [27]. He found a marked increase in face and particularly eye area looking in the baby of 5–7 wk of age; this is approximately the same period of time that mothers in our sample began to experience more closeness to their infants.

Genevieve Carpenter [15] has explored the infant's responses to the mother's face, in camparison to a mannequin and abstract head form, over the first 8 wk of life. Discrimination of mother's face is consistently apparent from the second week of life, as evidenced by the lower visual attention time paid to it, as compared to the other stimuli. This lack of attention is felt to reflect, in part, the formation of a familiar maternal schema in Piagetian terms. This schema might be thought of as the earliest evidence of an attachment in the infant. The interactive processes through which this is achieved are of great interest to our understanding of early object relations.

In the research cited thus far, I have stressed the role of the distance receptors, especially the visual and auditory modes, in attachment for both mother and infant. It appears that in humans these sensory channels mediate much of social intercourse [61], and Schaffer and Emerson [53], in an excellent study of the development of attachment, conclude that the "need-fulfilling" and attachment systems are separate. To what extent physical contact, particularly holding, is an important mode in our species remains to be documented. But even in the rhesus monkey, where physical closeness is clearly significant, the classical studies of Harry Harlow [28] demonstrated that infant monkeys reared with parent surrogates became attached to the terry cloth "mother" that provided contact comfort, rather than the wire mesh "mother" that offered food. Here again, the prepotency of a non-need-fulfilling mode was documented. From an evolutionary point of view, all primate babies can cling to their mothers almost from birth, whereas human infants cannot for many months. This fact may increase the importance of distance receptor interchange as a way of "holding" mother.

By the fourth month of life, the modal mother-infant pair are firmly attached to one another as evidenced both by maternal report and observable discrimination and preference for the mother. For example, infants at this age can clearly differentiate mother from stranger using selective smiling and vocalizing as indices. The quality of this attachment is critical since it sets the style and tone of future interpersonal relations. In the preceding sections, I have examined some maternal and infant factors in attachment as related to the gaze system, but mother-infant interaction is an exquisitely complex phenomenon in which the rhythms, tones, and spacing of the partners can lead to harmonic or dissonant ego-relatedness. Before turning to important events in the latter half of the first year, I shall summarize certain aspects of this interpersonal choreography that research in visual behavior has begun to reveal.

Approach-Avoidance Sequences

Earlier in this report I suggested that the chains of behavioral events between mother and infant, and the expectancies developed within those chains or sequences, were highly significant parameters to study. Martin Richards suggests that the central problem of mother-infant interaction is "the timing and phase relationships of the 2 participants' behavior" [46]. Mutual gazing, since it is an on-off system, lends itself to this kind of analysis. If gazing at one another connotes a "readiness to interact" [33], then gaze aversion can be viewed as avoidance. Indeed, Michael Chance views gazing as a cut-off act that permits two members of a species to remain in close proximity without flight or attack occurring [16].

Genevieve Carpenter [15] was struck by the infant's gaze behavior over the first 8 wk of life. She observed that in looking at the mother the following sequences often occurred: direct fixation—look away—peripheral gaze, with gradual rolling of the head and eyes for a brief central fixation; or look—look away—look—look away. Lowering of the eyelids, prolonged closing of the eyes, and turning away of the head and body with fussing were also observed. She felt that these approach-avoidance behaviors represented a "grappling with the visual target" in order to regulate the amount and intensity of visual input. Avoidance behaviors were consistently more frequent with the mother than the mannequin and abstract head form.

Carpenter interprets these results in relation to the so-called "incongruity hypothesis." This hypothesis states that a familiar percept that is viewed in an incongruous manner elicits disequilibrium (Piaget's violation of a schema) or fear [30]. In Carpenter's experiment, the mothers were viewed through a porthole, and they were silent and still, sometimes nodding. These behaviors were at odds with the *response expectancies* built up by the infants in their daily contacts with mother outside of the laboratory. The avoidance behaviors were utilized to reduce the intense levels of distress and arousal caused by maternal *response failures* or violation of the "face schema" [34]. Only consistent experiences over time with a mother who provides reasonable approximations of the expected can lead to the infant's establishing a stable internal representation of her, which he is both safe to live with and safe to leave. A critical determinant of the stability of that representation is the infant's sensitivity to violations of the expected. Unfortunately, reliable individual differences of this parameter have yet to be documented.

Daniel Stern [59] has carried out naturalistic observations of mother-infant gaze patterns using a primiparous mother and her 3½-mo-old twins. He noted characteristic sequences between mother and each of the twins. Although the direction of effects was difficult to assess, one of the twins avoided eye contact far more than the other. In turn, this avoidance behavior shaped mother's reciprocation, creating an early "set" on both partners' parts. It was of interest that at 12 and 15 mo of age, the "avoiding" twin was more fearful and dependent than his brother. One would guess that his internal representat on of and attachment to his mother was less stable than that of his twin. He may have experienced a relative paucity of comfortable "ego-relatedness" with her.

With the hope of more closely identifying the nature of these early experiences, I have recently completed a study of 35 mother-infant pairs. They were observed at 10-day intervals during the first 5 mo of life. Interactions that involved mutual gazing, vocalizations, and infant smiling were recorded. Since the analysis of these data is not completed, I can only share impressions. If mutual gazing in man, as opposed to other species, is used for approach behavior one can ask what makes this possible. I alluded earlier to the intimate associations of gazing with speech and smiling. Observations of these mother-infant pairs strongly suggest that both speech and smiling, on either partner's part, help to modulate the potentially arousing or disrupting effects of gaze alone. For example, if the infant is about to gaze away from his mother and she speaks, he may continue to look at her. Similarly, if she turns away, a vocalization on the infant's part increases the likelihood of her returning her gaze to his. If he smiles when his mother is gazing at him, there is a burst of maternal speech. With gaze as the conductor of this social orchestration, speech and the smiling response play a constant counterpoint. The patterns and contingencies of these object-relational sequences should deepen our understanding of the ontogeny of human attachment. This attachment is particularly noticeable by the increasing differentiation that the infant displays between his parents and others, most clearly exhibited during the second 6 mo of life by his fear of strangers and separation reactions. And there is evidence that relates these behaviors to his previous experiences.

The Fear of Strangers

The fear of strangers, or so-called "eight-month anxiety," was thought until recently to occur in the third quarter of the first year [39, 58]. Bronson's investigations [13, 14] place the onset of this behavior in the fourth month of life. In subhuman mammals the dramatic avoidance of other members of their species takes place after mother-infant attachment is firmly established. This avoidance behavior tends to maintain the bond by keeping the infant close to his mother and by preventing him from forming indiscriminate and potentially life-endangering attachments to others. Daniel Freedman hypothesizes an analogous function for stranger anxiety in humans [23]. Spitz [58] and John Benjamin [7] felt that separation concerns were a major determinant of the fear of strangers; the stranger was, so to speak, "non-mother." Current research, however, raises questions about this point of view [53]. Situational variables—such as the stranger's size, tone, intensity of voice, and physical appearance—clearly play a role in who elicits avoidance reactions [13, 14].

Innate constitutional factors are also important although the data here is sparse. Nevertheless, in one of the few studies that has convincingly linked infant behavior during the first 6 mo of life to later outcomes, Gordon Bronson [13, 14] has shown that precocious fear of visual novelty in male infants predicts social fearfulness up to 8 yr of age. Another fascinating experiment by Gene Sackett [52] emphasizes the importance of non-experiential contributions to the fear of strangers. He raised rhesus monkey infants in isolation from their mothers and peers. Periodically he exposed them to photographs of adult monkey faces, which included the typical species-specific threat expressions. At the age when normally raised infants begin to show avoidance of threatening strangers, the isolates reacted similarly to threat photographs. Sackett concluded that, at least in the rhesus, unlearned predispositions accounted for his findings.

Obviously, the fear of strangers is a complicated behavior with multiple determinants. One line of research has explored the role of the infant's early interpersonal experiences in this behavior. These investigations relate the presence and quality of the infant's attachment to his mother to later interactions with strangers. Bronson stresses that social avoidance can be seen in many infants around 4 mo of age. As I previously pointed out, at this age a baby evidences selective social responses to and, hence, discrimination of his primary objects of attachment. It may be that the stability or "strangeness" of these early internal representations (schemas) is central to subsequent fearfulness with others.

My colleague Frank Pedersen and I studied the same group of infants at 8 and 9½ mo of age that Howard Moss and I had observed during the first 3 mo of life [48]. We were interested in their reactions to strangers. The gaze system again proved a useful paradigm. These infants' gaze behavior with a stranger, how much and how long they looked at him, was highly predictive of all other approach-avoidance tendencies occurring at that time. Furthermore, when we examined relationships between the frequency of mother-infant gazing at 1 and 3 mo of age and later behaviors we found that, at least for males,[3] there was a strong positive relationship with stranger-infant gazing and similar ratings of fearfulness. In another study [42], we discovered that the amount of visual, auditory, and tactile stimulation delivered by mother to infant during the first 3 mo was inversely related to subsequent fearfulness.

Our findings in both of these studies are in keeping with research by other investigators. Namely, that the amount of stimulation an infant receives from his mother in early life shapes his developing social and exploratory behaviors. Furthermore, in keeping with both Piaget's theories on the optimal level of stimulation for schema development and the incongruity hypothesis, the capacity of an infant to integrate perceptions of a stranger should depend upon the stability of previous internal representations of the mother. In the language of learning theory, the infant's response expectancies developed in relation to his primary objects will generalize to his relationships with others.

These expectancies must also relate to the *quality* of the responses delivered. The degree to which maternal behaviors are contingent upon the baby's signals, and the fostering of ego-relating rather than orgiastic interchanges should correlate with stranger behavior. Rubinstein's study [50] is suggestive of such a correlation. She found a positive relationship between the mother's looking at, playing with, touching, holding, and talking to her baby in the fifth month and the infant's willingness to respond to objects presented by a stranger at 6 mo of age.

---

[3] Such *sex differences* are the rule in developmental research. They are at once tantalizing and frustrating to an investigator hoping to generalize about infant behavior.

The fear of strangers, since it seems prototypical of object-relational capacities, should hopefully predict approach-avoidance tendencies in older children and adults. With the exception of Bronson's studies, this has not proven to be the case. Pedersen and I, for example, were unable to find any relationships between our infants' reactions to strangers and their social behavior at 2½ yr of age. In general, despite the fact that most clinicians and researchers agree on the developmental significance of the first year of life, the prediction of subsequent behaviors from this age period has been disappointing.

Michael Rutter [51] has addressed himself to some of the reasons for this dilemma. One possible explanation is that the measure of partially developed behaviors in infancy are insufficient to account for the full-blown behavior assessed later in life. Another possibility is that subsequent modification of the behavior in question obscures the form that it takes in infancy. Further explanations include the problem of differential rates of maturation (well-documented between the sexes) and the question of whether or not tests in infancy are measuring the same thing as is measured by tests in later childhood or adult life. Thus, although highly significant longitudinal relationships among behaviors occurring *within* the first year of life are demonstrable, our knowledge of subsequent outcome is extremely limited to date.

Nevertheless, the importance of an infant's early ego-relating experiences within the first year of life in relation to his fear of strangers emphasizes the relevance of the attachment process. The appearance of detachment behaviors—the infant's thrust towards separation and beginning autonomy—seem to have equally significant determinants in his earlier interpersonal relationships.

Separation and the Problem of Object Constancy

In the third quarter of their first year, generally close to the time when the more dramatic evidences of fear of strangers become apparent, many infants exhibit signs of distress when separated from their mothers. Bowlby [9] has extensively reviewed the theories held to account for separation anxiety. A good deal of research related to the long-term effects of separation, in both animals and humans, has been carried out. The companion volume to Bowlby's book on attachment [11] will summarize most of this work. For present purposes, I shall focus on the relationships among an infant's early attachment experiences, his separation behavior, and the development of object constancy (i.e., a stable internal representation of his mother).

Bowlby views separation anxiety as a primary anxiety with survival value; its potential is innate although subject to modification by experience. The responses of the infant to separation represent the activation of response systems (crying, clinging, and following) that are ordinarily terminated by the mother's proximity or return. Failure of their termination leads to separation anxiety. To the extent that such anxiety is shaped by environmental events it has secondary and "expectant" components. These components should relate to the degree of stability of the infant's inner image of his mother. The greater that stability, the lower the intensity of his separation anxiety should be. Current research efforts by Mary Ainsworth and her colleagues have tended to support such relationships.

Ainsworth [1–3] has used a paradigm in which infants of 1 yr of age are brought into the laboratory with their mothers and exposed to both a stranger and separations from their mothers. The mother's absence increased the incidence of crying, searching, and proximity-seeking on reunion and suppressed exploration of the environment. Ainsworth was struck by the variability of response and by the presence of contact-resisting (ambivalent) and proximity-avoiding (defensive) patterns in some infants upon reunion with mother; prominent among these patterns were gazing away from and refusal to look at mother. During the first 3 mo of life these same infants had been extensively observed in feeding situations with their mothers. Ratings of the pacing and sensitivity of the mothers to their babies' cues were made at that time. Infants whose mothers were especially sensitive and responsive to them in the early feeding situation displayed attachments to their mothers without behavioral disturbance in relation to separation at 1 yr of age. Conversely, infants who exhibited either disinterest in their mothers or ambivalence and defensiveness upon her return had experienced relatively insensitive and unresponsive mothering during the first 3 mo. These data impressively relate the quality of early object relations to subsequent attachment behavior and separation reactions.

Piaget's concept of object permanence was discussed briefly before. Silvia Bell, a coworker of Mary Ainsworth, conducted a superb experiment that explored the development of the object concept in relation to infant-mother attachment [6]. A group of infants was observed in the same strange situation mentioned above and was also subjected to a battery of tests to determine the development of their ability to visually conceptualize the permanence of both toys and human objects (usually the mother). Bell found that the babies who responded to the separations with obvious signs of attachment to mother but without upset, ambivalence or defensiveness had accelerated conceptions of person permanence as opposed to inanimate object permanence. Furthermore, interviews with the mothers regarding their play with and interest in their infants revealed a positive relationship between sensitive and devoted mothering attitudes and practices and the babies' concept of person permanence. By inference, these attitudes and practices probably reflect the quality of the early relationship between mother and infant.

To summarize, it seems that at every point during the first year of life the quality of an infant's relationships with his primary objects—whether characterized as contingent, harmonic or ego-related—shape his abilities to cope with and master his interpersonal world. His internal world, however, remains largely a mystery. Clues to the nature of that world are revealed to us in the psychotherapy of the schizoid disorders and borderline states. In the concluding section of this report, I will describe certain characteristics of deviant development in the first year of life and some clinical observations that reflect the interpersonal experiences that may have given rise to them.

MANIFESTATIONS OF PATHOLOGIC DEVELOPMENT DURING THE FIRST YEAR OF LIFE

Older concepts of psychologic deficiency diseases during infancy put primary emphasis on the role of the mother as the causal agent. This set reflected both the bias of psychoanalytic reconstructive methodologies and the paucity of solid developmental research. In my own training, I cannot recall a complaint about a child who was a "difficult infant" that was not viewed as a reflection of parental inadequacy or dysfunction. Since these are the data that are most apparent to the clinician, and since deviant infant behaviors cannot be retrospectively validated, this perspective is understandable.

But current research efforts have lent more credibility to the importance of *infant effects*. For example, Moss [40] has demonstrated that male infants cry more during the first 3 mo of life and that this sex difference contributes to selective maternal handling. The impact of brain-damaged [44] or blind infants [22] upon their parents is substantial. An interactive model that stresses the *match* between mother and infant seems to offer a more accurate paradigm in which to examine disturbed mother-infant relations.

Gewirtz [24] differentiates between the concepts of *privation* and *deprivation* in his discussion of aberrant development during the first year of life. Privation implies a continuous state of inadequate mothering, while deprivation involves the loss of a preexisting condition. Chronic maternal depression (privation) as compared with an acute depression or psychosis (deprivation) are analogous situations. These concepts are pertinent, since infant disturbances that do not involve institutionalization of the baby or separation from the mother appear to account for the burden of deviant object-relating in infancy [66]. Atypical gaze behavior, vocalization, and smiling are pathognomonic of these syndromes. I find it useful to divide these syndromes into those in which either inappropriate approach behavior or extreme avoidance of social objects prevails. I believe that the early interpersonal experiences (and quality of attachment) is quite different in both cases.

At one extreme of disturbance one finds so-called "object-hungry" infants. These babies, in the second 6 mo of life, give no evidence of having formed an attachment to a primary object [8]. They exhibit neither fear of strangers nor separation reactions and smile indiscriminately. Indeed, they welcome and seek out novel or exciting stimulation. As children or adolescents they often present the exploitative (need-fulfilling) and impoverished interpersonal relations of the psychopath (addict). Early experiences and/or constitutional characteristics that predispose to this outcome are as yet poorly defined. It seems as if such individuals never move beyond the more indiscriminate phase of relating seen in the first 3 mo of life. I would speculate that in infancy these disorders might exhibit a state of *steady* but low intensity parental privation that is relatively free of anxiety, *Biologic* need-fulfilling is the mode of relating while "ego-relating" is negligible. Maternal disinterest rather then active intrusion or withdrawal may contribute to a poorly articulated attachment and the search for others.

Conversely, the syndromes of social avoidance-idiopathic failure to thrive, spasmus nutans, anaclitic depression and infantile autism [47, 49]— are characterized by gaze aversion and depression of speech and the smiling response. Transient or enduring social withdrawal and failure to relate are primary signs of these conditions. Although the determinants are complex, and the direction of effects difficult to determine, there are research findings and clinical observations that implicate *maternal response failure* as a contributing factor. I would suggest that these varieties of disturbance predispose to the development of schizoid disorders with an attachment that requires hypervigilance and intense separation concerns. Relationships in later life are indiscriminately threatening and there is a negligible sense of object constancy.

In two learning studies, 4-mo-old babies' smiling and vocalizations were increased by the experimenters' looking, smiling, and talking back when smiled at or vocalized to by the infant [12, 45]. During the extinction phase of these experiments, in which the observers stopped responding and stared impassively, a number of infants developed acute gaze aversion with cessation of smiling and vocalization. Carpenter's [15] observations of visual avoidance and distress in a similar paradigm support the significance of response failure (violation of expectancy and/or the incongruity hypothesis) as a determinant of these disorders.

Seay [56, 57], working in Harlow's laboratory, separated infant monkeys from their mothers by placing them in adjacent cages with an intervening plexiglass or opaque partition. The mother could be seen or heard, but more intimate contact was precluded. Among the signs of acute distress described, a decrease in making or attempting to make visual contact with the mother was prominent. In his first hour with me, one of my schizoid patients, who was keenly and painfully aware of my response failures with him, described a dream. He was driving toward his mother's house with his infant daughter, and the car crashed; at the moment of impact he and his child fused. As he lay on the sidewalk, desperate for help, television cameramen came to the scene and, after impassively recording the events, left. This dream reflected the longing for a response and the desperation engendered by its absence and to me seems similar to the conditions in the experiments noted previously. My patient discovered subsequently that his mother had sustained a long postpartum depression following his birth. *The physical availability of a socially unavailable mother* is a recurrent and devastating experience for such patients, and maternal depression or preoccupation frequently accompany the object-avoiding syndromes of infancy.

If maternal response failure is one component of these syndromes, Sackett's [52] study of monkey isolates, discussed earlier in relation to the fear of strangers, suggests another. It seems plausible that maternal facial expressions that express depression, resentment, and anxiety could be analogous to the threat faces that elicited innate avoidance reactions in the monkeys. Mother, so to speak, becomes the threatening stranger whose visage must, on an innate basis, be avoided by the infant. Whatever other variables, including individual differences between infants, are operative in the avoidance syndromes, these data suggest that the infant experiences internal disruption as a result of potentially meaningful ego-relating interactions that sustain "orgiastic" or instinctual intensity.

It has been my experience with schizoid and borderline patients that the approach behaviors of one or both parents are colored by a similar orgiastic hue. For example, incessant and unmodulated tickling or more overt forms of sexual stimulation are substituted for low intensity play and comfortable contact. These polarities of disruptive withdrawal and intrusive excitation, rather than disinterest, seem to occur together in such patients and have led me to a hypothesis about the quality of early object-relating in the schizoid disorders: that what Winnicott describes as ego-relatedness of a social and noninstinctual nature is mediated by highly charged interactions of both approach and withdrawal that release unmanageable instinctual responses in the infant. The prepotency of these responses prevents the formulation of a *stable* attachment or, in the case of infantile autism, suppresses all evidences of ego-relating behaviors—the potential object of attachment is fled from more than longed for. Unfortunately, there are as yet no prospective developmental studies to support this hypothesis and to locate the origins of these disorders in the first year of life. I suspect that in the next decade such studies may become available.

CONCLUSION

There are many maturational processes and developmental events in the first year of life that I have neglected in this paper. Yet it seems to me that human life, as opposed to existence, is lived in and takes its origins from an interpersonal world. It is within the context of early attachment experiences, so prolonged and subject to deviation in our species, that the self is born. Investigations of infancy offer the possibility of bearing witness to that birth process. In this respect the first year of life is becoming like "home," which T. S. Eliot [18] described as ". . . the place you return to and know it for the first time."

REFERENCES

1 Ainsworth, M. D. S.: Object relations, dependency and attachment: a theoretical review of the infant-mother relationship. Child Develop. 40:969, 1969.

2 ——, and Bell, S. M.: Some contemporary patterns of mother-infant interaction in the feeding situation. *In* Ambrose, J. A. (Ed.): Stimulation in Early Infancy. London, Academic Press, 1969.

3 ——, and Bell, S. M.: Attachment, exploration and separation: illustrated by the behavior of one-year-olds in a strange situation. Child Develop. 41:49, 1970.

4 Baldwin, A. L.: Theories of Child Development. New York, Wiley, 1967.

5 Bell, R. Q.: A reinterpretation of the direction of effects in studies of socialization. Psychol. Rev. 75:81, 1968.

6 Bell, S. M.: The development of the concept of object as related to infant-mother attachment. Child Develop. 41:291, 1970.

7 Benjamin, J. D.: Some developmental observations relating to the theory of anxiety. J. Amer. Psychonal. Ass. 9:652, 1961.

8 Bowlby, J.: Forty-four juvenile thieves. Int. J. Psychoanal. 25:1, 1957.

9 ——: Separation anxiety. Int. J. Psychoanal. 41:69, 1960.

10 ——: Attachment: Attachment and Loss, Vol. 1. New York, Basic, 1969.

11 ——: Loss: Attachment and Loss, Vol. II. New York, Basic, in press.

12 Brackbill, Y.: Extinction of the smiling response in infants as a function of reinforcement schedule. Child Develop. 29:115, 1958.

13 Bronson, G. W.: Sex differences in the development of fearfulness: a replication. Psychonomic Science 17:367, 1969.

14 ——: Infants' reactions to an unfamiliar person. Paper presented to the Society for Research in Child Development, Minneapolis, Minnesota, 1971.

15 Carpenter, G. C., Tecce, J. J., Stechler, G., and Friedman, S.: Differential visual behaviors to human and humanoid stimuli in early infancy. Merrill-Palmer Quart. 16:91, 1970.

16 Chance, M. R. A.: An interpretation of some agonistic postures; the role of "cut-off" acts and postures. Symposium of the Zoological Society of London 8:71, 1962.

17   Eibl-Eibesfeldt, I.: Ethology. New York, Holt, Rinehart & Winston, 1970.

18   Eliot, T. S.: The Four Quartets. *In* The Complete Poems and Plays (The Four Quartets). New York, Harcourt, Brace & Co., 1952.

19   Frantz, R. L.: Visual perception and experience in early infancy: a look at the hidden side of behavior development. *In* Stevenson, H. W., Hess, E. H., and Rheingold, H. L. (Eds.): Early Behavior, New York, Wiley, 1967.

20   Flavell, J. H.: The Developmental Psychology of Jean Piaget. Princeton, N.J., Van Nostrand, 1963.

21   Fraiberg, S.: Libidinal object constancy and mental representation. *In* Eissler, R. S. et al. (Eds): Psychoanalytic Study of the Child, Vol. XXV. New York, International Universities Press, 1969.

22   ———: Personal communication.

23   Freedman, D. G.: The infant's fear of strangers and the flight response. J. Child Psychol. Psychiat., 2:242, 1961.

24   Gewirtz, J. L.: A learning analysis of the effects of normal stimulation, privation and deprivation on the acquisition of social motivation and attachment. *In* Foss, B. M. (Ed.): Determinants of Infant Behavior. London, Methuen, 1961.

25   Goodall, J.: In the Shadow of Man. Boston, Houghton Miftlin, 1971.

26   Guntrip, H. J. S.: Psychoanalytic Theory, Therapy and the Self. New York, Basic, 1971.

27   Haith, M.: Personal communication.

28   Harlow, H. F.: The nature of love. Amer. Psychol. 13:673, 1958.

29   Harper, L. V.: The young as a source of stimuli controlling caretaker behavior. Develop. Psychol. 4:73, 1971.

30   Hebb, D. O.: On the nature of fear. Psychol: Rev. 53:250, 1946.

31   Hess, E. H.: Ethology. New York, Holt, Rinehart & Winston, 1962.

32   Hinde, R. A.: Animal Behaviour. New York, McGraw-Hill, 1966.

33   Hutt, C., and Ounsted, C.: The biological significance of gaze aversion with particular reference to the syndrome of infantile autism. Behav. Sci. 11:346, 1966.

34   Kagan, J.: Growth of the face schema: Theoretical significance and methodological issues. *In* Hellmuth, J. (Ed.): Exceptional Infant, Vol. 1. Seattle, Special Child Publications, 1967, p. 336.

35   Klaus, M. H., Kennell, J., Plumb, N., and Zuehlke, S.: Human maternal behavior at first contact with her young. Pediatrics 46:187, 1970.

36   ———, and Kennell, J. H.: Mothers separated from their newborn infants. Pediat. Clin. N. Amer. 17:1015, 1970.

37   ———, Jerauld, R., Kreger, N. C., McAlpine, W., Steffa, M., and Kennell, J.: Maternal attachment. New Eng. J. Med. 286:460, 1972.

38   Lorenz, K.: On agression. New York, Harcourt, Brace & World, 1966.

39   Morgan, G. A., and Ricciuti, H. N.: Infants' responses to strangers during the first year. *In* Foss, B. M. (Ed.): Determinants of Infant Behaviour, IV. London, Methuen, 1969.

40   Moss, H. A.: Sex, age and state as determinants of mother-infant interaction. Merrill-Palmer Quart. 13:19, 1967.

41   ———, and Robson, K. S.: Maternal influences in early social-visual behavior. Child Develop. 39:401, 1968.

42 ——,, Robson, K. S., and Pedersen, F. A.: Determinants of maternal stimulation of infants and consequences of treatment for later reactions to strangers. Develop. Psychol. 1:239, 1969.

43 Pedersen, F. A., and Robson, K. S.: Father participation in infancy. Amer. J. Orthopsychiat. 39:466, 1969.

44 Prechtl, H. F. R.: Neurological sequelae of prenatal and paranatal complications. In Foss, B. M. (Ed.): Determinants of Infant Behaviour. London, Methuen, 1961.

45 Rheingold, H. L., Gewirtz, J. L., and Ross, H. W.: Social conditioning of vocalizations in the infant. J. Comp. Physiol. Psychol. 52:68, 1959.

46 Richards, M. P. M.: Social interaction in the first weeks of human life. Psychiat., Neurol. Neurochir. 74:35, 1971.

47 Robson, K. S.: The role of eye-to-eye contact in maternal-infant attachment. J. Child Psychol. Psychiat. 8:13, 1967.

48 ——, Pedersen, F. A., and Moss, H. A.: Developmental observations of diadic gazing in relation to the fear of strangers and social approach behavior. Child Develop. 40:619, 1969.

49 —— and Moss, H. A.: Patterns and determinants of maternal attachment. J. Pediat. 77:976, 1970.

50 Rubinstein, J.: Maternal attentiveness and subsequent exploratory behavior in the infant. Child Develop. 38:1089, 1967.

51 Rutter, M.: Psychological development-predictions from infancy. J. Child Psychol. Psychiat. 11:49, 1970.

52 Sackett, G. P.: Monkeys raised in isolation with pictures as visual input: evidence for an innate releasing mechanism. Science 154:1468, 1966.

53 Schaffer, H. R., and Emerson, P. E.: The Development of Social Attachments in Infancy. Monographs of the Society for Research in Child Development, 29, 1964.

54 ——: The onset of the fear of strangers and the incongruity hypothesis. J. Child Psychol. Psychiat. 7:95, 1966.

55 Schaller, G.: The Year of the Gorilla. New York, Ballantine, 1964.

56 Seay, B., Hansen, E., and Harlow, H. F.: Mother-infant separation in monkeys. J. Child Psychol. Psychiat. 3:123, 1962.

57 ——, and Harlow, H. F.: Maternal separation in the rhesus monkey. J. Nerv. Ment. Dis. 140:434, 1965.

58 Spitz, R. A.: The First Year of Life. New York, International Universities Press, 1965.

59 Stern, D. N.: A micro-analysis of mother-infant interaction. J. Amer. Acad. Child Psychiat. 10:501, 1971.

60 Timbergren, N.: Social Behaviour in Animals. New York, Wiley, 1953.

61 Walters, R. H., and Parke, R. D.: The role of the distance receptors in the development of social responsiveness. In Lipsitt L. and Spiker C. (Eds.): Advances in Child Development and Behavior, Vol. II. New York, Academic Press, 1965.

62 White, R. W.: Ego and reality in psychoanalytic theory. Psychological Issues, Monograph II, 1963.

63 Winnicott, D. W.: The capacity to be alone. *In* The Maturational Process and the Facilitating Environment. New York, International Universities Press, 1965.
64 ———: The location of cultural experience. Int. J. Psychoanal. 48:368, 1966.
65 Wolff, P. H.: The developmental psychologies of Jean Piaget and psychoanalysis. Psychological Issues, Monograph 5, 1960.
66 Yarrow, L. F.: Maternal deprivation: toward an empirical and conceptual reevaluation. Psychol. Bull. 58:459, 1961.

Sequelae

The sequelae of high-risk infancy are many and varied and include failure to thrive, child abuse, sudden infant death, mental retardation, emotional disturbances, and learning disorders. While organic pathologic factors contribute to many of these disorders, the authors of the articles included in this section emphasize the psychosocial and predispositional aspects. We have already discussed the importance of a positive nurturing environment for the mother and child as a powerful determinant in developmental outcome. The mutual and reciprocal influence between infants and their parents will be further considered as we attempt to understand the long-range effects of prematurity.

Early separation of the mother from her infant may correlate with later inability to provide nurturing, leading to neglect, and as has been found in some cases, to child abuse. The findings of Kennell,[1] Klaus,[2] Stern,[3] and

[1] J. H. Kennell and M. H. Klaus, "Care of the Mother of the High-Risk Infant," *Clin. Obstet. Gynocol.* vol. 14, pp. 926–954 (1971).

[2] M. H. Klaus, J. H. Kennell, N. Plumb, et al., "Human Maternal Behavior at the First Contact with Her Young," *Pediatrics,* vol. 46, pp. 187–192 (1970).

[3] L. Stern, "Prematurity as a Factor in Child Abuse," *Hosp. Prac.,* May 1973.

Elmer[4] require prospective confirmation with larger samples, but the consequences of antenatal and perinatal risks would seem consistent with the hypothesis that a range of impaired maternal-child relationships may result from disturbance of the early mother-infant bond.

The first article selected for this chapter, "Reactions to the Threatened Loss of a Child," by Morris Green and Albert J. Solnit, is a classic in its field. The authors delineate a clinical constellation of children who have undergone life-threatening episodes and subsequently have manifested behavior problems as the "vulnerable child syndrome." They describe twenty-five children with a history of illness or accident from which they recovered, contrary to the expectations of their parents. The study was based on the hypothesis that children who have been critically ill or injured may be predisposed to psychological sequelae.

Other authors, also, have commented regarding early illness and sequelae. Levy[5] reports that critical illness early in life may lead to maternal overprotection and later psychological disturbance. Gibson[6] found that parents of children who have undergone surgery experience emotional reactions, the severity of which has little correlation with the surgical risk. Constanza's[7] data suggest that the child is made vulnerable not by life-threatening illness but by family members who react abnormally to the child's illness. It is also noted that altered parental perception of the child may follow such a traumatic reaction to the child's illness. In such a disturbed relationship, the child senses the parental expectation of his vulnerability and identifies with this distorted image of himself. He may then develop avoidance symptoms in order to stave off the imagined danger of growing up only to die and may remain at an infantile level of psychosocial adaptation in some areas of his development.

Parents of the vulnerable child are often unwilling to enforce reasonable discipline and tend to become overprotective and indulgent. The child, in response, may become disobedient, argumentative, and uncooperative. Other symptoms may occur during weaning, feeding, toilet training, and periods of separation, which relate directly to this lack of control on the part of the parents.

Authors studying the mothers of prematures suggest that these parents

[4] E. Elmer, "Studies in Child Abuse and Infant Accidents" *Ment. Health Prog. Rep.* HEW-NIHM. December 1971, pp. 58–89.

[5] D. Levy, *Maternal Overprotection,* W. W. Norton & Company, Inc., New York, 1966.

[6] R. M. Gibson, "Trauma in Early Infancy and Later Personality Development," *Psychosom. Med.* vol. 27, pp. 229ff. (1965).

[7] M. Constanza, I. Lipsitch, and E. Charney, "The Vulnerable Child Revisited," *Clin. Pediat.* vol. 7, pp. 680ff. (1968).

be given frequent opportunities to ask questions and to report observations for which they may seek clarification. Follow-up visits also provide opportunities for them to express reactions, concerns, fears, and questions which may develop during the time they spend "alone" with their premature child. The final goal, then, becomes the full acceptance of the child by the parents as healthy and normal once the crisis has passed.

In the second article, "Psychologic Sequelae of Early Infancy Health Crises," Dr. William B. Carey documents evidence which suggests that the development of psychopathology during childhood may result from illness during early infancy. His clinical observations support the theory that the earlier the illness occurs in the child's life, the greater the potential damage to the mother-child relationship.

Carey prefers such terms as "neonatal crisis syndrome" or "ominous infant phenomenon," since he believes they describe this clinical dilemma more accurately than "vulnerable child syndrome."

Having reviewed the recent literature, Carey draws three main conclusions with respect to early infancy health sequelae. First, he sees the mother's reaction to her baby's illness, rather than the physician's objective evaluation, as a major factor in the subsequent development of emotional problems in the infant at risk. Second, maternal vulnerability to emotional trauma is reflected in the type of psychosocial environment in which the mother and child find themselves. The mother's intellect, education, general health, and emotional support seem to play a major role in her ability to cope satisfactorily with a sick baby. Finally, he states that the psychobiological mother-child interaction, which results from an infant's early health crisis, can lead to a wide spectrum of psychologic sequelae in the developing child.

Our third article, "Failure to Thrive: A Retrospective Profile," by Shaheen, Alexander, Truskowsky, and Barbero, presents evidence of growth failure in forty-four patients admitted to a children's hospital during one year. The purpose of this report is to document the high incidence of children suffering from growth failure without specific organic etiology and to examine the various clinical and psychosocial histories of these children.

"Failure to thrive" is a term used by these authors to identify a syndrome which is elsewhere called "maternal deprivation." Relevant clinical studies suggest that important growth and developmental sequences can be adversely or positively affected by psychosocial components. Extrapolations drawn from clinical data also suggest that failure to thrive can be viewed on a continuum. The literature contains numerous references to failure to thrive coexisting with such problems as malnourishment, neglect, abuse, and accidental injury.

The fourth article, "Studies of Child Abuse and Infant Accidents," by Elmer, Gregg, Wright, Reinhart, et al., provides a detailed study of the syndromes included under the rubric of child abuse. Its place in this volume is justified by the high incidence of low-birthweight children who later become victims of child abuse. In this study, about one-third of the children abused by their parents weighed less than 5½ pounds at birth—an extraordinarily high percentage when compared with the national figure of 8 percent prematurity. The stresses and demands placed upon families of premature infants are often substantial and, at times, overwhelming. Too frequently, these families are the ones least able to respond adaptively; the result can be a gradual deterioration in parent-child relations, leading to child abuse. An awareness of these factors points to the need for supportive services during the postpartum period whenever such problems are suspected.

Even under the best of circumstances, there are many instances of long-term stress to which parents are subjected as a result of their infant being premature or small for date. Long-term follow-up studies of low-birthweight infants, especially the work done by Van den Berg and Yerushalmy,[8] Lubehenco,[9] Drillien,[10] and Wortis,[11] indicate a much higher incidence of congenital anomalies, minimal brain damage, physical handicaps, and emotional problems among these high-risk infants. In addition, according to Bergman's studies,[12] the tragic sequela of sudden infant death is greater among this group.

Ann Stewart and E. O. R. Reynolds, in "Improved Prognosis for Infants of Very Low Birth Weight," present the findings of a recent study program examining the use of the intensive-care unit with premature infants. The study included 197 infants weighing 1,500 grams or less, who were cared for in the neonatal unit of the University College Hospital, London, over a period of five years (1966 to 1970). Their work confirmed earlier findings by the authors that the prognosis of infants of very low birthweight has improved and that there has been a reduction of serious handicaps in survivors. They conclude that appropriate intensive care of these neonates is worthwhile from a social and economic as well as humanitarian standpoint.

The final article in this section, "Communication Skills in Five-Year-

[8] B. J. Van den Berg, and J. Yerushalmy, "The Relationship of the Rate of Intrauterine Growth of Infants of Low Birth Weight to Mortality, Morbidity, and Congenital Anomalies," *J. Pediatr.,* vol. 69, Oct. 1966, pp. 531ff.

[9] L. O. Lugehenco, F. Horner, L. Reed, et al., "Sequelae of Premature Birth." *Am. J. Dis. Child.,* June 1963, pp. 101–115.

[10] C. M. Drillien, "The Incidence of Mental and Physical Handicaps in School-age children of Very Low Birth Weight. II," *Pediatrics,* vol. 39, Feb. 1967, pp. 238ff.

[11] H. Wortis, and A. Freedman, "The Contribution of Social Environment to the Development of Premature Children," *Amer. J. Orth-psychiat.,* vol. 35, 1965, pp. 57–68.

[12] A. Bergman, B. Beckwith, and G. Ray, *Sudden Infant Death Syndrome,* University of Washington Press. Seattle, 1970.

Old Children with High-Risk Neonatal Histories," by Ehrlich, Shapiro, et al., includes a study of the speech, auditory, and intellectual development of eighty-one five-year-old children with birth weights of less than 2,500 grams and gestation ages of less than thirty-eight weeks. Despite normal intelligence, 54 percent of these children needed special help. Among the problems detected in this group were difficulties in word finding, articulation, and attention span. Respiratory distress, abnormal birth weight, and gestational age were directly related to the greatest incidence of these disabilities.

The findings of these investigators emphasize the need for infants at risk to be monitored with tests for auditory and visual figure-ground discrimination, as well as screened for language and perceptual functions known to be related significantly to high-risk conditions. The authors further suggest that such monitoring be done early in the child's development so that deficiencies in communication skills, which may precipitate later academic failure and social maladjustment, can be detected as early as possible.

Increasing knowledge in the management of seriously ill newborn infants points to the need not only for highly developed intensive care units but for a far more comprehensive follow-up of these infants. We have discussed the fact that very few opportunities exist for parents of premature infants to receive adequate information and attention after their children are brought home. The need for forming voluntary groups of parents to work toward this end cannot be underestimated. The crisis which most parents experience is often endured with inadequate assistance.

Socially and financially deprived children are often undernourished and intellectually understimulated. The absence of appropriate nutrition and mental stimulation has longstanding repercussions on the child's emotional development. Services for underprivileged children must be extended in order to diminish the serious hazards and harmful effects brought about by unsatisfactory social environments.

Reactions to the Threatened Loss of a Child: A Vulnerable Child Syndrome: Pediatric Management of the Dying Child, Part III

Morris Green, M.D.
Professor and Chairman, Indiana University School of Medicine
Albert J. Solnit, M.D.
Sterling Professor of Pediatrics and Psychiatry, Director, Yale University Child Study Center

So many people die who never died before.

Viennese saying

For more than six years, observations of pediatric patients in two regions of the country, Indianapolis and New Haven, have been made to examine the hypothesis that children who are expected by their parents to die prematurely often react with a disturbance in psycho-social development. The repetitive quality of the pathological reactions observed, the number of patients seen, and the relief which both child and parents experience when the problem becomes clarified through verbalization provide substantial clinical evidence that this hypothesis is a useful and significant one.

For purposes of presentation, these observations involve three patient groups: (1) children who are expected to die because they underwent a serious illness from which the parent did not believe the child would recover; (2) children who are expected to die because they represent for the parent, usually the mother, a figure from the past who died prematurely, e.g., a maternal grandmother who died when a patient's mother was nine years old; and (3) children who are expected to die because in their birth the mother's fear of her own dying became displaced on to the baby. (This expectation is enhanced if both the mother and child were in actual danger of losing their lives during the pregnancy or delivery, e.g., because of a placenta previa or a difficult delivery.) While a total of more than 50 children are included in these three groups, the authors are aware of many other stiuations in which this difficulty in the parent-child relationship, which we have termed a *vulnerable child syndrome*, is apparent in a more subtle or less clear fashion. The present report is concerned with the first group of children, i.e., those with a history of an illness or accident from which they were not expected to recover.

From *Pediatrics*, vol. 34 pp. 58–66 (July 1964).

CLINICAL FEATURES

Table I summarizes some of the clinical data in 25 of these cases (16 boys and 9 girls). In most instances, the doctor had told the parents that the child was going to die, was likely to die, or would not live very long. In some cases the parents had been advised to contact an undertaker. For reasons not founded in reality, these children following recovery are considered by their parents to be vulnerable to serious illness or accident and destined to die during childhood. The parents have the feeling that these children are not completely theirs but only on a tenuous loan. In an occasional instance the illness in the child is followed by an extended depression in the mother during which her ability to relate warmly and intimately with the child becomes markedly impaired. Some parents appear to experience a modified grief reaction when they become convinced or informed that their child will die. This reaction becomes incompletely aborted when recovery is apparent but is not completely dispelled for a long time. Some mothers give a history of recurring nightmares about losing their child.

PRESENTING SYMPTOMATOLOGY

1. Difficulty with Separation

Pathological separation difficulties are frequent. The child may be briefly intrusted to the care of a grandparent, but baby sitters are rarely used. In extreme cases mother and child never separate. Sleep problems are common: the child often sleeps in the parents' bedroom, either with the mother, with both parents, or in his own crib or bed which is kept next to the mother in her direct line of vision. The parents may report that the baby does not sleep well, but a closer inquiry often reveals that it is the parent who wakes up several times a night to check on the child, often managing to awaken him to be sure that he is alive. This fear of the child dying while asleep causes some mothers to hover about the child even during naps. Older children frequently complain of abdominal pain in the morning before school, especially on first going to school for a full day. A classical school phobia may be present.

Jerry A., a 3-year-old boy, was brought to the pediatric clinic because of his mother's mounting exhaustion, resulting from the child's inability or refusal to sleep since birth. The mother had come from some distance in ". . . a last ditch effort to preserve my sanity since I can't continue to get along without sleep." The child was physically well, active and developing normally in other respects. In the interviews the mother eventually made it clear to the pediatrician that at the time of birth she had expected to lose her only son because of a placenta praevia and prematurity. Over a period of two months, in five interviews, she discussed and remembered the details

Table I

Patient number	Sex	Current age	Current chief complaints	Nature of precipitating illness	Age when ill
1	M	17 mo	Temper tantrums	Dyspnea, poor feeding	Newborn
2	M	2⁴/₁₂ yr	Breath-holding spells	Seizures and apnea	Newborn
3	M	2¹/₂ yr	Feeding problem; overactive, sleep problem, stubbornness	Diarrhea	Early weeks of life
4	M	2¹⁰/₁₂ yr	"Intermittent fever"	Pneumonia	18 mo
5	M	3	Separation problem; does not talk, disciplinary problem	Pneumonia	15 mo
6	M	3	Severe insomnia	Prematurity and birth with placenta previa	At birth
7	M	4	Disciplinary problem; temper tantrums; hits mother	Croup	18 mo
8	F	4	Lack of discipline	Erythroblastosis fetalis	Newborn
9	M	5	Headaches; cyanotic when crying	Neonatal cyanosis; misdiagnosis of coronary artery disease	First two weeks
10	M	6	Restless; discipline problem; nervous tic; poor sleeper	Salicylate poisoning	2 yr
11	M	7	Not doing well in school	Head trauma	21 mo
12	F	8	Acute anxiety attacks; mild school phobia	Details not clear. Severe conjunctivitis & allergy	6 mo
13	M	8	Abdominal pain; effeminate behavior	Vomiting and anemia	First 3 mo
14	F	8	Headaches; pains in abdomen and extremities	Infectious gastroenteritis	14 mo
15	M	8	Panic before surgery at 8; impulsive behavior and underachievement at school after successful cardiac surgery	Congenital cardiac disease	From birth and at time of open heart surgery
16	F	10	Mild school phobia; unhappy, cries frequently; sleep problem	Tracheotomy to relieve laryngeal obstruction	3 mo

Table I (continued)

Patient number	Sex	Current age	Current chief complaints	Nature of precipitating illness	Age when ill
17	M	11	Obesity	Cyanotic episodes	Newborn
18	F	11	Nervous, frequent arguments between mother and daughter; history of severe feeding problem	Serious streptococcal illness	5 mo
19	M	12	Headache	Pneumonia	7 years
20	F	12	Recurrent diarrhea in response to stress	Diagnosis congenital heart disease during hospitalization for diarrhea	3 mo
21	M	13	Discipline problem; mild school phobia; school failure	Post-measles pneumonia	11 mo
22	M	14	Sleeplessness; extreme nervousness; also has diabetes	Malnutrition	Early weeks of life
23	M	14	Truancy; disciplinary problem; severe conflict between mother and boy	Vomiting and diarrhea	Newborn
24	M	14	Failure to do well in school	Perforated appendicitis with complications	6 yr
25	F	14	Refusal to take insulin or regulate diet	Diabetes mellitus	10 yr

of the birth that had threatened her life and that of her baby. She vividly described the obstetrician's concern, and his decision, "I may have to choose between you and the baby, so don't be surprised if the baby doesn't live." With this as a background, the pediatrician's questions tactfully but specifically evoked a description of the mother being unable to sleep at night unless she felt the baby was safe and sound. It became apparent that she unwittingly kept the baby awake each night through a series of visual, auditory, and tactile stimuli which conveyed her insistence that the baby not fall asleep, probably because of her fear that she would again feel the baby was dead. The pediatrician did not attempt to interpret the mother's reactions, but after each interview he gave advice about reduction of stimuli at bedtime for child and mother, always with the realistic reassurance that the child was safe. Within a month the mother and child were sleeping, and the mother began to refer to the past exhaustion and sleep disturbance as a bad dream.

2. Infantilization

In many cases, it is apparent that the parents are unable to set disciplinary limits. The parent is overprotective, overly indulgent, and oversolicitous while the child is overly dependent, disobedient, irritable, argumentative, and unco-operative. Feeding problems are common. Some of these children are physically and publicly abusive to the mother, e.g., hitting, biting, or scratching her. Although resentful and embarrassed by this behavior, the mother cannot control the child. It is common for such mothers, however, to restrict the child's physical activity, e.g., by keeping him in a playpen excessively, confining him in a fenced yard beyond the usual age for such precaution and forbidding bicycling and contact sports.

George T., a 6½-year-old boy, seen in the pediatric clinic with the presenting complaints of shaking of his head, restlessness, poor sleeping, and gritting of his teeth, was described by his mother as "hard to handle." During the interview the child sat on the mother's lap, kicking her on the shins with the heels of his shoes. He would not separate from her. At the age of 2½ years the child had ingested a large number of aspirin tablets and was rushed to a hospital emergency room where the doctors, according to the mother, told her that the child might die. She was not permitted in the treatment room until "three hours later." The mother recalled this experience as follows: "We felt certain that he was going to die. Finally, they said that we could come in. We saw him lying there—white and with his eyes closed. He looked dead. . . ." After this episode the mother had an altar built in the home to pray because she now thought that she would probably lose her son prematurely. She reported that he had had several subsequent "close calls" which re-enforced her need to restrict and closely supervise his activities.

3. Bodily Overconcerns

Hypochondriachal complaints, recurrent abdominal pain, and headaches or infantile fears which cause absence from school are frequent in the child while the mother is overly concerned about minor respiratory infections, keeps a close check on the child's bowel movements, and worries about "his poor color," the circles under the child's eyes, or his blueness when crying.

Mary B., 8-years-old, an only child, was brought to the pediatrician because of recurrent headaches and vague pains in her extremities and abdomen. The mother explained that Mary had always been sickly, suffering from repeated colds and stomach upsets. In the past year these symptoms interfered increasingly with school and social activities. The initial pediatric history and examination revealed an apprehensive child whose physical status and development were normal. During the first visit the mother used the word "sickly" and yet it was difficult to obtain a more specific notion as to what she meant. When the pediatrician asked about past illness, the mother initially described the colds and the headaches and bodily pains in terms that suggested the mother's apprehensions about her daughter's safety. The pediatrician commented that Mrs. B. seemed fearful that Mary was seriously ill. The mother said it always seemed serious and that she often felt foolish about her assessment of Mary's health. The doctor asked if Mary had ever been seriously ill, and Mrs. B.'s eyes filled with tears as she described her daughter's hospitalization at the age of 14 months for a severe diarrhea complicated by convulsions. The doctors had told Mr. and Mrs. B. that Mary might die, and for three days and nights as the child received medications and parenteral fluids and electrolytes, the parents, deeply religious, had made many vows as they prayed for the recovery of their only child. Implicit in the parents' vows was the foregoing of all aggression toward the child if her death would be postponed. "Will never do anything to upset her." The details of this traumatic experience emerged over a month's time, in the second and third interviews, as the pediatrician encouraged the mother to remember and tell him what had happened when ". . . Mary just about died." This encouragement by the physician had been preceded by an explanation of Mary's sound health, and followed by discussions of the child's need for firm guidance and appropriate discipline. The complaints disappeared in the next few months, as mother and child were seen once a month.

4. School Underachievment

Although formal learning difficulties have a more subtle association with the fear of a premature death, this relationship should be kept in mind. The expectation of a premature death is one cause for the hyperactive child who is blocked in learning at school. Often such underachievement is preceded by a separation anxiety in going to school, the child and mother sharing an unspoken agreement that the child is only safe in the presence of the mother. As separation anxiety becomes less prominent due to the practice of separation in going to school, the child is unable to concentrate freely on the learning exercises and content. When school failure is the main manifestation of this vulnerable child syndrome, pediatric evaluation often leads to a referral for psychiatric evaluation and treatment at an appropriate time after tactful, timely preparation.

THE PEDIATRIC INTERVIEW

The parents without exception do not spontaneously verbalize and are not aware of a relationship between the presenting complaints and their long-standing fear and belief that the child will prematurely die. Instead they "worry about him for no reason." Usually no intimation of this is given when the usual history of past medical illnesses is obtained. It is only in answer to such questions as, "How sick was he then?" "Was he seriously ill?" "Has your child ever been seriously ill?" "What did the doctor tell you during his illness?" or "Did you ever feel from what the doctor told you or from what you sensed that his condition was critical?" that they disclose this fear. This part of the anamnesis is frequently accompanied by a great deal of affect which dramatizes the apprehension and anxiety which many of these parents endure. While the parent appears to re-experience the frightening past history as she recalls, often in vivid detail, what the doctor said, and her own bewildering uncertainty often accompanied by feelings of nausea and emptiness, she also clearly is relieved to share with the physician these previously undisclosed fears.

PREDISPOSING FACTORS

Since not all children who recover from a critical illness develop this vulnerable child reaction, it was hypothesized that such families contain within their past or current history certain predisposing experiences which predate the serious illness. While the data permit a general estimation of such factors, a more exact quantification awaits further controlled investigations in which predictions are made after recovery of children from critical illnesses on the basis that certain predetermining factors are operative. Experiences to date suggest that this vulnerable child syndrome may follow a critical illness when the following historical facts or sets are also present.

    1   The patient is the first child born to older parents after they had resigned themselves to being childless because of many years of infertility or a succession of miscarriages or stillbirths. The parents do not expect to be able to have further children.

    2   The patient was born with a congenital anomaly.

    3   The patient was premature.

    4   The patient had an acquired handicap, e.g., epilepsy.

    5   The patient already has had a truly life-threatening illness, e.g., congenital virilizing adrenal hyperplasia, nephrosis, ulcerative colitis, or severe asthma.

    6   During pregnancy, the doctor had predicted that the fetus might die, e.g., because of maternal diabetes or because of a maternal-infant blood group incompatibility.

    7   The mother had a postpartum depression following the birth of the patient.

    8   Because of a hysterectomy or other sterilization procedure in either mother or father, the parents cannot have additional children.

    9   Conscious, strongly ambivalent feelings toward the patient are present, e.g., the mother of a baby born out of wedlock who had strong feelings of not wanting him.

10   An unresolved grief reaction related to the death of another child, a spouse, or some other close relative is present in a parent.

11   A hereditary disorder is present in the family, e.g., muscular dystrophy or cystic fibrosis.

12   There is a psychologic need in the mother to find something physically wrong with the patient, a displacement of unacceptable feelings toward the child, or of unacceptable thoughts and reactions associated with the birth of the child. Such a parent repeatedly brings her child for medical attention, usually to many doctors, for a host of complaints because of her certainty that the child has leukemia, a brain tumor, or some other elusive malignant disease even though a succession of doctors have been unable to make a diagnosis.

DETERMINANTS OF THE SYMPTOM PICTURE

Analysis of the case histories in this series suggests that the variability of the manifestations of this condition depends on the following factors:

1   The type of life-threatening disorder which the child experiences, e.g., the mother whose child recovers from a serious episode of diarrhea may view the later occurrence of abdominal pain with unwarranted alarm because of her expectation that a small child will die if he does not eat and absorb sufficiently, the abdominal pain being associated by the mother with impaired alimentation.

2   The child's constitutional characteristics, e.g., an asthmatic attack may be triggered in an allergic child in response to his mother's expectation of his premature death.

3   The psychological task that the child and his mother are focused on at a specific developmental level, e.g., a child may have a marked separation anxiety at the age of four, abdominal pain from five to ten, and feel depressed and pessimistic as he copes with his separation conflicts during adolescence.

4   The parents' experiences subsequent to the life-threatening illness, e.g., whether they have subsequent children and their experiences in regard to other deaths or threatened deaths in their family.

5   The child's subsequent health experiences, e.g., the child who is sickly with many infectious illnesses or is confronted with continuing defects has a different outlook, as does his parents, than the child who has vigorous physical health.

6   The nature of the parents' experiences with doctors, especially the physician who was responsible for the medical care of the child or who interpreted the life-threatening condition. The data suggest that the parents may find it most difficult to disentangle themselves from their lingering fears if this physician has an important reputation and/or serves as a consultant during the illness and then can no longer be seen, worked with, or doubted in terms of the magic of his power.

COMMENT

The data presented are consistent with the hypothesis that parental reactions to an acute, life-threatening illness in a child may have long-term psychologically deleterious effects on both parents and children. In one sense these reactions represent pathological after-effects of a persistent, disguised mourning reaction that was evoked by an earlier life-threatening illness of the child [1, 2]. Important developmental disturbances or somatic complaints arising after such an illness may thus be ascribable to determinants other than that illness, hospitalization, or surgery. This complex condition cannot be characterized simply because of the many factors that influence its manifestations and because of the variability of its symptomatology; however, there are three important, continuing themes that usually can be followed.

1   The past, life-threatening incident remains alive as an experience that attaches itself to many of the growing-up experiences; doom, failure, and disappointment are built into the anticipation by both mother and child of many new experiences, especially those that represent a significant advance in development, e.g., weaning, toilet training, separation, and school achievement. This reaction may either inhibit developmental progress or, by blocking such normal progression, cause deviant development. The most important and common reason for the persistence of this maladaptive orientation is the mother's resentment, guilt, and fear which have continued as residua from the time she tried to cope with the expectation that her child would die. This almost intolerably prolonged uncertainty and anxiety may be accompanied by the fleeting thought that everyone would be better off if the child would die. Such thoughts, of course, often augment the parents' guilt.

2   Although seemingly unrecognized by parents, the child regularly senses the mother's expectation of his vulnerability and accepts his mother's distorted mental image of himself. This is communicated in many subtle ways but mainly through the mother's moods and in her way of granting him autonomy and independence with fearful inhibiting reservations. It can also be observed in the mother's way of experiencing separation from the child.

Faced with an atmosphere in which the all-important adult, the parent, expects the child to die prematurely, the child may attempt to reduce this threatening danger by demonstrating that it has not happened or that the threat can be converted symbolically and displaced to a limited part of the body, e.g., abdominal pain. In the first instance the child attacks what he fears the most, that is, he challenges the expectation of death by behavior designed to prove that death will not occur. In the second instance of converting and displacing the threat to a limited part of the body, the child and parent have a definable symptom to take to the doctor for reassurance, in this way avoiding to some extent the painful awareness of the fear of dying. The child may also develop avoidance symptoms that stave off the "danger" of growing up to die and remain at infantile levels of psychosocial adaptation vowing like *Peter Pan:* "I won't grow up! I won't grow up!"

3 The child's symptoms usually represent among other things his and the mother's fear of separating and attempts at avoidance of separation. To do otherwise seems to imply the risk that one is inviting a realization of the expectation of death.

Robbins recently emphasized the need to consider the long-term consequences of a variety of kinds of incidents and the importance of associating causally events separated but related distantly in time: ". . . we are entering a new era in which we are facing the need for relating occurrences that are separated; not by days, weeks, or months, but by years. We must deal with relationships of greater complexity and subtlety and must consider the long-term consequences of a variety of kinds of incidents, many of which may now be considered benign and unimportant. . . . When we attempt to understand the genesis of behavior and emotional disorders, the need to relate distant events becomes especially important" [3].

It seems surprising that the pediatric or psychiatric literature contains relatively little concerning the long-term psychologic sequelae of acute, severe, non-fatal illness in children in contrast to the extensive bibliography on the effects of hospitalization and surgery. Recently, however, Rose and his colleagues described a "mothering disability" syndrome which developed in association with Rh blood group incompatibility or prematurity [4, 5].

MANAGEMENT

Once the *vulnerable child reaction* is recognized, the physician's authoritative statement, based on a thoughtful, cumulative history, physical and other pertinent examinations, that the child is physically sound represents the first therapeutic step. The next objective is to help the parents understand, first, that the symptoms are related to the child's being considered special in the family, and second, that this derives from the parental reaction to the acute, life-threatening illness. The ability of the parents to accept and utilize the physician's realistic assurance that the child is physically healthy and to understand the causal relationship between present behavior and past experience determines in great measure whether they can be helped in a pediatric environment or whether psychiatric treatment is necessary. It is important to point out that these parents are generally intelligent, well-educated, and emotionally healthy; often they are not experiencing problems with their other children. When they are able to recognize and accept the reasons for their unnecessary concern and for the child's responsive behavior, the mutual re-enforcement of anxiety and symptoms is interrupted. The parents become enabled to set limits for the child, discontinue the patterns of infantilization and overprotectiveness, make proper sleeping arrangements, deal more effectively with problems of separation, be more realistic about the child's complaints, and stop recounting to him or to others in his hearing about the time that they "almost lost him."

This vulnerable child syndrome dramatizes a clear opportunity for secondary prevention of emotional disturbances following severe, acute illnesses in children and points the way to primary prevention. Such illnesses are *psychologically* as well as *physically* hazardous. Discussion with the parents of the significance of an illness is a serious obligation. The physician's thoughtful statements in this regard must reflect to the best of his knowledge the exact state of affairs without over- or understatement. The designation "critically ill" should be employed only when clearly indicated. The parents should be informed of this by the doctor, preferably in person, rather than by a nurse or ward clerk who may feel a need to supply answers to the parents' questions. As soon as commensurate with improvement, the patient should be taken off the critical list. Unfortunately, an occasional physician will tend rather regularly in judging the seriousness of an acute illness to overestimate this and to share needlessly with the parents his own anxieties. This is a professional liability, especially when it is unrecognized by the physician. Certain routine hospital practices such as placing all prematurely born infants or all children with meningitis on the critical list may also be questioned. Physicians sometimes believe that they must employ the term "critically ill" in relation to all seriously ill children in order to "protect" themselves or their reputations in the event that the child unexpectedly dies. The authors concur with the advice given by a senior colleague, responsible over the years for the care of hundreds of seriously ill children, that in situations of this kind, the physician should not permit concern about this reputation to guide him in deciding when to call a child critically ill.

Once recovery has occurred, the physician must resist the temptation to impress the parents with seriousness of the illness from which the child has recovered. This is of especial importance in view of evidence that in some cases this vulnerable child syndrome is an iatrogenic disorder. Such retrospective comments as, "If he had gotten here an hour later, we wouldn't have been able to save him," or "I thought sure he would die," though commonly made and superficially innocuous, serve no helpful purpose and are potentially harmful.

Before discharge the physician should emphasize, if this is true, that recovery is or will be complete, that no special precautions will be necessary after a certain time and that the child will not be more vulnerable than other children to illness. The physician may also point out that after a child's recovery from a severe illness, many parents have a natural inclination to wonder if they could have prevented it in some vague way and, since the child was so sick, there is a natural inclination to treat him specially, a tendency that actually becomes disadvantageous to both the parents and the child. He should also indicate the importance of seeing the family again if the parents come to recognize such a bent on their part. When the physician concerned is a consultant and not the regular family physician, this invitation to return may be especially important. A definite return appointment should be made when the doctor suspects that the parents may not be able to carry this off on their own, e.g., when the physician knows of predisposing factors in the family history. While such preventive intervention may not be regularly effective, it would appear that some maladaptive reactions in this susceptible population may be aborted or confined. We would suggest that the parents be asked to return without the child to discuss their questions and observations of the child about which they wish clarification. This type of follow-up conveys specifically that the child is well and not in need of medical attention and provides the parents with an opportunity to ventilate reactions, concerns, fears, and questions that come up when they are "alone" with their recently ill child, now recovered, at home.

SUMMARY AND CONCLUSIONS

1   A group of clinical features constituting a *vulnerable child syndrome* is reported and described in 25 children with a history of an illness or accident from which they recovered although the parents were expecting a fatal outcome.

2   This paper describes a study of this group based on the hypotheses that children who are expected by their parents to die prematurely often react with a disturbance in phychosocial development and in the parent-child relationship.

3   Outstanding clinical features include difficulty with separation, infantile behavior, bodily overconcerns, and school underachievement.

4   Predisposing factors and determinants of the symptomatology are discussed along with suggestions for management and prevention.

REFERENCES

1   Solnit, A. J., and Green, M.: Psychologic considerations in the management of deaths on pediatric hospital services. I. The doctor and the child's family. Pediatrics, 24:106, 1959.

2   Solnit, A. J., and Green, M.: Pediatric management of the dying child. II. A study of the child's reaction to the fear of dying. *In* Modern Perspectives in Child Development. New York: International Universities Press, Inc., p. 217, 1963.

3   Robbins, F. C.: The long view. *Amer. J. Dis. Child.,* 104:499, 1962.

4   Rose, J. A., Boggs, T. R., Jr., Alderstein, A., *et al.:* The evidence for a syndrome of "Mothering Disability" consequent to threats to the survival of neonates: A design for hypothesis testing including prevention in a prospective study. *Amer. J. Dis. Child,* 100:776, 1960.

5   Rose, J. A.: The dimensions of comprehensive pediatrics. Pediatrics, 26:729, 1960.

Psychologic Sequelae of Early Infancy Health Crises

William B. Carey, M.D.
Department of Pediatrics, University of Pennsylvania Medical School at the Children's Hospital of Philadelphia

Although others had discussed the phenomenon previously, Green and Solnit [1] first coined the useful term, the "vulnerable child syndrome." They described 25 children who had behavior problems and who in their backgrounds had the common feature of an illness or accident, mostly in early infancy, from which they had fully recovered although their parents had expected them to die. The authors offered the hypothesis that the illness experience itself left the parents with the feeling that the child was henceforth unusually vulnerable to serious illness or accidents and might well die during childhood.

A recent paper, "The Vulnerable Children Revisited" [2], concluded that severe illness in infancy does not by itself predispose the child to behavior problems unless the family reacts abnormally. Before anyone accepts either of these apparently conflicting views as the last word on the subject, he should be fully acquainted with the great complexity of the problem. No investigation to date has studied properly the many variables longitudinally.

This report reviews the pertinent literature that is published and some that is unpublished, constructs a more complete theoretical framework of the elements involved, and makes some suggestions as to how the practitioner can best manage the situation until we have better data.

There are four main conclusions to be drawn from the information currently available.

From *Clinical Pediatrics,* vol. 8, no. 8 pp. 459–463 (August 1969).

1   The most important etiologic factor in any subsequent behavioral disturbance is the variable maternal reaction to the baby's illness—not the physician's opinion as to the objective severity of the illness.

It is the mother's reaction to the illness, not the doctor's, that affects the way she handles her child afterwards. Her concerns are not necessarily the same as the doctor's in either quality or extent.

VARIOUS REACTIONS TO MAJOR PROBLEMS

Reports have been published on postpartum reactions to prematurity [3], gross mental defect [4], cleft palate [5], congenital heart disease [6–8] and erythroblastosis [9]. All conditions have common features such as grief and guilt but they also have particular variations.

It seems that the more dramatic or early the illness the greater is the problem of adaptation for the mothers. For example, few newborn health crises have the emotional impact of erythroblastosis fetalis which requires exchange transfusions. Rose [9] has reported on a group of 88 mothers of such babies, interviewed when their children were four or five years old. Most of the mothers recalled traumatic emotional reactions beginning in the neonatal period with persisting distorted perceptions of the child.

Yet some major problems seem to present greater emotional hazards than others. Gibson [10] found this in studying the behavioral sequelae of various gastrointestinal abnormalities that required surgery in early infancy. The greatest disturbance, as determined by four projective tests, followed prolonged food intake problems and postsurgical anal manipulations.

OVERREACTING TO MINOR PROBLEMS

There is evidence, furthermore, from clinical experience and research that objectively trivial medical problems also can prove to be a real threat for the postpartum mother. For example, through ignorance and inadequate medical support she may conclude that the use of forceps for delivery made her "instrument baby" somehow special and less than normal.

One study [11] has suggested that even the threat of neonatal illness may be associated with behavior disturbance. Of 1,000 newborn infants 105 were placed in special nurseries for observation because of a variety of reasons such as possible infection and after Caesarean sections. None had any pregnancy complications, and none developed any neonatal illness. All were judged completely normal by physical examination on discharge and at one year. Yet, at one year of age 11.6 per cent had behavior deviation as compared to 4.4 per cent of those with a completely uncomplicated neonatal course, a highly significant difference. Even though this study did not appraise maternal attitudes in the neonatal period, its findings do raise the question of whether an illness needs to be life-threatening for the postpartum mother to be upset in an enduring way.

In a related investigation [12] of 62 infants with pregnancy or neonatal complications, the 23 mothers who expressed distress about the complications and feared death or defect in the infant were "more apt to be high in controlling behavior, (excessive) closeness and hostility." Their infants exhibited significantly more behavior deviation at 18 months. It is not clear why these women reacted differently from the others.

A dramatic parallel appears in the recently reported "PKU Anxiety Syndrome" [13]. Acute or chronic anxiety that their babies are or will become mentally retarded may persist in some of the parents who have received reports of a positive PKU test later proven false, despite repeated subsequent negative tests and considerable reassurance and support from their physicians.

A possibly similar phenomenon has been noted by Waldrop *et al.* [14] in a group of presumably normal nursery school children. Those with several minor physical anomalies, such as unruly hair or epicanthal folds, have shown more hyperkinetic, aggressive and intractable behavior, possibly because their appearance had resulted in their mothers being less supportive and more restrictive.

UNDERREACTING TO PROBLEMS

Of 19 mothers in an intensive longitudinal study of child rearing in Cleveland two expressed what was thought by the investigators to be inadequate concern or denial about rather severe problems in their babies [15]. One can expect that this reaction might occur in several situations: (1) probably most often when parents cannot bring themselves to accept the bad news at first; (2) if the parents believe that the doctor is expressing more concern than is called for by the problem, such as when they have had a previous good outcome from the same peril; and (3) when the physician has failed adequately to communicate his well-founded concern.

2 The maternal reaction to the health crisis is a compound of several factors beside the illness itself and the mother's vulnerability, particularly the quality of the medical care given.

MOTHER'S VULNERABILITY

The mother's vulnerability, her susceptibility to the emotional trauma of the illness, may come from having inadequate intelligence or knowledge or from her negative feelings about childrearing in general or this child in particular. Her feelings about her capacity as a mother may be affected profoundly by her own experiences while being reared. Her previous experiences with the patient and with other children may color her attitude toward him should a health crisis come [1, 16].

Levy [17] pointed out that maternal overprotectiveness often followed illness in the children of the 20 women he studied. He viewed the illness "not as a genetic factor but as a strengthening element in an attitude already present, weighing it, however, with the measure of the external event." He was not studying the effect of the child's illness on mothers not already exhibiting overprotective behavior.

The discrepancy between the doctor's concern and the mother's perceptions of the neonatal problem is possibly partly explained in the perspective of the maturational crisis theory [18]. Caplan has shown how women normally experience a disturbance of their emotional equilibrium during and immediately after pregnancy, making them capable of forming irrational attitudes in a way not found before or after. Using his terminology, we can speak of these illnesses and health threats as early infancy "health crises."

THE CHILD'S ROLE

The participation of the child in any pathologic interaction is overlooked too often. He may have residual damage to his central nervous system from the illness [19]. He may have allergies that produce diseases such as asthma and become the focus of maternal anxiety. The child with a difficult temperament would present far more cause for concern to his mother than the one who is easy-going [20].

THE EXTERNAL SITUATION

The general psychosocial environment of mother and child may affect the way she responds to the illness in the child. The emotional supports from her family at the time of the illness and in the months that follow may be of critical importance in determining how well she adapts to the stressful experience. Unrelated physical, psychologic or social problems in herself or her family may weigh her down and make adjustment difficult [1, 16].

Werner et al. [21] have pointed out that after perinatal stress of various forms "the quality of the home environment had a significant effect on both mental and social development by age two, and the effect increased with the severity of perinatal complications." Several investigations of the mental and behavioral outcome of premature infants have yielded similar conclusions [22–24].

MEDICAL CARE

If a mother has a health crisis to adjust to in her baby's early infancy, surely the understanding of it and emotional support provided by the physician are of great importance to her. He may be the deciding factor in resolving her emotional reaction in a healthy direction. If she is given insufficient information or not allowed to bring up her fears for discussion, she is likely to be left with a distorted view of her child. Pediatricians often pay insufficient attention to the way their words and actions influence the outcome of these events.

3   The variety of mother-child interactions resulting from these health crises apparently leads to a wide range of psychologic sequelae in the child.

As mentioned already, infants may sustain physical damage from early illnesses, such as impairment of the central nervous system [16]. Also, behavioral symptoms may be from a combination of physical and environmental factors. This discussion is confined to nonorganic psychologic sequelae.

Adequate data are not available now to permit a statement about the frequency of the various sorts of outcomes. We only mention the possibilities.

EXCELLENT OUTCOME

Eminence in adulthood can be the ultimate outcome of early infancy health crises for some individuals. Newton, Voltaire, Wesley, Keats, Victor Hugo, Pavlova and Churchill were born prematurely. Not expected to survive the immediate newborn period were: Samuel Johnson, Thomas Hardy, Picasso and Rousseau. Others who had life-threatening illnesses in infancy were Pascal and Schweitzer [25]. Whether such prominence came because of or in spite of the early health problems is open to speculation.

DEVIANT OUTCOME

Abnormal psychologic sequelae to early infancy health crises include both behavioral and psychosomatic problems.

Green and Solnit [1] described the vulnerable child syndrome as having the principal features of difficulty in separation, infantile behavior, bodily overconcerns and school underachievement.

Rose [9] found that the majority of his four- to five-year-old children who had had erythroblastosis were exhibiting problems in behavior control, mostly overcontrol and unaggressiveness. He also suggested that the mother's fears might make her withdraw from normal contact with the baby and by understimulation cause him to be environmentally retarded.

Psychosomatic problems such as infantile colic [26] and abdominal pain [27] appear related at times to early infancy health crises.

NORMAL OUTCOME

Probably a goodly number of children emerging from health crises in early infancy evolve into children and adults who are generally considered normal by themselves and others. What the percentage and circumstances of this favorable outcome may be nobody can say at this time. It may be that most mothers and infants do all right if the crisis is not too overwhelming and if the other circumstances are not too disruptive of the mother's ability to adapt.

4 Inadequate data should not lead the pediatrician to belittle the possible importance of these health crises, nor should it deter him from conscientious attempts to manage them to the best of his ability.

Various spokesmen [1, 16] have exhorted pediatricians to manage more skillfully the feelings of the mother in early infancy health crises. Kennell and Rolnick [28] give some excellent specific suggestions on discussing problems in newborn babies with their parents. Green and Solnit [1] offer a way of dealing with the vulnerable child syndrome later on, when the child has developed symptoms, and also some principles for prevention. Little, however, is available to the pediatrician in the form of general plans of management of proven value.

Rose [16] described the pediatrician's role as twofold: (1) to maintain the developmental capacity in the child, that is, to do anything he can for the infant's physical well-being; and (2) to provide the mother with emotional support by presenting her with the realities of the situation and by helping her adapt to these realities. To do the latter, he suggested, the pediatrician should allow her to verbalize any distorted perceptions of the child, a process which of itself should produce a healthy shift in her attitude.

In addition to this step it would seem logical to include: (1) approving her appropriate attitudes and plans; (2) trying to give insight into and suppression of her inappropriate attitudes and plans; (3) mobilizing family support to the maximum; and (4) calling for psychiatric or social work help if her own problems or social situation are getting in the way of a reasonable adjustment to the situation. The pediatrician's availability, interest, and willingness to listen may be most important. This approach does seem to make sense, though there is as yet no proof that it will improve the ultimate outcome of early infancy health crises.

REFERENCES

1 Green, M. and Solnit, A. J.: Reactions to the threatened loss of a child; a vulnerable child syndrome. Pediatrics 34: 58, 1961.

2   Costanza, M., Lipsitch, I. and Charney, E.: The vulnerable children revisited. Clin. Pediat. 7: 680, 1968.

3   Kaplan, D. M. and Mason, E. A.: Maternal reactions to premature birth viewed as an acute emotional disorder. Amer. J. Orthopsychiat. 30: 539, 1960.

4   Solnit, A. J. and Stark, M. H.: Mourning and the birth of a defective child. Psychoanal. Stud. Child. 16: 523, 1961.

5   Tisza, V. B. and Gumpertz, E.: The parents' reaction to the birth and early care of children with cleft palate. Pediatrics 30: 86, 1962.

6   Glaser, H. H., Harrison, G. S. and Lynn, D. B.: Emotional implications of congenital heart disease in children. *Ibid.* 33: 367, 1964.

7   Linde, L. M., Rasof, B., Dunn, O. J. and Rabb, E.: Attitudinal factors in congenital heart disease. *Ibid.* 38: 92, 1966.

8   Offord, D. R. and Aponte, J. F.: Distortion of disability and effect on family life. J. Amer. Acad. Child Psychiat. 6: 499, 1967.

9   Rose, J. A. and Adlerstein, A. E.: The factors affecting maternal adaptations in cases of blood group incompatibility between adult and offspring. Presented at Fourth International Congress of Child Psychiatry in Holland in August, 1962. Unpublished. Abstract in Amer. J. Dis. Child. 100: 776, 1960.

10   Gibson, R. M.: Trauma in early infancy and later personality development. Psychosom. Med. 27: 229, 1965.

11   Cecil, H. S., Carey, W. B. and Rigg, L. I.: Neonatal health complications and deviant behavior. Unpublished.

12   Cecil, H. S., Rigg, L. I., Coleman, L. T. and Fondi, M.: The psychological effects of pregnancy and neonatal health threats on child development. Presented at meeting of American Orthopsychiatric Association, New York, March 1969.

13   Rothenberg, M. B. and Sills, E. M.: Iatrogenesis; the PKU anxiety syndrome. J. Amer. Acad. Child Psychiat. 7: 689, 1968.

14   Waldrop, M. F., Pederson, F. A. and Bell, R. Q.: Minor physical anomalies and behavior in pre-school children. Child Develop. 39: 391, 1968.

15   Kennell, J. H.: Personal communication.

16   Rose, J. A.: The prevention of mothering breakdown associated with physical abnormalities in the infant. *In* Caplan, G., ed., Prevention of Mental Disorders in Children. New York, Basic Books, 1961. pp. 265–282.

17   Levy, D. M.: Maternal Overprotection. New York, Columbia University Press, 1943, p. 45.

18   Caplan, G. (ed.): Prevention of Mental Disorders in Children. New York, Basic Books, 1961, pp. 398–416.

19   Pasamanick, B. and Knobloch, H.: Epidemiologic studies on the complications of pregnancy and the birth process. In Ref. 18: pp. 74–94.

20   Thomas, A., Chess, S. and Birch, H. G.: Temperament and Behavior Disorders in Children. New York, New York University Press, 1968, p. 75.

21   Werner, E., Simonian, K., Bierman, J. M. and French, F. E.: Cumulative effect of perinatal complications and deprived environment on physical, intellectual and social development of preschool children. Pediatrics 39: 490, 1967.

22   Bacola, E., Behrle, F. C., de Schweinitz, L., Miller, H. C. and Mira, M.: Peri-

natal and environmental factors in late neurogenic sequelae. Amer. J. Dis. Child. 112: 369, 1966.

23 Wortis, H. and Freedman, A.: The contribution of social environment to the development of premature children. Amer. J. Orthopsychiat. 35: 57, 1965.

24 Drillien, C. M.: The incidence of mental and physical handicaps in school age children of very low birth weight. II. Pediatrics 39: 238, 1967.

25 Illingworth, R. S.: Lessons from Childhood. Baltimore, Williams and Wilkins Company, 1966, chapter 5.

26 Carey, W. B.: Maternal anxiety and infantile colic. Clin. Pediat. 7: 590, 1968.

27 Green, M.: Psychogenic, recurrent, abdominal pain. Pediatrics 40: 84, 1967.

28 Kennell, J. H. and Rolnick, A. R.: Discussing problems in newborn babies with their parents. Ibid. 26: 832, 1960.

Failure to Thrive: A Retrospective Profile

Eleanor Shaheen, M.D.
Staff Doctor, Child Health Department, University of Missouri

Doris Alexander, M.S.W., A.C.S.W. and Marie Truskowsky, R.N.
Children's Hospital of Philadelphia

Giulio J. Barbero, M.D.
Professor and Chairman, Department of Health, University of Missouri School of Medicine

Growth failure is an important manifestation of illness in childhood. An extensive list of somatic disturbances are recognized to result in growth failure, but there remains a group of children in whom no clear organic etiology can be demonstrated by traditional methods. It has long been observed that the problem of growth failure may arise in situations of environmental deprivation [1–10]. Such a syndrome has been called by various names such as environmental, sensory or maternal deprivation, and recently, failure-to-thrive in order to avoid specific etiologic implications [4, 11, 13]. In a recent report [14], the authors define features of this clinical syndrome of childhood as growth and developmental failure accompanied by psychosocial disruption followed by improvement on placement in a nurturing environment. The purpose of this present report is to present the incidence of children with growth failure without specific organic etiology in a children's hospital setting, and to examine various clinical and environmental aspects of these children.

From *Clinical Pediatrics*, vol. 7, no. 5, pp. 255–261 (May 1968).

METHOD OF STUDY

The children in this study were all hospitalized in the Children's Hospital of Philadelphia, a 164 bed teaching institution. Although it has many admissions from the local urban area, much of the patient load is derived by referral from practicing pediatricians and general practitioners of the surrounding communities.

The third percentile on the Children's Medical Center of Boston Anthropometric charts was arbitrarily chosen as the critical weight for a given age. All children falling below that point were included in this study. The charts of all children, except infants of low birthweight who were under six months of age on admission and adolescents above 13 years, were screened by weights initially for the period between July 1, 1963, and June 30, 1964.

During this period there had been 6,979 admissions, corrected to 5,700 individual children by excluding re-admissions. The exclusion of 128 children who were over 13 years of age and 70 prematures under six months left 5,488 children for the study.

As seen in Table 1, 287 (5%) of the 5,488 showed a weight below the third percentile at the time of admission. The charts of these 287 children were then reviewed more intensively and separated into various systemic categories to further single out the group of patients who could be characterized as having growth failure with no clear physical or laboratory findings to account for the disruption in growth. It was found that 15.2 per cent (44) of the 287 patients fell into the pure failure to thrive category, second in size only to the neurologic group among the various diseases or systemic entities (Table 2).

In our study a case was included in a particular systemic category whenever there was even slight evidence of that specific diagnosis, rather

Table 1   Number of Admissions in the Children's Hospital of Philadelphia with Weight below the Third Percentile from July 1, 1963 to June 30, 1964

Total admissions	5,488*
Total admissions below the third percentile	287 (5.0%)
Systemic disease group	243
Failure-to-thrive group	44

*Excluded:	Patients >13 years	128
	Prematures <6 months	70
	No weight data	16

Table 2   Diagnostic Distribution of Admissions under the Third Percentile in Weight

Neurologic	52
Failure to thrive	44
Cardiac	38
Gastro-intestinal	26
Cong. anomalies	22
Cystic fibrosis	17
Respiratory	16
Genito-urinary	14
Surgical	13
Endocrine	12
Blood and tumors	10
ENT and dental	14
Skeletal	2
Miscellaneous	7
Total	287

than in the failure-to-thrive group. This resulted perhaps in a lower incidence of the failure-to-thrive group than might occur from an anterospective study. The 44 medical charts in the failure-to-thrive group were further studied for delineation of various medical and psychosocial factors. Data were also secured from the hospital social work and financial departments and from community social service exchange files.

ANALYSIS OF FAILURE-TO-THRIVE GROUP

Our 44 cases consisted of children with clear growth failure, but without obvious organic disease; they showed nothing on physical examination indicative of a specific disorder or rapid cessation of any symptoms which they had prior to admission (anorexia, vomiting, or diarrhea most frequently). In addition to a history and physical examination. the majority had most of the following studies: gastro-intestinal x-rays of the esophagus, stomach, small and large intestine; intravenous urogram; skull and long bone x-rays; serum electrolytes; blood urea nitrogen; sweat test; urinalysis; urine culture; complete blood count; and xylose tolerance test—all of which were reported to be within normal range. In spite of negative clinical and laboratory findings, we felt that this group might be one of heterogeneous nature; nevertheless, it seemed useful to analyze these cases for various

Table 3 Age and Diagnostic Distribution of Admissions below the Third Percentile in Weight

Ages	Systemic disease	Failure to thrive
0–5 mos.	40 ⎤	9 ⎤
6–11	41 ⎱ 132	20 ⎱ 35
12–17	32 ⎰ 54%	33 ⎰ 80%
18–23	19 ⎦	3 ⎦
2–4 yrs.	49	4
5–7	52	3
8–13	10	2
Total	243	44

factors to determine any prevailing clinical features which subsequently could be examined in an anterospective study.

Age

Analysis of the group by age (Table 3) showed that 54.3 per cent of the systemic disease and 79.5 per cent of the failure-to-thrive group were below two years of age. It is interesting that failure to thrive was observed less frequently over two years of age in this population.

Birthweight

To clarify the possible role of low birthweight as an etiologic factor in subsequent low weight, an examination of the records of the 39 failure to thrive infants below two years of age revealed that 41 per cent were below 5 lb. 8 oz. at birth (Table 4). Full term gestational age had been attained by only three of these infants.

Table 4 Distribution of Birthweights of Patients with Failure to Thrive

Weight in pounds	Number of cases
3 lbs. 9 oz.–4 lbs. 8 oz.	3 ⎤
4 lbs. 9 oz.–5 lbs. 8 oz.	13 ⎦ 41%
5 lbs. 9 oz.–6 lbs. 8 oz.	13
6 lbs. 9 oz.–7 lbs. 8 oz.	6
7 lbs. 9 oz.–8 lbs. 8 oz.	4
No data	5
Total	44

Other Clinical Features

The failure-to-thrive group showed an equal distribution with respect to sex: 20 boys and 24 girls; race: 21 were Negro and 23 White; and hospital service: 22 were ward and 22 were private patients.

While the presenting complaint by the parent was failure to grow or gain weight in 16 cases, 28 presented with systemic symptoms. Seventeen had gastro-intestinal symptoms such as anorexia, vomiting and diarrhea; seven had symptoms of the respiratory system; and four had miscellaneous complaints. The symptomatic cases were characterized by cessation of clinical manifestations during the early period of hospitalization. Early recognition of the failure-to-thrive syndrome is most often clouded by those infants with somatic symptoms.

Pregnancy History

The pregnancy history was recorded in 37 cases and was complicated in 21 (57%). Complications included toxemia, premature delivery, nervous disturbances, staining and bleeding, intercurrent illness and amniotic fluid loss.

Social History

Social factors may play a role in certain cases of growth failure in infants. We examined five specific areas:

I   Family constellation
   A   Ordinate of patient
       The failure-to-thrive patient was the youngest child in his family in 35 of our 44 cases. In four families, the patient was an only child, and in another four, he was the oldest. No data were available on one foster child.
   B   Multiple or twin births
       Four of our failure-to-thrive patients were one of a twin pair. Twin births were also noted among siblings of another two of our patients.
   C   Age and spacing of siblings in relation to patient
       Table 5 shows that 47.6 per cent of our patients came from families of three or less children. In 12 cases, the birth of the patient and his next sibling occurred only one to two years apart, and in an additional ten cases, there was one year or less spacing between the patient and his sibling. At the other extreme, two cases had spacing of more than ten years between births. No data were available on five cases in which the patient had siblings.
   D   Age of parents
       At the time of hospitalization, maternal age was noted in 37 cases and paternal age in 35 cases (Table 6). It is interesting that our failure-to-thrive cases are *not* arising predominantly among very young parents.
   E   Two parent, single parent or other major caretaker

Table 5 Family Size of Forty-four Patients with Failure to Thrive

Number of children/family	Frequency
1	4 ⎫
2	8 ⎬ 47.6%
3	8 ⎭
4	5 ⎫
5	4 ⎬ 38.1%
6	7 ⎭
7	3 ⎫
8	1 ⎬ 14.2%
9	2 ⎭

Of the 44 cases studied, 31 (70.5%) were from two parent families; nine had a single parent; and the remaining four were under foster parent care. In only six instances was the mother employed outside the home.

II Socioeconomic status

Table 7 summarizes the occupational status of the father in 33 cases. In the six cases where the mother was employed outside the home, her occupation was housekeeper, babysitter, domestic service, nurse's aide, or power machine operator.

The important areas of educational status of the parents and income could not adequately be assessed due to lack of data. Thirteen medical histories did note financial stress, however. Especially significant was the fact that 21 of the 30 families having three or more children were dependent on public assistance for their livelihood or required state financing for hospitalization.

Table 6 Age of Parents with Failure to Thrive

	Mothers	Fathers
Under 20 years	6	1
20–29 years	18	14
30–39 years	10	13
40–49 years	2	4
50 years	1	3
Total	37	35

**Table 7 Occupational Status of Parents of Patients
with Failure to Thrive**

Father			Mother	
I	Semi-skilled and unskilled	8	I Housewife	38
II	Skilled	7	II Employed	6
III	Domestic and services	4		
IV	Waiters	2		
V	Self-employed	4		
VI	Salesman	3		
VII	Engineers	4		
VIII	Professional	1		
	Total	33		44

Substandard quality housing was noted in six cases. Five cases later became known to the relocation or housing authorities.

III Disruption in patient's immediate family

   A Health of parents

Of the 44 cases, 32 had adequate histories for study. Sixteen mothers had varying degrees of chronic and acute physical ailments, and nine exhibited emotional problems of varying degrees. The histories were less adequate in regard to the fathers, but seven were noted to have serious health complications. One father had been diagnosed as a failure-to-thrive in his own infancy. A few parents, now asymptomatic, had had serious illnesses in childhood. Five sets of parents had health complications in both members.

   B Health of siblings

Of the 16 failure-to-thrive cases with recorded health complications among their siblings, physical illness included allergies, celiac disease, pyelonephritis, cleft palate, cerebral palsy, club feet, asthma, epilepsy, sickle cell anemia, cardiac defects or other similar chronic conditions. More than one sibling in a family was affected in 11 of the 16 cases. Surprisingly, only two cases of failure to grow were discovered among siblings of our patients, and they eventually were described as normal in growth and development.

Four cases had siblings with severe emotional problems or mental retardation. In one of the four, two siblings were affected.

   C Death of parents or siblings

No parents were reported as deceased. Two cases had a deceased sibling; one died two hours after delivery and the other died at two months of age. Miscarriages were noted among three cases.

   D Disruption in caretaking of patient and siblings

Eight cases in addition to the four children in foster care had multiple caretakers or disruption in caretaking. One patient had been cared for by a "nurse relative" from age three months to age eight months in another state while the parents were establishing themselves in the Philadelphia area; another was frequently left alone and unattended; one patient whose mother worked was alternately cared for by the maternal grandmother and a 12-year-old aunt; another was cared for by a 16-year-old pregnant aunt while the mother worked; and in one family, local social agencies had to intervene by placing more than one child. One patient from this family expired after placement in foster care due to injuries inflicted by a ten-year-old grandson of the foster parents.

Disruption in caretaking was also characteristic of the children who had been placed in foster care prior to the patients' hospitalization.

E Illegitimacy of patient and siblings
Nine of our patients were born out of wedlock. In two additional cases, there were illegitimate siblings, but the mother had married by the time of the patient's birth.

F Unwanted or unplanned pregnancy
This area was recorded in only six cases, but significantly, four mothers had tubal ligations following the birth of the failure-to-thrive patient.

G Previous hospitalization of patient
There were previous hospitalizations among half of the cases. Three additional patients had prolonged stays in the nursery after delivery. There were repeated hospitalizations, each several weeks in duration among some. For example, one patient was hospitalized for growth failure three times in local hospitals and also in two specialty children's hospitals without specific organic etiology being found. The meaning of these previous separations of mother and child needs further evaluation.

H Parental perception of defect or damage in patient
In 24 cases, the mother expressed direct concern about some damage or defect in the patient. Eleven of these patients were felt to be slower than their siblings in total development. Fears were frequently expressed that the affected child had been damaged at birth or that he would die from his problem.

I Quality of caretaking
Poor caretaking was sufficiently evident to be commented upon in 12 charts. The descriptions were occasionally as pronounced as "strong suspicion of battering" with multiple fractures resulting in a medical report to authoritative agencies dealing with the problem, or "abandonment." Some parents were described as so preoccupied with other stresses that they were not adequately attuned to the patient's needs.

J Marital instability
Instability was reported in 15 of our 44 cases, usually noted only in terms of separation or descriptions of the father being frequently unavailable or nonsupportive.

K Geographical or social mobility
Only one case reported family disorganization while parents were locat-

ing in Philadelphia; in this case, the parents left the patient in another state under the care of a relative until the family settled.

IV Disruption in extended families

    A Health of close relatives

    Grandparents, aunts, and uncles were described as having an acute or chronic illness in 26 cases. No data were available in ten cases.

    B Death of close relatives

    Although the timing of death was seldom recorded and the family's pattern of coping with grief seldom noted, there were 20 cases in which death of close relatives had occurred, including two suicides. In addition to loss of patients' grandparents, parents had also suddenly lost their own siblings in five cases from such conditions as pneumonia, leukemia, childbirth, and tuberculosis. One mother had four deceased siblings including a set of twins.

    C Deprivation in extended family

    This area was recorded in only six cases. Gross situations recorded include divorce, foster care or dependency involvement of patients' families on the Department of Public Assistance or the courts. It is of interest that two sets of parents were both reared in foster care themselves, and each was currently in the process of separation, necessitating foster placement for their children.

    D Conflicts with extended family

    Conflicts were described in six cases. This was reported as pronounced domination or criticism of the parents by close relatives. In one instance, the mother stated that she had been forced to leave home by her own mother when she became pregnant.

V Pattern of community health and welfare agency involvement

    The Philadelphia-Camden Social Service Exchange registered each of the 44 cases for some assessment of the families' involvement with community agencies as another indicator of whether family disorganization was present. Some agency involvement was shown in 62 per cent of the 44 cases. Since nearly half of the patients resided outside of the metropolitan area where the social service exchange registration is not widely used, our figure is probably too low.

    Nineteen cases showed activity with as many as one to six agencies prior to hospitalization of the patient. Fifteen cases were reported to the Children's Hospital of Philadelphia Social Work Department during the patient's hospitalization (seven of the 15 had had no agency involvement prior to hospitalization). Nineteen showed agency contact after the patient's discharge, only one of which had no prior agency involvement. Agencies included the Philadelphia Society to Protect Children, Juvenile and Domestic Relations Courts, Department of Public Assistance, child placement agencies, Department of Public Welfare, Public Health Nursing, and Relocation Bureau.

In this study it was possible to tabulate approximately ten areas of stress (as tabulated in the analysis of cases) with which these families were coping. Any one of these could influence the parents' caretaking and relationship to our patients. Only four cases showed less than three areas of stress in the family. In six cases, eight areas of stress were noted; three revealed nine or more. It was possible to know a great deal about the external and situational stresses encountered by these families, but knowledge of internal family stresses is rudimentary in this retrospective review.

HOSPITALIZATION

Table 8 tabulates the weight changes occurring during hospitalization in 36 of our failure-to-thrive infants under two years of age. Eight stayed less than one week; 13 stayed between one and two weeks; eight remained three weeks; seven were hospitalized between three and five weeks. Only one out of 15 infants remaining over two weeks failed to gain weight by the end of the hospitalization, and of the total sample, 23 (63.8%) gained weight regardless of the length of hospitalization. All of the weights on discharge, despite the gains, were still below the third percentile on the growth curve. In many instances signs of progress in developmental milestones and disappearance of symptomatic manifestations were described.

FOLLOW UP ON 32 CHILDREN

Follow up growth data, six to 40 months after discharge from the hospital, were obtained on 32 of the original group of 36 children under two years of age. Contact was made through the referring physicians. No follow up data are available in four patients who could not be located. In 29, the duration

Table 8 Weight Changes during Hospitalization of Thirty-six Infants with Failure to Thrive

Days of hosp.	No. of patients	Gained			Lost	
		>1 lb.	<1 lb.	Same	>1 lb.	<1 lb.
1–6	8	2	1	3	0	2
7–13	13	2	4	1	0	6
14–20	8	4	3	0	0	1
21–27	3	3	0	0	0	0
28–36	4	4	0	0	0	0
		63.8%		11.2%	25%	

of follow up was greater than 15 months, while the other three were seen within six to 12 months after discharge. In each of the latter three cases, the weight had increased above the third percentile. The follow up data are outlined in Table 9. It shows that 78 per cent were above the third percentile in weight at the end of the follow up period.

With respect to height, 14 of the 23 cases in whom there were data available on follow up were below the third percentile when discharged from the hospital, but by the end of the follow up period, only six remained below the third percentile.

COMMENTARY

This retrospective survey was undertaken to obtain evidence of the frequency of growth failure in infants in the absence of demonstrable organic abnormality. The incidence is high in a pediatric hospital population, second only to neurologic disorders as a basis of growth failure. In spite of variations in type and duration of hospitalization, two-thirds of these infants gained weight during hospitalization. In long-term follow up, three-fourths of the infants were within normal limits in weight and height two years after hospitalization. Such observations indicate that the primary basis of growth failure without organic etiology is not irreversible.

Of further interest is the high incidence of psychosocial factors which are recorded in this retrospective survey. All such findings are of potential interest with respect to our clinical observations and those of others described recently as failure to thrive in children in which psychosocial disruption exists concurrently with the development of growth failure during early childhood.

Detailed prospective investigations are necessary to delineate various aspects of this picture more clearly. It is not yet clear what the primary association is between the growth and developmental failure and the envi-

Table 9   Weight and Height Observed in Follow Up of Patients with Failure to Thrive

	Weight		Height	
	Below 3rd percentile	Above 3rd percentile	Below 3rd percentile	Above 3rd percentile
At discharge	32	0	14	9
At follow up	7	25	6	17

ronmental disturbance. There may well be constitutional differences in these infants in contrast to their siblings, as well as specific aspects in their psychosocial situation. The importance of the present report is our finding of such a high incidence of this group. This places into proper perspective the need for clinical study and definition of failure to thrive by the physician. It further indicates the need for exploration of methods of therapy by the pediatrician, and for his intervention in a problem encompassed by various social disturbances.

REFERENCES

1 Bakwin, H.: Emotional deprivation in infants. J. Pediat. 35: 512, 1949.
2 Bowlby, J.: Maternal care and mental health. WHO, Monogr. Ser. No. 2, pp. 67–71, 1951.
3 Coleman, R. W. and Provence, S.: Environmental retardation (hospitalism) in infants living in families. Pediatrics 19: 285, 1957.
4 Leonard, M. F. et al.: Failure to thrive in infants. Amer. J. Dis. Child. 111: 600, 1966.
5 Patton, R. G. and Gardner, L. I.: Influence of family environment on growth: the syndrome of maternal deprivation. Pediatrics 30: 957, 1962.
6 Provence, S. and Lipton, R. O.: Infants in Institutions. New York, International Universities Press, Inc., 1962.
7 Spitz, R.: Hospitalism: an inquiry into the genesis of psychiatric conditions in early childhood. Psychoanal. Stud. Child. 1: 53, 1945; 2: 113, 1946.
8 Stewart, A. H. et al.: Excessive infant crying (colic) in relation to parent behavior. Amer. J. Psychiat. 110: 687, 1954.
9 Talbot, N. B.: Has psychologic malnutrition taken the place of rickets and scurvy in contemporary pediatric practice? Pediatrics 31: 909, 1963.
10 Widdowson, E. M.: Mental contentment and physical growth. Lancet 260: 1316, 1951.
11 Barbero, G. J., Morris, M. C. and Reford, M. T.: Malidentification of Mother, Baby, Father Relationships Expressed in Infant Failure to Thrive. In The Neglected-Battered Child Syndrome. New York, Child Welfare League of America, 1963.
12 Elmer, E.: Failure to thrive: role of the mother. Pediatrics 25: 717, 1960.
13 Yarrow, L.: Maternal deprivation: toward an empirical and conceptual re-evaluation. Psycho. Bull. 53: 459, 1961.
14 Barbero, G. J. and Shaheen, E.: Environmental failure to thrive: a clinical view. J. Pediat. 71: 639, 1967.

Studies of Child Abuse and Infant Accidents

Investigator: **Elizabeth Elmer, M.S.S.**
Assistant Professor of Social Case Work, School of Medicine, University of Pittsburgh

Co-Investigators: **Grace Gregg, M.D.**
Associate Professor of Pediatrics, University of Pittsburgh School of Medicine, Director, Developmental Clinic of Children's Hospital, Pittsburgh

                           Byron Wright, M.A. and John B. Reinhart, M.D.
University of Pittsburgh School of Medicine

Contributors: **Thomas McHenry, M.D., Bertram Girdony, M.D., Paul Geisel, Ph.D.**

Prepared by: **Clarissa Wittenberg**

Historically, the terrible toll taken by childhood illness and industrial accidents overshadowed the risk of children being injured by their parents. At one time children were believed to be in the grip of the devil because they had been conceived in sin, and harsh punishment was thought necessary to save them. Parents "owned" children and almost any punishment was considered legitimate. As our concepts of child development have become more sophisticated and our understanding of learning and discipline has advanced, harsh punishment has become less and less acceptable. Consequently the parent who beats his child is an object of censure. Today, we hold parents responsible for the well-being of children, and, therefore, the malnourished and medically neglected child becomes a subject of concern. Recognition that parents do abuse their children has grown, and hospitals and doctors are increasingly aware of the problem. Studies have been done to help define the problem and its dimensions, and to record the effects of abuse on children.

Children's Hospital of Pittsburgh is located in a large low-income district of the inner city and, like many other city hospitals, has an active emergency ward where many injured children are brought. Some of these children have multiple bone injuries. Early in the 1960's the staff began to systematically study the possibility of abuse in these cases. A research team headed by Miss Elizabeth Elmer began, in 1962, a study of 50 families with children suffering from bone injuries who had been admitted to the hospital over the previous 13 years. This was a follow-up study to determine what

Elizabeth Elmer, principal investigator, and Clarissa Wittenberg, author, "Studies of Child Abuse and Infant Accidents," in Julius Segal (ed.), *Mental Health Progress Reports*, no. 5, DHEW publ. (HSM) 72-9042, GPO 0-446-535, 1971, pp. 58–89.

happened to these children after their initial admission to the hospital. A second study followed which focused on infant accidents, and compared infants and families where accidental injury had occurred with those where neglect or abuse was present.

The problem of diagnosing abuse was attacked in the first study. Cases were selected for the follow-up study on the basis of their hospital admission record. Although abuse is a complicated subject involving both social and medical problems, the criterion of multiple bone injuries was selected for the purpose of a less controversial diagnosis. The family history was then examined and the families judged to be either abusive or nonabusive; those who could not be placed clearly in either group were considered unclassified.

The first study showed clearly that these children are in serious jeopardy, that many die and many become severely retarded and/or crippled and spend their lives in institutions. The first Study of Fifty Families resulted in an examination of what constitutes abuse. An examination of the "failure to thrive" child was begun and the role of accidental injuries noted. The second study focused on small babies not yet capable of getting into trouble on their own, thus illuminating the role of the parents in such accidents.

Both studies resulted in an examination of the theories and accepted ideas surrounding this issue. For instance, the working mother, commonly felt to contribute to child abuse, did not appear to be important. Neither were these children typically abused by extramarital partners or non-related figures; there was no "wicked stepmother" syndrome. While many parents were found to have serious emotional problems, few were mistreating the children for bizarre or extremely sadistic reasons. These children were rarely abused "coldly." Few of the parents were "bad" parents and total failures; most stayed with their families and eventually exhibited some success with their children. Neither did the parents typically injure all of their children. Abuse has been found to be a phenomenon related to the child-bearing period of the mother, and often the mother has been uninformed about contraception.

THE FIFTY FAMILY STUDY

A radiologist and a pediatrician selected 50 former patients for the study. Basic criteria included:

1 Injured bones, revealed by x-ray film, indicating the occurrence of more than one traumatic episode, in conjunction with—
2 Absence of clinical bone disease that might account for the condition.
3 A history of assault or gross neglect, or the absence of a history showing convincingly that the injuries were accidental or attributable to an

unusually traumatic delivery. A small group of children do suffer undiag-
nosed fractures at birth.

The final group was equally divided between male and female subjects,
of whom 36 were white and 14 Negro. This racial distribution approximated that of the hospital's clientele. A number of the children had come to the
hospital for other complaints, and bone injuries had been discovered in the
course of routine examinations.

The majority of subjects had been young babies at the time of their
admission. Seventeen were under 3 months of age when multiple injuries
were found. Nine were between 3 and 9 months of age. This is in contrast
to the curve for childhood accidents where the incidence rate for accidents
is minimal below the age of 9 months. It then begins a sharp climb, reaching a peak between 2 and 3 years when it begins to level off.

Fewer than 50 families were actually interviewed—due to deaths, institutional placements, and refusals. Only families who still had their children
were interviewed. Six families refused to cooperate. Thirty-one of the children in the original group, plus two siblings found to have bone injuries,
added up to a total of 33 children studied and 31 mothers interviewed.
Seven were foster mothers and one an adoptive mother. Essentially the
families were told that the object of the study was to examine the hospital's
treatment of patients, and an attempt was made to avoid focusing on the
suspected episodes of abuse in order to minimize suspicion and distortion.
It is of interest that the noncooperative parents were in general better educated than the rest of the group. They may have been more suspicious of
the hospital's motives or more guilty about their own behavior.

Information was accumulated from hospital records, current examinations, home visits, and interviews with the mothers. It was initially anticipated that the fathers would not be available for interviews. Fathers were
not interviewed formally, and it was felt that potentially information from
the fathers would have been of value.

Each of the children was given a current examination which included a
complete pediatric evaluation, psychological testing, a psychiatric interview, a hearing test, and an x-ray survey of skull, long bones, chest, pelvis,
and spine—with special attention to the sites of old bone injuries.

On the basis of all this information, the children were divided into
three groups. Twenty-two were considered abused, four nonabused, and
seven unclassified. Nonabused children were those whose early bone injuries had a plausible explanation other than assault by an adult. If agreement
could not be reached as to the cause of the injury, the child was considered
unclassified. For example, one such child had a record of birth injuries and
a hospital admission at 3 months with fresh fractures, but no account could

be obtained of abuse or accident. Unclassified families, then, while not labeled abusive cannot be considered nonabusive either.

Almost all of the families struggled to live on low incomes. Most had less than a high school education and correspondingly few job opportunities. In most cases the families had three or four children. About a quarter of the families in this study were on welfare; however, none of the nonabusive families were. The families lived in substandard, but not the worst, housing. Most lived in private dwellings or apartments, but none in trailers or rooming houses. Many of the families kept their homes in fairly good condition and the mothers tended to be good housekeepers. Physical squalor was not characteristic of this group.

The study families, particularly the abusive ones, suffered from marital stress. Many couples had been separated and reconciled many times without coming to any real resolution of their problems or differences. The abusive families tended to have more quarreling and drinking than the others. Several abusive mothers expressed fear of their husbands, and the investigators thought that in general their fear was well justified. One father, for instance, had a prison record for murder; another was observed to blow cigarette ashes in his baby's eyes and then to knock the child's head against a post. It is possible that mothers with poor self-control tend to be attracted to men with similar problems, or that the mothers want the fathers to appear in a bad light so as to appear sympathetic by comparison.

For disciplinary measures most of these families relied on physical means of control. Whipping and spanking were the most commonly used methods of discipline; scolding, withdrawal of privileges, shaming, and shaking were also common. Reasoning with a child or avoidance of the conflict were methods almost never used. *These parents tended to see even small infants as needing discipline and as consciously and deliberately misbehaving.* It was rare for anyone other than the mother, or the mother and the father together, to discipline a child—and very unusual for the father to deal with the children by himself.

The nonabusive families tended to use a few types of punishments consistently, while some of the abusive families used a broad range of disciplinary measures that they were searching for some effective way to manage their children.

Mothers who abused their children felt very negatively toward the child who had been injured. It is not known if they felt this way about all their children or only the one who was abused. In one exceptional case, the mother expressed sympathy for the child who had been abused by her husband.

The abusive mothers appeared to have more emotional problems of greater severity than the nonabusive ones. Depression was common with about half of the abusive mothers troubled by difficulties in eating or sleeping and having a tendency toward crying spells. The nonabusive mothers, in general, had fewer and milder symptoms.

Several of the abusive mothers admitted to uncontrollable actions in the past—including physical aggression against other women; sexual promiscuity; and secret, compulsive spending. These mothers, who themselves had serious problems of control, admitted being afraid of their husbands as well. By their own reports, more of the abusive mothers than the nonabusive were easily irritated.

The abusive mothers were lonely people, often with no place to escape from the pressures of home and children. In many cases they had poor relationships with their own parents. There were no friends or relatives to help. It was noted that the mothers actively discouraged friendships, and did not join even relatively impersonal groups such as the PTA.

Child abuse is a family affair, however, and regardless of the identity of the abuser, the rest of the family participates. The other parent is involved by virtue of lack of interference or tacit approval. In many cases siblings may have injured the child, but again the responsibility must rest with the parents. The family dynamics are important in these situations.

The following case history illustrates the type of family problems that surround child abuse:

A 19-year old mother brought a three-month-old baby, her third, into the hospital. The baby was wearing a cast, and his weight including that of the cast was 10 pounds. He had had a birth weight of 5 pounds, 3 ounces. His x-ray showed that he had an old fracture of the skull, an injury to his shoulder, fracture of the left arm, multiple injuries to knees, ankles, and long bones of both legs. In addition, he had a bulging fontanel suggesting subdural hematoma.

The mother expressed her horror that every time she picked up the baby he appeared to have something else wrong with him. The child had been in another hospital at six weeks of age when he had been injured falling off a bed onto a concrete floor. When the emergency room doctor saw the baby, he wanted the police called as he thought it obvious that the child had been beaten. The baby needed two subdural taps at that time.

The mother's explanation was that she had put the baby in the middle of a double bed while she went to another room to wash his crib. A 14-month-old sibling was in the room with the baby. She heard a thump and thought toys had been dropped, and then ran to find the baby on the floor. She assumed that he had "scooted off" the bed. The father was critical of the mother for not watching the baby.

The mother had been a favorite child and had attended church faithfully. Her family had had ambitions for her to get a good education. At sixteen, however, she became pregnant and was disowned by her parents. The minister of her church was also very critical of her. The baby was born after a six-month gestation period and died after three days. During this crisis the mother was alone as none of her family came to see her. She married the father, and became pregnant again and had a little boy. When he was three months old, she became pregnant again and delivered the baby who was the patient. This added up to three births within 22 months. Two children had been premature. In addition, her parents separated and blamed their troubles upon her "disgrace."

The Children

Most of the children were quite young at the time of their first admission to the hospital. This study has shown that many children die or suffer grave and irreversible damage, but also that some children survive this early abuse, and reach a phase where their parents can successfully care for them and they can attain a reasonably good physical condition.

Eight of the 50 children had died by the time of this study. Most had been under five months of age at the time of death; two had been slain by their mothers. Five children were in State institutions for the retarded. Many, who were in basically good health, had scars or deformities, but considering that they had been at the point of death and had suffered very serious injuries they were quite well-recovered. One child was suffering from malnutrition, and several had organic brain defects. A large number of children were observed to show signs of upper motor neurone disease, as manifested by hyperactive tendon reflexes as well as abnormal plantar reflexes. A few children had signs of cranial nerve involvement manifested by strabismus and nystagmus. These signs appeared to be related to injury in all of the children born at full term, except in the case of one who was jaundiced at birth and had had convulsions prior to the injury.

In the premature children with signs of neurological damage, the effect of prematurity itself cannot be discounted. Only two of the prematures were known to have had head trauma and symptomatic convulsions. In one child, prematurity was the only known condition that could account for central nervous system damage. The abused children had twice the incidence of neurological signs as was true of the rest of the group.

The investigators found that two of the children had been injured in substitute homes. In one case the substitute home was arranged through an informal agreement between the natural and the foster parents, and in the other an adoption agency chose the home for an infant who was born out of wedlock. The latter child was subsequently moved to another foster home. In all, 11 children in the study were moved to substitute homes for their own protection, following the abusive incidents.

Birth

Histories were obtained from the mother, and other available sources such as hospital records. *It was found that about a third of the children weighed less than 5.5 pounds at birth, indicating prematurity.* As the national figure for prematurity is 8 percent, the percentage in this study is extraordinarily high. It is known that birth weight varies by race and by socioeconomic status. The national rates are 7 percent prematurity for whites and 12 percent for nonwhites. In this study, however, the higher percentages of low birth weight occurred among the white families: 8 of the 24 white and only 2 of the 8 Negro children had birth weights of less than 5.5 pounds. Although the significance of the large number of premature babies is not known, one possible explanation is that premature infants, because of their incomplete development at birth, are more vulnerable to bone injuries than full-term infants. A pediatric radiologist, Dr. John Caffey, is of the opinion that there is more vulnerability in the first few weeks. The bones of a premature baby may be injured even with normal handling, for instance, during diapering. However, when chronological age plus the number of weeks of prematurity equals nine months, Dr. Caffey observes that vulnerability to bone injury becomes that of any full-term newborn.

The median age of the premature children in this study was 11 months at the time of hospital admission. This would indicate that their injuries were not due to immature bone development, but to other factors. Of the 21 abused children whose birth weight was known, seven were premature; none of the nonabused children were premature. It is known that premature babies are more difficult to care for than full-term ones; they may be more irritable and cry more due to their immature nervous systems. The mothers may be more apprehensive about picking them up because they are so tiny. In addition, the emergency situation that so often surrounds premature birth may be a serious strain on an already easily upset mother. Preparations for births are often incomplete when a premature baby arrives, and for a family with only marginal resources the strain can be severe.

Negroes, who often had extended families or else lived in overcrowded housing where other women were available, seemed to cope with the strains of prematurity better, with relatively fewer combinations of prematurity and abuse.

There is another issue, too, that must be considered: the more subtle problem of the mother's condition during pregnancy. A woman who is unhappy about herself, her marriage, her pregnancy, or her other children may take inadequate care of herself or be too overwhelmed to obtain help. In many cases these mothers may not even seek prenatal care.

Other questions arise: For instance, what causes one family to zealously protect, or even overprotect, a premature infant, and another family to abuse such an infant? Why, if a couple with abusive tendencies has other children, is the premature child selected for abuse?

Conditions at Time of Original Admission

At the time of admission to the hospital there was no difference between the chief complaints of the abused children and the others. The majority were brought to the hospital because of limitation of motion or pain in an extremity. The next most common complaint was convulsions, then "failure to thrive," and gastric symptoms. Convulsions and subdural hematomas, physical conditions that are often associated with brain damage, were diagnosed in eight children upon admission. Surgical procedures connected with subdural hematomas were necessary in seven cases. Two other children required orthopedic surgery due to bone injuries. One-third of the group had previous hospital admissions.

Records of growth show that poor growth and abuse are not always associated. However, many of the children showed an improvement in appetite and growth while they were in the hospital.

Condition at Time of Study

Retardation Forty-Five percent of the entire study group had IQs under 80. Twelve of the 22 abused children and none of the nonabused children fell in this low IQ group. This is more striking when one realizes that this group does not include five of the original children who were placed in State institutions for the retarded. Only children still at home were included in the study. The investigators stress that they have no way of knowing what was cause and what was effect in this relationship between abuse and retardation. Neurological impairment is important in retardation, and many of these children showed such signs. In addition, many had histories of poor early growth, a condition thought to be associated with later mental retardation.

Speech problems, which are often associated with both emotional difficulties and mental retardation, were found in this study to be more closely related to mental retardation than to emotional problems.

Emotional Characteristics The abused children had marked difficulty in impulse control as compared with others in the study. Many of the children, regardless of their classification, had poor self-concepts. Even the nonabused children had suffered serious injuries, pain, and traumatic experiences at an early age. Most had scars or physical deformities. It is not difficult to understand that they might view themselves poorly or feel inferior, especially if the parents had not been able to help them in a sensitive way.

Eight of the abused children had difficulty in controlling anger, and either had outbursts of rage or serious inhibition of negative feelings, manifested by very apathetic responses.

General Functioning   The abused children who remained in the same environments had a substantially greater number of problems than the nonabused children. Eight of these were retarded. The unclassified children had more general problems than the abused children who had been moved to foster homes. Seven children, whose physical development had been poor at the time of hospital admission and who had been moved from the home, had achieved an average level by the time of the study. To emphasize the importance of the home environment, two children who remained in the same poor homes showed average development on admission but below average development at the time of the study.

Families at the Time of Abuse

The abusive families by and large lived in far more difficult circumstances than did the nonabusive families. However, all these families had often lived under stress, and for some reason abuse was not a constant process. Rather, it breaks out and then abates. In many cases, the sex or ordinal position of the abused child had a special significance for the abusive parent. One child was a second girl, as her mother had been, and both were family scapegoats. In another family, the two girls were severely abused by the mother, but never the boys.

The birth of a sibling less than one year before or nine months after the incident of abuse was found to be important. Nine of the abusive mothers were pregnant at the time of the abused child's hospital admission, one abusive mother had miscarried just before the child was admitted, and two others had borne an infant other than the patient during the year prior to admission. In only one of the other 11 families, unclassified and nonabusive taken together, was there an interval of less than one year between the injured child's admission and the birth of a sibling.

The investigators found that the connection between abuse and the burdens of pregnancy and child-rearing is clear and important. They cite the theories of Bibring, who identified pregnancy as a biologically determined maturational crisis that is not always resolved with the birth of the baby, but usually continues for some time, even in the most auspicious circumstances. The investigators point out that *these families abuse their children primarily during the child-bearing phase of marriage.* Later they appear to cope in a better fashion. *It was found that those families who had successfully begun to use contraception were able to recover from their previous strain and to stop venting their feelings of frustration and rage upon their children.*

Several of the mothers who were abusive were quite disturbed, and some were under psychiatric care. In three cases the fathers were clearly very disturbed or antisocial.

Substitute Care

A change in environment often saves the life of a child who has been assaulted. Still, some children were abused while in foster care. It was found that foster parents who voluntarily took children who were injured, neurotic, or retarded often had an unhealthy need to have children who were excessively dependent upon them. Furthermore, while much good can be accomplished, even the best foster or adoptive parents cannot undo irrevocable damage already done to the child.

Some foster children, due to their previous abuse, have severe difficulties even after the original crisis is resolved. These are troubled children and symptoms can appear long after the original trauma. In addition, the protective care so helpful in the beginning can cause rebellion later if the foster parents are unable to modify their methods in accordance with the changing developmental needs of the growing child. However, most of the children in placement showed marked improvement in their physical health.

INFANT ACCIDENT STUDY

The majority of the abused children in the Fifty Families Study had been brought to the hospital as accident victims even though their injuries were caused by assault. A few innocent parents of children suffering authentic accidents had unfortunately been suspected and sometimes accused of abuse. The masquerading of abuse as an accident and the reverse was possible because neither phenomenon was clearly understood. The investigators decided to study infant accidents, including abuse, to try to pinpoint the characteristics distinguishing one from the other.

Subjects were infants under 13 months of age who had been brought to Children's Hospital for x-ray following an impact accident or abusive incident. Since the younger the baby the more important the role of the caretaker, it was felt that this study would yield information about parental maltreatment and neglect, and not be conplicated by the considerations of the normal accidents of the active toddler. One hundred and one children were seen, both inpatients and outpatients. Various issues were explored: for instance, the difference between families of abused or neglected children and those suffering accidents, with or without injury. The differences between retarded children who had been abused and retarded children who had not were also studied, with special attention to the mothering received by each group.

Abuse was suspected if the families' explanation of the injuries were not adequate, or if abuse was reported, or if more than one injury was present. Initial assessments were made of family stress. Pregnancy and very small children were considered stressful. The family was considered to be under strain, too, if either parent had a close relationship with another adult who was unrelated to the child. This issue was considered and observed because of a number of mass media reports of abuse involving step-parents or paramours. As in the first study, this did not turn out to be an important issue.

The family was also considered under stress if the baby had developmental problems such as a significant deviation in growth, language, motor or social development, or such troubles as feeding difficulties or excessive crying.

All of these issues are important as parental reports are heavily influenced by anxiety, guilt, and concern when a child is brought to a hospital. An accurate report of the precipitating incident is hard to obtain. It is necessary to look at the entire family structure to find the clues that differentiate the abusive family. When abuse is suspected, deficiencies and deviance will usually be found in other aspects of family life. This study focused upon family structure, interpersonal relationships, and child care practices, in order to illuminate these differentiating issues. Because the children were so young, the mother was considered the principal caretaker and her interaction with the baby was carefully examined. In order to assess the mother-baby relationship, the pair were observed—and also the mother was interviewed and asked to fill out questionnaires. The observations were felt to be of particular importance, as the mother's habitual behavior with the child is likely to be beyond her awareness and ability to report. The observations provided data to supplement and correct the information gained through the other methods.

Many issues involved with mothering were examined in addition to the traditional ones of providing food, shelter, and medical attention. The stimulation given the baby, the verbal responsiveness, the quality of play, and the ability of the mother to assess the changing needs of the child were all considered. As in the previous study, a high number of retarded children in this group was noted and some important observations about their mothers were made.

Attempts to have an equal number of boys and girls, white and non-white, were unsuccessful as the potential subjects did not fall this way. Most of the children presented for x-ray were white females. Black female babies rarely appeared and, in addition, it was more difficult to enlist the cooperation of the nonwhite families in the research. All social classes were represented, but the majority of the families were in the lower classes.

Although a few families had refused to participate in the first study, the refusal rate was even higher in the second. It was suspected that the increased public awareness of child abuse and the outcry and pressure that had been building up made some parents less cooperative. Also, even parents of accidentally injured babies experience great guilt leading to unwillingness to discuss the event. In the Infant Accident Study, it was found very difficult to keep the allegedly abusive parents as subjects. They rarely refused outright to come to an appointment or to allow a home visit, but they failed to appear or were away from home at the specified time.

Neglect played an important role, and several families who could not be considered abusive were still considered deficient in their care of their children based on observations made during the study. Some parents, for instance, left their children without competent babysitters when they were absent for prolonged periods of time, or failed to obtain needed medical care despite repeated and careful instructions as to the needs of the child.

The final study group consisted of 100 cases, 78 of which were followed through all phases of the study and 22 in which families participated in the initial and final procedures, with only a mailed questionnaire in the interim. One of the mothers had two children in the study, making the total number of children included 101.

The methods included initial screening of x-rays, several home interviews with the mothers, and observations of the mothers in examination, feeding, and teaching situations. A questionnaire was mailed, and several pediatric and developmental evaluations were made. In several situations the mother was put under mild stress. In one instance, where she was asked to teach her baby to stack a series of blocks, the task was generally too advanced for the child so as to determine her reaction when frustrated by the baby. In another, she was asked to fill out a questionnaire when accompanied by the baby, to learn about her attitude when she was intent on another task. Four of the research persons saw each baby and family, and they were seen in as many situations as was practical.

The babies were evaluated twice in the first two years of life, a time of extremely rapid growth and development. This allowed for observations of the effect of the environment in a way not possible at later stages of life. Effects of Poor Parental care are obvious very soon during these early stages.

Of the 101 babies, brought to the hospital, only 10 were entirely without signs or symptoms. These 10 had been brought to the hospital for examination and reassurance, that despite a potentially injurious event, no injury had occurred. The other 91 babies displayed a range of conditions from mild bruising symptoms related to the central nervous system, such as momentary unconsciousness with or without vomitting, seizures, paralysis, and coma. The proportion of abused children without symptoms was roughly equal to the proportion of nonabused.

In addition to x-ray examinations of the site of the presumed injury, 21 x-ray surveys of the entire skeleton were performed. Ten of these were part of a diagnostic work-up for failure to thrive, the rest because multiple injuries were suspected. Eighty-two children had no evidence of fracture, 12 had a single recent fracture, and 7 had multiple fractures. The proportion of children with multiple fractures was much greater among the abused than the nonabused children. It was thought that if skeletal surveys had been universally performed, they might have disclosed other unsuspected, clinically unimportant fractures, which would have helped to evaluate the quality of child care. However, it is difficult to justify x-ray examinations without symptoms of injury.

Twenty-four children were judged to be abused, or to be both abused and neglected. Ten children were thought to be neglected only. There were 67 nonabused, non-neglected children. All initial judgments concerning abuse and nonabuse were reevaluated at the end of the one-year study.

The research was focused on the effect of abuse on the growing infant. The main areas of investigation included mental and motor development, behavioral characteristics, health status, and physical growth. The baby was seen as being affected by at least two kinds of factors—those that are relatively unchangeable, such as conditions at birth, and those that are influenced by the caretaker. It was hypothesized that the abusive group, in comparison to the nonabuse group, would show more stress, less support, and greater authoritarianism.

As required by State law, when abuse was found, reports were made to the Child Welfare Services and the parents were informed. Reports were made on eight children. A few other families were already known to the Child Welfare Services when they came into the study. In several cases, the mothers had named their husbands as the abuser and had separated from them. Two mothers overtly rejected the children whom they had mistreated, and the study personnel helped them arrange for placement away from home. The protective agency removed eight children from their own homes.

Because it is often observed that sick children are irritable and difficult to care for, it was noted whether or not the child had an acute illness at the time of admission. Eighteen of the babies were sick with gastrointestinal and upper respiratory complaints when brought to the hospital. A few had anemia, and suffered other problems such as eye infections. By and large the babies were not suffering from infections, and the traumatic event was not related to the extra demands and needs of a sick child.

Twenty-four of the babies were admitted to the hospital, eleven of these for protection while further investigation of the family condition was carried out. Thirteen needed hospital medical-surgical care, some for incidental medical problems and some for injuries resulting from the accident or abuse.

The "failure to thrive" babies were studied from several standpoints. For some, metabolic and endocrine studies were done with inconclusive results. This condition, defined as occurring when a child has weight and height below the third percentile for his age and sex, is not well understood. Rarely are these children seen because of trauma; characteristically, the mother who brings them in is full of concern because a child has not reached the expected developmental landmarks. Often she is anxious because her child is not growing and will assert strongly that she feeds her baby well.

Home interviews in this study did substantiate that some of these mothers fed their babies adequately. Medical opinion is growing that this entity belongs with others where psychological phenomena and physical development interact pathologically, as in anorexia nervosa or infantile marasmus. Studies at Johns Hopkins Hospital have indicated that the problem lay in the hypothalmic area and that it was reversible without any hormonal or chemical treatment when the child was placed in a hospital, a relatively nurturing environment. It was postulated that emotional disturbance in these children may have had an adverse effect upon the release of the pituitary tropic hormone via the central nervous system. In the Infant Accident Study, "failure to thrive" babies whose environment was changed tended to achieve normal growth, but rarely normal development.

Initial Pediatric Evaluation

Upon initial evaluation, 54—or slightly over half the children—were found to have either no medical problems or only the insignificant ones expected during the first year of life. Two-thirds of the abused children, however, had serious health problems. Slightly fewer than half the babies had a number of actual and/or potential health problems including prematurity, moderate or high perinatal stress scores, significant medical problems, and histories of acute illness. Children in the abused group had a disproportionately greater number of health problems per child than the nonabused children.

The abused group was also distinguished initially from the nonabused by their poor physical growth. In part their retarded growth was probably due to prematurity (9 or 37 percent were premature by birth weight, gestation, or both), but even giving credit for weeks of prematurity did not bring them to normal level.

An estimate of how well the child was cared for in general was judged by the manner in which baby appointments and immunizations were attended to by the caretaker. Nineteen had not been seen regularly, if at all. Twenty-eight of the mothers had not kept their babies' immunization schedule up-to-date, and some babies had not received any immunizations at all. Most of the faulty child care was concentrated in the abused group. However, upon questioning it was found that 92 percent of all the mothers were able to recognize symptoms of poor health in their children and to find suitable medical services for them when they became ill.

Thirteen babies were considered poorly dressed, dirty, or illkempt when they were brought for their pediatric visit. The number of abused children in this category was much greater than the number of nonabused.

Accidents versus Abuse—Initial Findings

Eighty-eight caretakers gave an accident history. *Twelve abused children were among those with credible accident histories, an overlap that illustrates the complexity of diagnosis in these cases.* Thirteen other children either had totally unexplained injuries or they were x-rayed because of suspected abuse, but no injuries were found; none of these had an accident history.

The assumption was made that adequate protection by the caretakers could completely abolish true accidents. The investigators realized, however, that this is unlikely and even undesirable, as a child reared in such a protective environment might have many other problems.

Three-fifths of the accidents were termed "active" because the baby's motor activity was an important contributing factor. Active accidents were subdivided into three categories: "open field" in which the babies propelled themselves into danger—for example, falling down the stairs when a gate had been left open; falls from appropriate furniture, such as couches or dressing tables; and falls from inappropriate furniture, such as the tops of washing machines—caused for instance, when a baby in an infant seat wiggles and the seat slides off the slippery top of the washing machine. It was thought that most of the active accidents might have been prevented by the use of built-in safety devices, such as belts to confine babies on dressing tables.

Passive accidents were those in which the baby's contribution was minor and the responsibility of the caretaker greater. Subdivisions of passive accidents included babies dropped by their caretakers, those suffering "Act of God" events, such as being hit by a stray baseball, and those who were admittedly assaulted by another person.

The accidents were described, then the abused group was compared to the nonabused, non-neglected children who had suffered accidents. Points of comparison, in addition to general health and injuries already mentioned, were behavioral characteristics, age, and ordinal position. The families were compared as to social class, stress at the time of the incident, and health of the mothers.

The only infants who differed behaviorally were the babies who had active, open-field accidents. They were predominantly negative in mood, not distractible, and moderately or highly active. This combination of traits can be seen to result in babies who are difficult to protect from harm. By contrast, the other subjects, including the abused children, were positive in mood, easily distracted, and moderately active. The babies represented in the "open field" accidents were also the oldest (median age, 42 weeks) and, therefore, their motor development was more advanced.

Most of the babies in the accident group, active or passive, were only children in their families, while on the average the abused child was the second child. This suggests that parents of a first child are not as aware of potential hazards as they might be, and also indicates that in abuse cases—in addition to evaluation of the stress of having several small children—the possibility should be considered that one small child might injure another.

Ninety-two percent of the abusive parents were identified with Class V (low) according to the Hollingshead Two-Factor Index. Forty-eight percent of the nonabusive, nonneglectful families studied fell in this class.

Regardless of the type of injurious event, the mothers typically had special stress added to chronic factors of strain. The abusive mothers mentioned baby irritability generally and the other more often mentioned disrupted schedules, fatigue, etc. Over 50 percent of the mothers of abused children had significant health problems, for example, mental retardation, emotional difficulties, seizures, and heart disease. Such major health conditions were found in only 20 percent of the nonabusive mothers.

In attempting to determine the quality of the mother-child relationship, the investigators studied the caretaking process. This process makes manifest much about the mother's interaction with the child and gives some measure of her general ability to function. The ability of the mother to monitor the environment for her helpless baby changes in relationship to many things. The mother, of course, operates within her own milieu and class structure, and this partially defines good mothering for her. The events that occur, the health and stability of the mother, the abilities she is potentially able to bring to bear to help her child, and her ability to perceive accurately his needs all affect her care of the child. Her degree of affection as well as her convictions about child rearing also enter in. Undoubtedly, too, the resources of the mother to provide support, affection, and aid for her are crucial.

Stress is seen as a major issue in child abuse, the caretaker being under insupportable stress in most such situations. In the case of the accidents, it has been noted that most of the mothers were reacting to stress in varying degrees—the abusive mothers, however, were under greater stress, had less support, and fewer personal resources. The interrelationship of stress, support, and the ability to cope can be seen as a continuum.

It must be remembered that the early years of child rearing are heavily demanding. Little money is available, and many young people are unprepared to become parents. Shifts occur in families even when children are desired and planned for, and greater strain is felt with unwanted babies. The investigators view most young families as being at a point of lowest tolerance for stress at a time when they are subjected to the highest stress during the years when children are being born. However, it must be realized that what constitutes stress for one individual can be handled by another. Unfortunately, some types of chronic stress are brought on by poverty, which rarely permits growth or learning and usually undermines a family's ability to function. The investigators were most interested in everyday stress, as opposed to extraordinary or emergency stress, because they felt that chronic stress was of key importance in child abuse.

The demographic data about the abusive families was a documentation of the degree of chronic stress. Almost half the abused children were black, and most of the combined abuse and neglect occurred among black families. Because of the larger numbers of children with comparatively few fathers in these homes, the families fall into a group known to be especially vulnerable to many kinds of stress. According to socioeconomic status, all the families in the combined abuse and neglect group are classified in the two lowest classes of the Hollingshead scale of social position.

There were ten families that were considered neglectful but not abusive, and it was found that in some ways they resembled both the abusive and nonabusive families.

The nine families demonstrating abuse but not neglect were predominantly lower class, with two members of the middle and upper classes; the ten families showing neglect alone included four classes from Class I, the highest of Hollingshead's classifications. One of these families was classified as neglectful because they habitually left the baby in the company of an active 30-month old sibling without adult supervision. Another family was called neglectful because their child was encouraged to perform physical feats distinctly beyond his limited ability, such as hanging from the pantry shelf by his fingers.

An assessment was made of the medical condition of the child and the mother's reaction to it. It was found that of the ten "neglect only" mothers, eight showed only slight reactions to medical problems. The mothers of the abused children reported feeling great stress due to their babies' medical conditions. The focus of these mothers on their babies' health was seen by the investigators as being realistic in view of the extremely poor health of these children.

There was one group of 24 women, primarily made up of black mothers, who were unusually bland or under-reacting to medical problems in both themselves and their children. One such mother had noted an abnormality in her baby's eye for more than a week, but hadn't sought medical advice about it. The investigators had several ideas, but no definite answers to explain this attitude. A middle-class mother, they believe, tends to emphasize her attentiveness to her child whether or not it is warranted. This is not always the case with the lower socioeconomic class mother. The investigators also note that many of the "upper reactors" were poorly educated and suggest that perhaps they did not really understand the potential hazard of some of the conditions. However, seven of the "under reactors" belonged to middle- and upper-class groups and were well-educated. An analysis of the "under reactors" by social class showed no significant class association. It is also suggested that the apparent apathy may be a defense against implied criticism and intrusion by the outsider or a way of coping with what would otherwise be overwhelming anxiety. It may also indicate a true indifference or a general state of apathy which includes, but is not limited to, the child.

The type of stimulus perceived as stressful and the reaction to it are highly individualized matters. To avoid imposing any preconceived hierarchy of stress, the investigators inquired what had happened to the mothers or their families since conception for the index child. The events divided naturally into Hill's four categories: physical difficulties, separations from persons or possessions, accession events such as a new person moving into the house, and social disgrace. The mothers' reactions were dichotomized as 1) mild or non-existent, or 2) strong. The number of stress events and associated reactions were combined to yield a total score for each individual. Mothers in each group were ranked and the groups compared.

In general, recent events were given highest stress ratings by the mothers. Acute conditions were reported as more stressful than chronic ones, and events involving the immediate family as more stressful than those involving extended family or friends. The proportion of mothers reporting no stress whatsoever was greater among the neglectful than the nondeviant, and only 4 percent of the abusive reported no stress.

Accidents, moves, and physical illness were the greatest sources of stress for the abusive mothers; also, prominent among the accidents were attacks upon the mothers by others. Several women reported having been beaten by their husbands. One abusive mother claimed to have been raped on her way to the hospital with her baby. Although the report seemed questionable, it was similar to others in its preoccupation with violence, either factual or fantasized.

A common source of stress for the abusive and other families was a change of residence. Typically the family moved during the woman's pregnancy to obtain more room. In both the abusive and nondeviant groups, the moves in late months of pregnancy resulted in strain on the mothers and at times brought on premature deliveries.

Illness was often reported and sometimes—especially in the group of abusive mothers—reported not as chronic conditions, but related to pregnancy for the index child. The abusive mothers felt very strained by the pregnancy of the child in question and ranked pregnancy as a higher stress even than deaths.

According to the physician's rankings of physical disorders associated with pregnancy, the abusive mothers who reported the most stress actually had the least, thus indicating a higher psychological sensitivity. Six of the abusive mothers who reported difficult pregnancies were caring for other young babies when they were pregnant and, also, had fewer people available to help them.

Potential support factors included a satisfactory male relationship; the presence of a man in the house—whether spouse, common-law partner, or father; a continuous association with a male during pregnancy; help from the man in relation to the baby; a stable source of income; a continuous source of medical care; participation in religious activities and involvement with neighborhood activities. The abusive families and the others differed significantly in the amount of support available. The abusive families had the least support.

Statistically significant factors were continuous association with the father during pregnancy and help from a male—whether husband, father, or friend—in relation to the baby. The current presence of a male in the home on a stable basis did not appear to be a significant positive factor; nor was marital stress a significant negative factor. During pregnancy the help of the father appeared to be mainly psychological, but once the baby arrived the mother received more support when some male did something concrete to assist in the care of the baby.

The effects of race on stress and support were assessed. When support was low, black mothers reported significantly more medical stress than white mothers; they suffered more physical problems than the whites. The white mothers, however, reported significantly more social stress when support was low. This comparison would seem to reflect the perception of the woman, white or black, as she viewed herself in relation to her peer group.

The mothers were scored for general negative and positive reations to their babies, and several trends appeared. The abusive mothers tended toward extreme reactions, judging the babies to be either all good or all bad, while the non-abusive parents saw their children more realistically as both pleasing and annoying. The abusive mothers were relatively silent with regard to their children's development. Fifteen of the 19 abused children showed early signs of retardation.

Modes of Punishment, Discipline, and Teaching

It was predicted that the abusive mothers would use harsher methods of punishment and would have less interest in teaching their children than the other mothers. The results were not so clear cut.

Forty-one percent of all the mothers used some form of physical punishment with babies less than 6 months old, usually slapping the hands or the buttocks. At 9 months, physical punishment intensified. By 24 months, 87 percent of all the mothers were using this method of physical punishment at least part of the time.

The type of behavior punished varied with social class. Mothers in the two highest classes punished principally for aggressive acts; middle-class mothers for activity, dangerous or otherwise; and lower-class mothers, for conduct such as excessive demands, disobedience, or crying. Generally the abusive mothers, most of whom were lower class, punished for unacceptable conduct. Across all groups, girls were consistently punished earlier: by the age of 9 months, 31 percent of the girls, but only 5 percent of the boys were being punished; by 18 months, the figures rose to 70 percent and 50 percent for the girls and boys, respectively.

The investigators had become aware that most mothers are extremely sensitive to their babies' aggressive acts against them as mothers. When asked how they would respond if their infants struck them or spat upon them, the overwhelming majority of the mothers of babies 6 months of age or older said they would retaliate in kind, ". . . to show him that he is *not* to do that kind of thing." Three mothers of babies who were less than 6 months of age also said the same. Eighty percent of the abusive and 63 percent of the nondeviant mothers said they would hit back against infant aggression.

Regardless of their social class, most mothers asserted that a baby should know right from wrong by the age of 12 months, and one-third of the mothers specified 6 months. This belief implies a common lack of realistic information about infant development and when babies learn concepts of right and wrong. These mothers also perceived the babies as having "tempers" and other directed feelings at a much younger age than is actually possible.

The mothers involved in this study usually discriminated very little between discipline and teaching. When asked how they would attempt to teach the baby some new behavior representing a real learning effort for him, they most frequently responded in terms of scolding or spanking to get him to learn after first giving verbal instructions. The investigators feel that infants are punished physically more often than is realized. When it is common practice to strike babies, however lightly, with the goal of teaching them, the laws of probability indicate that some babies are going to be struck too hard and that some will be injured.

Values Related to Mothering

The mothers were questioned as to their expectations concerning the child. The majority preferred their babies to be "good"; that is, respectful, grateful, obedient, and not rebellious. These were the particular goals of the abusive and neglectful mothers; they were not interested in creativity, etc.

There were varied opinions among them as to what constituted an "ideal mother." All the abusive and the neglectful mothers mentioned keeping the baby clean and giving him material things. A few mentioned the importance of being a "proper" woman. They described the ideal woman in negative terms as somebody who does not run around or sit at bars. The abusive group often described the ideal father in terms of discipline or financial support. Several women said that the ideal father should not beat the mother.

Quite a few mothers felt that affection should be restrained: that there is danger in being too affectionate toward babies. This trait was more marked in the abusive and the neglectful mothers.

The index of values related to mothering clearly and significantly distinguished between the abusive and the nonabusive groups, correctly classifying 77 percent of all the families. Among the abusive mothers, emphasis was placed on cleanliness and materialistic values. They tended to perceive themselves and their husbands in stereotyped roles, a perception suggesting difficulties in forming and maintaining close relationships. Their fear of showing too much affection toward their babies was another manifestation of the same difficulty. These characteristics, together with the common need to have an obedient, compliant baby, established the abusive mothers as more authoritarian than the nonabusive women.

The Baby

The contribution of the baby to the mother-child relationship is extremely important. A smiling baby who is responsive may keep even a detached mother involved. While many types of behavior are important, it was decided that four behavioral characteristics would be examined: mood, level of activity, approach or the way the baby related to a new person or new object, and distractibility. These characteristics were studied during the initial and the final pediatric examinations.

Among all the children the distribution of positive and negative mood showed a decided difference according to sex and developmental age. Regardless of their developmental age, half the boys were positive, half negative. The girls were strikingly negative when developmentally young but became positive as they matured. Abused boys were markedly negative compared to their nonabused peers. Abused girls were more positive than nonabused girls; however, the abused females as a group were developmentally older than the nonabused.

Eight abused children, four boys and four girls, were separated from their parents by the time of the second testing. All were predominantly negative in mood. According to the study data, this seemed associated less with their removal from home and more with the mood to be expected from the above findings. The four negative boys were similar in mood to the majority of abused males, while three of the negative girls were developmentally young and thus apt to be more negative.

The factors of sex, age, and abuse which affect predominant mood need considerably more study before the interrelationships will become clear. Nevertheless, these findings suggest that boys and girls may indeed respond to abuse in quite different ways.

It was not possible to find associations between mental development and behavioral patterns. Some of the children were advanced developmentally, some at age level, and some retarded. Some in each group were positive in mood and could be distracted.

Distractibility depends upon whether or not a child can be intrigued away from something he is doing, especially if it is a hazardous activity. In this case, it is a positive quality, as opposed to hyperactive distractibility which interferes with concentrated learning.

All of the babies who were positive in mood and distractibility were positive in approach; that is, interested or curious or pleased at meeting new people and new things. Among the nonabused children who had negative or mixed scores on mood and distractibility, a racial difference occurred on the approach scores. The whites of both sexes were predominantly positive in approach, while the blacks of both sexes were predominantly negative. The investigators noted that the examining doctor was a white woman and wondered if this could be a factor influencing these results.

Activity levels did not distinguish between abused and nonabused children. The babies who were both abused and neglected were low in approach and play behavior and high in negative activity. The "abused only" or "neglected only" had wider repertoires of behavior. However, of the "neglected-only" children, a large proportion either remained high or became high in activity. It was observed that the mothers were largely ineffectual in controlling their children; they tended to pile on command-after-command while the children became more anxious, active, and difficult. The ability of these mothers to limit the activity of their children, who seemed to be in special need of help in controlling or directing their activities, seemed very meager.

Observations of Interaction

The mothers were observed with their babies during a feeding period at home and in a teaching situation in the pediatrician's office. It was learned that mothers vary considerably in their perceptions of what is dangerous to their babies. While the mothers were in the doctor's office, the babies were often attracted to the doctor's kit containing instruments. Most mothers did not permit their children to handle these, yet failed to see the danger in the sharp corner of a drawer that the children loved to pull out. The examining table was also a danger, as mothers often turned away while their babies who were lying on it waited to be dressed.

The actions of each baby and mother were tallied and analyzed according to content, mode, and context. Mothers of retarded children concentrated on feeding them and behaved more positively toward the child as the baby ate. They did not talk spontaneously to the child as much as the mothers of non-retarded children. The investigators believed that this reflected the mother's concern that the child eat rather than play or socialize. There was an overwhelming tendency for mothers of retarded *abused* children to show low verbal response to the babies' vocalizations, but an opposite trend was shown by mothers of retarded *nonabused* children. The age of the baby was not a factor in the mother's tendency to verbalize when the baby made sounds. Some babies responded to their mothers' speech, others did not, and again this was not related to baby age.

It is probable that an involved mother gives her baby many types of stimulation in addition to the verbal. The verbal response, however, seems to be a good indicator of the total social environment provided for the baby. Mothers with a good education were much more verbally responsive than those with a poor education.

A significant association appeared between mothers who responded verbally and the higher rates of development among these babies. The investigators note that such an association has not previously been reported but they point to several conditions that may affect it. The children of well-educated, intelligent mothers may have superior genetic endowment. Also, babies who have had a great deal of verbal experience do better on tests, which often require ability to follow verbal instructions.

With regard to control, the abusive mothers tended to give their children great latitude until their patience wore thin, when they would abruptly threaten or strike their children. The neglectful mother seemed to burden the child with repetitive commands and threats to which he paid little attention, apparently sensing that the mother did not know how to control him, or for some reason was unable to do so. As he became more active, the mother became more frenetic.

The abusive and neglectful mothers tended to care for the babies, but made neither broader responses nor extra reactions to their children. They tended toward stereotyped responses.

The teaching situation, which was essentially an artificial one, aroused some anxiety. However, the observers of the feeding, who knew the mothers, thought that they behaved much the same as they had in the past. This was substantiated by the significant positive correlations between the feeding and teaching observations with respect to maternal-verbal responses among all cases; mothers of nonretarded children; high social class; and females.

Final Evaluation of the Babies

The most important final difference between the abused and the nonabused babies appeared in the scores on the Bayley Mental Scales. There was significantly more retardation among the abused children when compared with the nonabused. The likelihood of retarded mental development among the abused children was greatly increased when they were also judged to be neglected by their parents. The fairly high rate of mental retardation found in all groups of children in this study may mean that the hospital outpatient population is biased in this direction.

The final checkups showed little difference in height and weight increases between the abused and nonabused children. However, this was true largely because one-third of the abused children had been removed from their homes and placed in benign and nurturing homes. All but one showed remarkable catch-up growth. There was a significant association between height and mental development ratings, with retarded mental development occurring more frequently among children below the 10th percentile in height.

In terms of family characteristics, the single factor most strongly related to the mental development ratings was the amount of income per person in the household. The percentage of children within the retarded, normal, and advanced groups coming from families with less than $100 a month per person was 74 percent, 46 percent, and 7 percent respectively. Although abused children more often come from families with low incomes, the relationship between income and mental development was not altered significantly when controlled for the occurrence of abuse. When children with retarded and normal development were combined, 79 percent of the abused and 52 percent of the nonabused children came from low-income families: this represents a statistically significant difference.

Among those with advanced development, the majority of the children were white; among those with slow development, the majority were black.

Although stress was found important, no statistical association between ratings of social stress and ratings of mental development appeared. However, the number of supportive resources for the mother was related to mental development. Among the families of retarded abused children, 69 percent were low in support while only 31 percent of the families of nonabused retarded children had similar low ratings. When stress hits a family with few sources of support and assistance, then the problems become more intense.

The presence of the father is also important. The group who were advanced mentally all had their fathers at home, while only 59 percent of the retarded had fathers living with them. The father was absent in the cases of 64 percent of the retarded children who were abused.

Regarding the probability of retardation, three factors in addition to abuse are important: low monthly income per person, significant physical problems in the baby, and low verbal responsiveness in the mother. When any two of these factors plus abuse was present, 100 percent of the children were retarded. Among children without any of these factors, only 21 percent were retarded.

The second evaluations showed that, remarkably enough, there are children who appear normal despite abuse, and it is also evident that there is a range of intensity in abuse. Some children are subjected to pervasive and long-standing abuse, while for others the abusive incident is isolated in an otherwise favorable environment. *The investigators caution that an overall characterization of the abused child demands both pediatric and family assessment. The physical and mental effects of abuse can be mimicked by other conditions, and also the physical and mental state may not fully expose the abusive atmosphere of the home.*

Diagnosis of Abuse

A crucial factor in the diagnosis of abuse is the willingness of the physician to consider abuse as a possible cause of a child's injuries and to examine him accordingly. Dr. Grace Gregg, a pediatrician and an investigator in this study, points out that a diagnosis of abuse requires a history that fails to explain the injury, the elimination of systemic disease, and an assessment of the type of care that would allow such a condition to develop. "Failure to thrive" children must be looked at with an eye to abuse and neglect. It is important where there are multiple injuries that each be accounted for. Multiple bone injuries are considered a key indication of abusive treatment. It must be remembered, however, that some bone changes do not show up immediately on x-ray and may be hidden until about 12 to 14 days. Furthermore, x-ray can tell the condition of the bones, but not how they were injured nor the motivation of the person responsible for the injury. In some cases a parent can roughly and abruptly grab a child to prevent an injury and accidentally hurt him. However, while this type of accident can happen once, a series of such incidents would be highly suspicious. Also, the idea that siblings can injure infants is unpopular, but must be considered.

Malnutrition is a key indication of abuse or neglect, but evidence of malnutrition is difficult to identify when intake becomes adequate, unless photographs are taken.

Familiarity with the normal injuries of children is indispensable to adequate diagnosis. Superficial injuries above the elbows, shins, and knees that do not resemble dermatologic conditions should be examined to see if they have been caused by rough handling, human bites, cigarette burns, etc. All bones and joints should be examined, not merely those pointed out as injured.

Legal Issues

By June 1967, 52 child abuse reporting laws were in existence in all 50 States, the Virgin Islands, and the District of Columbia. Puerto Rico added a law soon thereafter. In most cases mandatory reporting by medical personnel, occasionally by schools or social workers, and investigation by law enforcement agencies was typical. In some states the professional can be fined or imprisoned if he fails to report a case of child abuse.

At first glance it looks as though the situation has been acknowledged and adequately covered. However, this is far from the case. The Children's Bureau looks upon child abuse reporting laws as case-finding devices. How successful they are for this purpose is difficult to assess. Some problems have, however, been identified. For instance, diagnostic guidelines are not well-drawn. There is the possibility of an inappropriate accusation, perhaps a law suit. Medical training is often limited in terms of teaching the type of social-family assessment that is required in many child abuse cases. This type of case can be tremendously time-consuming and time is a rare commodity in most medical practice.

Another problem is that of confidentiality. The child abuse laws place the child's right to safety above the traditional rights of the patient—in this case, the parent—to protected communications. A social class difference may slant the manner in which a case is treated. For example, in many States hospitals and physicians are required to report a case if an abused child is brought for care. Private doctors, however, are not exposed to the same public attention and might—and do—manage private patients differently. A doctor who reports a patient stands to gain ill-will and lose the family for treatment. He may feel he can give more help by not reporting the case and staying involved as an interested and concerned family doctor. Patients who can afford private care can also "shop" around. They can go to different physicians and the full extent of the child's history of trauma might be hidden in this way.

The goal is not, it must be remembered, merely full reporting. The goal is the protection of the child. The two are related, but not the same.

The investigators feel that professionals who report a family in good faith should be granted immunity in the event of a law suit. Other changes should allow for concern for the other children in the family.

The lack of community placements for such endangered children also make some people reluctant to confront an abusive parent, as it is realized that all too often the child must return home with an even more enraged and abusive parent.

There is considerable question as well, as to whether or not the police should be given responsibility for establishing whether abuse has occurred. In many cases this type of approach with the goal of proving guilt and establishing criminal behavior is unfruitful. As this research has shown, the problem may be subtle; a child may have been left with inadequate supervision or the parent may have shown poor ability to anticipate the child's pattern of activity. The caretakers may be extremely immature or disturbed, and thus cannot be considered directly responsible for injury to the child. Nonetheless the child may be in great jeopardy. But it is questionable whether most police have the orientation, time, or training to investigate these issues.

Prevention is largely ignored, as is appropriate follow-up and assistance to families in need of community aid. Expanded protective services are much to be desired. Assistance with related problems such as contraception should also be available.

Punishment of the parents or probation, which often means only the most minimal surveillance, rarely accomplishes much toward the most important goal—protection of the child. Punishment for doctors or hospitals may very well be self-defeating and discourage reporting. The most fruitful approach is via education. Physicians need to be sensitized to the issues and hospital procedures need to be changed so as to permit early identification of the endangered child. Referrals to social agencies should be facilitated and child care resources developed. Where a murder or brutal attack has taken place, then the police are appropriate; where an overwhelmed mother has a child who continually injures himself due to lack of supervision, another resource such as the help of a trained homemaker might be more appropriate.

Prevention of Child Abuse

To save a child from the serious effects and irremedial damage caused by abuse and neglect, it is necessary to recognize the situation when it occurs. Professionals need to be alert when they notice that young families are having their children too quickly, with no relief between pregnancies. The danger signs of marital strain, poverty, isolation, and overwhelmed mothers need to be heeded. Premature births with indications of family strain should be of great concern; all possible assistance and surveillance should be given these parents. Parents with children showing developmental difficulties should be given similar help.

It is important that education be restructured so that every young woman has some idea how children grow and develop. Classes should be held early in school, possibly at the elementary and junior high level, ensuring that all prospective mothers will be at least basically informed and, if possible, have supervised experience with child care. It cannot be too strongly stressed that far too many women think a young baby is responsible for his acts and can react intellectually like an adult. The whole concept of physical punishment for infants requires re-thinking in the light of knowledge about child development. Again, it must be realized that, despite ideas that physical punishment is a lower-class phenomenon, this practice was found in all classes. And males must be taught the importance of their contribution to the stability of the family and the emotional life of the child.

Education in family planning should be made available if we are to prevent parents from becoming so overwhelmed that they destroy their own children. Appropriate birth control methods should be made easily available. Unwanted children are in grave danger of abuse and all its long-term residual damages.

Education of legal personnel, especially that of judges, is necessary. The investigators note that even in cases which represented blatant abuse as manifested by multiple skeletal trauma with central nervous system damage, when they petitioned for removal of the child from the home the authorities were more concerned about the rights of the parents than the welfare of the babies. Some children were returned to the custody of their parents after their fractures had healed and their general condition improved without any assessment of the family at all. The courts do not seem to be truly aware of the risk to the child—that it might not merely be a question of a single meaningless act, but that abuse may constitute an active expression of a wish to be rid of the child. The overwhelming odds against complete recovery from parental abuse seem to escape appropriate attention. The horror of many situations and the intense feelings they arouse may cause some people to try and mend the parent-child relationship in order to wish the whole situation away. It is not always true that the natural parent is best for the child, nor is it true that any parent is better than none. Parents, on the other hand, need not be treated as criminals because they have abused their children. A total assessment of the entire situation and its pressures needs to be made.

One issue, that of community support, demands special attention. As family patterns change and mobility increases, social institutions such as the church lose their strong hold on family life. People who tend to be isolated become even more so. It is probably true that many parents who do not beat their children would also benefit if a neighbor could help them out when they are overwhelmed, or if a network of friendly visitors would somehow fill this void. Volunteers could be used to extend the work of the public health nurses and the hospital clinics to ensure that both mild supervision and help would be available to young mothers. Homemaker services can be extremely important. Community programs and neighborhood associations could also be helpful if the prohibition about interfering or getting involved could somehow be broken down constructively. It is possible that an auxiliary to the police department could be useful.

The interrelationship of poverty, isolation, and too many unplanned-for small children is important. Too often, little is done to reach the very people who are too weak to ask for help. Newspapers and TV, too, often carry only the sensational story and not the steady compilation of data that might enable us to make reforms in our welfare systems, our birth control clinics, hospital regulations, courts, and foster home programs—data that might enable us to prevent such tragedies and save these children.

REFERENCES

Caffey, J. Multiple fractures in the long bones of infants suffering from chronic subdural hematoma. *American Journal of Roentgenology,* August 1946.

De Francis, Vincent. *Child Abuse—Preview of a Nationwide Survey.* The Children's Division. American Humane Association, Denver, Colorado, 1963.

Elmer, Elizabeth. Identification of abused children. *Children,* U.S. Department of Health, Education, and Welfare, September-October 1963, 180–184.

——— Hazards in determining child abuse. *Child Welfare,* January 1966.

——— Child abuse: Overview of the problem and avenues of attack. Paper presented at the 5th Annual Mental Health Institute. St. Louis, Missouri, July 1966.

——— Abused children and community resources. *International Journal of Offender Therapy.* 11, 1, 1967.

——— *Children in Jeopardy.* Pittsburgh: University of Pittsburgh Press, 1967.

Elmer, Elizabeth & Gregg, Grace, M.D. Developmental characteristics of abused children. *Pediatrics,* October 1967, 40(4) [Part 1], 596–602.

Gregg, Grace, M.D. Physician, child-abuse reporting laws; and injured child, psychosocial anatomy of childhood trauma. *Clinical Pediatrics.* Philadelphia: J. B. Lippincott Co., December 1968.

Hill, Reuben. Social stresses on the family. *Social Casework,* 1958, 39, 139–150.

Powell, G. F., M.D., Brasel, J. A., M.D. & Blizzard, R. M., M.D. Emotional deprivation and growth retardation simulating idiopathic hypopituitarism: 1—clinical evaluation of the syndrome. *The New England Journal of Medicine,* June 8, 1967, 276(23), 1271–1278.

Powell, G. F., M.D., Brasel, J. A., M.D., Raiti, M.D., & Blizzard, R. M., M.D. Emotional deprivation and growth retardation simulating idiopathic hypopituitarism: II—Endocrinologic evaluation of the syndrome. *The Journal of the American Medical Association,* April 27, 1964, 88, 358–362.

U.S. Department of Health, Education, and Welfare. The child abuse reporting laws: A tabular view. Washington, D.C., 1966. (Reprinted with revisions in 1968).

Improved Prognosis for Infants of Very Low Birthweight

Ann L. Stewart, M.B., Ch.B., and E. O. R. Reynolds, M.D., M.R.C.P.
Medical Research Council, Human Biochemical Genetics Unit, Gatton Laboratory, University College, London

Increasing knowledge of how to manage seriously ill newborn infants has been followed by the establishment of intensive care nurseries in many large hospitals. While these nurseries undoubtedly save more lives than less highly developed units [1], there is concern about the mental and physical well-being of the survivors. In the past, low-birthweight infants who form the largest group requiring intensive care, have had a poor prognosis for normal development [2–5]. The smaller the infant, the worse the outlook; for example, Drillien [5] found that 83% of infants weighing less than 1,250 gm at birth proved abnormal at follow-up. Drillien [3] and more recently Holt [6] have suggested that measures taken to increase the survival rate of infants of very low birthweight would result in an increasing number of handicapped children entering the community, where they would become a burden on their families and upon society. While not all have taken such a dismal view of the efficacy of perinatal intensive care [7], those looking after the smallest infants have been faced with a dilemma similar to that which relates to the management of infants with severe congenital malformations: is it worthwhile using sophisticated methods of treatment to preserve life if the ultimate prognosis is so questionable?

In order to obtain information on this point, a follow-up study of infants weighing 1,500 gm or less at birth was started in our hospital at the beginning of 1966, after the introduction of an intensive care program which was designed to foresee and prevent, as well as treat, any abnormality which might be lethal or damage the infant. An increase in survival rate followed and in 1971 a preliminary report on the progress of the infants was published [8] showing that most appeared to be developing normally. At that time, the number of infants under surveillance was small and they were still very young. The purpose of the present report is to describe the outcome for all infants weighing 1,500 gm or less born in our hospital or admitted to the neonatal unit from other institutions during the five-year period from 1966 to 1970 inclusive. The surviving infants are now aged 2 years 10 months to 7 years 10 months, old enough for the identification of those who have handicaps which will prevent them from functioning as normal individuals in society [3]. In order to delineate areas where improve-

From *Pediatrics*, vol. 54, no. 6, pp. 724–735 (December 1974).

ments of care are required, details of all infants who died are included, and the methods of perinatal management which were employed are described. Where infants have been found to have an abnormality at follow-up, a relationship with perinatal events has been sought.

MATERIALS AND METHODS

Study Population

During the five-year period from 1966 to 1970, 123 live-born infants who weighed 1,500 gm or less at birth were born in University College Hospital (UCH). An infant was classified as live-born if any cardiac or respiratory activity was detected after delivery. Another 74 infants were admitted from 19 hospitals situated over a wide area in and around London. Criteria used by these hospitals to decide upon the transfer of a particular infant in addition to the very low birthweight are not known, but because of the special interest of the staff of the neonatal unit are likely to have included the presence of respiratory illness.

Obstetric Care at UCH

The condition of the infants who were growing poorly *in utero* was checked by means of hormone assays such as maternal urinary estriol excretion and by ultrasonic biparietal diameter measurements. The optimum time for the delivery of fetuses who were at risk *in utero* was decided after consultation between obstetricians and pediatricians. Women admitted in preterm labor were treated with bed rest, sedation, and drugs such as isoxuprine in an attempt to prevent delivery. If labor continued, the fetal heart rate was repeatedly checked, often using an ultrasonic fetal heart detector. Fetal blood samples were taken [9] when indicated for measurement of acid-base status, and continuous heart rate monitoring was used in a few infants towards the end of the five-year period. Forceps were often applied during delivery in order to protect the head. Breech deliveries were conducted as rapidly as was consistent with safety, in order to avoid asphyxia during umbilical cord compression.

Women booked for delivery in other hospitals which did not have facilities for neonatal intensive care were, if they went into preterm labor and if their obstetricians requested it, transferred to UCH for delivery.

Neonatal Care

Because the infants were under the care of the same senior medical and nursing staff throughout the period of study, uniformity of care was assured.

Resuscitation at Birth Pediatricians were warned in advance of the delivery of a low-birth-weight infant and were present in the delivery room. Every effort was made to prevent hypoxia. After birth the infant was kept warm and the airway was cleared: if no respiratory efforts were made, the heart rate was below 80 beats per minute, and there was little or no tone, endotracheal intubation was carried out. The lungs were held inflated with oxygen at a transpulmonary pressure of 30 cm of H_2O for several seconds and then rhythmically inflated at a frequency of about 40 per minute to a pressure sufficient to produce adequate chest movement, usually about 15 cm of H_2O. When the infant's condition did not rapidly improve, 2 to 5 ml of 5% sodium bicarbonate solution were injected slowly into the umbilical vein. External cardiac massage was used in infants with a very slow heart rate and nalorphine (0.25 mg) was injected intravenously when an infant whose mother had had a substantial amount of opiate analgesia was slow to breathe. Endotracheal tubes were often left *in situ* until the infant arrived in the neonatal unit, which was very close to the delivery room, so that breathing could be further assisted if necessary.

Transfer of Infants Infants transferred from other hospitals were almost always collected in a portable incubator by a member of the medical or nursing staff trained in resuscitation. Before and during the journey steps were taken to ensure that the infant was properly warmed and oxygenated. The blood glucose level was usually checked with Dextrostix[1] and oral or intravenous glucose solution was given if indicated. When the history and clinical state of the infant suggested severe acidosis, small intravenous doses of 5% sodium bicarbonate solution were also given. Infants who were apneic or whose breathing appeared very precarious were intubated so that intermittent positive pressure ventilation could be used in transit. Since early 1968 the portable incubator has been equipped with a mechanical ventilator in order to facilitate the transfer of apneic infants [10].

Temperature Control The infants were nursed in incubators and maintained in the neutral thermal range [11]. They were moved into cots when they had reached a conceptual age of about 34 weeks or a weight of about 1,800 gm.

Hydration and Feeding Fine nasogastric feeding tubes were passed as soon as possible after admission and feeding was started, usually with human milk obtained from the infant's mother. The smallest and illest infants were given small amounts of milk every five or ten minutes, and the more robust ones were fed hourly. As the infants grew the intervals between feedings were increased. At about 10 days cow's milk formula feeding was

---

[1] Destrostix, Ames Co., Stoke Poges, Bucks, England.

introduced for most infants. The nasogastric tubes were changed to the other nostril weekly. For the first few days of life when the total fluid requirement was not tolerated orally, a parenteral infusion of 10% dextrose with electrolytes was also provided. Umbilical venous catheters were often used during 1966 but subsequently the infusions were given either through an umbilical artery catheter or a peripheral vein. The total fluid administered to the infant on the first day of life was about 65 ml/kg/24 hr and the volume was increased to 150 ml/kg/24 hr by the 7th to 10th days. An attempt was made to raise the caloric intake to 100 calories/kg/24 hr or more by the 7th to 10th days. Bottle-feeding was instituted as soon as the infant could suck adequately.

Oxygen Therapy Measurement of arterial oxygen tension, carbon dioxide tension, and pH were made within two hours of birth, and subsequently as indicated in almost all the infants. Arterial samples were obtained from indwelling umbilical artery catheters or by percutaneous puncture of peripheral arteries, and the estimations were performed on equipment present in the unit. The inspired oxygen concentration was measured with oxygen analyzers and regulated to produce an arterial oxygen tension (Pao_2) in the range of 50 to 90 mm Hg. Umbilical artery catheters were removed at 48 hours or sooner, except in a few infants with severe hyaline membrane disease when they were left in place for up to five days. Peripheral artery sampling often continued for several weeks. Metabolic acidosis was totally or partially corrected by intravenous injections of 5% sodium bicarbonate solution (600 mM/liter) and infusions of hypotonic sodium bicarbonate solution (100 mM/liter). We aimed to correct a base excess less than about -6 mEq/liter to 0 in the smallest, illest infants, particularly if they had severe respiratory problems. If the infant was asymptomatic, however, a metabolic acidosis of this or sometimes greater severity was often not treated.

Monitoring and Management of Apneic Attacks In the early years cardiac ratemeters were used for monitoring, and cardiac slowing was the signal employed to detect apnea. In 1968 impedance pneumographs were sometimes used and in 1969 apnea alarm mattresses were introduced [12]. After that time all infants were monitored with apnea alarm mattresses set to detect apnea after a delay of 5 to 15 seconds and cardiac ratemeters were frequently used as well. The nursing staff carefully observed the infants and in the event of apneic attacks stimulated them to breathe by maneuvers such as flicking the sole of the foot. If breathing did not rapidly resume, the lungs were inflated with oxygen. Systems using bags and masks were used intermittently as a substitute for intubation, but were not generally accepted because they were less effective in rapidly overcoming hypoxia, and distension of the stomach with vomiting was sometimes provoked. As soon as an intubated child resumed breathing the endotracheal tube was removed. If breathing remained inadequate he was mechanically ventilated. Since 1968 some infants have had their arterial blood pressure monitored by attaching a strain-gauge transducer to an umbilical artery catheter.

Mechanical Ventilation   The indications for using mechanical ventilation, which was needed principally for hyaline membrane disease, were very strict. Initially the only indications were apnea or a deterioration in clinical condition accompanied by peripheral vasoconstriction, bradycardia, or gasps superimposed on a slowing respiratory frequency. More recently, since mid-1969, we have also ventilated infants whose Pao_2 fell below 35 mm Hg while they were breathing a concentration of oxygen greater than 95%. The ventilator usually employed was the Bennett PR_2.[2] Details of our ventilator management have been given elsewhere [13, 14]. The only important change which occurred during the years 1966 to 1970 was that at the end of 1969 means were found to ventilate infants with hyaline membrane disease at much lower peak airway pressures than we had previously used and it also became possible to ventilate some of them with lower concentrations of oxygen [14, 15].

Management of Hypoglycemia, Jaundice, and Hypocalcemia   Blood glucose levels were measured in all infants using Dextrostix. Laboratory determinations were made when indicated. Enough extra oral or intravascular glucose was given to maintain the blood glucose level above the lower limit of detection with Dextrostix (initially 40 mg/100 ml, later 25 mg/100 ml). Bilirubin measurements were made in all jaundiced infants. The level of indirect-acting bilirubin which was regarded as an indication for exchange transfusion was lowered somewhat as the five-year period progressed. For example, at 28 weeks of gestation a level below 17 to 18 mg/100 ml was considered safe in 1966, whereas in 1970 we sometimes performed exchange transfusions to prevent the level reaching 15 to 16 mg/100 ml, particularly if the infant had severe hyaline membrane disease, or a tendency to apnea. Towards the end of the period phototherapy and occasionally phenobarbital were used to control jaundice. The plasma calcium level was measured in all babies who appeared "jittery." If hypocalcemia (plasma calcium <7.0 mg/100 ml) was found, calcium gluconate solution was given orally or by intravenous infusion.

Infection and Antibiotics   Increasing attention was paid over the years to the early detection of infection and greater numbers of blood cultures

---

[2] Bennett Respiration Products Inc., Santa Monica, California.

and lumbar punctures were performed. In 1966 the antibiotics most commonly used to treat serious infections were ampicillin and cloxacillin; subsequently, kanamycin and cloxacillin were employed. Prophylactic antibiotics were given to infants when the fetal membranes had been ruptured for more than 24 hours until 1968 (usually ampicillin), and to infants being treated by mechanical ventilation until 1970 (usually kanamycin and cloxacillin). These practices were then abandoned.

Problems of Hemostasis   One milligram of phytonadione (vitamin K_1) was given intramuscularly to all infants on admission. Coagulation studies were performed only if the clinical state of the infant suggested an abnormality of hemostasis until late 1970. At that time routine measurements of coagulation status were introduced.

Parents   Parents have always been allowed unrestricted visiting but until 1968 they were only rarely allowed into the intensive care area although they could see their children through a glass partition. Since that time we have encouraged them to enter the intensive care area and to handle their infants, even if they were being cared for in incubators.

Follow-up

Infancy (Less than 3 Years of Age)   After leaving the hospital, the children were seen regularly at a special clinic in the children's outpatient department by one of us (A.L.S.) who had not been involved in their inpatient care. At each visit they were weighed, measured, and examined clinically and their development was assessed according to Knobloch, Pasamanick, and Sherard's Developmental Screening Inventory [16] from which a Developmental Quotient (DQ) was calculated. Intervals between clinic visits were dictated by the clinical state of the child, and the competence and confidence of the parents, but never exceeded three months during the first year of life. If growth and development were considered to be normal at the age of 18 months, the interval between assessments was increased to six months. Development was then assessed according to Sheridan's chart [17].

The Preschool Period (3 and 4 Years of Age)   During the fourth year of life, the first psychological assessment was made, usually in the children's outpatient department by a clinical psychologist who knew nothing of the child's perinatal history, except the period of gestation and the birthweight. Birth rank and parental occupation were also made available to the psychologist. Assessment was usually made with the Revised Stanford Binet (form LM) Intelligence Scale [18]. The Merrill-Palmer Scale [19] was also used for children who spoke no English or occasionally for very shy children.

Older Children (More than 4 Years of Age) Following the first psychological assessment, the children were contacted annually, and the majority attended the outpatient department. At these visits they were measured, examined clinically, and their progress both at home and at school was discussed with the parents. A few children were retested using the Weschler Preschool and Primary Scale of Intelligence [20] after school entry, particularly if they had been unable to speak English at their first assessment.

Special Assessments Throughout the period of the study any child who was thought to be abnormal in any way was referred for investigation to colleagues with a special interest in the particular abnormality. Investigations carried out included hearing assessments, ophthalmic examinations, and refraction. Children thought to have cerebral palsy or an abnormality of mental development were assessed by a consultant in mental and physical handicap and a child psychiatrist.

Children Living Abroad Reports from parents and local medical attendants were obtained annually. In some cases the methods of assessment differed from our own and there were insufficient data to derive developmental or intelligence quotients. These results are reported separately.

Controls and Parents An attempt to collect a control population was abandoned because satisfactory matching for important factors such as ethnic group, social class, maternal age, and parity proved impossible in our hospital which carries out less than 2,000 deliveries per year. In any case, at this stage of the study we can only hope to rule out with certainty handicaps sufficiently severe to interfere with normal function in society. This degree of handicap does not require a control group to establish abnormality.

The intelligence of one parent of each child was tested using the Weschler Adult Intelligence Scale [21]. The assessment was carried out on the same occasion as the child's first psychological assessment, by a separate psychologist. Except in cases where only one parent spoke English, the parents themselves decided which one was to be tested.

RESULTS

The results are summarized here. Further details are available.[3] . . .

---

[3] See NAPS document 02453 for eight pages of supplementary material. Order from ASIS/NAPS c/o Microfiche Publications, 440 Park Avenue South, New York, N.Y. 10016. Photocopies are $5.00. Microfiche are $1.50 (payable in advance to Microfiche Publications). Outside of the United States and Canada add postage (photocopy, $2.00; microfiche, $0.50).

Table I   Twenty-eight-Day Survival Rate by Birthweight of 197 Infants Born in 1966 to 1970

| Birthweight (gm) | UCH | | | Outborn | | | Total survived % |
| | No. of infants | | | No. of infants | | | |
	Live	Dead	Survived %	Live	Dead	Survived %	
501–750	0	14	0	1	4	20	5
751–1,000	7	15	32	6	13	32	32
1,001–1,250	24	15	61	14	8	64	62
1,251–1,500	36	12	75	21	7	75	75
Total	67	56	54	42	32	57	55

The Perinatal and Neonatal Periods

Sixty of the total of 197 deliveries during the five-year period were to primagravidae, 108 mothers had had previous live or stillborn infants, and 29 had previous abortions only. Abnormalities of pregnancy included threatened abortion or antepartum hemorrhage (64 cases) and pre-eclamptic toxemia (13 cases). Shirodkar sutures had been inserted during 15 pregnancies. Details of the social and obstetric histories of the mothers, and the gestation, birthweight, and sex of the whole population of infants are given.

Survival Rate and Prenatal or Perinatal Events   Eighty-eight infants died in the first 28 days of life. A further 11 infants died subsequently aged 29 days to 25 months (median, 3 months), leaving 98 children who have survived for longer than 2¾ years. Tables I and II summarize figures for neonatal (> 28 days) survival rate by birthweight and gestational age. The survival rate appeared to be highest among infants born by cesarean section (69%), followed by forceps-assisted vertex delivery (65%), vertex delivery without forceps (53%), and breech delivery (47%). These differences were not, however, statistically significant.

There were considerable variations in neonatal survival rate from year to year. For example, although the survival rate during the five-year period for infants weighing 1,001 to 1,500 gm was 69%, the range in individual years was from 48% to 85%. No differences were apparent in the survival rates of inborn and outborn infants in the years 1966 to 1970. The neonatal survival rate for infants born in UCH is probably increasing . . . and in the most recent five-year period, 1968 to 1972, 75% of infants weighing 1,002 to 1,500 gm have survived. Appendix Table IV shows perinatal mortality rates

Table II   Twenty-eight-Day Survival Rates by Gestational Age of 197 Infants Born from 1966 to 1970*

| Gestation (completed weeks) | UCH | | | Outborn | | | Total survived % |
| | No. of infants | | Survived % | No. of infants | | Survived % | |
	Live	Dead		Live	Dead		
<24	0	4	0	0	0	0	0
24–25	0	10	0	3	8	27	14
26–27	5	14	26	3	5	38	30
28–29	16	17	48	11	10	52	50
30–31	23	6	79	10	5	67	75
32–33	13	4	76	12	2	86	81
34–40	10	1	91	3	2	60	81
Total	67	56	54	42	32	57	55

*The length of gestation was assessed from the date of the mother's last menstrual period and from the neurological and physical characteristics of the infant.

for infants born in UCH and neonatal survival rates both for inborn infants and for those admitted from elsewhere in each of the five study years.

The overall incidence of major birth defects, defined as structural or biochemical abnormalities interfering with normal function, was 6%; that of minor defects, namely structural abnormalities which did not interfere

Table III   Summary of Numbers of Children with and without Handicap at a Mean Age of 5 Years 2 Months (Range, 2 Years 10 Months to 7 years 10 Months)

Total no. of children		95
Children without handicap		86(90.5%)
Children with handicap		
Physical handicap only		
Partially sighted	1	
Spastic diplegia	3	
Total		4(4.2%)
Mental, with or without physical handicap		
IQ <68	3	
Minimal cerebral dysfunction, IQ 79	1	
Hemiparesis, IQ 70	1	
Total		5(5.3%)

Table IV Relation of Subsequent Handicap with "Presumed Severe Hypoxia" and Jaundice*

Infants	Total no.	No. of handicapped	Handicapped (% of total)
Without "presumed severe hypoxia"			
Without jaundice	48	0	0
With jaundice	10	1	5
Total	67	1	1
With "presumed severe hypoxia"			
Without jaundice	17	2	18
With jaundice	11	6	54
Total	28	8	29

*Hypoxia: base excess—15 mEq/liter or less in the first sample obtained within two hours of birth or apnea at any age (other than immediately after delivery) necessitating endotracheal intubation; jaundice: maximum serum billirubin 10 mg/100 ml.

with normal function, was 8%. . . .

The relationship between the sex of the infant and intrapartum or postnatal events to survival rate is shown. . . . Although the survival rate in females (60%) was higher than in males (50%) this difference was not statistically significant ($X^2 = 1.79$, $P < 0.2$). The survival rate of the infants who weighed less than the 10th percentile for gestation [22] was higher than for those whose weight lay on or above the 10th percentile ($X^2 = 5.65$, $P < 0.02$).

Seventy-nine of the 197 infants were intubated at birth. A total of 74 infants were breathing spontaneously and adequately within five minutes of delivery; 15 between five and nine minutes; and 29 at ten minutes or later. Spontaneous breathing was never established in 27 infants who died. Although there was no significant difference between the mean rectal temperature on admission to the unit of survivors (35.3 ± SE 0.1 C) and of infants who died (34.4 ± 0.2 C), a temperature below 35 C was associated with a reduced survival rate ($X^2 = 10.08$, $P < 0.005$).

The presence of a severe intrapartum or postpartum metabolic acidosis, presumably caused by hypoxia, and defined as a base excess (BE) after correction for any bicarbonate given during resuscitation of -15 mEq/liter or less in the first sample obtained within two hours of delivery, was associated with a much reduced survival rate ($X^2 = 13.16$, $P < 0.001$). Only five (21%) out of 24 such infants survived, and none of the 11 with a base excess lower than -20 mEq/liter survived. Similarly, the infants with hyaline membrane disease who needed mechanical ventilation fared poorly, only 14 (31%) surviving. Preterm apnca (apnea apparently due to immaturity) rather than the severity of the pulmonary abnormality was thought to be the main reason for ventilation in infants with hyaline membrane disease who survived after being ventilated. Preterm apnea by itself carried a very good prognosis for life whether or not mechanical ventilation was required.

Among surviving infants, the mean of the maximum weight loss expressed as a percentage of the birthweight was 9.5 ± SE 0.6%. There fluid intake reached 150 ml/kg/24 hr at a mean age of 9.4 ± 0.3 days and their caloric intake 100 calories/kg/24 hr at 8.7 ± 0.3 days. The infants had regained their birthweight at a median age of 19 days (range, 0 to 34 days) and they were fully bottle-fed at a median age of 50 days (range, 3 to 84 days). Complete bottle-feeding was achieved by the equivalent of 40 weeks of gestation in all but four infants.

The relation of prenatal or perinatal events to survival rate may be summed up as showing adverse effects of a severe metabolic acidosis, presumably due to hypoxia, shortly after birth; a low body temperature on arrival in the unit; and hyaline membrane disease sufficiently severe to necessitate mechanical ventilation. Apart from the deleterious effects of decreasing birthweight and gestational age, no other adverse influences affecting survival could be identified.

Autopsy

By far the most common diagnoses at autopsy were hyaline membrane disease and intraventricular hemorrhage, either or both of these findings being regarded as the main cause of death in 56 (58%) of the infants. The main findings and the clinically diagnosed causes of death in the 18 infants weighing less than 800 gm who were not autopsied are given in Appendix Table VII.

Follow-up

Three of the 98 long-term survivors who had returned with their parents to Nigeria, Ghana, and Germany could not be traced. Data were available for the remaining 95 children including detailed assessments of 85 children who were attending our own clinic and 4 who have been assessed by colleagues on our behalf. During the first four years the child's age was regarded as his chronological age less the weeks that he had been born before term. For infants aged 5 years or more this correction was no longer considered to be necessary.

The term *handicap* as used below is defined as an abnormality sufficiently severe to interfere with present or future normal function in society.

Growth Measurement of height (89 children) and weight (95 children) between the ages of 2 and 6 years (mean, 4 years 9 months) have been compared with Tanner and Whitehouse's standards for London children [23]. No corrections were made for ethnic group or for parental height. The height of 13 (15%) of the children lay on or above the 75th percentile, 37 (42%) were between the 25th and 74th percentiles, 21 (23%) between the 10th and 24th percentiles, and 18 (20%) below the 10th percentile. For weight the distribution was similar: 9 (11%) were on or above the 75th percentile, 28 (33%) lay between the 25th and 74th percentiles, 26 (31%) were between the 10th and 24th percentiles, and 22 (25%) were below the 10th percentile. Taking only the 20 infants who were light-for-dates at birth ($<$ 10th percentile), ten remained below the 10th percentile for height or weight or both.

Intelligence Quotients   The distribution of the IQs of the 65 older children obtained at a mean age of 3 years 6 months (range, 2 years 11 months to 5 years 9 months) . . . was no different from that of their parents. Sixty (92%) of the children had an IQ of 80 or above.

The IQs of three handicapped children fell within the very inferior (IQ $<$ 68) range . . . , including a girl who had been transferred from a normal primary school to a special school, and two boys one of whom attended a normal school and the other a special school for the severely mentally handicapped. The mental development of two other handicapped children with IQs in the inferior range (68 to 83) was also regarded as potentially abnormal. One child, a girl, had a specific language-learning difficulty. She was also partially deaf (see below), but this was thought to be insufficient to account for her problems and a diagnosis of minimal cerebral dysfunction was made. The other child, a boy with cerebral palsy and an IQ at the lower end of the inferior range, may need special educational provision for mental as well as physical handicap.

Development of Younger Children   Twenty-four children born in 1970 were too young for IQ testing. The results of the last DQ measurements performed using the Knobloch *et al.* Screening Inventory [16] at a mean age of 16 months (range, 12 to 18 months) gave 4 children a DQ of 80 to 89, 8 a DQ of 90 to 99, and 12 a DQ of 100 or more. Sheridan's chart [17] which was used for subsequent assessments does not allow the derivation of a DQ. However, apart from two handicapped children with spastic diplegia (see below) whose development was satisfactory in all other than motor areas, the children were continuing to develop normally at a mean age of 3 years 3 months (range, 2 years 10 months to 3 years 7 months).

Cerebral Palsy   A total of four handicapped children had cerebral palsy, including three girls with spastic diplegia. The eldest child was fully mobile and attended a normal primary school. The fourth child, a boy, had a right hemiparesis, and his IQ was at the lower end of the inferior range.

Convulsions Four children had had one febrile convulsion each. There were no children with epilepsy.

Hearing One handicapped girl had a hearing loss of 40 dB, due to chronic inflammatory disease of the middle ear.

Vision One handicapped girl was partially sighted as a result of congenital cataracts. The etiology of the cataracts is unknown and virus studies were negative. Her intelligence was within the normal range. Another girl had Duanes syndrome, with a total left VI nerve palsy. The results of surgery were cosmetically excellent and handicap consequent on visual abnormality is considered to be unlikely. Nine children including two siblings and another child with affected siblings had refractive errors. Eight of the nine presented with squints. None were handicapped by their refractive errors.

Incompletely Assessed Children Living Abroad Six children, including three siblings, were living abroad and have been incompletely assessed. At ages between 2 years 10 months and 6 years 11 months (mean, 5 years 4 months) they were all regarded as normal children by their parents and local medical attendants.

Summary of Physical and Mental State of Surviving Children Table III summarizes the physical and mental state of the total population of 95 children.

Cause of Handicap The presence of handicap was very significantly related to the occurrence of presumed severe hypoxia (Table IV) in the perinatal or neonatal period, paricularly if accompanied by jaundice. We suspected that severe hypoxia had occurred in two circumstances; firstly when a base excess less than -15 mEq/liter was found in the first sample obtained within two hours of delivery indicating intrapartum or postpartum hypoxia; and secondly, when an infant became apneic and required endotracheal intubation. Among the 28 infants who fell into one or both of these categories, eight (29%) were found to be handicapped (X^2 vs non-"hypoxic" infants $= 13.87$, $P<0.001$). Eleven of the 28 "hypoxic" infants were jaundiced, with maximum indirect serum bilirubin levels above 10 mg/100 mg (mean, 14.2 mg/100 ml; range, 11.4 to 18.4 mg/100 ml; of 11, six (54%) were handicapped (X^2 vs "hypoxic" nonjaundiced infants $= 4.08$, $P<0.05$). No other statistically significant adverse relationship with obstetric or perinatal illnesses, either alone or in combination, affecting the incidence of handicap could be identified. There were no handicapped children among the 23 who had run an uncomplicated course, and only one proved to be handicapped among the 44 who had had illnesses or complications such as hyaline membrane disease (18 infants), hypoglycemia (5 infants), jaundice (19 infants), or a delay in regaining the birthweight of more than 21 days (14 infants), but had not suffered from "presumed severe hypoxia."

DISCUSSION

The program of care for infants of very low birthweight which was employed in our unit when this study began was intended to anticipate and prevent, as well as treat, any abnormality which might be lethal or result in damage to the central nervous system. This program, which has continued to develop subsequently, was particularly concerned with the prevention of hypoxia both before and after delivery. For example, facilities were provided for prompt resuscitation at birth, the monitoring of breathing, rapid analysis of arterial oxygen tension, and mechanical ventilation. The nursing staff was trained in resuscitation using, if necessary, endotracheal intubation, so that apneic spells could rapidly be overcome, even if no member of the medical staff was present. The infants were hydrated and fed from the first day of life, and biochemical abnormalities such as hypoglycemia and hyperbilirubinemia were avoided whenever possible.

Survival Rate

The survival rate of the infants increased after the introduction of these methods of care. For example, only 45% to 50% of those weighing 1,001 to 1,500 gm survived in the 1950s and early 1960s [8], whereas the survival rate for inborn and outborn infants averaged 69% and 70%, respectively, during 1966 to 1970, the five-year period under review (Table I). . . . During this period 50% of those infants who were born at gestational ages of 28 to 29 weeks survived (Table II). Among inborn infants the survival rate has probably continued to increase. . . . Since our hospital is a referral center for high-risk pregnancies, as well as for infants requiring intensive care, and since our survival figures are well above the national average [24], we infer that the use of intensive care methods is largely responsible for our improved results.

Follow-up

Most of the earlier follow-up studies of infants of very low birthweight concerned those who had survived from a time when little was known of their normal or abnormal physiology and facilities for intensive care were not available. Certain features of the management of the infants in the perinatal period may at that time have been actively harmful: for example, the limitation of inspired oxygen concentration to below 40% under all circumstances in order to reduce the incidence of retrolental fibroplasia [25], and the practice of starving the infants in the first days or weeks of life, which was probably responsible for promoting metabolic abnormalities such as hypoglycemia and hyperbilirubinemia [26], as well as depriving the developing brain of an adequate supply of calories [27]. These early studies gave a uniformly poor prognosis for survivors who had weighed less than 1,500 gm at birth, with handicap rates ranging from 33% to 60% [2–5, 28].

The present study has confirmed our preliminary report [8] that the prognosis for infants of very low birthweight can now be very much better. Only nine (9.5%) of the 95 children have handicaps which will prevent them from functioning normally in society (Table III), and the distribution of the IQs of the older children was no different from that of their parents. . . . Among these nine, only five or possibly six had abnormalities of mental or physical development which required, or may require, special educational facilities. All the children were beyond the age when Drillien had identified major handicap in her 1958 study [3] and 45 of them were attending school. It is, therefore, most unlikely that any serious handicaps remained undiscovered, although we cannot, of course, be sure that learning difficulties or minor abnormalities of, for example, coordination, may not be detected later. We propose to keep the children under surveillance and test them accordingly.

Cause of Death

In spite of our efforts to prevent it, by far the most important immediate cause of death was hypoxia, due either to intrapartum or postpartum asphyxia, or hyaline membrane disease requiring mechanical ventilation. . . . Coexisting intraventricular hemorrhage, itself probably caused by hypoxia [29], was frequently found at autopsy. The only other important factors which influenced survival rate were birthweight and gestational age. Not surprisingly, the highest mortality was among the smallest infants (Table I), and only 23% of those weighing 501 to 1,000 gm survived. Birth defects were rarely a cause of death . . . [30], serious infection was uncommon . . . , and no relation could be found between specific abnormalities of pregnancy and survival rate. . . .

Cause of Handicap

The number of handicapped children was small; nevertheless, a clear relation between the presence of handicap and the occurrence of neonatal illnesses, particularly those presumed to have caused severe hypoxia, was established (Table IV . . .). It was striking that there were no handicapped children among the 23 who were free of serious neonatal difficulties and only one of the 44 who suffered from a variety of problems such as hyaline membrane disease, preterm apnea, hypoglycemia, and jaundice but who had apparently not had any severe hypoxic episodes proved to be handicapped. These findings applied equally to infants who were light-for-dates and to those who were solely preterm. By contrast, eight out of the nine handicapped children had probably suffered severe hypoxia around the time of birth (as judged by the discovery of a large metabolic acidosis soon after delivery), or subsequently (as indicated by the development of apnea necessitating endotracheal intubation). The incidence of handicap in infants with either or both of these findings was 29% (Table IV). Hypoxia, therefore, seemed not only to be the most important cause of death, but also the most important cause of handicap. Seven of the nine handicapped children were jaundiced and the incidence of handicap among the 11 children in whom presumed hypoxia and indirect serum bilirubin levels between 10.8 and 18.4 mg/100 ml both occurred was 54% (Table IV). Serum bilirubin levels as high as this without hypoxia appeared innocuous. The reason for the apparent potentiation of the adverse effect of hypoxia by jaundice may have been, in some cases at least, that low pH was responsible for detaching bilirubin from albumin so that it could penetrate into the brain [31].

No other significant associations between handicap and social or obstetric factors, or perinatal events, could be discovered. Since starvation in the neonatal period has been implicated in the causation of handicap or reduced IQ in low-birth-weight infants [27, 32] particular attention was paid to the possibility that poor weight gain might predispose to handicap. Although five of the nine handicapped children were still below their birthweight on the 21st day . . . , so too were 20 of the nonhandicapped children ($X^2 = 2.87$, N.S.), even though we tried to increase their caloric intake as rapidly as possible. Four of the five also suffered from hypoxia and jaundice. We doubt, therefore, whether the degree of undernutrition experienced by the infants in the present study (who were fed from arrival in the unit) was sufficient to cause handicap. While it is highly probable that severe starvation can damage the developing brain [33], another explanation for the association of delayed weight gain and subsequent handicap and low IQ which seems at least as probable from our data is that both are caused by severe illness, particularly if accompanied by hypoxia and jaundice.

Implications and Conclusions

Studies from other centers [34, 35] confirm our findings that the application of intensive care methods to infants of very low birthweight is associated both with an increase in survival rate and a reduction in the proportion who will be handicapped. We therefore conclude that much of the high mortality and morbidity found by previous workers was caused by preventable perinatal events, and we also conclude that the intensive care of these infants is worthwhile for social and economic as well as purely humanitarian reasons. It follows that facilities for carrying it out should be provided on a wide scale. Because less than 2% of live-born infants in this country weigh 1,500 gm or less at birth and because they are so susceptible to hazards which may kill or handicap them, we believe that they should whenever possible be delivered in major centers which are properly equipped to provide optimal care both before and after birth. Failing this, they should be transferred immediately after delivery to neonatal intensive care units. With improvements in the methods for the transfer of small or sick infants, the risks of transfer will often be less than the dangers of remaining in a hospital with inadequate facilities.

Many infants of very low birthweight still die and our handicap rate of 9.5% remains unacceptably high. Since this study indicates that intrapartum or postpartum hypoxia is largely responsible for death and handicap in these infants, advances in methods which combat hypoxia, or the illnesses which cause it, are likely to produce the greatest further improvement in prognosis. For example, the increasing use of intrapartum monitoring will ensure that more infants are born in good condition. Also, since the survival rate in the present investigation appeared to be highest in infants delivered by cesarean section and lowest among breech deliveries . . . ., who are likely to have suffered the worst hypoxia, it seems that a low threshold for cesarean section can safely be encouraged when a very small fetus is at high risk *in utero.*

During recent years substantial advances have been made in the management of the most important lethal postnatal cause of hypoxia, hyaline membrane disease. The prenatal detection of infants at risk for the illness [36] allows some pregnancies to be prolonged until the lungs are sufficiently mature to avoid the likelihood of developing it and the antenatal treatment of infants with immature lungs may soon become feasible [37]. The introduction of methods for maintaining alveolar inflation during spontaneous breathing [38] and of better methods for mechanical ventilation [39] have much improved the chances for infants with the established illness in our unit in the years since the study period ended. Because of the association of jaundice together with hypoxic episodes and subsequent handicap, we have intensified our efforts to prevent and treat jaundice in infants who are either thought to have suffered hypoxia or who are considered to be at risk for it.

Other changes in management which have taken place and which may be expected to cause a further improvement in prognosis include the introduction of parenteral nutrition [40], which has proved very useful in the management of the smallest infants, and the routine measurement of coagulation status, which allows infants at risk for bleeding to be treated prophylactically.

REFERENCES

1 Usher, R. H.: Clinical implications of perinatal mortality statistics. Clin. Obstet. Gynec., 14:885, 1971.

2 Knobloch, H., Rider, R., Harper, P., and Pasamanick, B.: Neuropsychiatric sequelae of prematurity. JAMA, 161:581, 1956.

3 Drillien, C. M.: Growth and development in a group of children of very low birth weight. Arch. Dis. Child., 33:10, 1958.

4 Lubchenco, L. O., Horner, F. A., Reed, L. H., Hix, I. E., Metcalf, D., Cohig, R., Elliott, H. C., and Bourg, M.: Sequelae of premature birth. Am. J. Dis. Child., 106:101, 1963.

5 Drillien, C. M.: The long-term prospects of handicap in babies of low birth weight. Hosp. Med., i:937, 1967.

6 Holt, K. S.: The Quality of Survival: Institute for Research into Mental Retardation. Occasional Papers 2, 3, 4. London: Butterworth, 1972.

7 Schlesinger, E. R.: Neonatal intensive care: Planning for services and outcomes following care. *Pediatrics,* 82:916, 1973.

8 Rawlings, G., Reynolds, E. O. R., Stewart, A., and Strang, L. B.: Changing prognosis for infants of very low birth weight. Lancet, 1:516, 1971.

9 Saling, E.: Neues Vorgehen zur Untersuching des Kindes unter der Geburt. Arch. Gynaek., 197:108, 1962.

10 Blake, A. M., Collins, L. M., Langham, J., and Reynolds, E. O. R.: Portable ventilator-incubator. Lancet, 1:25, 1970.

11 Hey, E. M., and Katz, G.: Optimum thermal environment for naked babies. Arch. Dis. Child., 45:328, 1970.

12 Blake, A. M., Collins, L. M., Langham, J., and Reynolds, E. O. R.: Clinical assessment of apnoea alarm mattress for newborn infants. Lancet, H: 183, 1970.

13 Adamson, T. M., Collins, L. M., Dehan, J., Hawker, J. M., Reynolds, E. O. R. and Strang, L. B.: Mechanical ventilation in newborn infants with respiratory failure. Lancet, H:227, 1968.

14 Reynolds, E. O. R., and Taghizadeh, A.: Improved prognosis of infants mechanically ventilated for hyaline membrane disease. Arch. Dis. Child., 49:505, 1974.

15 Reynolds, E. O. R.: Effect of alterations in mechanical ventilator settings on pulmonary gas exchange in hyaline membrane disease. Arch. Dis. Child., 46:152, 1971.

16 Knobloch, H., Pasamanick, B., and Sherard, E. S.: A developmental screening inventory for infants. *Pediatrics.* 38(Suppl.):1095, 1966.

17 Sheridan, M.D.: The developmental progress of infants and young children. Rep. Pub. Health Med. Subj. No. 102, 1968.

18 Terman, L. M., and Merrill, M. A.: Stanford-Binet Intelligence Scale. London: Harrap, 1961.

19 Stutsman, R.: Mental Measurement of Pre-school Children. New York: Harcourt, Brace and World, Inc., 1931.

20 Wechler, D.: Wechler Pre-school and Primary Scale of Intelligence. New York: Psychological Corporation, 1967.

21 Wechler, D.: Wechler Adult Intelligence Scale. New York: Psychological Corporation, 1955.

22 Lubchenco, L. O., Hansman, C., Dressler, M., and Boyd, E.: Intrauterine growth as estimated from live-born birth weight data at 24 to 32 weeks of gestation. *Pediatrics,* 32:793, 1963.

23 Tanner, J. M., and Whitehouse, R. H.: Standards for height and weight of British children from birth to maturity. Lancet H:1086, 1959.

24 Alberman, E.: Stillbirths and neonatal mortality in England and Wales by birthweight 1953–71. Health Trends, 6:14, 1974.

25 Cross, K. W.: Cost of preventing retrolental fibroplasia? Lancet, H:954, 1973.

26 Davies, P. A., and Russell, H.: Later progress of 100 infants weighing 1,000 to 2,000 g. at birth fed immediately with breast milk. Develop. Med. Child Neurol., 10:725, 1968.

27 Davies, P. A., and Davis, J. P.: Very low birth weight and subsequent head growth. Lancet, H:1216, 1970.

28 McDonald, A. D.: Children of very low birth weight. Medical Education and Information Unit of the Spastics Society. London: Research Monograph No. 1, 1967.

29 Cole, V. A., Durbin, G. M., Olaffson, A., Reynolds, E. O. R., Rivers, R. P. A., and Smith, J. F.: Pathogenesis of intraventricular haemorrhage in newborn infants. Arch. Dis. Child., 49:722, 1974.

30 Stewart, A.: The risk of handicap due to birth defect in infants of very low birth weight. Develop. Med. Child Neurol., 14;585, 1972.

31 Stern, L., and Denton, R. L.: Kernicterus in small premature infants. *Pediatrics,* 35:483, 1965.

32 Drillien, C. M.: Babies of very low birthweight. *In* The Growth and Development of the Prematurely Born Infant. Edinburgh: E & S Livingstone Ltd., 1964.

33 Winick, M.: Malnutrition and brain development. J. Pediat., 74:667, 1969.

34 Calâme, A., and Prod'hom, L. S.: Prognostie vital et qualité de survie des prématurés pesant 1500g et moins à la naissance soignés en 1966–1968. Schweiz. Med. Wochenschr., 102:65, 1972.

35 Alden, E. R., Mandelkorn, T., Woodrum, D. E., Wennberg, R. P., Parks, C. R., and Hodson, W. A.: Morbidity and mortality of infants weighing less than 1,000 grams in an intensive care nursery *Pediatrics,* 50:40, 1972.

36 Gluck, L., Kulovich, M. V., Borer, R. C., Brenner, P. H., Anderson, G. G., and Spellacy, W. N.: Diagnosis of the respiratory distress syndrome by amniocentesis. Am. J. Obstet. Gynec., 109:440, 1971.

37 Liggins, G. C., and Howie, R. N.: A controlled trial of antepartum glucocorticoid treatment for prevention of the respiratory distress syndrome in premature infants. *Pediatrics,* 50:515, 1972.

38 Gregory, G. A., Kitterman, J. A., Phibbs, R. H., Tooley, W. N., and Hamilton, W. K.: Treatment of idiopathic respiratory distress syndrome with continuous positive airway pressure. N. Engl. J. Med., 284:1333, 1972.

39 Blake, A. M., Collins, L. M., Durbin, G. M., Hunter, N. J., McNab, A. J., Reynolds, E. O. R., and Sellens, G.: Simplified mechanical ventilation for hyaline membrane disease. Lancet, H:1176, 1973.

40 Shaw, J. C. L.: Parenteral nutrition in the management of sick low birth weight infants. Pediatr. Clin. N. Am., 20:333, 1973.

Communication Skills in Five-Year-Old Children with High-Risk Neonatal Histories

Carol H. Ehrlich, Ph.D.
Director, Audiology and Speech Pathology and Adjunct Professor, University of Denver Children's Hospital

Esther Shapiro, Ph.D.
Child Psychologist, Children's Hospital Mental Health Center, Denver, Colorado

Bud D. Kimball, Ph.D.
Regional Audiologist, Southeast Alaska Communicative Disorders Program, Public Health Service Hospital, Mt. Edgcumbe, Alaska

Muriel Huttner [1]
Formerly of Children's Hospital, Denver, Colorado

Communication skills involving auditory and visual perception, the learning and conceptualizing of a verbal symbol system (language), and the actual production of speech are critical to social adjustment and academic learning. Deficiencies in communication skills result in academic failure, social maladjustment, and the need for special care programs, often at considerable cost to society. Disabilities of speech, language, and hearing are often not detected or treated until a child reaches school age. A growing consensus of opinion holds that by this time the critical period for learning language is largely past (Lenneberg, 1967; Tervoort, 1964; Elliott and Armbruster, 1967; McNeill, 1966), and gains made by subsequent special training do not seem to compensate for the time lost during infancy and preschool years.

Early identification of these communication problems in children has

From *Journal of Speech and Hearing Research*, vol. 16, no. 3, pp. 522–529 (September 1974).
[1] Deceased.

therefore been deemed important. Agreement has not been reached, however, about the most efficient means of achieving early identification. Screening devices have been used, but there are still unresolved questions of whether screening adequately identifies the problem, and if it does, what population to screen and how to make this population available. Special surveillance of high-risk babies is another possible course of action, not necessarily exclusive of other approaches. The prospective Collaborative Study of Cerebral Palsy and Other Neurological and Sensory Disorders of Infancy and Childhood which began in 1959 was undertaken to define various high-risk populations and their developmental sequelae. Subnormality was reported in some areas, and while all results will not become available for several years, the collaborative study makes clear the validity of the high-risk approach to early identification.

A wealth of material is available demonstrating mortality risks of certain newborn conditions. When morbidity is reported, it is usually expressed in terms of systemic disorders such as seizures, cerebral palsy, cardiovascular malfunction, blindness, deafness, and mental retardation. The recent literature includes some reports of less obvious but highly significant behavior and learning disabilities, and as clinicians we see enough evidence of this to warrant further careful study of the high-risk population.

Accordingly, this preliminary study investigated the skills of five-year-old children who were labeled "at risk" after birth on the basis of one or more of the following neonatal conditions: (1) abnormal birth weight or gestational age, (2) blood incompatibility, (3) respiratory distress, and (4) hyperbilirubinemia. The study centered on the following questions: (1) Does the high-risk infant have a greater than normal chance of demonstrating specific learning and perceptual disorders? (2) Which conditions imply the greatest risk of such disorders? and (3) Which function or functions are most apt to be affected?

METHOD

Subjects

The children selected for study met one or more of the following criteria: (1) birth weight less than 2500 grams, (2) gestational age less than 38 weeks, (3) small for gestational age (SGA) according to the classification of Battaglia and Lubchenko (1967), (4) blood incompatibility in either Rh or ABO factors, (5) respiratory distress diagnosed by the neonatologist, and (6) hyperbilirubinemia greater than 15 mg% unconjugated bilirubin.

The 1966 abstracts from the Newborn Center, an intensive care unit at Children's Hospital of Denver, were combed for all records meeting these criteria, excluding those with other conditions which could have disturbed development (that is, myclomeningocele and hydrocephalus, heart or CNS

Table 1 High-Risk Data of Subjects

N	Condition	Average	Range	Normal
48	Premature			
	Gestational age	32.6 weeks	27–37 weeks	40 weeks
	Birth weight	1781 g	1049–2455 g	>2500 g
44	Hyperbilirubinemia	20.36 mg%	15.2–27 mg%	<13–14 mg%
26	Respiratory distress	7.28 pH	7.14–7.41 pH	7.38–7.42 pH
	(12 cases of which were hyaline			
	membrane disease)			
35	Blood incompatibility	—	—	—
20	Rh	—	—	—
15	ABO	—	—	—
32	Female	—	—	—
49	Male	—	—	—

abnormalities, chromosomal defects, known maternal history such as rubella, lues, and so on). Subjects were sought from among 180 such children; attrition by death, moving without available contact, and unwillingness to participate reduced the pool so the ultimate sample for the study numbered 81. Their specific high-risk data and sex distribution are displayed in Table 1. Sixty-four percent of the children were of upper socioeconomic status and 36% were lower socioeconomic status, according to the Minnesota Occupational Scale developed from paternal occupation data (Institute of Child Welfare, 1950).

All study children were five years of age, plus or minus two weeks, at the time of testing. This age was chosen because (1) basic grammatical language structure is normally established by this time (Menyuk, 1969; Chomsky, 1970; Lowell, 1967; McNeill, 1970); (2) standardized tests are available which tap perceptual, language, and intellectual functions, so test results can be quite specific; (3) performance by this age has been found to have a high predictive value for later intellectual functioning (Welcher, Mellitis, and Hardy, 1971); and (4) performance could be measured before formal academic training begins so a fair baseline could be measured.

Several normal five-year-old children were included in the nonmedical appointments. Examiners saw all children without knowing which of the high-risk or normal categories they fit, and it was hoped thereby to remove bias in testing.

Testing

Twenty-nine measures or observations were made, including a physical examination with pediatric neurologic screening . . . , speech-language-audiologic testing, and psychometrics. The order of the last two sections was alternated to minimize the effects of fatigue on the overall results. Standardized test instruments were the Wechsler Preschool and Primary Intelligence Scale (WPPSI), the Arthur Adaptation of the Leiter International Performance Scale (LIPS); the Peabody Picture Vocabulary Test, Form A (PPVT); the Templin-Darley Articulation Screening Test; and the Illinois Test of Psycholinguistic Abilities (ITPA). The normative data from the WPPSI, LIPS, Templin-Darley, and ITPA were drawn from children whose socioeconomic backgrounds were equivalent to or slightly lower than those of the study children. The WPPSI data base approximated the 1960 census, with 58% USES and 42% LSES. The LIPS standardization was derived from a homogeneous middle-class group. The Templin-Darley test followed the 1950 census distribution with 30% USES and 70% LSES. The ITPA was standardized with middle occupational levels slightly overrepresented at the expense of lower levels. While not identical to the background of the children yielding the various test norms, the study children's socioeconomic levels either approximated or slightly exceeded them. Audiology tests included monaural pure-tone and speech reception thresholds, monaural speech discrimination in quiet (PB-K ½ list), and diotic speech discrimination in noise (PB-K ½ list with white noise at a signal/noise ratio of 0 dB). In addition, remarkable hyperactivity, short attention span, and word-finding difficulties were noted. Testing was done appropriately by a clinical psychologist, a speech pathologist, and an audiologist. A double-walled IAC sound suite with either an Allison 22 or a Grason Stadler 1701 audiometer was used for all audio examinations.

A pass-fail record from all tests of high-risk subjects was treated with chi-square and binomial sign procedures in order to determine the significance of risk of specific perceptual and language/learning disorders for each high-risk category. Failure on the physical examination was noted because of systemic problems or inability to perform a neurologic screening item. Performance below the normal range on any subtest constituted failure on the standardized tests. Failure in auditory discrimination was a quiet score below 88% (based on data reported by Ehrlich and Tartaglia, 1973) or a noise score below 70% (based on mean and range data from normal listeners studied by Keith and Talis, 1972). Failure on (or the presence of) hyperactivity required observation by both the psychologist and speech pathologist of driven or uncontrollable physical activity, and a judgment of short attention span also had to be made by both. Word-finding difficulty was noted if the child's expressive language was marked by circumlocutions and searching pauses even though his receptive vocabulary was normal according to the PPVT.

Following the testing, one of three reports was made to the child's physician: (1) performance was quite normal and the child should handle the demands of school well; (2) performance in certain areas was below normal but the child demonstrated sufficient compensatory strength so the only immediate need was to watch him carefully as he moved through school; and (3) performance was remarkably poor either in certain areas or overall, and special intervention in the form of additional tests and/or therapy was indicated.

RESULTS AND DISCUSSION

Six of the 81 study children demonstrated neurologic and sensory problems, and two of these were multiply involved. Mild retardation in the 70–80 range was noted in three children, cerebral palsy twice, visual impairments twice, and a moderate sensorineural hearing loss twice.

The incidence of cerebral palsy (almost 2.5%) only slightly exceeded the incidence rate from the collaborative perinatal study (1.5%) which was not limited to high-risk babies. Retardation occurred less frequently than expected (3.7%). Significant hearing loss occurred in 2.5% of the sample, as compared with 0.5% in the Israeli study of high-risk babies (Feinmesser and Bauberger-Tell),[2] 18% in the Lubchenco et al. (1972) study of very low birth weight babies, and 11.5% in a series of babies with respiratory distress who were treated with positive pressure ventilation (Johnson et al.).[3]

IQs ranged from 87 to 145, averaging 112, using the highest single measure as the index of potential. Full-scale IQs from the WPPSI averaged 103 with a range of 74 to 136. LIPS scores averaged 107 with a range of 68 to 145. Whichever index is used, it is clear that the high-risk children were at least as bright as the normal population, and a good case could be made for their being brighter.

It is surprising, then, to find that only 13 (16%) of these children were functioning normally, 24 (30%) were regarded to bear close watching, and follow-up testing and therapy of 44 (54%) of the children were recommended to their doctors.

In the group needing therapy and more testing, 61% were boys and 39% were girls, a ratio identical to that of the total group studied. The stability of the ratio suggests that high-risk neonatal conditions may not affect children's development differentially by sex.

The physical examination identified 21 of the 81 children (26%) who failed certain items. These included hearing, 1; balance, gait, or hopping, 12; pronation/supination, 5; and drawing/copying, 2. One had asthma and two drooled. Eighteen of these 21 children were also identified by speech-

---

[2] M. Feinmesser and L. Bauberger-Tell, personal communication on detection methods for hearing impairment in infants and young children (1971).

[3] J. D. Johnson, W. J. Daily, R. G. Malachowski, and P. Sunshine, personal communication on the aid of mechanical ventilation in the neonatal period (1972).

Table 2 Significant Disabilities as a Function of Neonatal Condition for 15 Measures of Physical Condition and Perceptual Language and Intellectual Function. The Four Conditions Considered Here Were Abnormal Birth Weight/Gestation Period (Condition A), Blood Incompatibility (Condition B), Respiratory Distress Syndrome (Condition C), and Hyperbilirubinemia (Condition D); Children Are Categorized According to the Number of Neonatal Conditions Present.

Condition	N	Auditory discrimination	Visual memory	Visual figure-ground	Auditory memory	Physical examination	Vocabulary, expressive	Block design	Word-finding	Articulation	Sentence memory	Similarities	Mazes	Sound blending	Geometric design	Short attention span
A alone	8	*	‡	—	†	†	—	—	—	—	—	—	—	‡	—	—
B alone	8	†	—	—	†	—	—	—	—	—	—	—	—	—	—	—
C alone	6	†	‡	—	—	—	—	—	—	—	—	—	—	—	—	—
D alone	4	‡	—	—	—	—	—	—	—	—	—	—	—	—	—	—
A and B	3	—	—	—	—	—	—	—	—	—	—	—	—	—	—	—
A and C	12	†	‡	†	‡	†	†	—	‡	—	†	†	—	—	—	—
A and D	9	*	—	—	†	†	—	—	—	—	—	—	‡	—	‡	—
B and C	0	—	—	—	—	—	—	—	—	—	—	—	—	—	—	—
B and D	16	†	—	—	†	—	—	—	—	—	—	—	—	—	—	—
C and D	1	—	—	—	—	—	—	—	—	—	—	—	—	—	—	—
A, B, and C	0	—	—	—	—	—	—	—	—	—	—	—	—	—	—	—
A, B, and D	7	*	—	†	—	‡	—	—	‡	—	—	—	—	‡	—	—
A, C, and D	6	*	*	†	—	—	—	†	—	—	—	—	—	—	—	—
B, C, and D	0	—	—	—	—	—	—	—	—	—	—	—	—	—	—	—
A, B, C, and D	1	—	—	—	—	—	—	—	—	—	—	—	—	—	—	—
Total	81	—	—	—	—	—	—	—	—	—	—	—	—	—	—	—
Any A	46	*	*	†	†	*	‡	—	—	‡	—	—	—	—	—	—
Any B	35	*	—	—	†	—	—	—	—	—	—	—	—	—	—	—
Any C	26	*	*	*	—	†	†	*	—	—	—	—	—	—	—	—
Any D	44	—	†	‡	—	‡	—	—	—	—	—	—	—	—	—	—

*Significant beyond 0.1% level.   †Significant beyond 1.0% level.   ‡Significant beyond 5.0% level.

language and psychological testing, with subsequent recommendations for therapy. The physical examination did not identify 22 other children whose problems in speech-language and psychology were regarded as significant and warranting therapy.

Chi-squared tests obtained on all test measures as a function of neonatal condition clearly indicate that deviant performance exceeded expectations for this group of children. In every case in which there were sufficient data to perform the statistical test, there was a significant association between presence of the condition and deviant performance. Therefore, further statistical analyses were performed.

Table 2 presents the results of binomial sign tests of the data by neonatal condition, revealing that significant dysfunctions occurred primarily in children with histories of respiratory distress and abnormal birth weight/gestational age. Auditory discrimination in noise or in quiet, auditory memory, visual figure-ground discrimination, and visual memory were the most commonly impaired functions. It should be noted that these are similar functions in the two major sense modalities. Other significant problems were found in the physical examination, expressive vocabulary, block design, word finding, articulation, memory for sentences, similarities, mazes, sound blending, geometric design, and short attention span.

The findings imply several needs: (1) More attention needs to be focused on auditory and verbal functions by physicians, parents, and preschool teachers. (2) Babies at risk because of respiratory distress or prematurity should be monitored with tests of auditory and visual figure-ground discrimination and memory in particular and should also be screened for the other language and perceptual functions found to be related significantly to these high-risk conditions. This monitoring may be done at four years of age as suggested by Welcher et al. (1971). (3) Screening tests for these functions must be designed and standardized in order to make monitoring programs feasible.

REFERENCES

Battaglia, F. C., and Lubchenco, L. O., Practical classification of newborn infants by weight and gestational age. *J. Pediat.*, 71, 161 (1967).

Chomsky, C., *The Acquisition of Syntax in Children from 5 to 10, Research Monograph Number 57*. Cambridge: MIT Press (1970).

Ehrlich, C. H., and Tartaglia, J., Three pediatric auditory discrimination measures: A correctional study. *J. Colo. Speech Hearing Ass.*, 7, (1973).

Elliott, L., and Armbruster, V. C., Some possible effects of the delay of early treatment of deafness. *J. Speech Hearing Res.*, 10, 209–224 (1967).

Institute of Child Welfare, *The Minnesota Scale for Paternal Occupations*. Minneapolis (1950).

Keith, R. W., and Talis, H. P., The effects of white noise on PB scores of normal and hearing impaired listeners, *Audiology II,* 177–186, (1972).

Lenneberg, E. H., *Biological Foundations of Language.* New York: Wiley (1967).

Lowell, E. L., Psychoeducational management of the young deaf child. In F. McConnell and P. H. Ward (Eds.), *Deafness in Childhood.* Nashville: Vanderbilt Univ. Press (1967).

Lubchenco, L. O., and Associates, Long-term follow-up studies of prematurely born infants. I. Relationship of handicaps to nursery routines. *J. Pediat.,* 80, 501–508 (1972).

McNeill, D., Capacity for language acquisition. *Volta Rev.,* 68, 17–33 (1966).

McNeill, D., Development of language. In *Manual of Child Psychology.* Vol. 1. New York: Wiley (1970).

Menyuk, P., *Sentences Children Use.* Research Monograph Number 52. Cambridge: MIT Press (1969).

Tervoort, B., Development of language and the critical period in the young deaf child. *Acta otolaryng.,* Suppl. 26, 247–251 (1964).

Welcher, D. W., Mellitis, E. D., and Hardy, J. B., A multivariate analysis of factors affecting psychological performance. *Johns Hopkins Collaborative Perinatal Project: Proceedings of a Symposium* (1971).

Chapter 6

Critical Issues in Comprehensive Care for Mothers and Infants

The preceding selections in this book have set forth many of the psychosocial challenges and dilemmas presented by high-risk mothers and infants. In this final chapter we shall explore some of the efforts made to prevent or reduce pathological outcomes of pregnancy and prematurity. Furthermore, this section includes an article pertaining to the biomedical ethics of intensive care for newborn infants and, finally, a legal analysis of decision making in involuntary euthanasia of defective newborns.

Comprehensive health care for pregnant women and their babies remains an unfulfilled promise for too many of those who need it most. In these articles, new approaches are offered which extend the professional services of nurses and social workers.

Some medical centers with infant intensive-care units are providing programs which bring together parents of high-risk infants. These groups are both therapeutic and educational, helping the parents with their emotional conflicts while preparing them for the infant care at home. Nurses and social workers combine their skills to provide these parents with the psychosocial counterpart to the medical care being offered. The need to explore contributions which can be made through paraprofessional and homemaker services is also essential if outreach and follow-up programs are to be effective.

In the first article, "One Hundred Pregnant Adolescents: Treatment Approaches in a University Hospital," by Helen O. Dickens et al., the authors outline the methods they use to give comprehensive physical and emotional care to young mothers before, during, and after delivery. The authors include public-health statistics which indicate that the mortality rate of black infants is twice that of Caucasians. Furthermore, black mothers die at about four times the rate of their white counterparts. We are also reminded that 40 percent of nonwhite households live at or below what the Social Security Administration defines as the poverty level. The authors emphasize the need for a preventive approach which is educational as well as medical. The article provides guidelines for other groups which may wish to implement such a program.

The statistics pertaining to teenage pregnancy leave no doubt that this group is especially prone to produce premature babies with all the attendant complications and pathological sequelae which inevitably follow. In the United States, over 600,000 babies are born annually to adolescent girls, of whom 225,000 are seventeen or younger. Although half of the girls under eighteen are unmarried, most of the young mothers (85 percent) choose to keep their babies. Most of these women become pregnant again and 60 percent of them are on the welfare rolls within five years.

"Reducing Neonatal Mortality Rate with Nurse-Midwives," by Barry S. Levy, Frederick S. Wilkinson, and William M. Marine, discusses the effective utilization of nurse-midwives. During the project described in this article, prenatal care increased and the rate of prematurity and neonatal mortality decreased in the population tended by nurse-midwives. The authors recommend that similar nurse-midwife programs be set up elsewhere, at least on a trial basis. These projects could be established in areas where poverty, a critical physician shortage, and a high prenatal and neonatal mortality rate exist.

The role of nurse-midwives in reducing maternal-infant mortality has been demonstrated abroad and in the United States. The effectiveness of such agencies as the Frontier Nursing Service has been well known since 1935. Unfortunately, too few states permit nurse-midwives to practice.

The third article, "High-Risk Pregnancy, II: A Pattern of Comprehensive Maternal and Child Care," by Howard N. Jacobson and Duncan E. Reid, suggests the use of the "family nurse practitioner." This classic article, published in 1964, illustrates the vision of the authors in planning for comprehensive maternal-child care. The family nurse practitioner whom they propose in their article is becoming a reality, but the role she can play in providing health care is still evolving.

The article, "Critical Issues in Newborn Intensive Care: A Conference Report and Policy Proposal," by A. R. Jonsen et al., reflects the growing concern with questions relating to euthanasia. The life-saving and life-maintaining techniques which have become almost routine medical procedures bring with them extremely difficult moral and ethical questions concerning such matters as definition of death and decisions regarding the utilization or termination of life-support apparatus. Neonatal intensive care has given rise to many of these perplexing dilemmas. The authors suggest four moral "fields of force" which they believe should be included in decision making regarding the life and death actions taken in neonatal intensive care units.

The final reading in this section is, "Involuntary Euthansia of Defective Newborns: A Legal Analysis." The author, Law Professor John A. Robertson, considers the various decision-making processes which lead to the withholding of ordinary medical treatment from severely defective newborns. He recognizes that this form of involuntary euthansia has become a pervasive practice. His conclusion is that a need exists for the establishment of legally defined criteria and procedures in these cases. One result would be that these life and death decisions would be removed from the informal authority of physicians, nurses, and parents. Robertson weighs the legal rights of the infants against the rights and obligations of society, parents, and medical personnel. The author offers the medical reader an opportunity to view these issues from the perspective of a member of the legal profession.

Thus, this volume concludes with two articles which represent pioneering efforts to meet the sobering moral, ethical, and legal challenges posed by the technological advances in the treatment of high-risk infants.

One Hundred Pregnant Adolescents: Treatment Approaches in a University Hospital

Helen O. Dickens, M.D.
Associate Professor of Obstetrics and Gynecology, University of
Pennsylvania School of Medicine

Emily Hartshorne Mudd, M.S.W., Ph.D.
Professor Emeritus of Family Study in Psychiatry, University of Pennsylvania
Hospital

Celso-Ramon Garcia, M.D.
Professor and Director of Human Reproduction, University of Pennsylvania
School of Medicine

Karen Tomar, M.S.W.
Division of Human Reproduction, University of Pennsylvania School of
Medicine

David Wright
Resident in Pathology, University of Pennsylvania Hospital

INTRODUCTION

The purpose of this paper is to explore various aspects of teenage pregnancy: the health and feelings of the young mother before, during, and after delivery, her wishes concerning care of her baby and desire for more babies, her response to the possible use of contraceptives, her return to school or job training, and her continuing development of self-worth in responsible living. It was desirable to assess the effect of intensive and personalized contact before delivery and for a year thereafter with the pregnant teenager as it might enhance the health and self-respect of the young mother and baby as well as the continuation of her schooling or job training, and her prevention of repeated unwanted pregnancies. Although data presented represent a sample of the total population delivered at the University Hospital, this review should point out the potentially significant areas of difficulty among the two University Hospital approaches with pregnant adolescents.

Public health statistics for the United States [1] and medical reports indicate that black infants die at twice the rate of whites, and that black mothers die at four times the rate of their white counterparts, with teenage mothers considered in the high risk category [2–7]. We are also told that almost 40% of non-white households live below what the Social Security Administration calls "the poverty level," attain less schooling and less em-

From *American Journal of Public Health*, vol. 63, no. 9, pp. 794–800 (September 1973).

ployment [8]. Inasmuch as a "relatively" high percentage of women delivered in the hospital of the University of Pennsylvania are black, with many in their teens, a significant proportion of whose medical expenses are covered by various Government subsidies, an obvious opportunity was presented to elicit further information concerning these conditions, their causes and their possible alleviation [9].

Dr. Sarrel, of Yale, emphasized in 1967 the depressing cycle which was set in motion by teenage pregnancy when no special attention was given to the young mother. In his words, "an out-of-wedlock pregnancy in these teenagers signaled the beginning of a cycle—a cycle consisting of failure to continue education, dependence on the state welfare system, never creating their own stable family, and continuing the reproduction of illegitimate offspring. The result was that of a young, frightened girl, 'caught' by a pregnancy, being transformed into a depressed, defeated and dependent unmarried mother of five or six young children" [10].

Within the Department of Obstetrics and Gynecology at the University Hospital, there have been two separate facilities available to the pregnant teenager for her care; the regular Prenatal Clinic serving all ages and, since September, 1967, a special adolescent or Teen-Obstetrical Clinic offering more intensive and personalized care before and after delivery. Study of fifty patients "randomly" selected from among those served by *each of these two clinics* should throw light on whether the patients have reasonably good health during and after pregnancy, whether delivery is without undue complications and the baby is normal, whether the young mother returns to school, takes job training and/or marries and cares for her child. It also should indicate whether the patient takes responsibility, through use of contraceptives offered following the birth of her baby, to prevent unwanted repeat pregnancies and develops a position of respect for herself and her family in her community.

THE CLINICS

The Teen Obstetrical Clinic was initiated and is directed by Dr. Helen O. Dickens, a black Board-certified obstetrician-gynecologist who believed the pregnant, usually unmarried, teenager to be uncomfortable, disadvantaged, and fearful in a clinic containing many women of her mother's age. In achieving her goals, between September, 1967 and September, 1970 Dr. Dickens was aided by the part-time assistance of a team composed of three rotating hospital nurses, one pediatrician, one case worker, one group worker, one school counselor, and three medical students. The clinic was held on Saturday mornings to facilitate attendance of girls still in school. Weekly discussion groups were offered to the girls, their mothers when willing, and the fathers of the babies when available. These covered information on pregnancy, delivery, baby care, contraception, support, school, and other realistically practical areas as brought up by the patients. About ten antepartum and five postpartum girls attended an average clinic session, a ratio of one staff to each one and one-half girls. In addition Dr. Dickens, assisted by medical students, talked with and/or examined each girl on each clinic visit.

The regular Prenatal Clinic, up to February 1971, has operated four afternoons weekly with average attendance of ninety to one hundred patients per clinic session. Clinic Staff consisted of one senior physician, five residents, four medical students, fifteen nurses, of whom four were registered nurses, three practical and eight nursing assistants, three and one-half social workers and seven family planning workers, a ratio of one staff to three patients. There were fewer personnel in 1967–68.

In 1968 the Head Nurse, Ms. Mary Theresa Green, initiated a Nursing Care Plan for each patient. This consisted of a half-hour individual interview during which a so-called "Portrait" was made with each patient's needs listed. This covered whether the child was wanted or not, past use of contraception and future desire in this area, problems in regard to support, care of the child, education, housing, etc. and an estimate of what the patient needs to be taught in nursing classes. If special continuing problems were indicated, the patient was referred to one of the staff case workers. In addition, a continuing weekly class meeting for eight sessions was programmed for each "expectant parent." This included discussion of antepartum care, nutrition, maternal and fetal changes during pregnancy, labor and delivery, family planning and baby care.

THE POPULATION

The study population to be reviewed were eighteen or under (84% between 15 and 17) and in their *first pregnancy*. One hundred subjects were randomly selected from the total adolescent obstetrical population of 730 followed at the University of Pennsylvania during the three-year period, September 19, 1967—September 19, 1970.

The sample included 21 girls in 1967, 21 in 1968, 34 in 1969 and 24 in 1970. Half of the population, fifty girls, were selected at random from the University Hospital Teen Obstetrical Clinic, picking every fourth case from the Clinic's then total population of 200. The second fifty girls were selected also at random from the Hospital's regular Prenatal Clinic which registered 530 adolescents during this period. Both groups, as already mentioned, were primarily girls in their *first* pregnancy.

Social and demographic characteristics of the two groups of fifty girls selected from each of these clinics were remarkably similar as to race, marital status, education, religion, as well as with whom the girls lived at the time they first registered in the hospital.

Race   In the Teen Obstetrical Clinic 49 girls were black: 46 in the Regular Prenatal Clinic: the remaining 5 were white.

Marital Status   Seventy-three of the adolescent girls remained single. Eight were married when they first came to the hospital, ten girls were married during pregnancy, and nine were married after the birth of the baby.

Religion   Eighty-two of the girls had Protestant affiliations, 17 were Catholic, 1 Jewish, and on 4 there was no information.

Education   As would be expected in this age span, the girls were attending Grades 7–12 with 2 high school graduates in each group. Eighty-six girls were attending school at the time of their first registration in the hospital.

Live with   Most of the girls (84%) lived with their mothers, 42% had fathers living in the home, and 67% also had siblings in the home. Thirty-six girls had other relatives in the home such as aunts, cousins, and godmothers.

PRENATAL CONTACTS

As we explore the hospital contacts after initial registration we note some differences in the intensity of contact with clinic staff between girls in the Teen-Obstetrical Clinic and members of their families, and the girls in the regular Prenatal Clinic. Table 1 shows the percentage of girls involved from each clinic and the greater number of contacts of the Teen-Obstetrical Clinic girls and their family members. The case work interviews covered the same general subjects for the girls in each clinic with some variation as to how often a particular subject was discussed. For instance, school and educational problems, parental problems, and supportive services were well-covered. Marital problems, sex relationships, baby care and job advice were less well-represented in the regular Prenatal Clinic.

In addition to interviews with case workers, classes held by nurses in both clinics discussed prenatal care, nutrition, maternal and fetal changes during pregnancy, labor and delivery, family planning and baby care. In the Teen-Obstetrical Clinic 2 husbands, 2 putative fathers, and three relatives were also seen, in addition to the mothers of the patients, and an experienced group worker met with 34 of the girls for from 1–14 meetings.

Table 1   Educational and Therapeutic Factors Antepartum

	Teen Obs. Clinic		Regular Prenatal Clinic		Total
	No. of contacts	%	No. of contacts	%	%
Casework interviews teenagers	192	98	140	96	97
Mothers of patients	1+	62	1+	66	64
Others	1+	78	1+	0	44
Attended nursing classes	4	56	4	56+	56
Continued in school	—	30	—	18	24

A black male social worker held discussion groups for the available fathers of the babies and a female group worker continued meetings with the mothers of the patients [11].

A variety of activities similar to efforts in other cities [12, 13] to involve girls in new and broadening "fun interests" were initiated in the Teen-Obstetrical Clinic as volunteer help and funding permitted. Some of these preceded the birth of the baby, such as knitting classes, trips to concerts and a ballet performance. Some were during the period after the babies' birth, such as dance class, swimming picnics, presentation by Plays for Living, and the initiation of a play given by the girls themselves, after hours of rehearsal, which was focused on the life of the Clinic Director. A beautician visited to encourage good grooming. In a more serious vein, speakers came to the clinic to discuss the legal rights of teenagers and their babies. The girls were often amazed and stimulated by these completely different experiences. Such contacts, unfortunately, were not available to the regular Prenatal Clinic adolescents.

During pregnancy 61% of the total of 100 girls dropped out of school. However, 15 girls from the Teen-Obstetrical Clinic and 9 from the regular Prenatal Clinic continued school in one of the programs for pregnant girls begun by the Philadelphia School Board in early 1968. Some of these dropouts occurred in 1967 and early 1968 before girls were permitted to stay in school after six months of pregnancy. It is also possible that after mid-1968 some of the more highly motivated teenagers elected to attend the Continuing Education Program of the Philadelphia School Board and sought delivery in other hospitals.

Evidence of interest and responsibility taken by the girls is shown in their record of clinic attendance before delivery. In both the Teen-Obstetrical Clinic and the regular Prenatal Clinic the girls averaged at least three months attendance in the Clinic program prior to delivery although a few girls registered in early pregnancy and a few not until near term [14].

MEDICAL FINDINGS

The average number of prenatal visits was eight per girl. On the average, the girls in the special Teen-Obstetrical Clinic made two more prenatal visits than the girls followed in the regular Prenatal Clinic. This may be indicative of more interest generated by the special teenage program. Every single girl had a Pap smear taken and 86% had chest X rays reported. The teenage girls in the regular Prenatal Clinic demonstrated exactly the same average weight gain during pregnancy (25.2 lbs.) as the girls in the Teen-Obstetrical Clinic. The weight gain is slightly higher than the desired standard and it is worthy of note that 27% of the 100 girls were treated for excessive weight gain during pregnancy.

The frequency of major complications of pregnancy and delivery for the regular Prenatal Clinic teenagers were somewhat greater than those of the Teen-Obstetrical Clinic. In neither group were there any maternal deaths or stillbirths. However, in the regular Prenatal Clinic one infant died within twenty-four hours after delivery from acute respiratory distress and another infant left the delivery room severely depressed with an Apgar of three. Overall, the patients in the regular Prenatal Clinic presented a greater rate of prematurity (15% compared to 8% in the Teen-Obstetrical Clinic); the average infant birth weights were remarkably similar (6 lbs. 10 oz. compared to 6 lbs. 15 oz.); and the average 1 and 5 minute Apgar scores were slightly lower (7.0 and 9.0 compared to 7.9 and 9.5). Five Caesarian sections were performed in the total 100 girls studied; there were three cases of cephalo-pelvic disproportion, one case of acute fetal distress, and one of diabetic ketoacidosis. Concerning minor complications of pregnancy; urinary tract infection, hydramnios, and toxemia of pregnancy, the girls in both clinics showed a very low incidence of problems. See Table 2.

However, two problems stood out; 25 per cent of the 100 teenage girls had anemia during pregnancy of less than 10 gm per cent of hemoglobin despite a program that recommended iron and vitamin supplementation and almost uniformly supplied it free; and as already noted, 27 per cent required treatment for excessive weight gain during pregnancy. It is likely

Table 2   Complications in Teen-Age Pregnancies as Reported by Other Authors*

Name	Nonwhite %	Toxemia during antepartum period %	Prematurity %	Perinatal loss %
Aznar & Bennett	90	9.8	18.7	5.0
Marchetti & Menaker	99	19.7	14.8	3.8
Morrison	95	21.0	16.0	3.8
Poliakoff	72	17.7	17.4	5.9
Sarell[++] & Klerman	97.5	5.0	10.8[†]	0.8
Present series	95	5.0	12	1.0

*From H. M. Hassan, and F. M. Falls, Am. J. Obst. & Gynec. 88:256, 1964.
†Percentages based on 119 pregnancies, 120 live births and 1 stillbirth.
‡Any infant weighing under 2,500 grams was classified as premature to insure comparability with the other studies which did not specify criteria.

that these problems represented a dietary inadequacy among the uninstructed or poor-to-do accentuated by their feelings of insecurity.

Finally, in the immediate postpartum period, prior to hospital discharge, only 7 per cent of the one hundred girls developed urinary tract infections, 5 per cent uterine infections and 18 breast infections. Within one year after delivery the only significant developments were: 6 per cent urinary tract infections and 6 per cent inflammatory disease.

Table 2 as modified from the Table presented by Hassan and Falls and added to by Sarrel [15] indicates how the medical findings in this study compare with those reported in other studies.

POSTPARTUM ACTIVITIES

Both the Teen-Obstetrical Clinic and the regular Prenatal Clinic offer active follow-up programs after the birth of the baby. Family Planning Clinic staff workers show the film "To Plan Your Family" while the young mother is on the maternity floor and later sees each patient individually to review questions still of concern. The Social Service workers also visit each girl during her postpartum stay in the hospital where they will assess the girl's response to her baby and any unresolved plans for the baby care and the total living situation and the girl's feelings concerning birth control.

When the girl leaves the hospital she is given an appointment for her postpartum checkup and informed that she may implement family planning procedures at that time should she so desire. In the Teen Clinic this appointment is set in two weeks following delivery; regular clinic at four weeks. This latter group receives a written reminder from the Family Planning Clinic while the girls in the Teen Obstetrical Clinic are called by the Social Worker who will continue to follow them for one year. If the appointment is not kept both clinics will attempt to encourage a return for medical follow-up by phone or mail.

Table 3 indicates the percentage of girls in each clinic who after the birth of their babies were involved in therapeutic and educational activities which indicated their relationship to assuming responsibility. These activities included: who kept their babies, accepted or refused contraceptives, attended group classes or casework interviews, who were known to have returned to school, failed to keep their follow-up appointment and who had repeat pregnancies.

In the Teen-Obstetrical Clinic the girls average 4 postpartum casework interviews for each, ranging from one to fourteen visits. Subjects discussed in order of interest were: the current situation, postpartum checkup, family planning education, baby care, parental relations, job advice, marital problems and needs for acceptance from peers, staff and others. Outside speakers from the City Health Department covered venereal disease and drug addiction. For girls in the regular Prenatal Clinic, a lesser range of subjects was covered by the casework interviews—primarily information on the current situation and schooling. It was not deemed necessary by the caseworkers to see 25 of the 50 girls. There were no group meetings arranged for these girls during the follow-up period.

Table 3   Educational and Therapeutic Factors Postpartum*

	Teen obs. clinic, %	Regular prenatal clinic, %	Total, %
Kept their babies	100	92	96
Group classes or case interviews	66	50	58
Accepted contraceptives	80	68	74
Refused contraceptives	10	16	13
Failed follow-up	10	18	14
Known to have returned to school	56	10	33
Repeat pregnancies	20	26	23

*Results in Table 3 suggest that girls in the Teen-Obs. Clinic, who received extra attention and care, fared better postpartum

DISPOSITION OF THE INFANT

In the total group of 100 as shown in Table 3, 96 per cent kept their own babies; all 50 from the Teen-Obstetrical Clinic and 46 from the regular Prenatal Clinic [16]. Of the four babies not kept, one died, one was taken by relatives, and two (one black and one white) were placed for adoption.

FAMILY PLANNING

As already reported, the possibility of family-planning instruction is mentioned first to the girls by the nurses or family planning staff health educator toward the end of their pregnancies in the Prenatal Classes conducted by the nurse and in casework interviews if desired. In the Teen-Obstetrical Clinic family planning is integrated into the group work program where emotional attitudes and community myths are discussed. It is routinely discussed again on the hospital ward after delivery by family planning personnel. Better Family Planning, Inc., an all black community organization assigns two of their neighborhood staff as members of the family planning staff of the hospital to work with postpartum and postoperative patients on the wards who are interested in contraceptive methods. Table 3 shows that 74 per cent of the girls received the contraceptive of their choice, 40 from the Teen-Obstetrical Clinic and 34 from the Prenatal Clinic [17]. The large majority, 57 out of 74, were given oral contraceptives, 15 were fitted with an IUD, and one was given a foam prescription. Five girls were supplied oral contraceptives while still in the hospital, the remaining girls, on the average, five weeks after delivery, although in the Teen-Obstetrical Clinic there was a range of 2–12 weeks with increasing emphasis on early return. Sixteen of these girls experienced problems with the oral contraceptive initially given (e.g., bleeding, rash, headache). A few stated personal or family worries over the method[1] and on three girls there was no information. In this problem group, some girls went from the pill to an IUD and the reverse, and some were given another type of pill.

In the Teen-Obstetrical Clinic 10 per cent of the girls refused all forms of birth control, 16 per cent in the Prenatal Clinic. A few girls were refused contraceptives because at the time they delivered, before the Spring of 1968, the hospital staff was not permitted to give contraceptives to a girl younger than 18 without parental consent. In the Teen-Obstetrical Clinic there was no information on 5 girls and in the Prenatal Clinic 9 girls never appeared for their postpartum follow-up and were not seen thereafter by hospital

---

[1] Senate subcommittee hearings on "the Pill" were held in March, 1970. Exhaustive newspaper, radio, and television publicity followed, disturbing many pill takers and their families.

staff in spite of follow-up letters from the Family Planning Staff begun in 1968.

The above figures lead to the almost inevitable conclusion that some of the girls will become pregnant again. From the Teen-Obstetrical Clinic, through September 1970, 20% of the girls are known to have become pregnant a second time 14½ months, on the average, after the first birth. Six of these ten girls had used or selected an oral contraceptive, 3 had refused any birth control method, 1 girl was fitted with an IUD. Among the Prenatal Clinic group there were 26% of the girls who had repeat pregnancies approximately 19 months after their first baby. Subsequently 3 out of this 13 had a second repeat pregnancy making a total of 16 pregnancies in all. Eight of these 13 girls had used or selected an oral contraceptive, 2 pregnancies were planned, 1 girl had an IUD, 1 did not come for follow-up, 1 was in 1968 and then administratively deemed "too young" for birth control. Although a total of 14% of the girls from the two groups, who had been supplied with oral contraceptives, became unexpectedly pregnant, this was from 24% who had selected the pill as their method of choice. Fifteen girls had elected the IUD and 2, (13%) were known to be pregnant.

Intervening time between acceptance for publication and publishing, gave the authors the valuable opportunity to further follow-up and evaluate postpartum activities through May 31, 1972—an extension of 20 and ½ months follow-up. The original study and figures were computed through September 19, 1970. In the Teen-Obstetrical Clinic through May 31, 1972, 42% of the girls are known to have become pregnant a second time on the average of 18 months after the first birth. One girl had three repeat pregnancies and three had two repeat pregnancies making a total of 26 repeat pregnancies. Twenty-two repeat pregnancies resulted in live births and four in therapeutic abortions. Seventeen of these 21 girls with repeat pregnancies had accepted contraceptives (14 "pill", 3 IUD), three had refused any birth control method, and one had not come for postpartum follow-up. Among the regular Prenatal Clinic through May 31, 1972, 42% of the teenagers had repeat pregnancies approximately 17 months after the first baby; six girls had two repeat pregnancies making a total of 27 repeat pregnancies. Nineteen of these resulted in live births and eight in abortions (four spontaneous, three therapeutics, 1 septic). Twelve of these 21 girls with repeat pregnancies had selected contraceptives (9 "the pill", 2 IUD, 1 foam).

It is obvious that any method requiring almost daily thought and care has added difficulties for young teenage girls unfamiliar with and unprepared to assume personal responsibilities. Some of the nurses, social workers and other clinic staff also feel that the recommendation from adults in authority to use contraceptives may tie in to the adolescent's whole conflictual system of behavior, including revolt from any directive. Thus the girls may be drawn consciously or unconsciously to forget her daily pill, to allow her supply to run out, or to resist using money for this [18, 19]. Other staff feel the need of these semi-deprived girls and the general dreariness of their life permits them to feel a certain satisfaction in the attention and the excitement of the pregnancy and to enjoy their ability to have a baby of their own. In this connection, it is of interest that infants from both the repeat pregnancy groups were kept by their mothers and in 10 of the 42 instances the mothers were married and indicated the possibility that the pregnancies had been desired.

DISCUSSION

This review suggests that the approaches and procedures used in the Department of Obstetrics and Gynecology at the Hospital of the University of Pennsylvania for the treatment of teenage mothers, give results which compare favorably to the results reported from other specialized clinics for pregnant teenagers as shown in Table 2. Little demonstrable difference was found during the prenatal period and immediate postpartum period between the Teen-Obstetrical Clinic patients and the teenage patients treated in the regular Prenatal Clinic. This held in regard to participation in medical visits and educational classes before delivery, and in medical findings before, during, and after delivery. Small differences were found in postpartum cooperative behavior between the groups who were accorded special individual care and those who were not (see Table 3). These findings are suggestive although not dramatic.

With dedicated nursing staff and the enlargement of the Family Planning Clinic in 1968 under a grant through the Population Council, Inc. and the Office of Economic Opportunity sponsorship, with staff talking to women on the delivery floor after the babies' birth, and with special contacts at the follow-up and thereafter, it could be argued that the so-called Regular Prenatal Clinic gives almost equivalent interest and care to that given by the specialized clinic. It seems clear that staff education has occurred without formal classroom training. With a change in attitudes, manner of speaking to patients, time and patience to listen to their problems without a personal culturally built-in bias in giving an answer, a broader approach has been arrived at.

In establishing a Clinic or Comprehensive Program that deals with a different population or a special problem, i.e., age, poverty, mores, family planning, one of the important facets is to familiarize the medical, social service, nursing and collateral staff with the patients' background and their problems [20, 21]. They need to realize that a population which is not accustomed to planning for something to happen in their lives, find it much more difficult to structure themselves to plan for something *not* to happen [12, 22]. It is believed that the influence of the special Teen-Obstetrical Clinic has changed in part the manner in which all Clinic obstetrical patients are handled so that the philosophy of the special clinic has pervaded other areas. Return to school, added social service, more nursing education classes, earlier family planning and return to jobs or job training are becoming routine, not only in our hospital clinics but in City Health Centers as well.

It is encouraging to report reasonably good results from the two clinics of the Department of Obstetrics and Gynecology which treat pregnant teenagers. The hard core percentage of repeat pregnancies within the time the patients were under supervision in the two University Hospital clinics and elsewhere seems to remain close to 20% in early follow-up. However, the importance of longer follow-up studies for more complete evaluation is stressed. An additional follow-up study in the University Hospital clinics of nearly two years beyond the original follow-up period revealed the repeat pregnancy rate had more than doubled, from 20% to 42%. As the large majority of these repeat pregnancies were unwanted, it is obvious that currently available contraceptives and/or methods for their use are not successful with many teenagers [23]. Physicians and collateral workers in this field have emphasized the vital role of the doctor and other clinic personnel in allaying the anxieties of the unwed mother, helping to restore her self-esteem, to increase her education, her job performance, and the stability of her family life. This philosophy is being brought to bear in all specialized clinics and is being taught in these clinics to medical students, residents and collateral personnel.

The importance of a preventive approach to this social problem of the unwed mothers and unwanted fatherless babies and the need for community cooperation at all levels has also been elaborated. May we suggest an intensive educational approach in one or two of the communities from which the majority of a hospital's patients are drawn. It is recognized that the sister of the unwed mother is particularly vulnerable to behavior similar to that of her pregnant sister. By contacting a family with sisters an offer could be made to hold informal discussion groups on human relationship problems, sex and birth control counseling for sisters and teenage friends in a home of their choosing, in a nearby community church or settlement, and/or in the Teen-Obstetrical Clinic [24]. Mothers of the girls and hopefully, available fathers would be invited to a second discussion group held in the same time period. In some instances these groups might be combined and thus bring into the open feelings, bias and anger, hopes and aspirations, as well as reliable information. These discussions should be available to the parents and the young male potential father on their home ground as they are to the teenage girl.

A man and a woman leader used in groups sometimes separately, sometime together, has been found to increase the possibility of constructive give and take [25]. We also suggest using former patients, who have made a successful adjustment to family life and work following the birth of their baby, as co-leader or resource person for a group. Classes might be held at the Teen-Obstetrical Clinic to orient future potential neighborhood group discussion leaders. Certain medical, social work, nursing and other students might also be involved in these groups and learn through them at first hand of dietary and other family and living conditions affecting the health of the teenager in the less advantaged community.

Thanks to a grant for the training of medical and collateral personnel working with minority groups and family planning these suggestions are in the process of being undertaken in 1972 by the Department of Obstetrics and Gynecology, University of Pennsylvania. This program will be reported later in detail.

COMMENTS

Some observations have been made that in spite of our broad education, improved prenatal health and available contraception, it appears that there is much to be learned with this age group. Liberalized family planning for teens hopefully would decrease the incidence of the unwed mother in the high school but now we can see a need in the elementary school.

We find that the young teenage mothers (12–15) are much more difficult to work with—especially the pill takers who become non-takers because they have many more important teenage activities to become a part of. The older teenager is much more apt to be a pill taker over a long period of time.

Then there is the teenager who becomes distrustful of our methods when she conceives with an IUD. Psychiatric support is needed around accepting therapeutic abortion or pregnancy after IUD failure, but on the whole it is important to work with the anger of this patient.

Certain questions can be posed: "Is early teen pregnancy to be likened to malaria which was controlled only when the environment was controlled, or is it to be likened unto small-pox which was controlled only with the development of a vaccine?" This then may bring up the issue of where funding should be directed. Can our researchers find a more efficient contraceptive or method of delivery of a contraceptive for teens? Or shall we liken this question to gonorrhea which is out of control in our large cities for want of a really satisfactory way of prevention in sexually active younger teens, or is education to pill taking our most satisfactory way of prevention of an ancient problem but more applicable to older teenagers.

The work done in Teen-Obstetrical Clinic is work after the fact. Much greater emphasis must be placed *before* the pregnancy occurs. We seek here and there, a community group to teach and give services, expending much more time and effort, when we have a captive audience for prevention in the schools from which these pregnant students are coming into our clinic. Education must somehow be moved from the biology class into the dispensary.

SUMMARY

One hundred pregnant teenagers were studied in the Hospital of the University of Pennsylvania, 50 from the regular Prenatal Clinic, 50 from the Teen-Obstetrical Clinic.

Findings indicate little difference between the two groups in prenatal health and attendance, during delivery, or in the infants' condition. Suggestive differences appeared in the early postpartum follow-up. Slightly higher percentages of girls from the more personalized Teen-Obstetrical Clinic offering group and other supportive services attended classes, accepted contraceptives, returned to school. Fewer had repeat pregnancies. However, a follow-up of both groups after approximately two and one-half years showed that the percentage of repeat pregnancies had increased substantially and was identical for both groups.

Suggested are preventative educational and therapeutic approaches with non-pregnant sisters and friends of teen patients through the neighborhood discussion groups led by black and other workers and assisted by former adjusted patients from the Teen-Obstetrical Clinic. Due to a training grant from a private Foundation received in 1972 following this study, these suggestions are being initiated in the Department of Obstetrics and Gynecology, University of Pennsylvania and will be reported in detail at a later date.

REFERENCES

1 Block, Irvin. The Health of the Poor. Public Affairs Pamphlet No. 435, 1969.
2 Aznar, Ramon and Bennett, Alwyn E. Pregnancy in the Adolescent Girl. Amer. J. Obstet. Gynec. 81:934–940, 1961.
3 Claman, A. David and Bell, Milton A. Pregnancy in the Very Young Teenager. Amer. J. Obstet. Gynec. 90:350–354, 1964.
4 Coates, John Boyd, III. Obstetrics in the Very Young. Amer. J. Obstet. Gynec. 11:68–72, 1970.
5 Furstenberg, F., Jr. Premarital Pregnancy Among Black Teenagers Transaction, 1970 7(7), 52–55.
6 Semmens, James P. Implications of Teenage Pregnancy. Obstet. Gynec. 26:77–84, 1965.
7 Zacler, Jack; Andelman, Samuel L.; and Baur, Frank. The Young Adolescent as an Obstetric Risk. Amer. J. Obstet. Gynec. 103:305–312, 1969.
8 Shiller, Alice. The Unmarried Mother. Public Affairs Pamphlet No. 440, October, 1969.
9 Pugh, Thomas J. and Mudd, Emily H. Personal and Family Problems of Black Men and Women, Their Feelings Toward Using Community Services. J. Religion and Health 10:256–277, July, 1971.
10 Sarrel, Phillip. The University Hospital and the Teenage Unwed Mother. AJPH 57:1308–13, 1967.

11 Bienvenu, Millard J., Jr. Parent-Teenager Communication. Public Affairs Pamphlet No. 438, September, 1969.

12 Mulliserve, Howard M. Programs for the Pregnant School Girls. Children's Bureau, Washington, D.C., 1968.

13 McMurray, Georgia L. Project Teen Aid. A Community Action Approach to Services for Pregnant Unmarried Teenagers. AJPH 58:1848–1853, 1968.

14 Raugh, Joseph L. Management of Adolescent Pregnancy and Prevention of Repeat Pregnancies. HSMHA Health Reports, 1971 86(1), 66–73.

15 Sarrel, Phillip and Klerman, Lorraine V. The Young Unwed Mother. Amer. J. Obstet. Gynec. 105:575–578, 1968.

16 Lewis, D. and Lewis, M. Ethical and Moral Considerations in the Management of the Unwed Pregnant Minor. Social Psychiatry, 1971, 6(1), 40–45.

17 Chang-Silva, Augusto W.; Mudd, Emily H.; and Garcia, Celso-Ramon. Psychosexual Response and Attitudes Toward Family Planning. A Study of One Hundred Pregnant Women. Obstet. Gynec. 37:289–296, 1971.

18 Balsam, Alan and Lidz, Ruth W. Psychiatric Consultation to a Teenage Unwed Mothers Program. Conn. Med. 33:447–452, 1969.

19 Gabrielson, Ira W.; Klerman, Lorraine W.; Currie, John R.; Tyler, Natalie C.; and Jekel, James F. Suicide Attempts in a Population Pregnant as Teenagers. AJPH 60:2289–2301, 1970.

20 Kinch, Robert A., II; Wearing, Morris F.; Love, E.J.; and McMahon, Dianne. Some Aspects of the Pediatric Illegitimacy. Amer. J. Obstet. Gynec. 105–20–31, 1969.

21 Osofsky, Howard J.; Rajan, Renga; Wood, Peggy W.; and DiFlorio, Robert. An Interdisciplinary Program for Low Income Pregnant School Girls: A Progress Report. J. Reproductive Med. 5:103–109, 1970.

22 Pohlman, Edward H. Psychology of Birth Planning. Cambridge: Schenkman Publishing Co., Inc., 1969.

23 Harrison, C. P. Teenage Pregnancy—Is Abortion the Answer? Ped. Clin. N. Amer., 16, 20:363–369, 1969.

24 Brogan, Nadine. Today Many Teenagers Are Learning All About Contraception. New York Times, July 10, 1972. Page 26.

25 Sacks, Sylvia T. Pastoral Educators Prepare to Lead Youth: The New Sexuality. Amer. J. Orthopsychiat. 40:493–502, 1970.

Reducing Neonatal Mortality Rate with Nurse-Midwives

Barry S. Levy, M.D.
Acting State Epidemiologist, Minnesota Department of Health, and Medical Epidemiologist, Center for Disease Control, Minneapolis

Frederick S. Wilkinson, M.D.
Staff, Permanentee Medical Group, Oakland, Calif.

William M. Marine, M.D., M.P.H.
Department of Preventive Medicine and Community Health, Emory University School of Medicine

More infants die in the United States than older people with diabetes, breast cancer, and tuberculosis combined [1]. In 1968, when our infant mortality rate was 21.7 per 1,000 live births, over 75,000 American-born infants died during their first year of life [2]. Our rank among 7 "advanced" countries in infant deaths has declined from fourth to seventh since 1950 [3].

About two thirds of infant deaths in the United States occur during the first month of life [4]. Since most of these first-month, or neonatal, deaths are associated with prematurity, significant reduction in neonatal mortality rate depends on reduced prematurity [5].

It has been demonstrated that prematurity (and in turn neonatal deaths) can be reduced by providing prenatal care to more pregnant women. Although 12 visits are generally recommended [6, 7], studies have shown that infants whose mothers have had any prenatal care have a lower risk of being premature [8, 9] and, hence, a lower risk of dying during the first month of life. In addition to more prenatal care, another way of reducing neonatal deaths may be with improved care during labor and delivery, and during the infant's first few days of life.

These objectives of improved and more extensive care might be easily achieved were it not for the shortage and maldistribution of physicians in maternal and infant care in the United States. With the available physician manpower and the predicted increase in American births, Hellman recently estimated that by 1980 about half of all deliveries in this country would be on the ward services of hospitals without assignable physicians [10]. This shortage in manpower for deliveries reflects similar shortages for prenatal and postnatal care.

One proposed solution to these shortages is the more extensive use of nurse-midwives, or nurse obstetric assistants (NOA's) as they are sometimes

Reproduced with permission from *American Journal of Obstetrics and Gynecology*, vol. 109, 50–58 (1971); copyright by the C. V. Mosby Company, St. Louis, Mo.

called. A nurse-midwife is a registered nurse who has had additional formal training (from 6 to 24 months) in maternal and infant care so that she can manage normal pregnancies. Nurse-midwives are never independent practitioners; they always function within the framework of a physician-directed health service. With NOA's managing normal pregnancies, physicians can concentrate on the few abnormal pregnancies.

The effectiveness of nurse-midwives in reducing infant mortality has been demonstrated abroad, and in the U. S. by the Frontier Nursing Service in Kentucky since 1935 [11]. With few states allowing nurse-midwives to practice, however, few opportunities were available to test further the feasibility and the potential benefits of nurse-midwives. Such an opportunity became available from 1960 to 1963 with the nurse obstetric assistant (NOA) program at Madera County Hospital in California.

The Madera County NOA Program. This program was established in response to critical problems at the county hospital in the late 1950's. Serving mainly the medically indigent in a poor agricultural county of about 40,000, the 148 bed hospital was plagued with serious physician and nurse shortages. The full-time staff had been ranging from two to five general practitioners. There were no Board-certified specialists in any field in the entire county. More than half of the pregnant women received late prenatal care or none at all, and it was estimated (but not documented) that about one fifth of the 400 annual deliveries there were not attended by physicians. The prematurity and neonatal mortality rates were much higher than at the two other hospitals in the county [12].

Attempting to solve these problems, the Health Department established a 3 year, $68,400, demonstration nurse-midwife (NOA) program with special legal permission from the State for the nurse-midwives to perform normal deliveries. From July, 1960, through June, 1963, two nurse-midwives managed most normal pregnancies, from prenatal care to labor and delivery, and the care of mothers and infants after delivery. But beyond "routine" care, they overcame many cultural and educational barriers to motivate many more women to seek prenatal care. When a woman first came to the prenatal clinic, she was examined by a physician. If no abnormality were found, she was then assigned to a nurse-midwife for the remainder of her pregnancy. By the middle of the program, the two nurse-midwives were managing the vast majority of the pregnancies and performing 78 per cent of the hospital deliveries. They were assisted by hospital staff physicians, who managed complications as they developed, and by obstetricians and pediatricians from a neighboring county who consulted for a total of a half-day, on the average, each week. At the end of the 3 years, the program was initially evaluated. Significant improvements during the program included: (1) more prenatal care given more frequently to a larger proportion of expectant mothers; (2) a greater proportion of mothers returned for routine 6 week postpartum examinations; (3) a decrease in the prematurity rate (based on a birth weight of 5½ pounds or less); and most importantly, (4) a decrease in neonatal mortality [12].

Despite these improvements, the program was not continued beyond its initial 3 year demonstration period. The Council of the California Medical Association refused to support a permanent change in the State law which would have permitted nurse-midwives to practice as they had during the program. Soon after the program, there were indications that the situation had deteriorated with the neonatal mortality rate for all births in the county increasing from 17.6 (per 1,000 live births) in 1963 to 30.0 in 1964, the first full year after the program [13].

This retrospective study (performed in 1968) was done to determine whether the situation had, in fact, grown worse after the discontinuation of the program. It is a second evaluation of the NOA program, comparing parameters of medical care and infant health and deaths, during and after the program. The discontinuation of a medical care program that was thought to be beneficial is a rare occurrence in American medicine, and thus offers an unusual opportunity for critical examination of possible cause-and-effect relationships.

MATERIALS AND METHODS

Two studies were done comparing parameters during and after the program: (1) a County Records Study, comparing data abstracted mainly from birth and death certificates for January, 1961, through June, 1962 (during) and 1965 (after), and (2) a Vital Statistics Records Study comparing data abstracted mainly from state birth and death records for January, 1961, through June, 1963 (during) and January, 1964, through June, 1966 (after). There was a high correlation between data of the two studies and between data from different sources, such as birth certificates and hospital charts.

County records study. Data gathered in the initial earlier evaluation (before vs. during) of the program for January, 1961–June, 1962 (during) was used along with data we gathered, using the same methods of data collection, for the 1965 (after) period. From all county certificates of live birth and fetal death, data were abstracted on mothers' obstetric histories and demographic characteristics and infants' birth weights (with prematurity defined on the basis of a birth weight of 5½ pounds or less). We did not use the increasingly accepted definition of prematurity based on weeks of gestation because this information was missing from many birth certificates.

All infant deaths of infants born in Madera County in the "during" and "after" periods were recorded. Infant deaths were traced by Bureau of Vital Statistics records and the *California Death Index*. Each infant death was matched with its birth certificate to confirm it as a Madera County birth. Because of the relative stability of the county population and our efforts to determine if infants born in the county to noncounty residents died anywhere in the state, we felt that few, if any, infant deaths were missed.

For all Madera County Hospital live births and fetal deaths, data on prenatal and postpartum care were abstracted from mothers' hospital charts. The 60 per cent of county births not occurring at the county hospital were grouped together under the category "other." (Only 2.5 per cent of these did not occur in hospitals.)

Public health nurse records were used to determine how many of the mothers had postpartum home visits.

Vital statistics records study. From state Bureau of Vital Statistics records, data were accumulated for live births and fetal deaths for January, 1961–June, 1963 (during) and January, 1964–June, 1966 (after). Infant deaths were determined as in the county records study. This study provided data for longer time periods, but in slightly less detail than did the county records study.

Other data. County welfare department personnel were interviewed regarding eligibility requirements for county hospital clinics. Information was obtained, from public health nurse files, on the number of mothers attending the county hospital prenatal clinic. The number of county hospital outpatient clinic visits, inpatient days, and average daily census, and number and turnover of hospital physicians were obtained from the hospital administrator.

RESULTS

Prematurity and Deaths

As seen in Table I (A), Vital Statistics records study data show that the prematurity and neonatal mortality rates of county hospital births increased significantly after the program. The prematurity rate increased by almost 50 per cent, and the neonatal mortality rate more than tripled.

There were no significant changes in the fetal mortality rate (based on stillbirths after the twentieth week of gestation), in the total infant mortality rate, nor in the postneonatal mortality rate (based on deaths from the end of the first month to the end of the first year of life).

While the prematurity and neonatal mortality rates increased among county hospital births after the program, there was no significant change in any of the mortality or prematurity rates among infants born elsewhere in the county, as shown in Table I (B).

Analysis of county records study data (1965) showed that premature infants had more than a tenfold greater chance of dying during the first year of life than mature infants: of the premature infants, 16.4 per cent died during the first year of life; of the mature ones, only 1.4 per cent died.

Table I Prematurity and Mortality Rates in Relation to Nurse-Midwife Program: Vital Statistics Records Study*

	(A) County hospital births			(B) Other births in county	
	1959 (based on initial evalua- tion data)	January, 1961– June, 1963	January, 1964– June, 1966	January, 1961– June, 1963	January, 1964– June, 1966
Prematurity (%)	11.0	6.6†	9.8†	6.0	7.4
Deaths (per 1,000 births)					
Fetal	29.0	22.2	27.3	17.5	17.0
Neonatal	23.9	10.3‡	32.1‡	17.8	20.6
Postneonatal	6.0	16.5	8.0	5.2	5.0
Total infant	29.9	26.8	40.2	23.0	25.6
Total births	345	991	768	1,370	1,233
Live births	335	969	747	1,346	1,212

*Rates for all parameters except fetal deaths and prematurity are per 1,000 live births. Rates for fetal deaths are per 1,000 total births. Prematurity expressed as a per cent.

†p < 0.02.

‡p < 0.005.

Prenatal Care

Over-all Use of County Hospital Clinic When the program became fully operational in late 1960, there was a large increase in the number of expectant mothers attending the prenatal clinic. . . . In 1961, total visits reached an annual peak of 1,905, compared with 1,231 in 1959. The ratio of prenatal clinic visits to total births rose significantly, from 3.57 in 1959 to 4.62 in 1961. Visits reached a quarter peak of 560 in July–September, 1961. In January, 1961–June, 1963 (during), the average number of visits for women receiving prenatal care was 4.5; in January, 1964–June, 1966 (after), it fell significantly to 3.6.

After the program, the number of visits dropped sharply, even below preprogram levels. At the same time that there was an abrupt decrease in the number of prenatal clinic visits at the county hospital in mid-1963, there was a 27 per cent decline in total outpatient clinic visits. In February and May, 1963, eligibility criteria for the use of county hospital outpatient clinics (including the prenatal clinic) were made stricter. No detailed written information is available to document these changes, but a welfare department employee, who was involved in determining eligibility before and after these changes, observed in an interview that these changes had a great effect on reducing clinic utilization. She also stated that there were minor changes for those receiving categorical aid starting in early 1962, but that these affected only a small fraction of mothers using the county hospital.

Individual Use of County Hospital Clinic The amount of prenatal care women received after the program decreased. As seen in Table II, the percentage of women receiving no prenatal care doubled after the program

Table II   Madera County Prenatal Care for Total Births (Proportion by Time Period and Place of Occurrence): Vital Statistics Record Study

	County hospital*		Other	
Trimester begun	January, '61–June, '63 (%)	January, '64–June, '66 (%)	January, '61–June, '63 (%)	January, '64–June, '66 (%)
First or second trimester	53.7	38.7	77.7	75.4
Third trimester	34.6	37.2	14.5	13.1
No known care	11.7	24.1	7.8	11.5

*Chi square = 60.32, $p < 0.0001$.

(p < 0.001) and the percentage of women beginning care during the first two trimesters decreased by about one-fourth (p < 0.001). There was a uniform increase after the program in the proportion of mothers of different parity receiving no prenatal care.

Decreased prenatal care was reflected also by a higher incidence of no known care for expentant mothers with previous fetal deaths after the program (10 of 48, or 20.8 per cent), as compared with during the program (4 of 51, or 7.9 per cent).

None of these changes in prenatal care occurred among mothers giving birth elsewhere in the county.

Review of mothers' county hospital charts provided yet further corroboration of decreased utilization after the program. As seen in Table III, there was a significant decrease of mothers making six or more prenatal clinic visits and a significant increase of those with no known clinic visits.

Prenatal Care Related to Prematurity and Deaths   Over 4,300 births in of prenatal care on prematurity and fetal deaths. It was found, as seen in Table IV, that mothers having no prenatal care had significantly higher risks of giving birth to stillborn infants (more than three times as high) and to premature infants (almost twice as high). Even subtracting fetal deaths, the prematurity rate is much greater without prenatal care (10.2 per cent) than with any prenatal care (5.9 per cent).

The greatest increase among mortality indices among Madera County

Table III   Prenatal Care by Number of Prenatal Clinic Visits for Madera County Hospital Live Births: County Records Study

No. of prenatal visits	Per cent related to NOA program	
	During (January, 61– June, '62)	After (1965)
None and unknown*	14.9	24.7
1	9.5	13.6
2–5	40.3	36.7
6 or more†	35.3	25.1
	598 births	299 births

*Chi square = 52.75, p < 0.001, when data analyzed by difference in proportion receiving no known prenatal care in the two periods.
†Chi square = 8.776, p < 0.02, when data analyzed by difference in proportion receiving 6 or more prenatal clinic visits in the two periods.

Table IV   Prenatal Care related to Fetal Deaths and Prematurity for Total Births in Entire County for during (January, 1961–June, 1963) and after (January, 1964–June, 1966) the program: Vital Statistics Records Study

Total births		Fetal deaths		Prematurity	
		No.*	Rate per 1,000	No.†	%
3,812	With prenatal care	60	15.7	252	6.6
550	No prenatal care	28	50.9	61	11.1

*$p < 0.01$.   †$p < 0.001$.

Hospital births after the program was in neonatal deaths (see Table I). Although the proportion of mothers receiving no prenatal care doubled after the program (Table II), the increased neonatal mortality rate was not only confined to mothers who received no prenatal care. As seen in Table V, the neonatal mortality rate of infants whose mothers had no prenatal care (only care during labor and delivery and afterward) almost doubled after the program; but the neonatal mortality rates of infants whose mothers began prenatal care during the first two trimesters increased almost fourfold after the program.

Postpartum care

The increased amount of postpartum care brought about by improved coordination through public health nurse home visits during the program was maintained afterward. No objective data could be obtained to indicate amount of postnatal care to infants.

Changes in Madera County Population and Health Care Resources

The total population of the county and its composition were relatively stable. The county hospital maternity population was also stable, with a higher percentage of Mexican-American and Negro mothers, mothers under the age of 20, and fathers employed in farm labor, as compared with the population delivering elsewhere in the county. There were no significant changes in the characteristics of the county hospital maternal population after the program. However, while the overall county births decreased by 15 per cent after the program, the number of births decreased by 23 per cent at the county hospital and *only* by 10 per cent elsewhere in the county.

The physician population in the county was also quite stable, increasing only from 20 to 25 from 1958 to 1965, and then decreasing to 23 in 1967, with the vast majority still being general practitioners. In 1958, only one physician did specialty work in obstetrics and gynecology; in 1961 and

1963, there were no physicians practicing this specialty; and in 1965 and 1967, one physician did specialty work in both surgery and obstetrics.

At the county hospital, the average number of full-time staff physicians per year went from a low of 2.9 in 1959 to a high of 5.1 in 1962. The hospital had no interns or residents. The number of staff physicians was approximately the same during and after the program. The inpatient to physician ratio during the program was 23.2, and decreased to 16.9 after.

COMMENT

Significant increases in neonatal mortality rate and prematurity among county hospital births occurred after the discontinuation of the NOA program (Table I, A). There were no significant changes among the other indices for county hospital births, although there was a trend of an increased postneonatal mortality rate during the program and a decreased postneonatal mortality rate after it.

Since this was a retrospective study with many uncontrolled variables, we investigated several possible explanations for the increased neonatal mortality and prematurity rates after the program.

First, we found no unusual events, such as nursery epidemics or an increased multiple-birth rate, to account for these increased rates. In addition, there was no countywide trend of increased prematurity and neonatal deaths since these rates did not change among infants born elsewhere in the county (Table I, B).

Second, there was no significant change in the number or types of doctors on the county hospital staff nor in the entire county after the program to account for these increased rates.

Third, we noted that the total births at the county hospital declined by 23 per cent after the program while the total births elsewhere in the county only declined by 10 per cent. This raises the possibility that some low-risk mothers who were delivered normally at the county hospital went elsewhere to be delivered after the program, possibly as a result of the stricter eligibility criteria then. Such a shift would have left a higher percentage of high-risk mothers at the county hospital, possibly accounting for these increased rates. No evidence among data gathered on the maternal population during and after the program, however, indicated such a shift. But even if one were to assume that such a shift occurred, it alone cannot reasonably account for the increased rates: there are still significant increases when one extrapolates a uniform decrease in birth rates after the program for both the county hospital and elsewhere in the county.

While prematurity and neonatal mortality rates increased among county hospital births after the program, prenatal care for mothers being delivered there decreased. Twice as many women received no known prenatal care after the program and far fewer women made six or more visits (Tables

II and III). Part of this decrease in prenatal care may have been due to the stricter eligibility criteria.

The prenatal care of one identifiable group of mothers at high risk, those having previous fetal deaths, reflected the over-all decrease in prenatal care. This suggests that the decrease in prenatal care, which affected the county hospital maternity population in general, also affected those with high-risk pregnancies.

Pooled data on all county births for 5 years (Table IV) indicate the lower risk of fetal deaths and prematurity among women receiving any prenatal care, and further corroborate studies by others [7, 8, 14]. The value of prenatal care per se, then, is clearly established. However, the relation of the content and quality of prenatal care and of care during and after delivery to prematurity and death is another matter.

Indirectly we measured this content and quality of care during pregnancy and after delivery by calculating the neonatal mortality rates for infants whose mothers had about the same amount of care during and after the program. As seen in Table V, the neonatal mortality rates of infants whose mothers began prenatal care in the first two trimesters (who received about the same amount of care) was almost four times greater after the program than during it. This suggests that the quality of care, both prenatal care and care during and after delivery, was lower after the program. Table V also indicates that the neonatal mortality rate of infants whose mothers had no prenatal care at all (only care during and after delivery) almost doubled after the program. Since the amount of care for all these infants was about the same, this increased trend suggests that the quality of care during and after delivery was lower after the program.

We found then that there were significantly higher prematurity and

Table V   Neonatal Deaths for Madera County Hospital, Live Births Related to Prenatal Care during and after the NOA Program: Vital Statistics Record Study

Trimester prenatal care begun	During NOA Program January, 1961 June, 1963			After NOA Program January, 1964–June, 1966		
	Live births	Neonatal deaths	Neonatal deaths (no./1,000)	Live births	Neonatal deaths	Neonatal deaths (no./1,000)
First or second trimester	520	5	9.6	288	11	38.2
Third trimester	337	2	5.9	281	4	14.2
No known care	112	3	26.8	178	9	50.6
Total	969	10	10.3	747	24	32.1

*$p < 0.01$ for neonatal mortality rate difference before and after program.

neonatal mortality rates, significantly less prenatal care, and probably a lower quality of maternal and infant care for births occurring at the county hospital after the discontinuation of the nurse-midwife program. We believe that the discontinuation of the nurse-midwife program created new manpower shortages in the prenatal clinic, on the maternity ward, and in the newborn nursery. These manpower shortages, it appears, brought about both lower quantity and probably lower quality of care for mothers and infants. And, finding no other reasonable explanations, we conclude that this lower quantity and probably lower quality of care were the main causes of the increased prematurity and neonatal mortality after the program.

As Hellman recently predicted, the physician shortage in maternal and infant care is likely to grow much worse in the next decade unless appropriate steps are taken. Currently, only six states and New York City in this country permit nurse-midwives to practice. On the basis of our study, we recommend that similar nurse-midwife (or NOA) programs be set up elsewhere, at least on a trial basis, especially where there are critical physician shortages and high prematurity and neonatal mortality rates.

REFERENCES

1 U.S. Public Health Service, Department of Health, Education, and Welfare: Monthly Vital Statistics Report 18: 13, 1970.
2 World Health Organization: World Health Statistics Rep. 22: 479, 1969.
3 Chase, H. C.: Amer. J. Pub. Health 57: 1735, 1967.
4 U.S. Public Health Service, Department of Health, Education, and Welfare, Annual Vital Statistics Reports, 1966–1968.
5 Clifford, S. H.: New Eng. J. Med. 271: 243, 1964.
6 California Medical Association: San Francisco Examiner, July 22, 1963, p. 34.
7 Committee on Maternal and Child Care: J. A. M. A. 193: 310, 1965.
8 Oppenheimer, E.: Amer. J. Pub. Health 51: 208, 1961.
9 Hepner, H. J., and Shaver, R.: Rocky Mountain Med. J. 57: 45, 1960.
10 Hellman, L. M.: Ann. N. Y. Acad. Sci. 166: 896, 1969.
11 Metropolitan Life Insurance Company: Quart. Bull. Frontier Nurs. Serv. 11: 13, 1935.
12 Montgomery, T. A.: Amer. J. Obstet. Gynec. 105: 309, 1969.
13 California Vital Statistics Report, 1964.
14 Montgomery, T. A., Hammersly, M., and Lewis, A.: Calif. Med. 99: 241, 1963.

High-Risk Pregnancy, II: A Pattern of Comprehensive Maternal and Child Care

Howard N. Jacobson, M.D.
Professor, Department of Community Medicine, College of Medicine and Dentistry of New Jersey

Duncan E. Reid, M.D.
Formerly William Lambert Richardson Professor of Obstetrics and Chairman of the Department of Obstetrics and Gynecology, Harvard Medical School, Chief-of-Staff, Boston Lying-In Hospital

The status of maternal and child health is a reliable index of the caliber of overall medical care within a society, nation or ethnic group. The quality of maternal and child care also reflects in large measure the socioeconomic conditions that prevail. Because poverty continues to exceed abundance the major health problems of the world continue to have their origin in deficiencies in maternal and child care.

Even in a nation of abundance, there are areas of poverty that in a small, homogeneous country may not influence the quality of care appreciably. But in a nation with a large, heterogeneous urban population, the socioeconomically underprivileged may reach proportions where the community is unable to provide the health services that modern medicine can offer.

As in the emerging nations, deprived citizens in this reputedly affluent nation rightfully demand the fruits of scientific progress. Despite the gratifying reduction in maternal mortality in this country through general advances in medicine and medical facilities it has been appreciated for the past two or more decades that mortality rates are several times higher in the nonwhite than in the white groups. Perhaps more accurately stated, the mortality and morbidity rates are higher among the poor—white and nonwhite—than in the economically more privileged groups, and this difference increases.

These inequalities in maternal and child-health services have become more apparent as greater attention has been focused in recent years on perinatal mortality and on the study of the factors, genetic and environmental, that may influence growth and development of and cause damage to the fetus and newborn infant as exemplified by malformation, cerebral palsy and mental retardation.

Those responsible for maternal and child care in this nation are challenged to act as a consequence of serious doubts about the adequacy of the present maternity services for the population as a whole. But the solutions

From *The New England Journal of Medicine*, vol. 271, no. 6, pp. 302–307 (August 6, 1964).

are not simple or easily reached, for the problems posed ramify into the entire social and political structure. It is the contention of many that any threat to this nation of being "buried" by a totalitarian political system is more likely to come from forces originating from within its boundaries, arising from socioeconomic pressures of unlimited population, rather than from influences beyond its borders. Without the control of population size attempts to eliminate poverty, juvenile delinquency and other social evils will probably prove futile and might end in total failure. To offer a remedy, based solely on economic support, might well accelerate population growth.

Hence, any program to improve maternal, child and family health must be concerned with aiding parents to plan the sizes of their families. Surely, simply to be born and struggle to survive is hardly the purpose of life. Rather, is it not a portion of humanity's constant effort to provide those of future generations with increased opportunities to develop the special talents and abilities with which each individual is endowed?

It is the purpose of this communication to consider briefly the shortages in maternal and child-health services and their socioeconomic effects and to offer a practicable program to help rectify them. Any program designed to correct present deficiencies in prenatal care must be developed within a setting appropriate to meet future needs. The program need not be patterned after those of other countries, but rather should be especially suited to meet the health needs of this nation.

THE PRESENT SITUATION

In 1962 the rate of infant mortality in the United States had apparently increased in contrast to a decrease in mortality seen in most Western countries [1]. Lesser [2] has commented, "In seven of our ten largest cities there were significant increases in infant mortality between 1950 and 1960, ranging from 5.6 per cent to 26.4 per cent" [2]. Now, a substantial difference exists between the national rate of 25.4 per 1000 live births and the lowest rates found in Europe (15.3 per 1000 in Sweden and in The Netherlands) [1]. Engel [3] recently estimated that if American services nationally were of equal quality to those provided in The Netherlands or Sweden, 40,000 infants would be saved annually. Because infant mortality within the first year of life occurs mainly in the first week such early deaths are greatly influenced by prematurity. This factor is commonly associated in many cases of central-nervous-system deficits.

As stated by Clifford [4], the prevention of prematurity is basic to any program directed toward reduction of both morbidity and mortality in the newborn and overall fetal wastage. The rates of premature deliveries vary enormously in different institutions within a single city and in different cities within the boundaries of the country. Data from four institutions participating in the Collaborative Perinatal Research Project of the National Institutes of Health . . . reveal over a 100 per cent difference between the lowest institutional prematurity rate of 5.7 and the highest rate of 13 per cent. Although it is usually stated that prematurity is more common among the Negro population, it can be seen that there is as much difference between groups of white patients as there is between white and nonwhite. The significance of these data stems from the knowledge that the rate of premature births is much higher in the lowest socioeconomic group of any society.

To emphasize further the socioeconomic factors involved, data for the year 1955 show that in the nonwhite population in the United States the perinatal mortality was 44.5 per 1000 live births. However, the figures from the United States white population (28.9 per 1000 live births) are quite comparable to those from Sweden (29.4) or from The Netherlands (29.2) [5]. Thus, the results in the upper socioeconomic group in the United States compare favorably with those found in other Western countries.

The scope of the socioeconomic aspects can be further described by a quotation from President Kennedy's Panel Report:

> Large numbers of expectant mothers in the United States, particularly among the lower socioeconomic groups in both urban and rural areas, receive little or no prenatal care and suffer from extremely inadequate health supervision during the postnatal period. This is becoming a serious problem, especially in our larger cities, and is directly related to the relative increase in the number of low-income families that has resulted largely from the middle-class exodus to suburban counties. In a large eastern seaboard city, ten thousand women who gave birth to children in 1962 received indifferent or no prenatal care. In the District of Columbia last year [1961], one-half of the births at the city hospitals occurred to women who had received no prenatal care, an increase from less than a third in 1952. In Baltimore, the percentage of births with late or no prenatal care increased from 8.2 per cent in 1951 to 21.4 per cent by 1958. In New York City, it is reported that the number of births without prenatal care is increasing by 2 per cent a year, and it is estimated that by 1965 one-half of all women delivering in Manhattan will be medically indigent [6].

It is evident that there are many variables to consider when comparisons are made between perinatal-mortality figures from the United States and those from European countries. In the United States the population is heterogeneous, in contrast to the rather homogeneous population of most Western European countries, and the extent of employment of the population differs, which is perhaps a reflection of the automation and increasing urbanization in the United States.

Perhaps no one has summarized better the problems ahead than Whitney Young, Jr., executive director of the National Urban League:

> There are forces at work, such as automation, urbanization, and a host of others, that, on the surface, are indifferent to race. Unless we identify these

problems, and take steps to meet them, we will find the masses of Negroes five years from today with a mouthful of rights, living in hovels with empty stomachs [7].

Obviously, this bleak outlook is not restricted to race or color as the scientific revolution expands under the impetus of the "new boss-man, the machine" [7].

A closer examination of unemployment figures reveals the disturbing fact that the rate among men in the age group marrying and starting families—that is, twenty-four or less—is more than twice as high as it is in men twenty-five and over. Although they are only one fifth of the labor force they make up over one third of the unemployed [8].

PROJECTED SITUATION

To anticipate future needs for maternal and infant services, an appropriate place to begin is with an examination of expected population changes. In 1970 the population of the United States will be close to 210,000,000 (209, 000,000 to 215,000,000 in other estimates), and by 1980, will be near 260, 000,000 people [9]. The immensity of the problems facing those providing maternal and children's services is revealed only when the figures are analyzed in terms of the proportions at various ages. As stated by Kirk [9], "The aged will continue to increase rapidly in number, but the largest absolute growth of population will be among children and, later, among young adults [italics ours]." The President's Manpower Report reached a similar conclusion [8].

To put this expected increase in population into still sharper focus, in 1960 there were 17,152,000 women between the ages of twenty and thirty-five. For 1975, nearly 25,000,000 women in that age group have been predicted [8].

The figures in Table 1 show the pattern of the increase in this age group and demonstrate that almost an 80 per cent increase can be expected to occur.

In the year 1960 there were 4,257,850 live births [1]. At the 1960 birth rate of 23.7 per 1000 population the total predicted in 1980 would be some 7,658,000 live births. It must be noted, however, that the birth rate has fallen consistently since 1957, from a high of 25.3 per 1000 to the most recent figure of 22.4 in 1962, and the trend appears to be continuing, for the national rate was 21.0 per 1000 population in November, 1963 [10]. If the birth rate should fall into line with rates found in West European countries, which have rates ranging from 13.7 (Sweden) to 17.9 (United Kingdom) [1], this would be a reduction in birth rate (taking a mean figure of 15 per 1000 population) of 35 per cent. Instead of the 7,658,000 births predictable at the 1960 birth rate, there would be 35 per cent less, or 4,980,000, but still 700,

Table 1 Increase in the Number of Women between the Ages of Twenty and Twenty-five to be Expected in 1980*

Age yr.	1960	1980
20	1,124,267	2,025,592
21	1,119,904	2,022,662
22	1,098,484	2,008,775
23	1,073,125	1,970,775
24	1,104,157	1,954,887
25	1,101,747	1,942,816
Total	6,621,684	11,925,507

*Based on the 1960 United States Census.

000 above the present annual numbers. Thus, even if the rate should fall to that of some European countries, the total number of annual births would be substantially increased.

MEDICAL MANPOWER NEEDS, PRESENT AND FUTURE

Compounding the problem of developing any form of health program is the question of where the trained personnel will come from and who will provide the additional services.

The urgency of this question was pointed out by the President's Panel Report, in which was stated, "The existing shortage of scientific manpower [for example, physicians, nurses, social workers, and nutritionists [8]] and the prediction of an even greater shortage in the future, necessitates every effort to make the best possible use of those men and women already trained and qualified for scientific careers" [6].

In terms of medicine in general, the Rockefeller Panel Report stated that "we are short of doctors in many parts of the country and also of many categories of medical specialists" [11]. The need would be even greater except for the immigration of physicians from other lands. In this connection, Folsom [12] noted that "17 per cent of the physicians entering practice in the United States in 1959 were educated abroad. . . ."

The problem was most forcefully presented in the Manpower Report of the President, which states, "Just to maintain the 1960 ratio of physicians to population in 1970 will require a *net growth* [italics ours] of more than 50,000 doctors, about 20 per cent over the 1960 supply of 257,000, according to estimates of the U. S. Public Health Service" [8].

But the difficulties for those responsible for providing maternity and children's services do not stop here. The proportion of physicians providing maternal care is also sharply declining. Some 60 to 70 per cent of the births in this country are attended, at least in some areas, by general practitioners. As Donabedian and Axelrod [13] state, "The rise in specialization has resulted in continued decline in the number and status of the family physician." Only some 20 per cent of present medical graduates enter general or family medicine.

Thus, the projected increases in the number of physicians in itself will not correct present inadequacies in maternal and child health or meet the future demands for such service. As in other areas of medicine, attention must be given to the question of how to relieve the physician of many of his routine duties. If this could be safely accomplished, it would permit him to devote his energies to being a hospital-patient consultant. In fact, to provide quality care or supply any care where none now exists, a method must be found in which much of the routine care can be carried out under a physician's supervision rather than through his exclusive participation.

A PROPOSAL

One of the significant departures in this proposal from the traditional pattern of American maternal care is the introduction of a person whom we shall arbitrarily designate as the "family nurse practitioner," who would provide most of the medical supervision in the prenatal and postnatal periods in a community-centered clinic, located within the geographic area from which the patients would come. The parent hospital would be responsible for the consultative and inpatient service. Before developing the proposal further, we shall present the assumptions and principles upon which the program is based.

Any system of medical care must be judged by what it does for the patient. Here, we stress service to women and their children within the family setting. The program to be accepted must meet the needs of the patient, including maintenance of self-respect, convenience and simplicity. As pointed out by Bierman, [14] the maintenance and strengthening of family life "cannot possibly be achieved without comprehensive medical care programs in public assistance—programs in which all essential services are available. . . ."

We believe that every pregnant woman has the right to be—and should be—delivered in a hospital equipped with the proper facilities to care for her and her newborn infant. These include anesthesia, to be administered by an anesthesiologist, especially in complicated cases, who is fully aware of the problems peculiar to obstetric anesthesia, a blood bank and the other ancillary services necessary to ensure the maximum safety of the mother and her infant. She should be delivered with a physician in attendance who is qualified to manage complications if they arise, for accidents, unheralded and unforseen, may occur even in normal labor [15], causing fetal asphyxia that may reach proportions that cause irreversible cerebral damage. We believe that this nation has the ability to provide for this right.

Having expressed our conviction that every woman has the inherent right to be delivered in a hospital properly staffed and equipped for that purpose, we emphasize the fact that the major inadequacy in maternity services in this country resides more in the area of prenatal care than in hospital care. This is not to say that hospital care cannot be improved as well, but so far as the major emphasis is placed on hospital functions, the emphasis is misplaced. Thus, the hospital must serve additional functions, community wide in scope.

We believe that a maternity service not only has the responsibility of its inhospital functions but also must extend its services and facilities for prenatal and postnatal care into the community through health units that it should support, supervise and control. Indeed, in recent times the concept of community health units has been approved and sanctioned by most of the groups and organizations presented with these problems [16]. Brockington [17], presenting the views of the World Health Organization, has clearly summarized this point of view:

> The first essential is to shift back the focus of medical care to the community and to lessen emphasis upon hospitals; to create everywhere sources for community health in terms of the family at home and at work. The establishment of health units—for day-to-day work in preventive and curative medicine, has the greatest possibilities for general use. In this way medical and social care are firmly united.

To come to grips with the socioeconomic factors that influence family health, especially in the area of maternal and child care, these health units or satellite clinics must be within ready reach of the patients and their families. Only by being a part of the community can those responsible for the provision of care fully appreciate the total health needs.

THE SATELLITE CLINIC

Related services of equal quality are necessary for any program of maternity care to achieve its potential. Thus, all the consultative services and facilities of the parent hospital must be available for the patients of the satellite clinics as they are to inhospital clinic patients. These related services should include case finding, case maintenance, social service, nutritional service, rehabilitation of or assistance to unwed mothers, adoption services, family services, including homemaker service, and genetic counseling. The activities of the satellite clinics would be carefully coordinated with state and municipal agencies and with private agencies providing community health services. Any program undertaken must provide for the careful follow-up study of infants.

Management in the clinic is predicated on careful screening and identification of the "high-risk" obstetric patient. In recent years it has been amply demonstrated that this is possible. In brief, the alerting items are risk because of very young or "elderly" age, because of excessive parity, outcome of last pregnancy (that is, perinatal death or prematurity) and overall pattern of reproductive performance in relation to fetal wastage, toxemia, ante-partum bleeding, erythroblastosis fetalis and medical and genetic problems [5].

The screening would be done at the initial visit by a physician of the parent hospital on the basis of the history and physical examination.

Women found by careful assessment to be of "high risk" (20 per cent, plus or minus, of the total) would be managed by physicians within regular hospital clinics. The "family nurse practitioner," whose training and qualifications are described below, would care for the 70 to 80 per cent of "normal" patients in the satellite clinic through the remainder of pregnancy as long as the patient remained normal or until she entered the hospital in labor. Thus, within the framework of hospital-sponsored community satellite clinics, the core of the program is centered in this specially trained person. It is hoped that this arrangement would maintain or improve the caliber of hospital care, for it would permit the physician to devote nearly all of his time to inhospital duties where the acute and complicated cases should be managed.

QUALIFICATIONS AND FUNCTIONS OF THE "FAMILY NURSE PRACTITIONER"

As previously stated, any solution to correct the present and projected unfilled demands for maternal and child-health care among the medically indigent must find a way to utilize to the fullest the physician's time and effort. Because of the vastness of the need his attempts to serve are often perfunctory at best. The time required in performing duties of a routine nature leaves him little time to deal with a patient's emotional and personal problems. Actually, the patient may feel more free to discuss these with a "family nurse practitioner" whom she would come to know more intimately.

Thus, we suggest that the scope and responsibilities of nursing be increased with the development of the concept of a "family nurse practitioner" who would be a regular staff member of an obstetric-gynecologic hospital service and would have much of the obstetric responsibility of a maternity clinic previously regarded as solely within the province of the physician.

The "family nurse practitioner" must have additional preparation in general medicine, psychiatry, pediatrics and obstetrics, as well as public-health nursing to enable her to function effectively in the community setting. Her obstetric education would stress the normal physiologic changes in pregnancy and how they may influence medical and surgical conditions. She should be especially knowledgeable regarding the various ante-partum complications. Her preparation would put less emphasis on the methods and technics of delivery and more on creating an awareness and appreciation of the changing tempo of the patient's physical and emotional needs in the various periods of pregnancy. Moreover, she would act as adviser to the family concerning the total health needs. Not only would she be responsible for the prenatal care of selected normal patients but also she would assess health needs and bring health education to the community. She must be skilled in communication, for she would be called upon to represent the program in community services. It is expected that the "family nurse practitioner" would attend and participate in interdisciplinary case conferences, both in the satellite clinic and in the hospital. She would be expected to participate in inservice teaching and assist with clinical supervision and teaching of student nurses.

It may be appropriate here to say what the "family nurse practitioner" would not be. She would not be trained to be nor would she serve in the capacity of a midwife or as an "obstetric nurse assistant," the latter having recently been introduced into American obstetrics. Too often the obstetric nurse assistant is distracted by the economic advantages associated with private practice. Being oriented toward the conduct of labor and delivery, she is a valuable ally of the busy private practitioner, and she can substitute totally for him if the need arises. This is not to decry such an arrangement, but it adds little in the correction of inadequacies in maternal and child care among the urban medically indigent.

Thus, the "family nurse practitioner" would differ from the classic nurse midwife in that her activities would be confined to the clinics and the community health services, and she would not be required to attend or to perform either home or inhospital deliveries. It is encouraging that neighboring schools of collegiate nursing find that the concepts and philosophies embodied in the "family nurse practitioner" in relation to improving maternal and child care and overall community health have great appeal.

DISCUSSION

In addition to the anguish imposed on the family, permanent central-nervous-system damage to the newborn infant has a strong economic overlay. Except for relief or modification of symptoms these conditions appear not to respond to curative measures. If cerebral palsy and mental retardation can be eliminated in large measure through prevention is it not more humanitarian as well as more economically wise to spend whatever is necessary in the treatment of patients with complications of pregnancy from which many of these cases are derived—not the least of which is the reduction of premature births? In many cases this may call for long-term, costly hospitalization of the expectant mothers.

Certainly, the full achievement of a person's potential can be blocked or retarded at any of a number of stages in his growth and development. The stage of intrauterine life and the physical events surrounding birth can be the most decisive. In recognition of this, it has been stated that it is the individual's initial right to be biologically well born [5]. Depending on the perception of this right, a maternal and child health service could be a make-do, temporary or undersupported effort, or it could command the attention and resources that we claim it is entitled to have and other less affluent societies already provide.

Perhaps at no other time in human history has a society had so many choices available for the use of its resources for the common good. Thus, one must examine what is meant by statements of rights and of what people are entitled to have. Whatever solution emerges will be couched within society's moral evaluation of these stated rights. As Tawney [18] put it, "An appeal to principles is the condition of any considerable reconstruction of society, because social institutions are the visible expressions of the scale of moral values which rules the minds of individuals, and it is impossible to alter institutions without altering that moral evaluation."

As with national uncertainties about the implications of statements of the rights of man, it is not entirely clear what the health rights of a newborn infant are. However, before any meaningful solution to ambiguities of these rights, one must deal with the more general question: Are the general statements that health services are a right of all people really acknowledged, or rather are they believed to be privileges that a society can withhold or grant? Whether health services are a right of the people or a privilege granted by society must be squarely faced and dealt with before solutions based on principles—and thus solidly shored—can be developed with the expectation that they will contain the necessary elements of permanence. Lacking a firm basis in principle, solutions can only be based on expediency, and thus be subject to the moods and whims of particular times, and too often to the sociopolitical atmosphere within a locale.

When health problems of a public nature are considered, it is customarily held that they are mainly matters of concern to health and welfare agencies and not necessarily to medical schools. With the recognition that the basic issues expressed in the health needs of a community are inseparable from the larger issues of concern to the nation, medical schools and their affiliated teaching hospitals must become more active workers in the overall efforts to solve them.

The university-affiliated teaching hospitals have always been associated with the care of the medically indigent. With the rising costs of its operation, the voluntary university hospital finds it more difficult to finance adequately its teaching activities and begins to curtail its services and to screen patients for admission. Because of these economic considerations, the idea is commonly expressed that private patients can serve as a source for clinical teaching material, totally or in part. We do not wish to debate this here, but such a pedagogical philosophy may, and too often does, tend to remove the voluntary teaching hospital still further from its responsibility for the care of the medically indigent. With the projected increase in the population, together with an estimated 3,000,000 workers replaced in the near future through the increased application of automation, it is unrealistic to believe that voluntary health programs will solve the problem. All this suggests that *the financing of a teaching service and the care of the medically indigent should be considered within the framework of the single overall problem and included together in the eventual solution.* It is our personal belief that the time is at hand when the Government, as well as private sources, must provide funds for financing teaching beds in the university-affiliated voluntary hospital. This is the most pressing problem facing medical education in the clinical years. Therefore, is it not time to examine the disparity between support for research and that for service to patients?

To return to the main purpose of this paper, we believe that a carefully designed maternity service offers opportunities to serve beyond the provisions of the care of the pregnant patient. Certainly, education of mothers regarding the laws of health should permeate into the family unit. Hence, there should be general agreement that this field of medical activity presents a great opportunity to initiate a program of preventive medicine and health education.

SUMMARY AND CONCLUSIONS

It has become apparent in the past decade or more and for a variety of reasons that the time has come for a major change in the methodology to improve and extend the scope of medical care for expectant mothers and children among the less fortunate. A program, supported and conrolled by the parent hospital, is suggested that will attempt to resolve present inadequacies and provide for anticipated demands for service. By direct contact with the home environment it is hoped that, through mutual understanding and trust, the family will realize that means are at hand to cope with its socioeconomic as well as its medical ills. In more specific terms, poverty is known to beget poverty. Any attempt to eliminate it must be concerned initially with the stabilization of the population in keeping with the number of children desired by parents. Dr. Frederick C. Irving, a discerning clinician who was known as a person with convictions freely expressed, is recalled to have said, "What this world needs is not more babies but better babies."

The proposed program contains three main features. The first is that the responsibility of the hospital would be greatly extended into the community by the establishment of, or a more effective use of, community health centers. Secondly, to increase the accessibility of services and unite medical and social care more firmly, most of the routine maternity and child care would be provided in these community-located health units. Finally, specially prepared "family nurse practitioners" would provide much of the routine prenatal and postnatal care, thus relieving the physician for inhospital and consultant duties. But beyond these activities, this person would assess the health needs of and advise the family concerning its sociomedical problems. Thus, as the family doctor would be, so the "family nurse practitioner" would be vitally concerned with the total welfare of the family. This program, rooted in the community, represents a necessary first step toward meeting the mounting health needs of an urbanized society.

In our view such comprehensive care is not more than the citizens are entitled to have. But these services cannot be provided for those inadequately insured or unable to pay. We believe that society must carefully study this problem and find immediate solutions within the framework of what constitutes acceptable medical care and, equally important, within the framework of its relation to the sociologic and ethical implications of the problem.

REFERENCES

1 *Demographic Yearbook,* 1962. Fourteenth issue. 665 pp. New York: United Nations, 1963.
2 Lesser, A. J. Current problems of maternity care. First Jessie M. Bierman Annual Lecture in Maternal and Child Health. Presented at University of California, Berkeley, California, May 10, 1963.
3 Engel, L. We could save 40,000 babies a year. *The New York Times* (November 17). 1963. (Magazine section.) p. 31.
4 Clifford, S. H. High-risk pregnancy: I. Prevention of prematurity *sine qua non* for reduction in mental retardation and other neurologic disorders. *New Eng. J. Med.* 271:243–249. 1964.
5 Reid, D. E. *A Textbook of Obstetrics.* 1087 pp. Philadelphia: Saunders. 1962.
6 President of United States. *National Action to Combat Mental Retardation (Statement by the President Regarding the Need): President's Panel on Mental Retardation.* Washington, D. C.: Government Printing Office. 1962.

7   Reston, J. Ironies of history and American Negro. *The New York Times* (May 15). 1964.

8   United States Labor Department. *Manpower Report of the President and Report on Manpower Requirements, Resources, Utilization, and Training by Department of Labor Transmitted by Congress March 1963.* 204 pp. Washington, D. C.: Government Printing Office. 1963. (Publication No. 0–676922.)

9   Kirk, D. Anticipating health needs of Americans: some demographic projections. *Ann. Am. Acad. Political & Social Sc.* 337:126–136, 1961.

10 United States Department of Health, Education, and Welfare. *Health, Education, and Welfare Indicators.* Washington, D. C.: Government Printing Office. February and March. 1964.

11 Rockefeller Brothers Fund. *Prospect for America: The Rockefeller panel reports.* 486 pp. New York: Doubleday, 1961.

12 Folsom, M. B. Goals of national health program for meeting health needs. *Ann. Am. Acad. Political & Social Sc.* 337:11–19, 1961.

13 Donabedian, A., and Axelrod, S. J. Organizing medical care programs to meet health needs. *Ann. Am. Acad. Political & Social Sc.* 337:46–56, 1961.

14 Bierman, P. Meeting health needs of low-income families. *Ann. Am. Acad. Political & Social Sc.* 337:103–113, 1961.

15 Leading article. Perinatal mortality. *Lancet* 2:1207, 1963.

16 Role of hospitals in programmes of community health protection: first report of Expert Committee on Organization of Medical Care. *Tech. Rep. World Health Organ.* 122:3–34, 1957.

17 Brockington, C. F. *World Health.* 405 pp. Harmondsworth, Middlesex, England: Penguin Books, 1958.

18 Tawney, R. H. *Acquisitive Society.* 188 pp. Harcourt, 1946.

Critical Issues in Newborn Intensive Care: A Conference Report and Policy Proposal

A. R. Jonsen, S.J., Ph.D.

R. H. Phibbs, M.D.

W. H. Tooley, M.D.

M. J. Garland, Ph.D.
Health Policy Program and the Department of Pediatrics, University of California, San Francisco

Ethical problems concerning newborn infants have received considerable attention in recent years [1–3]. Two particular types of cases have been much discussed: agressive management of spina bifida [4–8] and the advisability of correction of physical anomalies in infants with genetic defects [9–13]. Another less dramatic, but more common and particularly troubling, problem concerns clinical decisions regarding resuscitation and maintenance of small, severely asphyxiated preterm infants, especially those with respiratory distress who require prolonged assisted ventilation. Just a few years ago most very small infants died of asphyxia in the first moments of life or during the first days of life from hyaline membrane disease. However, developments in newborn intensive care have markedly reduced the fatality rate from both asphyxia and hyaline membrane disease.

Life-saving intervention in an infant's existence inevitably raises certain questions about the desirability of saving certain lives, *e.g.*, those that may be marked by physical and intellectual abnormalities. Should doctors (or parents, or society) discriminate among endangered neonates, attempting to save some and not others? If so, what norms should guide this discrimination?

While these and other such questions cannot be answered solely on the basis of medical information, they cannot be considered apart from clear knowledge of the possibilities and limits of medical efforts on behalf of the infants in question. This is true both on the level of individual decisions and on the level of larger policy decisions.

On May 19, 1974, a small conference was convened in the Sonoma Valley, in California, to consider the ethical problems raised by neonatal intensive care. It brought together 20 persons . . . from different disciplines: medicine, nursing, law, sociology, psychology, ethics, economics, social work, anthropology, and the news media, some of whom have direct

From *Pediatrics*, vol. 55, no. 6, pp. 756–000 (June 1975).

responsibility for newborn intensive care, but all with a professional interest in problems of childhood.

Part I of this article summarizes the materials presented to the Conference participants: five illustrative cases, papers on the major considerations, and four clinical questions. While the discussions of cases, papers, and questions are not reported here, the tables showing participant responses to the four clinical questions are given [Tables I to IV].

Part II presents a "moral policy for neonatal intensive care." This section, consisting of certain ethical propositions and procedural recommendations, was not developed at the Conference but written subsequently by the authors, who take full responsibility for it. The substance of this moral policy arises from our reflections on those two days of conversation and argument. We sent this to the participants for review. Their response was generally favorable, but there were several significant dissenters. However, we felt that the participants, whose contributions formed the matrix in which the policy was shaped, would accept it as an accurate reflection of the mood and tone of the Conference.

The purpose of the moral policy is not to close the agonizing debate over the moral issues of neonatal intensive care. On the contrary, it is intended to stimulate that debate and to propose a framework within which certain questions can be posed more precisely and pointedly than in the past. We have limited our discussions and the subsequent policy statement to problems of decision faced by those who are involved in the clinical care of newborns.

Neonatal intensive care units exist and decisions are being made constantly. Those responsible for these decisions are beginning to ask certain questions. It is to these questions that we address ourselves, quite consciously excluding the major social, political, and economic decisions which must be made about neonatal intensive care. However, we refer to them, especially in the procedural recommendations, and they always lurk in the background. The data required for their discussion are still scarce, and the gradual accumulation of this information will be profoundly affected by stances taken on the nature of clinical decisions. These must be clarified first.

PART I: CONFERENCE REPORT

Case Studies

Five cases were selected to illustrate ethical problems that might emerge in the course of providing intensive care to newborn infants.

In the first two cases both infants were born after a 28- to 29-week gestation. In each, at least one parent urged that the infant not be resuscitated but be allowed to die on the grounds that prematurely born infants are likely to end up retarded or otherwise markedly handicapped. In both cases, the attending physicians argued in favor of providing intensive care, and won the consent of the parents to this line of action. The infants were both vigorously resuscitated and did well in the neonatal period. Now, one is normal at 4 years of age while the other is severely retarded and probably autistic. These cases provide background for the first clinical question: *Is It Ever Right Not To Resuscitate an Infant at Birth?* Because of the initial parental stance, these cases also raise the problem of identifying the proper locus of decision-making authority and of dealing with the tensions that can accompany the exercise of that authority.

In the third and fourth cases the infants were delivered after 32 weeks gestation, weighing 1,750 and 1,800 grams. They were severely depressed at birth, with Apgar scores of 1 at 1 minute and an arterial blood pH of 6.90 at 5 minutes of age. Both were vigorously resuscitated and now one is normal at 5 years of age. The other required prolonged ventilatory assistance, had a large intracranial hemorrhage, and developed hydrocephalus, with only 1 mm of cortex visible by pneumoencephalography. Although both these infants appeared the same at birth, by 2 weeks of life one had clear evidence of severe, irreversible brain damage, a rapidly enlarging head, was still receiving assisted ventilation, and was a candidate for a ventriculoperitoneal shunt. These two cases highlight the problem of early detection of severely handicapping problems and stress how difficult it is to judge from an infant's initial condition whether he will be healthy or defective ultimately. These cases provide the basis for discussion of the second clinical question: *Is It Ever Right To Withdraw Life Support From a Clearly Diagnosed Poor-Prognosis Infant?*

The fifth case concerned an infant who was the first of twins, born after a 28-week gestation, weighing 1,000 grams. He developed severe respiratory distress and had clear evidence of large intracranial hemorrhages at 2 and 4 days of age. Because of a large shunt, the ductus arteriosus was litigated at 10 days of age. He had retrolental fibroplasia and was blind at 2 months of age. He required continuous assisted ventilation to maintain a carbon dioxide below 60 mm Hg. By 4½ months of age, inspiratory pressure of 40 mm Hg and an inspired oxygen concentration of 60% were required to adequately ventilate his diseased lungs. At 4½ months of age, respiratory support was withdrawn. The infant's parents and physicians agreed that should he have a cardiac or respiratory arrest, he would not be resuscitated. His arterial carbon dioxide tension gradually rose to 150 mm Hg at 5 months of age; he developed seizures, and died at 5½ months of age. This case illustrates the problems associated with a decision not to continue life support and is the basis for the third clinical question: *Is It Ever Right To Intervene Directly To Kill a Dying Infant?*

Major Considerations

In addition to the cases, background material was organized around five themes: (1) development of neonatal intensive care; (2) legal and policy perspectives on neonatal intensive care; (3) early indicators of development; (4) family concerns; and (5) economics of neonatal intensive care. These themes were used later to focus the Conference discussions.

Development of Neonatal Intensive Care   Dr. Clement Smith, former editor of *Pediatrics,* prepared a summary of the development of neonatal intensive care and its attendant ethical concerns.

He stated that recent progress in newborn intensive care has extended the concern of neonatologists beyond mere prevention of death to the question of the value of that life for which infants may now be saved. The longer these once unpreventable deaths are deferred, and the more the factor of expense aggravates the problem, the less acceptable is any course except continuation of treatment. Ideally, reduction of neonatal death should be accompanied by reduction in the persistence of permanent handicaps. Yet, some infants are saved from early death only for an existence which few persons would consider worth living. Dr. Smith concluded that so many variable circumstances surround these problems that many physicians find it difficult to meet them with any single moral rule—except perhaps the Golden one.

Legal and Policy Perspectives   F. Raymond Marks, J.D., a lawyer with the Childhood and Government Project at Boalt Hall School of Law, University of California at Berkeley, submitted an essay as background for this theme (with assistance from Lisa Salkovitz, also of the Childhood and Government Project).

He maintained that the dilemma facing parents, doctors, and society in neonatal intensive care units is similar to that faced and resolved by the United States Supreme Court in the abortion decision. A defective child, like a fetus, may be unwanted. The maintenance of a defective child, like carrying a fetus to term, may involve not only broad social costs but a threat to its family's viability. The decisions to be made in the intensive care nursery are human and societal, based on medical estimates. Marks' paper identified the actors, their interests, and their decision-making capacities. In the question of the survival of a defective child, parents are the true risk-takers and burden-bearers, and this problem calls for informed and reflective consent. Parents must speak for the child, whether for the claim of the right to live or the right to die, as well as for the family unit in balancing medical estimates with economic and other family considerations. Marks argued for a social policy that would withhold legal personhood from certain carefully defined categories of high-risk infants until a clear diagnosis and prognosis can be made concerning them and until their parents have made an informed decision whether or not they want to keep and nurture these infants.

Early Indicators of Development   Dr. Jane Hunt, Developmental Psychologist with the Institute of Human Development, who has followed children from the University of California-San Francisco Intensive Care Nursery, prepared material on this third theme.

She indicated that neonatal intensive care has improved the chances for survival and has reduced the numbers of survivors with severe brain damage. An accurate early prognosis of development is not generally possible, because some subtle but permanent insults to the brain are not evident until later in life, while other demonstrable insults have transient or reversible effects. However, increasingly accurate prognostic evaluations can be made between 1 and 4 years of age. Accurate prognosis depends on better understanding of the loci and extent of brain damage, the behavioral implications of this damage, the potential of undamaged brain areas, and the environmental factors that determine the realization of that potential. Environmental variables include such disparate elements as nutrition, sensory and motor stimulation, and social interaction. Comprehensive special education programs, instituted early in life and focused on specific disabilities and abilities, can yield good results.

Family Concerns   Marna Cohen, M.S.W., Social Worker with the University of California-San Francisco Department of Pediatrics, presented material on the fourth theme.

There is a wide range of individual, initial reactions to the birth of a premature, sick, or defective baby. The initial parental response is partly determined by the nature of the infant's illness or defect, proceeds in stages from shock to adaptation, and encompasses denial, anger/depression, bargaining, acceptance/grief, and adaptation. The authenticity of parental participation in decisions about how far to extend treatment is related to the stage which parents have reached in this process. Timing is a key ingredient to parental involvement in necessary decisions and bears directly on the ultimate resolution of the grief process. The use of available community support for the defective child and his family is important. Unfortunately, these supports are generally inadequate, although the level and quality of assistance varies from state to state.

Economics of Neonatal Intensive Care   Marcia J. Kramer, M.A., of the National Bureau of Economic Research, Inc., of New York City, and the Department of Economics at Swarthmore College, presented material on the economics of neonatal care.

She emphasized that provision of neonatal intensive care necessarily diverts limited resources from other uses. Because the activities given up by choosing to develop neonatal intensive care may be of greater moral worth than the provision of this care itself, it is morally imperative that cost criteria be established for this, as for any other, service. However, the means for doing so lie outside the province of technical economic analysis. The principle of consumer sovereignty is basic both to the market mechanism and cost-benefit analysis, yet an infant is not morally equivalent to a commodity whose value derives solely from the utility it yields to others.

Ethical problems are by no means confined to the determination of moral cost ceilings; in fact, they permeate every phase of the economic analysis of neonatal intensive care. Computation of the expected net cost associated with a decision to offer treatment, for instance, is heavily conditioned by judgments about the duration of the commitment implied by neonatal intensive care, the anticipated quality of post-neonatal special care, and the alternative to neonatal intensive care. Cost-effective decision-making also requires that relative values be attached to each possible outcome, since rates of survival and long-term disability vary greatly from one condition to the next. Because a positive neonatal intensive care decision presupposes that the incidence of costs is acceptable, both interpersonally and intergenerationally, distributional norms must be made explicit.

Four Clinical Questions

Four questions were raised which focused on the clinical situation. They were asked in the broadest possible terms in order to allow the participants to define the limits of their own responses.

The questions address the issues of initial intervention, withdrawal of life support already initiated, active lethal intervention, and allocation of the limited resources of a neonatal intensive care unit.

1   Many infants are born in need of virorous resuscitation. The decision whether or not to treat them must be made immediately. Given a situation where such therapy is readily available, *Is It Ever Right Not To Resuscitate an Infant at Birth?*

2   Many infants who are candidates for intensive care therapy at birth have underlying anomalies, lesions, or disease states that are not readily apparent when the decision to initiate therapy is made; also, complications sometimes develop in the course of therapy that result in severe neurological damage. Given the situation of an infant who is receiving intensive care but who has a clearly recognized defect, *Is It Ever Right To Withdraw Life Support From a Clearly-Diagnosed, Poor-Prognosis Infant?*

3   Assuming that a decision is made to let a given infant die, on the basis of a clear diagnosis and poor prognosis, and that the infant is now, and will be for some period of time, self-sustaining, *Is It Ever Right To*

Intervene Directly To Kill the Dying Infant? (Insofar as one accepts as valid the distinction between *active* and *passive* euthanasia, this question concerns *active* euthanasia, *i.e.,* taking some directly lethal action against the life of the infant.)

4 An intensive care nursery may have no more room when an infant is born who needs intensive care and no equivalent facilities are available within a reasonable distance. Suppose that one of the infants who is already receiving intensive care is clearly diagnosed and has a poor prognosis, and that the other infant is judged with reasonable certitude to have a better prognosis, *Is It Ever Right To Displace Poor-Prognosis Infant A in Order To Provide Intensive Care to Better-Prognosis Infant B?*

All participants approved, in principle, not resuscitating some infants and withdrawing life support in certain cases; 17 said "yes" to active euthanasia in some circumstances, 2 answered "no," and 1 was "uncertain." The question of choosing between endangered neonates on the basis of poor prognosis versus good prognosis drew 18 "yes" and 2 "no" responses.

Consensus in these responses is on the surface only; much variability appears in the conditions employed to establish boundaries for the responses [Tables I to IV]. Conditions focus variously on the child's status, consequences to the family of a defective child, costs to society of caring for defectives, and such procedural matters as peer consultation and review, open policy in the delivery room and nursery, and informed consent of parents. Some participants objected that the questions focused unwisely on individualistic problems of conscience in isolation from pertinent social issues, such as priorities for resource allocation.[1]

PART II. A MORAL POLICY FOR NEONATAL INTENSIVE CARE

When individuals face decisions on matters about which they have moral convictions, they act in accord with those convictions or violate them, or

---

[1] Dr. Laura Nader, Ph.D., Professor of Anthropology at University of California at Berkeley, was critical of the Conference on this score: "Let me touch upon some problems. We cannot dismiss the economics of neonatal intensive care by simply stating 'an infant is not simply a commodity whose value is defined by its utility.' Questions should be raised: who benefits economically from neonatal intensive care—the companies that produce the machinery, the doctors who work at this labor, insurance companies, the hospital, the parents, the families of the neonate, the neonate? Furthermore, what are the preventative possibilities, and why was this not relevant? Can the number of such 'infants' be reduced by monitoring drug, geneology, and environmental inputs? What of the process affecting a chain of professionals and clients alike, decisions being made in and out of the health field? The scarce resources question was dismissed without adequate discussion—it was 'off the track.' We never pursued the question, how has our society come to be spending so much time and money on neonatal intensive care without similar attention to born healthy, but later not so healthy, deprived children—is this development related to special interests that may be ours although we are unaware of them? If so, what are they?" (personal communication).

find compromises, excuses, or extenuating circumstances to resolve the dilemmas of conscience. However, when many individuals with diverse moral convictions face a series of decisions about similar cases, there should be a way to accommodate the diversity of private beliefs within some degree of broad agreement about how such cases should be managed. We call this effort making a moral policy [14]. This policy should describe not only substantive moral principles with which the majority can agree, but also the social arrangements which would facilitate discussion and action on the basis of those principles. Thus, a moral policy mingles statements of principle with procedure.

This moral policy presents the elements with which one can make a reasonable ethical argument, the elements of which are certain moral rules, attributions of responsibility and duty, and medical, psychological, social, and economic facts.

A word of warning: this moral policy may seem unreal. This is the inevitable result of considering moral decisions apart from the agony of living through the decisions. It reflects abstraction from the actualities of fear, self-interest, exhaustion, the dominance of some and the truancy of others charged with responsibility and duty. But the air of unreality is, we believe, the necessary cool moment which philosophers say should precede any reasonable judgment. That judgment will have to be made amid the hard realities, but it may be better made in the light of reflection on these propositions.

Ethical Propositions

  1 Every baby born possesses a *moral value* which entitles it to the medical and social care necessary to effect its well-being.

  2 Parents bear the principal *moral responsibility* for the well-being of their newborn infant.

  3 Physicians have the *duty* to take medical measures conducive to the well-being of the baby in proportion to their fiduciary relationships to the parents.

  4 The State has an *interest* in the proper fulfillment of responsibilities and duties regarding the well-being of the infant, as well as an interest in ensuring an equitable apportionment of limited resources among its citizens.

  5 The responsibility of the parents, the duty of the physician, and the interests of the State are conditioned by the medicomoral principle, "do no harm, without expecting compensating benefit for the patient."

  6 Life-preserving intervention should be understood as doing harm to an infant who cannot survive infancy, or will live in intractable pain, or cannot participate even minimally in human experience.

  7 If the court is called upon to resolve disagreement between parents and physicians about medical care, prognosis about quality of life for the infant should weigh heavily in the decision as to whether or not to order life-saving intervention.

8 If an infant is judged beyond medical intervention, and if it is judged that its continued brief life will be marked by pain or discomfort, it is permissible to hasten death by means consonant with the moral value of the infant and the duty of the physician.

9 In cases of limited availability of neonatal intensive care, it is ethical to terminate therapy for an infant with poor prognosis in order to provide care for an infant with a much better prognosis.

Commentary

These propositions identify four moral "fields of force" of which cognizance must be taken in decisions about sustaining neonatal life. Each field is designated by a term with strong ethical connotations: *value, responsibility, duty,* and *interest.* These terms suggest that the various parties in the neonatal situation have diverse roles and relationships.

Moral value indicates that the infant, although unable to comprehend, decide, communicate, or defend its existence, requires by its very existence to be approached with attitudes of respect, consideration, and care. The infant is designated as a being in its own right and morally, if not physically, autonomous. Its life is not merely a function of others.

The term *responsibility* signifies that those who engender and willingly bring an infant to birth are morally accountable for its well-being. They are closest to the infant and must bear the burdens of its nurture, especailly if it is ill or defective. This principle is stated with full recognition that some parents will not or cannot exercise this responsibility. Nonetheless, it states an ideal and a demand which medical professionals should acknowledge in their attitude and in their institutional arrangements.

The term *duty* applies to the professional relationships of a physician who has two clients, the infant and the parents.[2] This relationship is fiduciary, entered into freely by the physician with the parents who entrust their infant to the medical judgment of the physician for the sake of promoting the infant's well-being. Informed consent usually controls fiduciary relationships. However, an infant, the proper patient in this relationship, is unable to be a consenting partner. Thus, parental decisions normally control the relationship. However, the physician, responding directly to the moral value of the infant-patient, may at times be duty-bound to resist a parental decision.

---

[2] Nurses have a special professional relationship to the infant, the parents, and physicians in the provision of intensive care. Their role in decisions about continuation of therapy for endangered infants merits full discussion and articulation with an understanding of the roles of physicians and parents. Other, nonmedical, persons, such as social workers and clergy, also play important roles in the decision-making process; these become apparent when one focuses on the decision process itself. For the present discussion we have set aside these other considerations in order to focus directly on the parent-physician relationship.

Physicians may feel that their duty extends not only to a particular infant under care but also to all children. For such a reason, some physicians may be devoted to scientific research aimed at improving the quality and effectiveness of neonatal care for all. While this dedication is necessary and praiseworthy, it may, on occasion, influence decisions about the care of a particular patient. The need for observation and data may push a clinician, even unconsciously, to extend a course of care beyond reasonable limits of benefit to the patient.

The designation of fields of force of parental responsibility and physician's duty means that the ultimate decisions, morally, lie with the parents. This does not, in fact, mean that parents will make those decisions always. They may absent themselves physically or psychologically. They may even abdicate their moral right to make decisions by failure to acknowledge the well-being of the infant upon which their responsibility is predicated. In such cases, the duty of the physician is expanded to include the heavy burden of rendering final decisions.

Interest designates the concern of the State, in particular, and society at large that actions of individuals respect certain values and fulfill certain responsibilities and duties. The State also has an interest in the fair and efficient distribution of benefits throughout that society as well as the promotion of health and well-being of its citizens. If promotion of the child's well-being unavoidably jeopardizes other equally worthy endeavors, a reconciliation of the competing interests must be sought. These concerns remain in the background unless a perceived threat to the common good requires remedial or preventive intervention.

We conceive of these moral fields of force as attracting and repelling certain kinds of actions. Thus, the value of the infant attracts respect, consideration, and care and repels indifference, violence, and neglect. Responsibility attracts specific forms of care for the infant and repels unconcern. The fields of force converge in decisions about neonatal survival, so that the valued infant is the focus of parental responsibility, physician duty, and State interest. Each of these has its limits; each is subordinate to the moral value of the infant.

Responsibilities, duties, and interests require many specific actions. For example, it is the responsibility of parents to nourish the infant, the duty of the physician to cure the infant's illness, and the interest of the State to punish neglect of the infant. However, we propose that the medico-moral principle "do no harm" is most appropriate to guide decisions regarding neonatal survival. Its appropriateness rests on the following considerations:

First, the principle, stated in the negative, admits of no exceptions. Positive formulations of moral obligation, such as "preserve life," admit of exceptions and must be qualified by listing grounds for exception. The traditional medical principle, "do no harm" is a universal. The problem, then, is not in finding grounds for exception but in defining harm [15].

Table I Question 1: Would It Ever Be Right Not to Resuscitate an Infant at Birth?

	Limiting conditions	
	Child's situation	
Yes/no	**General physical status**	**General "human" status**
Yes, unanimous	1 If baby is dying (or is "dead") and there is no hope of correcting the present lethal condition or foreseeable related complications so that, if resuscitated, the baby would probably die in infancy 2 If baby is in pain which resuscitation will only prolong	1 If the quality of life is and will be intolerable as judged by most reasonable men. The infant's life will predictably involve greater suffering than happiness and it will probably be without self-awareness or socializing capacities 2 If the infant has no chance (or small chance) of normal life 3 If the infant is clearly below human standards for meaningful life
	Medical indications	
	1 If infant is anencephalic 2 If the infant has severe central nervous system disorders 3 If the infant has gross physical anomalies (e.g., no limbs) 4 If the infant has a (large) meningomyelocele 5 If the infant has Down's Syndrome (and other chromosomal abnormalities) 6 If the infant is extremely premature or has an extremely low birthweight. (Three cut-off lines proposed: (1) 900 grams; (2) 750 grams or 26 weeks gestation; (3) 500 grams or 22 weeks gestation)	7 If the infant has (major) hydrocephaly 8 If there has been a catastrophe in the birth canal 9 If the infant is porencephalic 10 If there is multiple absence of sense organs 11 If the infant is dead as evidenced by tissue decay 12 If there has been no fetal heartbeat for more than five minutes before birth

*All conditions listed here presuppose that the infant is severely defective.

Family situation*	Miscellaneous conditions*
1 If the death of the infant would minimize the suffering of the parents	1 If, insofar as possible, the parents participate in the decision
2 If the death of the infant would avoid unbearable financial costs to the family	2 If there is an open and consistent delivery room policy about nonresuscitation
3 If the death of the infant would avoid emotional burden to its siblings	3 If there is prior informed consent from parents not to resuscitate under specific conditions
4 If the parents already have a defective child	4 If delivery room policy not to resuscitate is kept flexible in response to the state of the art
	5 If, insofar as possible, an advocate for the infant assists in the decision whether to resuscitate
	6 If costs to the state of infant's survival are considered
	7 If, in cases where gross and obvious structural anomalies are not present, decisions not to resuscitate would be reviewed by a board of physicians and others

Table II   Question 2: Would It Ever Be Right to Withdraw Life Support from a Clearly Diagnosed, Poor Prognosis Infant?

Yes/no	Limiting conditions	
	Child's situation	
	General physical status	**General "human" status**
Yes, unanimous	1 If the infant is diagnosable as having gross defects (coupled with item 2 or 3 below) 2 If the infant is slowly dying; continued therapy only delays death 3 If the infant is and will probably remain unable to sustain itself 4 If continued therapy prolongs present pain	1 If the quality of life of the infant is and will be intolerable as judged by most reasonable men. The infant's life will predictably involve greater suffering than happiness and it will most probably be without self-awareness or socializing capacities 2 If the infant will be totally handicapped and dependent 3 If the infant will be markedly impaired with small chance for normal existence 4 If the infant is defective and *unwanted* by its parents and unneeded by society
	Medical indications	
	1 If the infant has suffered irreparable damage to crucial organs, especially the brain 2 If the infant has meningomyelocele with no cord or bladder function 3 If the infant has hypoplastic (dysplastic) kidneys 4 If the infant is unable to be weaned from respirator 5 If the infant has a genet-	ic defect linked to severe mental retardation requiring institutionalization 6 If the infant has hypoplastic lungs 7 If the infant has cardiac abnormalities for which no corrective or palliative treatment is possible 8 If the infant suffers from short gut syndrome 9 If the infant is anencephalic

*All conditions listed here presuppose that the infant is severely defective.

Family situation*	Miscellaneous conditions*
1 If the survival of the infant would threaten the quality of life of the parents and the family as a whole 2 If the survival of the infant would impose excessive financial costs on the family 3 If the parents desire more speedy death for the dying infant 4 If the parents do not want to rear a severely handicapped child 5 If the parents are judged unable to nurture severely handicapped infant	1 If the parents participate in the decision 2 If court arbitration is employed to resolve conflict between the physician and the family regarding the decision 3 If strong and continued support is available to parents who decide to have life support withdrawn 4 If there is an open and consistent nursery policy regarding such decisions 5 If the obligation to give care and comfort is understood to continue until death occurs 6 If the death of the infant would serve to overcome the demoralizing effect on the nursery staff of prolonged treatment of a hopeless case

Table III Question 3: Would It Ever Be Right to Intervene Directly to Kill a Self-Sustaining Infant?

	Limiting conditions	
	Child's situation	
Yes/no	**General physical status**	**General "human" status**
Yes, 17†	1 If the infant is irretrievably dying a lingering death 2 If the infant is dying painfully, or is in extreme pain or its life would be pain ridden 3 If the infant has gross physical anomelies	1 If the quality of life of the infant is and will be intolerable as judged by most reasonable men. The infant's life will predictably involve greater suffering than happiness and it will most probably be without self-awareness and socializing capacities
No, 2‡		
Uncertain, 1§		2 If the infant will be totally (or markedly) handicapped and dependent 3 If the infant is defective and unwanted by parents and unneeded by society
	Medical indications	
	1 If the infant is anencephalic 2 If the infant is hydrocephalic with little or no cortex 3 If the infant has massive brain damage 4 If the infant has a flat E.E.G. 5 If the infant has severe central nervous system disorders	6 If the infant has uncorrectable cardiac abnormalities, e.g., hypoplastic left heart syndrome 7 If the infant has Down's syndrome 8 If the infant has chromosomal disorders 9 If the infant has short gut syndrome

Family situation*	Miscellaneous conditions*	
1 If the quality of parental life is threatened by the continued survival of the infant	1 If parents consent to the action	8 If the means is chosen primarily because it offers the least painful death to infant and sec-ondarily, because it offers least suffering to those around the dying infant
2 If the quality of familial life is threatened by the continued survival of the infant	2 If the obligation to pro-vide care and comfort is understood to continue to the moment of death	
3 If the parents desire the death of the infant	3 If the decision is under-stood to be the respon-sibility of the physician, advised by a neutral party, and the decision is made known to the parents	9 If the parents adminis-tered the syringe of KCl prepared by the judge with all the lawyers, priests, economists, phychologists, and journalists within a 50 mile radius as wit-nesses and no physi-cians, nurses or medi-cal or nursing students were allowed to be present.
	4 If *in loco parentis* the decision is made by the physician and a court appointed guardian	
	5 If, where feasible, there is prior review of the decision by a commit-tee	
	6 If, where feasible, the responsible physician consults with an experi-enced colleague	
	7 If consideration is given to overcoming the de-moralizing effect on the nursery staff of pro-longed or cruel dying	

*All conditions listed here presuppose that the infant is severely defective.

†Many, especially the physicians, who responded "yes" indicated that they would not do it themselves, but would not condemn another for doing it. Others indicated their yes was intellec-tual, but they were emotionally uncomfortable with the action.

‡Two reasons cited: (a) *Subjectively* impossible for respondent, (b) only passive euthanasia is permissible.

§Uncertain because, although the act intends mercy, society seems wisely unwilling to approve of this kind of power in the hands of physicians.

Table IV   Question 4: Would It Ever Be Right to Displace Poor Prognosis Infant A in Order to Provide Intensive Care to Better Prognosis Infant B?

		Limiting conditions
	Child's situation	
Yes/no	**General physical status**	**General "human" status**
Yes, 18	1 If there is a gross difference in prognosis between two infants	1 If infant A would certainly have a poor quality, grossly abnormal life
	2 If infant A is *dying*, and infant B is truly viable (intact or nearly so)	2 If infant A has at best a 5% chance for meaningful existence.
No, 2†	3 If infant B would die without intensive care but otherwise has a good chance for intact survival	
	4 If infant A is in pain, has been treated for a reasonable period of time, and has certain prognosis for grossly abnormal life if he survives.	

Medical indications
1 If infant A is less than 1000 gm, has severe respiratory distress syndrome and has had a central nervous system bleed; and infant B is 1800 gm and has severe respiratory distress (1)
2 If infant A is hopelessly toxoplasmic and infant B has neonatal tetanus (1)
3 If infant A is older, exposed to prior stress, less mature and diagnosed as having presumed brain damage; and infant B is younger, more mature, and has no presumed brain damage (1)

Secondly, most medical interventions effect some harm, either transient or permanent; that harm is usually justified by an expected compensatory benefit. If no benefit can be reasonably expected or if the benefit does not compensate for the harm, the intervention is unethical. The assessment of whether the benefit does compensate for the harm lies principally with the patient, who must suffer the harm. In the case of infants, the assessment

Family situation*	Miscellaneous conditions*	
1 If infant A's survival would constitute a negative impact on its family's social and economic condition	1 If parental consent is obtained where possible 2 If certain POLICY MATTERS are operative: a) some form of *prior review mechanism* is required (e.g., peer, arbitration panel, neutral party, court order) b) there is *demonstrable certitude* that displacement is *necessary* to provide care for infant B and that there is a *vast difference in prognosis* for the two infants	c) the policy for allocating resources is clear, open and cautiously applied d) there is a clear impartially applied formula for calculating who stands to gain the most from the therapy 3 If the situation is an *emergency,* the physician must decide and act on the basis of putting his efforts where they are likely to produce the greatest benefit to the greatest number

Additional comments

1 This situation is not a *moral* problem but a tragic, necessary situation to be approached practically (like the life boat situation with too many wanting to get in). The *moral* problem would appear on the larger social scale if an affluent society permitted such needless, tragic scarcity to be chronic.
2 Displacement is *permissible* in this situation, but would not be so for adults who must be given security that they will not be bumped from life support machines to accommodate "better prognosis" late-comers.

*All conditions listed here presuppose that the infant is severely defective.
†Two reasons cited: (a) Not a matter of morality but of practicality; no right/wrong; (b) policy favoring such action is too easily abused.

must be made by those who bear responsibility and duty within a context of broad social understanding.

In the context of certain irremediable life conditions, intensive care therapy appears harmful. These conditions are identified in the sixth proposition as inability to survive infancy, inability to live without severe pain, and inability to participate, at least minimally, in human experience.

The first condition recognizes the possibility that some infants may be born with irreparable lesions incompatible with life. They are already in the dying state and, while care should never be neglected, efforts aimed at prolongation of life are best viewed as harming rather than helping such an infant. The second condition envisions the case of an infant who is in constant severe pain which cannot be alleviated either by immediate treatment or as the result of a long course of treatment. The third condition is perhaps the most controversial. Participation in human experience means the assessed expectation that the infant has some inherent capability to respond affectively and cognitively to human attention and to develop toward initiation of communication with other [12]. It deals with presence or absence of capacity, not degrees of deviation from statistical normality.

Our concept of the abilities which count as signs of these human qualities are quite broad. While we are reluctant to quantify or describe in detail the levels of affective and cognitive activity, we would prefer to err on the side which favors the life of the child. A baby with Down's syndrome would fulfill the criteria, whereas one with a trisomy 18 will not [9, 16].

The eighth principle intimates that the question of the morality of active euthanasia is far from settled. We do not intend to settle it here. The formulation of this principle allows for the opinion that the moral value of the infant represents a sanctity against which no lethal action can be judged ethical. The principle also recognizes the opinion that the primary duty of the physician, healing, is incompatible with any lethal action. This formulation allows for the invocation of the double effect doctrine, acceptable to many, which distinguishes between *intended* and *permitted* effects of an action. It also allows for the distinction, favored by some, between acts of commission and acts of omission. All these issues can be defended or criticized [17–23].

We suggest that there may be a significant moral difference between an infant whose therapy has been terminated and an adult whose condition is diagnosed as hopeless, or (in a rapidly vanishing example) condemned to death. For the adult, the time intervening between verdict and death may be of great personal value. For the infant, the intervening time has no discernible personal value.

The ninth proposition responds to the problem of the allocation of limited resources as it sometimes occurs in the intensive care nursery. Up to this point, moral considerations have focused on the well-being of the individual infant. Now, a new element is introduced, *i.e.,* the comparison between two individuals. It becomes difficult to apply the rule "do no harm," since either decision will effect some harm without providing a compensatory benefit to the one harmed.

The traditional medicomoral rule of triage (screening of the wounded or the ill to determine priority for treatment) may illuminate this dilemma.

Casualties in military and civil disasters are divided into those who will not survive even if treated, those who will survive without treatment, and the priority group of those who need treatment in order to survive. A further triage among the priority group would give preference to those who can be reactivated quickly or who are in crucial positions. Considerations of the common good become relevant in such decisions.

Similarly, in the comparative selection of infants for treatment, the interest of the State can be invoked as an ethical consideration since the State has an interest in the recognition of values, in fulfillment of responsibilities and duties, in the fair and efficient distribution of benefits, and in the promotion of a healthy population. These interests are directed toward a common good which, in situations such as this, may be the predominant consideration. Thus, given the impossibility of treating all infants in need, those should have preference who give the greatest hope of surviving with maximal function.

The use of this principle must be approached with grave caution. First, common good considerations are, in practice, often disguised special interest considerations. Favored treatment of certain persons or classes is judged, by those identified with those persons or classes, to contribute to the common good. Secondly, the hope of survival with maximal function is predicated not only on physical potential of the infant but on the socioeconomic world into which it enters. Thus, estimates of the quality of future care may bias selection. Thirdly, selection of better-prognosis infants can be strongly motivated by the physician's interest in compiling favorable statistics and a more rapid selection decision than the condition of an infant may warrant. Thus, the principle of neonatal triage, while instructive in general, is fraught with the risk of serious bias.[3]

Procedural Recommendations

A moral policy requires both ethical propositions and procedural recommendations. Procedural recommendations suggest certain institutional and social arrangements which will facilitate deliberation and action on the basis of the ethical propositions. These recommendations discuss the neonatal problem on a different level than the ethical propositions. There, we were concerned with the *microdecisions* made by those bearing responsibil-

---

[3] Dr. Jane Hunt, Ph.D., Psychologist at the University of California at Berkeley, registered vigorous opposition to this proposition. "I maintain (neonatal triage) turns out *not* to be a proper ethical question because there is *no* ethical solution. One rule is as good as another, unlike the military triage. You can never articulate a policy which separates "common good" from "special interest" because the latter can be put forward as cogent arguments for the former. For example, consider the comparison between the wanted and the unwanted infant" (personal communication).

ity and duty about particular infants at risk. Here, we move to the *macrodecisions* about social and institutional arrangements. Here, issues of State interest, social costs, and economic considerations are most relevant.

We had excluded direct and extensive consideration of public policy questions concerning allocation of scarce medical resources, priorities between preventive and curative medicine, and between medical care and other forms of care affecting personal health from the Conference deliberations. Nonetheless, they must be mentioned.

1 Research in neonatology should be coordinated at the national level in the interests both of efficiency and caution.

2 Neonatal intensive care should be organized on a regional basis so that its quality and access are relatively equal among various communities, so that continuing information on techniques can be shared, and so that adequate epidemiological data can be gathered and compared.

3 On the basis of clinical experience, professionals in neonatal intensive care should refine those converging clinical criteria which render more specific the general conditions of prolonged life without pain and the potential for human communication. These criteria should be communicated broadly within the pediatric, obstetric, and mental health community.

4 Resuscitation criteria should be established with full awareness of the economic and medical implications of providing this care. Estimates should be made of the financial cost to society of prolonging life, at a humane level, depending upon the condition at birth.

5 Delivery room policy, based on certain criteria, should state conditions for which resuscitation is not indicated. This policy should be made known to health professionals and to parents who may be at particular risk (possibly to all parents).

6 Parents at risk should be counseled about the possibilities. Since they bear primary responsibility for their infant, explanatory and supportive counseling is mandatory before and, in the event of a sick infant, after birth. While recognizing that parents often will be unable or unwilling to make decisions, medical professionals must always accept, in principle, that the responsibility should be borne by the parents and attempt to facilitate but not force them to make the decision.[4]

7 The decision to terminate care for the infant requires sufficient time for observation, mature assessment and parental involvement in the

---

[4] Dr. Clement Smith, M.D., noted the unanimity with which nonmedical members of the conference insisted that life-and-death decisions must be made by the parents, while doctors of medicine with almost equal unanimity saw that as an avoidance of the physician's own responsibility—which may inflict a lifetime of regret whichever course the parents decided upon. He would prefer, and in this he believes most physicians would agree, that the doctor, through intimate participation and full discussion with the parents, interpret their beliefs or wishes clearly enough to act according to those indications rather than confront parents directly with the act of decision (personal communication).

decision. Thus, it is more ethical, although perhaps more agonizing, to terminate care after a period of time than to withhold resuscitative measures at the moment of birth. This should be an accepted and publicly acknowledged policy in pediatric and obstetric practice.

8   Regional neonatal intensive care units should establish an advisory board consisting of health professionals and other involved and interested persons. This board is not to be charged with particular decisions about specific infants; this remains the responsibility of the parents with advice and concurrence of the physician. The Board would discuss the problems of the unit and make a periodic retrospective review of the difficult decisions. They would assess the criteria for diagnosis and prognosis in terms of medical validity and social acceptability. They would provide, by bringing a variety of experience, belief, and attitude, a wider human environment for decision-making than might otherwise be available. To implement such a procedure, a neonatal intensive care unit could review its experience prospectively for each case in which a decision had to be made. All data pertinent to the decision could be recorded in a case summary, which would be reviewed monthly, describe the current process of ethical decision-making in the unit, and provide a basis for any changes which might be planned.

9   Since some infants may be abandoned by their parents or, because of their condition, be maintained in an institution, neonatology must concern itself with the adequacy of such institutions. The advocates of intensive care must become the advocates for the development of humane continuing care and for sufficient funding of programs to support families whose children require special attention at home or in institutions. Neonatology cannot be developed in isolation from the continuing specialized care which, unfortunately, will be needed by some of the survivors of life-threatening neonatal disorders.

In the neonatal intensive care situation some people have to act in the best interests of others who cannot act for themselves. Rational assessment of such a situation is an important contribution to the work of safeguarding the rights of these infants. We have espoused a definite position, but do not presume to have spoken the final word, in order to invite reflection and debate. We hope this will promote more sensitive appreciation of the needs and rights of all the participants in the drama of newborn intensive care.

REFERENCES

1   Report of the 65th Ross Conference on Pediatric Research: Ethical Dilemmas in Current Obstetric and Newborn Care. Columbus, Ohio: Ross Laboratories, 1973.
2   Duff, R. S., and Campbell, A. G. M.: Moral and ethical dilemmas in the special care nursery. N. Engl. J. Med., 289:890, 1973.
3   Shaw, A.: Dilemmas of "informed consent" in children. N. Engl. J. Med., 289:885, 1973.

4 Lorber, J.: Criteria for selection of patients for treatment. Read before the Fourth International Conference on Birth Defects, Vienna, 1973.

5 Smith, G. K., and Smith, E. D.: Selection for treatment in spina bifida cystica. Br. Med. J., 4:189, 1973.

6 Freeman, J.: To treat or not to treat: Ethical dilemmas of treating the infant with myelomeningocele. Clin. Neurosurg., 20:134, 1973.

7 Freeman, J. M.: Is there a right way to die—quickly? J. Pediatr., 80:904, 1972.

8 Cooke, R. E.: Whose suffering? J. Pediatr., 80:906, 1972.

9 Gustafson, J. M.: Mongolism, parental desires, and the right to life. Perspect. Biol. Med., 16:529, 1973.

10 Smith, D. M.: On letting some babies die. Hastings Center Stud., 2:37, 1974.

11 Tooley, M.: Abortion and infanticide. Philos. Public Affairs, 2:37, 1973.

12 McCormick, R. A.: To save or let die—the dilemma of modern medicine. JAMA, 229:172, 1974.

13 Englehardt, H. T., Jr.: Euthanasia and children: The injury of continued existence. J. Pediatr., 83:170, 1973.

14 Callahan, D.: Abortion: Law, Choice, and Morality. London: Macmillan, 1970, p. 341.

15 Gert, B.: The Moral Rules. New York: Harper & Row, 1966, pp. 60 and 104.

16 Gustafson, J. M.: A Christian approach to the ethics of abortion. Dublin Rev., Winter, 1967–1968, p. 358.

17 Bennett, J.: Whatever the consequences. Analysis, 26:82, 1966.

18 Foot, P.: The problem of abortion and the doctrine of the double effect. Oxford Rev., 5:5, 1967.

19 McCormick, R. A.: Ambiguity in Moral Choice. Milwaukee: Marquette University Press, 1973.

20 Bok, S.: Euthanasia and the care of the dying. Bioscience, 23:, 1973.

21 Myers, D. W.: The legal aspects of medical euthanasia. Bioscience, 23:467, 1973.

22 Crane, D.: Physicians' attitudes toward the treatment of critically ill patients. Bioscience, 23:471, 1973.

23 Cassell, E. J.: Permission to die. Bioscience, 23:475.

Involuntary Euthanasia of Defective Newborns: A Legal Analysis

John A. Robertson
Assistant Professor of Law, University of Wisconsin

One of the most perplexing dilemmas of modern medicine concerns whether "ordinary"[1] medical care justifiably can be withheld from defective newborns. Infants with malformations of the central nervous system[2] such as anencephaly, hydrocephaly, Down's syndrome, spina bifida, and myelomeningocele often require routine surgical or medical attention merely to stay alive. Until recent developments in surgery and pediatrics, these infants would have died of natural causes. Today with treatment many will survive for long periods, although some will be severely handicapped and limited in their potential for human satisfaction and interaction. Because in the case of some defective newborns, the chances are often slim that they will ever lead normal human lives, it is now common practice for parents to request, and for physicians to agree, not to treat such infants. Without treatment the infant usually dies.

Nontreatment of defective newborns has occurred throughout history, but only recently has the medical profession openly acknowledged the scope and alleged desirability of the practice. In 1973, Doctors Raymond S. Duff and A. G. M. Campbell documented 43 cases of withholding care from defective infants at the Yale–New Haven Hospital,[3] thereby breaking what they characterized as "public and professional silence on a major social taboo."[4] Subsequently, similar cases across the country have re-

---

Abridged from *Stanford Law Review*, vol. 27, no. 2, pp. 213–69 (January 1975).

Editors' note: Some footnotes in the original have been omitted without indication; footnotes have been renumbered.

[1] Few persons would argue that "extraordinary" care must be provided a defective newborn, or indeed, to any person. The difficult question, however, is to distinguish "ordinary" from "extraordinary" care. In this Article "ordinary" care refers to those medical and surgical procedures that would normally be applied in situations not involving physically or mentally handicapped persons.

[2] The need for ordinary treatment will also arise with noncentral nervous system malformations such as malformations of the cardiovascular, respiratory, orogastrointestinal, urogenital, muscular and skeletal systems, as well as deformities of the eye, ear, face, endocrine glands, and skin. . . . Often these defects will accompany central nervous system malformations. The medical-ethical dilemma discussed in this Article has arisen chiefly with regard to central nervous system problems, perhaps because the presence of such defects seriously affects intelligence, social interaction, and the potential for development and growth, and will be discussed only in the context of the major central nervous system malformations. Parents of physically deformed infants with normal intelligence might face the same choice, but because of the child's capacity for development, pressure to withhold ordinary treatment will be less severe.

[3] Duff & Campbell, *Moral and Ethical Dilemmas in the Special-Care Nursery,* 289 New Eng. J. Med. 890 (1973).

[4] *Id.* at 894.

ceived widespread public attention.[5] Recently, the Senate Subcommittee on Health held hearings at which eminent physicians attempted to justify the practice.[6] Pediatric textbooks discuss clinical indicators for withholding treatment,[7] and physicians writing in medical journals have advocated nontreatment in certain situations.[8] Thus, nontreatment of defective infants, now occurring in hospitals throughout the United States and England, is rapidly gaining status as "good medical practice."[9]

This development is significant because it represents the only large-scale instance of involuntary euthanasia[10] now being practiced by the medical profession, at a time when most physicians and the public retain strong opposition to involuntary euthanasia in other circumstances.[11] This does not imply that the decision to withhold care is lightly made. The clash between the norms of preventing suffering and preserving life is too great to ignore, and has engendered much soul searching and ethical analysis on the part of parents, physicians, and nursing staffs. Duff and Campbell, for instance, described in detail their efforts to help parents reach informed choices: "In lengthy frank discussion, the anguish of parents was shared

---

[5] See Boston Globe, Feb. 25, 1974, at I, col. I; Newark Star Ledger, Oct. 3, 1973, at 32, col. 8; note 20 infra. See also R. TRUMBO, AN ACT OF MERCY 145 (1973); TIME, Mar. 25, 1974, at 84.

[6] N.Y. Times, June 12, 1974, at 18, col. 4.

[7] F. INGRAHAM & D. MATSON, NEUROSURGERY OF INFANCY AND CHILDHOOD 35–39 (1954).

[8] See, e.g., Gimbel, Infanticide: Who Makes the Decision, WIS. MED. J., Vol. 73, No. 5, at 10 (1974). . . .

[9] Although some reservations have been expressed, see, e.g., Cooke, Whose Suffering?, 80 J. OF PEDIATRICS 906 (1972), public furor as evidenced in anti-abortion campaigns has yet to erupt. See Grunberg, Who Lives and Who Dies?, N.Y. Times, Apr. 22, 1974, at 35, col. 2.

[10] The term "involuntary euthanasia" is used here to denote the absence of consent of the person from whom treatment is withheld as opposed to "voluntary euthanasia," where the subject gives full, knowing consent to another person's causing his death. Involuntary and voluntary euthanasia can also be distinguished on the following grounds: Involuntary euthanasia is passive and indirect, as where care or sustenance is withheld; voluntary euthanasia is active and direct as where the act that causes death is actually performed rather than omitted. This Article deals only with issues arising from involuntary, passive euthanasia of defective newborns. Although "involuntary" may be redundant in the case of newborns who are in any case incapable of consent, the term is retained to emphasize the absence of consent from the subject.

[11] The only situation calling forth a comparable consensus for withholding ordinary medical care arises in the case of the moribund, particularly the elderly moribund, where treatment would at best prolong the dying process or maintain a life with little chance of social interaction or development. See Fletcher, Ethics and Euthanasia, 73 AM. J. OF NURSING 670 (1973); Fletcher, Legal Aspects of the Decision Not to Prolong Life, 203 J.A.M.A. 65 (1968); Fletcher, Prolonging Life, 42 WASH. L. REV. 999 (1967); Williams, Euthanasia and Abortion, 38 U. COLO. L. REV. 38 (1966). This practice may often be correctly described as involuntary euthanasia, for the patient may be unconscious or not have previously consented to the cessation of ordinary medical care, and undoubtedly involves more patients than nontreatment of defective newborns.

and attempts were made to support fully the reasoned choices, whether for active treatment and rehabilitation or for an early death." [12]

Indeed, no sensitive person can fail to sympathize with the plight of the parents, or blithely pass judgment on the choice they make. After months of expectancy, they are informed that the newborn infant has serious mental and physical defects and will never know a normal existence. The shock of learning that one's child is defective overwhelms parents with grief, guilt, personal blame, and often hopelessness.[13] They are suddenly confronted with an uncertain future of financial and psychological hardship, with potentially devastating effects on their marriage, family, and personal aspirations. If asked to approve a medical or surgical procedure necessary to keep the child alive, it is perhaps understandable that the parents view a life capable only of minimal interaction and development as the greater evil and refuse to provide consent.[14]

But, while one may empathize with the parents of a defective infant one cannot forget that the innocent life of an untreated child is also involved. Like any infant, the deformed child is a person with a right to life—a right that is the basis of our social order and legal system. In fact, the plight of the infant is probably greater than that of the parents. Handicapped at birth, it stands to lose ameliorative treatment, loving care, and probably life itself. Moreover, with the parents' rejection, no one remains to protect or even articulate its interests. Whatever the morality of the ultimate choice, it seems unfair to subject the life of a helpless infant to the unguided discretion of parent and physician, particularly when they may have conflicting interests. Indeed, in other circumstances, the right of parents to

---

[12] Duff & Campbell, *supra* note 3, at 891.

[13] Cohen, *The Impact of the Handicapped Child on the Family,* 43 SOCIAL CASEWORK 137 (1962); Fletcher, *Attitudes Toward Defective Newborns,* HASTINGS CENTER STUDIES, Vol. 2, No. I, at 21 (1974); Goodman, *Continuing Treatment of Parents With Congenitally Defective Infants,* SOCIAL WORK, Vol. 9, No. I, at 92 (1964); Mandelbaum & Wheeler, *The Meaning of a Defective Child to Parents,* 41 SOCIAL CASEWORK 360 (1960).

[14] In the curious manner in which art often prefigures life, Franz Kafka anticipated the emotional and ethical dilemma of parents of the defective newborn in his short story, *The Metamorphosis,* more than 50 years ago. Kafka, *The Metamorphosis,* in THE METAMORPHOSIS AND OTHER STORIES 67–135 (Shocken ed. 1961). While the story concerns Gregor Samsa, an adult commercial traveller, the situation dramatized by Kafka captures most of the pressures facing parents of defective children. The middle-class Samsa family awakes one morning to find that their son, Gregor, sole support of the family, has been transformed into an insect-like monstrosity. They are shocked by this strange trick of fate and recoil in horror, attempting to hide their shame by isolating Gregor in his room. His sister and mother feel sympathy. They leave him milk and bread, and sometimes sit with him. But revulsion soon takes over. As the psychic and economic burdens mount, the family sinks into depression and lethargy. Gregor realizes their embarrassment, and to save them from further grief decides to die. On his death, the Samsa family suddenly awakes, dismissing the charwoman and boarders who knew of their shame, and begins life anew.

injure their children, even if done benevolently, is sharply limited,[15] and the rights of physical and mental defectives are now strenuously protected.[16] From the infant's perspective withdrawing care would appear to be a serious infringement of a basic right.

In resolving the emotional and ethical dilemmas that confront parents of defective infants, it is surprising that law and legal values have rarely been invoked. The law's long experience with protecting minority rights and its concern with procedure and decisionmaking processes may offer a path out of this troublesome thicket. Yet, Duff and Campbell, while attempting to aid parents in making an informed choice, neglected to advise as to legal duties and the legal ramifications of withholding medical care.[17] Perhaps the most appropriate solution to this problem is, as they suggest, to allow parents and physicians wide latitude in decisionmaking.[18] This decision, however, can be reasonably made only after we understand and evaluate existing legal policy, and consider how law can best resolve the dilemma. . . .[19]

[O]ne cannot conclude that parents and physicians have nothing to fear when they decide not to treat a defective newborn. Rather, as the practice is more openly acknowledged and debated, some criminal prosecutions are likely to occur, at least while the legal issues are still being clarified. Although the right-to-life groups have focused on abortion and not yet entered this area, they may rechannel their efforts in the future, particularly as they suffer defeat on the abortion issue. In many instances complaints by a few citizens, who find involuntary euthanasia of defective newborns to be morally repulsive, might suffice to focus the district attorney's awareness on the issue and possibly engender prosecution.[20]

---

[15] Thus, Jehovah's Witness parents, who believe that blood transfusions are a transgression of God's law and hence not in their children's best interests, may generally not prevent a child from receiving a transfusion if essential to prevent substantial harm to the child. *See* Jehovah's Witnesses v. Kings County Hosp., 278 F. Supp. 488 (W.D. Wash. 1967), *aff'd,* 390 U.S. 598 (1968); People *ex rel.* Wallace V. Labrenz, 411 Ill. 618, 104 N.E. 2d 769, *cert. denied,* 344 U.S. 824 (1952); State v. Perricone, 37 N.J. 463, 181 A.2d 751, *cert. denied,* 371 U.S. 890 (1962). Similarly, parents who believe that a public school education is not in the best interests of their child are limited in the educational alternatives that they may select, because of the state's judgment that the absence of certain forms of education will harm the child. *Cf.* Wisconsin v. Yoder, 406 U.S. 205 (1972).

[16] *See* Jackson v. Indiana, 406 U.S. 715 (1972); Lessard v. Schmidt, 349 F. Supp. 1078 (E.D. Wis. 1972), *vacated and remanded,* 414 U.S. 473 (1974); Mills v. Board of Educ., 348 F. Suppl 866 (D.D.C. 1972).

[17] One may question whether parents in a legal sense provide informed consent to withhold treatment when they have not been informed that they risk criminal liability. This raises a serious issue of medical ethics that Duff and Campbell apparently ignored. *See* Roberts v. Young, 369 Mich. 113, 119, N.W.2d 627 (1963); Walz & Scheuneminn, *Informed Consent to Therapy,* 64 Nw. U.L. Rev. 628 (1969).

[18] Duff & Campbell, *supra* note 3, at 894.

[19] *Editors' note:* The deleted section offers a legal analysis of the criminal liability of the parties involved in the decision to withhold treatment.

[20] The events leading up to the Boston abortion prosecution are instructive in showing

II. EVALUATION OF ALTERNATIVE LEGAL ARRANGEMENTS

A. The Issue

It is reasonably clear that parents who withhold ordinary care from a defective infant, as well as physicians, nurses, and hospital officials who acquiesce in this decision, risk liability for crimes ranging from homicide to neglect and violation of the child-abuse reporting laws. The chance of prosecution at the present time, however, is small.

One may ask whether either full or partial enforcement of the law is a desirable mode of regulation, or whether some alternative legal arrangement would better resolve the conflicting values in the defective-infant situation. Duff and Campbell, for instance, argue that "[i]f working out these dilemmas in ways such as [we] suggest is in violation of the law, . . . the law should be changed,"[21] an opinion apparently shared by many other physicians.[22] Other persons consider withholding care from the newborn as morally unjustifiable, and presumably prefer to see the law fully enforced. Still others suggest that new laws be enacted to handle the situation. Possible modifications include amending the homicide and neglect statutes and creating a separate offense of withholding treatment from defective newborns; subjecting to further review the decision not to treat an infant; or designating a decisionmaker wholly independent of parents and physicians to make these decisions.[23]

The appropriate legal response to the defective-infant situation depends on our expectations of what law can and should accomplish. A minimum requirement should guarantee certainty of rule and rule enforcement, thereby informing people of the limits of their discretion and enhancing freedom by permitting them to take legal rules into account. In addition to certainty, however, the law should create a system of expectations that

---

the forces that might lead to prosecutions. On June 7, 1973, an article describing research at the City Hospital in Boston involving fetal tissue from 33 therapeutic abortions was published. *See* Philipson, Sabath & Charles, *Transplacental Passage of Erythromycin and Clindamycin,* 288 NEW ENG. J. MED. 1219 (1973). An anti-abortion group noted the article and complained of experimentation on live fetuses to the mayor, attorney general, and several legislators, and called a press conference to publicize the issue. *See* Scheckan, *BCH Fetus Case: Research at Stake,* Boston Globe, June 2, 1974, at I, col. I. The Boston City Council, which has authority over the hospital, began an investigation and held a public hearing. The hearing brought the issue to the attention of Suffolk County District Attorney, Garret Byrne, who also began receiving information from sources within the hospital concerning certain types of activities by some doctors. *Id.* His office investigated and learned of two dead fetuses for whom no death certificates had been filed, as required by state law. While the abortions had been lawfully performed, evidence indicated that either the fetus had been intentionally killed during the procedure, or had been removed alive from the mother and then allowed to die. This information was presented to a grand jury and an indictment resulted. *Id.*

[21] Duff & Campbell, *supra* note 3, at 894.

[22] *See* note 8, *supra.*

[23] *See generally* notes 93–109 *infra* and accompanying text.

resolves conflicting interests consistent with prevailing morality and our sense of what is just and right. An arrangement exacting too heavy a cost in the values of life; personal, parental and professional autonomy; scarce resources; or other strongly held values will be unacceptable.

What legal rule best comports with dominant values, while doing minimal violence to conflicting interests and providing certainty of application? This question can be answered only by considering two other questions that are at the core of the defective-infant dilemma. The first is whether there is a definable class of beings, such as defective newborns, from whom, under prevailing moral standards, ordinary medical care may be withheld without their consent. If withholding care can never be justified, the sole policy question then is whether existing legal categories best implement that goal or whether a new offense and penalty structure should be created. The second question arises if we conclude that withholding care in some instances is morally justified or socially desirable and asks who among parents, physicians, or other decisionmakers is best equipped to decide when care is to be withheld. Legal rules in this regard must focus on criteria, procedures, and decisionmaking processes for implementing a social policy of involuntary passive euthanasia. Until we thoroughly canvass these questions, decisions about legal policy cannot reasonably be made.

This Part first considers two arguments in favor of withholding necessary but ordinary medical care from defective infants, and concludes that neither is persuasive. It then considers whether, given the appropriateness of failing to treat some infants, parents and physicians should be given discretion to make such decisions, and suggests an alternative solution to the issue of who should decide.

B. Arguments in Favor of Withholding Ordinary Medical Care from Defective Infants

I. Defective Infants are not Persons Children born with congenital malformations may lack human form and the possibility of ordinary, psychosocial development. In many cases mental retardation is or will be so profound, and physical incapacity so great, that the term "persons" or "humanly alive"[24] have odd or questionable meaning when applied to them. In these cases the infant's physical and mental defects are so severe that they will never know anything but a vegetative existence, with no discernible personality, sense of self, or capacity to interact with others.[25] Withholding

---

[24] Commentary, *The Ethics of Surgery in Newborn Infants*, 8 CLINICAL PEDIATRICS 251 1969); *cf.* Grunberg, *Who Lives and Dies?*, N.Y. Times, Apr. 22, 1974, at 35, col. 2.

[25] *Id.* While the proposition appears to draw some support from Bracton's statement in a noncriminal context that a monster is not a human being, "Quia partus monstruosus est cum non nascatur ut homo," *cited in* G. WILLIAMS, THE SANCTITY OF LIFE AND THE CRIMINAL LAW 20–21 (1957), no case has ever held that a live human offspring is not a human being because of certain physical or mental deficits, and therefore may be killed. *See* G. WILLIAMS, *supra*, at 20–24. The state, in the exercise of its *parens patriae* power to protect persons incapacitated by

ordinary medical care in such cases, one may argue, is justified on the ground that these infants are not persons or human beings in the ordinary or legal sense of the term, and therefore do not possess the right of care that persons possess.

Central to this argument is the idea that living products of the human uterus can be classified into offspring that are persons, and those that are not. Conception and birth by human parents does not automatically endow one with personhood and its accompanying rights. Some other characteristic or feature must be present in the organism for personhood to vest,[26] and this the defective infant arguably lacks. Lacking that property, an organism is not a person or deserving to be treated as such.

Before considering what "morally significant features" might distinguish persons from nonpersons, and examining the relevance of such features to the case of the defective infant, we must face an initial objection to this line of inquiry. The objection questions the need for any distinction among human offspring because of

> the monumental misuse of the concept of 'humanity' in so many practices of discrimination and atrocity throughout history. Slavery, witchhunts and wars have all been justified by their perpetrators on the grounds that they held their victims to be less than fully human. The insane and the criminal have for long periods been deprived of the most basic necessities for similar reasons, and been excluded from society. . . .
> . . . Even when entered upon with the best of intentions, and in the most guarded manner, the enterprise of basing the protection of human life upon such criteria and definitions is dangerous. To question someone's humanity or personhood is a first step to mistreatment and killing.[27]

Hence, according to this view, human parentage is a necessary and sufficient condition for personhood, whatever the characteristics of the offspring, because qualifying criteria inevitably lead to abuse and untold suffering to beings who are unquestionably human. Moreover, the human species is sufficiently different from other sentient species that assigning its members greater rights on birth alone is not arbitrary.

This objection is indeed powerful. The treatment accorded slaves in the United States, the Nazi denial of personal status to non-Aryans, and count-

---

infancy, neglect, or mental incompetence, recognizes that many "persons" incapable of leading an ordinary or normal life are nevertheless persons with rights and interests to be protected. *See, e.g.,* Herr, *Retarded Children and the Law: Enforcing the Constitutional Rights of the Mentally Retarded,* 23 SYR. L. REV. 995 (1972). Even a slave was protected by the law of homicide even though incapable of full social interaction. *See, e.g.,* Fields v. State, I Yager's Rep. 156 (Tenn. 1829). Thus, a judge in Maine recently had little difficulty in concluding that a deformed child with multiple anomalies and brain damage was "at the moment of live birth . . . a human being entitled to the fullest protection of the law." Maine Medical Center v. Houle, No. 74–145, at 4 (Super. Ct., Cumberland Cty., Feb. 14, 1974).

[26] *See* Tooley, *Abortion and Infanticide,* 2 PHIL. & PUB. AFFAIRS 37, 51 (1972).

[27] Bok, *Ethical Problems of Abortion,* 2 HASTINGS CENTER STUDIES, Jan. 1974, at 33, 41.

less other incidents, testify that man's inhumanity to man is indeed greatest when a putative nonperson is involved.[28] Arguably, however, a distinction based on gross physical form, profound mental incapacity, and the very existence of personality or selfhood, besides having an empirical basis in the monstrosities and mutations known to have been born to women,[29] is a basic and fundamental one. Rather than distinguishing among the particular characteristics that persons might attain through the contingencies of race, culture, and class, it merely separates out those who lack the potential for assuming any personal characteristics beyond breathing and consciousness.

This reply narrows the issue: should such creatures be cared for, protected, or regarded as "ordinary" humans? If such treatment is not warranted, they may be treated as nonpersons. The arguments supporting care in all circumstances are based on the view that all living creatures are sacred, contain a spark of the divine, and should be so regarded. Moreover, identifying those human offspring unworthy of care is a difficult task and will inevitably take a toll on those whose humanity cannot seriously be questioned. At this point the argument becomes metaphysical or religious and immune to resolution by empirical evidence, not unlike the controversy over whether a fetus is a person.[30] It should be noted, however, that recognizing all human offspring as persons, like recognizing the fetus to be a person,[31] does not conclude the treatment issue.[32]

Although this debate can be resolved only by reference to religious or moral beliefs, a procedural solution may reasonably be considered. Since reasonable people can agree that we ordinarily regard human offspring as persons, and further, that defining categories of exclusion is likely to pose special dangers of abuse, a reasonable solution is to presume that all living human offspring are persons. This rule would be subject to exception only if it can be shown beyond a reasonable doubt that certain offspring will never possess the minimal properties that reasonable persons ordinarily associate with human personality. If this burden cannot be satisfied, then the presumption of personhood obtains.

For this purpose I will address only one of the many properties proposed as a necessary condition of personhood—the capacity for having a sense of self—and consider whether its advocates present a cogent account of the nonhuman. Since other accounts may be more convincingly articulated, this discussion will neither exhaust nor conclude the issue. But it will

[28] See Alexander, Medical Science under Dictatorship, 241 NEW ENG. J. MED. 39 (1949).
[29] T. BECK & J. BECK, ELEMENTS OF MEDICAL JURISPRUDENCE 422 (11th ed. 1960).
[30] See Tribe, Foreword—Toward a Model of Roles in the Due Process of Life and Law, 87 HARV. L. REV. I, 18–20 (1973).
[31] See Thomson, A Defense of Abortion, I PHIL. AND PUB. AFFAIRS 47 (1971).
[32] See notes 44–91 infra and accompanying text.

illuminate the strengths and weaknesses of the personhood argument and enable us to evaluate its application to defective infants.

Michael Tooley has recently argued that a human offspring lacking the capacity for a sense of self lacks the rights to life or equal treatment possessed by other persons.[33] In considering the morality of abortion and infanticide, Tooley considers "what properties a thing must possess in order to have a serious right to life,"[34] and he concludes that:

> [h]aving a right to life presupposes that one is capable of desiring to continue existing as a subject of experiences and other mental states. This in turn presupposes both that one has the concept of such a continuing entity and that one believes that one is oneself such an entity. So an entity that lacks such a consciousness of itself as a continuing subject of mental states does not have a right to life.[35]

However, this account is at first glance too narrow, for it appears to exclude all those who do not presently have a desire "to continue existing as a subject of experiences and other mental states." The sleeping or unconscious individual, the deranged, the conditioned, and the suicidal do not have such desires, though they might have had them or could have them in the future. Accordingly, Tooley emphasizes the capability of entertaining such desires, rather than their actual existence.[36] But it is difficult to distinguish the capability for such desires in an unconscious, conditioned, or emotionally disturbed person from the capability existing in a fetus or infant. In all cases the capability is a future one; it will arise only if certain events occur, such as normal growth and development in the case of the infant, and removal of the disability in the other cases. The infant, in fact, might realize its capability[37] long before disabled adults recover emotional balance or consciousness.

To meet this objection, Tooley argues that the significance of the capability in question is not solely its future realization (for fetuses and infants will ordinarily realize it), but also its previous existence and exercise.[38] He seems to say that once the conceptual capability has been realized, one's right to desire continued existence permanently vests, even though the present capability for desiring does not exist, and may be lost for substantial periods or permanently. Yet, what nonarbitrary reasons require that we protect the past realization of conceptual capability but not its potential

---

[33] Tooley, *supra* note 26, at 49.

[34] *Id.* at 37.

[35] *Id.* at 49.

[36] *Id.* at 50.

[37] Tooley concedes that the infant attains this capacity in the first year of life, though further research is necessary to identify the exact time. *Id.* at 64.

[38] *Correspondence,* 2 PHIL. & PUB. AFFAIRS 419 (1973).

realization in the future? As a reward for its past realization? To mark our reverence and honor for someone who has realized that state? Tooley is silent on this point.

Another difficulty is Tooley's ambiguity concerning the permanently deranged, comatose, or conditioned. Often he phrases his argument in terms of a temporary suspension of the capability of conceptual thought.[39] One wonders what he would say of someone permanently deranged, or with massive brain damage, or in a prolonged coma. If he seriously means that the past existence of a desire for life vests these cases with the right to life, then it is indeed difficult to distinguish the comatose or deranged from the infant profoundly retarded at birth. Neither will ever possess the conceptual capability to desire to be a continuing subject of experiences. A distinction based on reward or desert seems arbitrary, and protection of life applied equally well in both cases. Would Tooley avoid this problem by holding that the permanently comatose and deranged lose their rights after a certain point because conceptual capacity will never be regained? This would permit killing (or at least withholding of care from) the insane and comatose—doubtless an unappealing prospect.[40] Moreover, we do not ordinarily think of the insane, and possibly the comatose, as losing personhood before their death. Although their personality or identity may be said to change, presumably for the worse, or become fragmented or minimal, we still regard them as specific persons. If a "self" in some minimal sense exists here then the profoundly retarded, who at least is conscious, also may be considered a self, albeit a minimal one. Thus, one may argue that Tooley fails to provide a convincing account of criteria distinguishing persons and nonpersons. He both excludes beings we ordinarily think of as persons—infants, deranged, conditioned, possibly the comatose—and fails to articulate criteria that convincingly distinguish the nonhuman. But, even if we were to accept Tooley's distinction that beings lacking the potential for desire and a sense of self are not persons who are owed the duty to be treated by ordinary medical means, this would not appear to be very helpful in deciding whether to treat the newborn with physical or mental defects. Few infants, it would seem, would fall into this class.[41] First, those suffering from mal-

---

[39] *Id.* at 421–23.

[40] A somewhat similar approach to the definition of personhood by Richard McCormick also fails to cogently distinguish the case of the deranged. McCormick argues that if the potential for human relationships "is simply nonexistent or would be utterly submerged and undeveloped in the mere struggle to survive, that life has achieved its potential" and ordinary care need not be provided. McCormick, *To Save or Let Die—The Dilemma of Modern Medicine,* 229 J.A.M.A. 172, 175 (1974). But would we sanction withholding antibiotics from an insane person suffering a serious infection simply because his capacity to enter into human relationships had become minimal?

[41] Warkany, for example, reports the incidence of anencephaly, the absence of all or most of an infant's brain, as approximately 1 in 1,000 for children born in hospital wards, but

formations, however, gross, that do not affect mental capabilities would not fit the class of nonpersons. Second, frequently even the most severe cases of mental retardation cannot be reliably determined until a much later period;[42] care thus could not justifiably be withheld in the neonatal period, although this principle would permit nontreatment at the time when non-personality is clearly established.[43] Finally, the only group of defective newborns who would clearly qualify as nonpersons is anencephalics, who altogether lack a brain, or those so severely brain-damaged that it is immediately clear that a sense of self or personality can never develop. Mongols, myelomeningoceles, and other defective infants from whom ordinary care is now routinely withheld would not qualify as nonpersons. Thus, even the most coherent and cogent criteria of humanity are only marginally helpful in the situation of the defective infant. We must therefore consider whether treatment can be withheld on grounds other than the claim that such infants are not persons.

2. No Obligation to Treat Exists when the Costs of Maintaining Life Greatly Outweigh the Benefits If we reject the argument that defective newborns are not persons, the question remains whether circumstances exist in which the consequences of treatment as compared with nontreatment are so undesirable that the omission of care is justified. As we have seen [in the omitted portion], the doctrine of necessity permits one to violate the criminal law when essential to prevent the occurrence of a greater evil. The circumstances, however, when the death of a nonconsenting person is a lesser evil than his continuing life are narrowly circumscribed, and do not include withholding care from defective infants.

Yet many parents and physicians deeply committed to the loving care of the newborn think that treating severely defective infants causes more harm than good, thereby justifying the withholding of ordinary care.[44] In their view the suffering and diminished quality of the child's life do not justify the social and economic costs of treatment. This claim has a growing commonsense appeal, but it assumes that the utility or quality of one's life can be measured and compared with other lives, and that health resources may legitimately be allocated to produce the greatest personal utility. This

---

notes that "remarkable variations have been reported from different areas." J. WARKANY, *supra* note 2, at 189.

[42] *Id.* at 39.

[43] But other factors might lead to treatment at this later point in time. For example, if care and nurturing occur immediately after birth, a strong mother-child bond is built, which might prevent mothers from deciding to withhold care when a serious defect is discovered weeks later. Barnett, Leiderman, Globstein & Klaus, *Neonatal Separation: The Maternal Side of Interactional Deprivation,* 45 PEDIATRICS 197, 197–99 (1970); Kennel & Klaus, *Care of the Mother of the High Risk Infant,* 14 CLIN. OBSTET. & GYNECOL. 926, 930–36 (1971).

[44] *See* Duff & Campbell, *supra* note 3.

argument will not be analyzed from the perspective of the defective patient and others affected by his care.

a. The Quality of the Defective Infant's Life   Comparisons of relative worth among persons, or between persons and other interests, raise moral and methodological issues that make any argument that relies on such comparisons extremely vulnerable. Thus the strongest claim for not treating the defective newborn is that treatment seriously harms the infant's own interests, whatever may be the effects on others. When maintaining his life involves great physical and psychosocial suffering for the patient, a reasonable person might conclude that such a life is not worth living. Presumably the patient, if fully informed and able to communicate, would agree. One then would be morally justified in withholding lifesaving treatment if such action served to advance the best interests of the patient.[45]

Congenital malformations impair development in several ways that lead to the judgment that deformed retarded infants are "a burden to themselves."[46] One is the severe physical pain, much of it resulting from repeated surgery that defective infants will suffer.[47] Defective children also

---

[45] The perspective that the mere saving of life is not enough unless the lives are worth saving" is well represented in the medical literature. Lorber, in discussing the process of selecting spina bifida infants for treatment, states: "Severe degree of paralysis is the most generally adopted reason for withholding treatment, but incontinence, severe hydrocephalus, gross deformities and social conditions are also taken into account. . . . There is no doubt that the future quality of life of many patients with myelomeningocele depends at least partly on the speed, efficiency and comprehensiveness of treatment from birth onwards—and often throughout their lives. Nevertheless, there are large numbers who are so severely handicapped at birth that those who survive are bound to suffer from a combination of major physical defects. In addition, many will be retarded in spite of everything that can be done for them. It is not necessary to enumerate all that this means to the patient, the family and the community in terms of suffering, deprivation, anxiety, frustration, family stress and financial cost. The large majority surviving at present have yet to reach the most difficult period of adolescence and young adult life and the problems of love, marriage and employment." Lorber *Results of Treatment of Myelomenigocele,* 13 DEVELOP. MED & CHILD NEUROL. 279–303 (1971) at 279, *citing* Rickham & Mawdsley, *The Effect of Early Operation on the Survival of Spina Bijida Cyshica,* DEVELOP. MED. & CHILD NEUROL. 20 (Supp. 11, 1966) at 20. He summarizes the results of treating 524 cases of myelomeningocele on an unselected basis: "In summary, at the most 7 per cent of those admitted have less than grossly crippling disabilities and may be considered to have a quality of life not inconsistent with self-respect, earning capacity, happiness and even marriage. The next 20 per cent are also of normal intelligence and some may be able to earn their living in sheltered employment, but their lives are full of illness and operations. They are severely handicapped and are unlikely to live a full life-span. They are at a risk of sudden death from shunt complications or are likely to die of renal failure at an early age. The next 14 per cent are even more severely handicapped because they are retarded. They are unlikely to earn their living and their opportunities in life will be severely restricted. They will always be totally dependent on others." *Id.* at 286. He concludes that "[i]t is unlikely that many would wish to save a life which will consist of a long succession of operations, hospital admissions and other deprivations, or if the end result will be a combination of gross physical defects with retarded intellectual development." *Id.* at 300.

[46] Smith & Smith, *Selection for Treatment in Spina Bifida Cystica,* 4 BRIT. MED. J. 189, 195 (1973).

[47] *See* Lorber, *supra* note 45, at 284.

are likely to develop other pathological features, leading to repeated fractures, dislocations, surgery, malfunctions, and other sources of pain. The shunt, for example, inserted to relieve hydrocephalus, a common problem in defective children, often becomes clogged, necessitating frequent surgical interventions.[48]

Pain, however, may be intermittent and manageable with analgesics. Since many infants and adults experience great pain, and many defective infants do not, pain alone, if not totally unmanageable, does not sufficiently show that a life is so worthless that death is preferable. More important are the psychosocial deficits resulting from the child's handicaps. Many defective children never can walk even with prosthesis, never interact with normal children, never appreciate growth, adolescence, or the fulfillment of education and employment, and seldom are even able to care for themselves. In cases of severe retardation, they may be left with a vegetative existence in a crib, incapable of choice or the most minimal response to stimuli. Parents or others may reject them, and much of their time will be spent in hospitals, in surgery, or fighting the many illnesses that beset them. Can it be said that such a life is worth living?

There are two possible responses to the quality-of-life argument. One is to accept its premises but to question the degree of suffering in particular cases, and thus restrict the justification for death to the most extreme cases. The absence of opportunities for schooling, career, and interaction may be the fault of social attitudes and the failings of healthy persons, rather than a necessary result of congenital malformations. Psychosocial suffering occurs because healthy, normal persons reject or refuse to relate to the defective, or hurry them to poorly funded institutions. Most nonambulatory, mentally retarded persons can be trained for satisfying roles. One cannot assume that a nonproductive existence is necessarily unhappy; even social rejection and nonacceptance can be mitigated.[49] Moreover, the psychosocial ills of the handicapped often do not differ in kind from those experienced by many persons. With training and care, growth, development, and a full range of experiences are possible for most people with physical and mental handicaps. Thus, the claim that death is a far better fate than life cannot in most cases be sustained.

This response, however, avoids meeting the quality-of-life argument on its strongest grounds. Even if many defective infants can experience growth, interaction, and most human satisfactions if nurtured, treated, and trained,

---

[48] Ames & Schut, *Results of Treatment of 171 Consecutive Myelomeningoceles—1963 to 1968,* 50 PEDIATRICS 466, 469 (1972); Shurtleff & Foltz, *A Comparative Study of Meningomyelocele Repair or Cerebrospinal Fluid Shunt As Primary Treatment in Ninety Children,* DEVELOP. MED. & CHILD NEURO. 57 (Supp. 13, 1967).

[49] *See* E. GOFFMAN, STIGMA: NOTES ON THE MANAGEMENT OF SPOILED IDENTIFY 57–129 (1963).

some infants are so severely retarded or grossly deformed that their response to love and care, in fact their capacity to be conscious, is always minimal. Although mongoloid and nonambulatory spina bifida children may experience an existence we would hesitate to adjudge worse than death, the profoundly retarded, nonambulatory, blind, deaf infant who will spend his few years in the back-ward cribs of a state institution is clearly a different matter.

To repudiate the quality-of-life argument, therefore, requires a defense of treatment in even these extreme cases. Such a defense would question the validity of any surrogate or proxy judgments of the worth or quality of life when the wishes of the person in question cannot be ascertained. The essence of the quality-of-life argument is a proxy's judgment that no reasonable person can prefer the pain, suffering, and loneliness of, for example, life in a crib at an IQ level of 20, to an immediate, painless death.

But in what sense can the proxy validly conclude that a person with different wants, needs, and interests, if able to speak, would agree that such a life were worse than death? At the start one must be skeptical of the proxy's claim to objective disinterestedness. If the proxy is also the parent or physician, as has been the case in pediatric euthanasia, the impact of treatment on the proxy's interests, rather than solely on those of the child, may influence his assessment. But even if the proxy were truly neutral and committed only to caring for the child, the problem of egocentricity and knowing another's mind remains. Compared with the situation and life prospects of a "reasonable man," the child's potential quality of life indeed appears dim. Yet a standard based on healthy, ordinary development may be entirely inappropriate to this situation. One who has never known the pleasures of mental operation, ambulation, and social interaction surely does not suffer from their loss as much as one who has. While one who has known these capacities may prefer death to a life without them, we have no assurance that the handicapped person, with no point of comparison, would agree. Life, and life alone, whatever its limitations, might be of sufficient worth to him.[50]

---

[50] *Cf.* Gleitman v. Cosgrove, 49 N.J. 22, 227 A.2d 689 (1967). The court denied plaintiff's right to collect damages for being born with deformities when a defendant physician was allegedly negligent in informing the plaintiff's mother of rubella, which would have led her to seek an abortion. The court stated: "It is basic to the human condition to seek life and hold on to it however heavily burdened. If Jeffrey could have been asked as to whether his life should be snuffed out before his full term of gestation could run its course, our felt intuition of human nature tells us he would almost surely choose life with defects as against no life at all." *Id.* at 30, 227 A.2d at 693.

Similarly, in the case of *In re* Hudson, 13 Wash. 2d 673, 126 P.2d 765 (1942), a child was held not to be neglected when her parent refused to consent to life-endangering surgery to correct a gross deformity that made normal development and interaction impossible: "As we read the evidence, it is admitted by all concerned that . . . the child may not survive the ordeal of amputation; nevertheless, every one except the child's mother is willing, desirous, that the

One should also be hesitant to accept proxy assessments of quality-of-life because the margin of error in such predictions may be very great. For instance, while one expert argues that by a purely clinical assessment he can accurately forecast the minimum degree of future handicap an individual will experience,[51] such forecasting is not infallible,[52] and risks denying care to infants whose disability might otherwise permit a reasonably acceptable quality-of-life. Thus given the problems in ascertaining another's wishes, the proxy's bias to personal or culturally relative interests, and the unreliability of predictive criteria, the quality-of-life argument is open to serious question. Its strongest appeal arises in the case of a grossly deformed, retarded, institutionalized child, or one with incessant unmanageable pain, where continued life is itself torture. But these cases are few, and cast doubt on the utility of any such judgment. Even if the judgment occasionally may be defensible, the potential danger of quality-of-life assessments may be a compelling reason for rejecting this rationale for withholding treatment.[53]

b. The Suffering of Others In addition to the infant's own suffering, one who argues that the harm of treatment justifies violation of the defective infant's right to life usually relies on the psychological, social, and economic costs of maintaining his existence to family and society. In their view the minimal benefit of treatment to persons incapable of full social and physical development does not justify the burdens that care of the defective infant imposes on parents, siblings, health professionals, and other patients. Matson, a noted pediatric neurosurgeon, states:

> [I]t is the doctor's and the community's responsibility to provide [custodial] care and to minimize suffering; but, at the same time, it is also their responsibility not to prolong such individual, familial, and community suffering unnec-

---

child be required to undergo the operation. Implicit in their position is their opinion that it would be preferable that the child die instead of going through life handicapped by the enlarged, deformed left arm. That may be to some today the humane, and in the future it may be the generally accepted, view. However, we have not advanced or retrograded to the stage where, in the name of mercy, we may lawfully decide that one shall be deprived of life rather than continue to exist crippled or burdened with some abnormality. That right of decision is a prerogative of the Creator." *Id.* at 684, 126 P.2d at 771. *See also* Cooke, *Supra* note 9, at 906–08.

[51] *See* Lorber, *supra* note 45, at 299.

[52] In Lorber's series, 20% of 110 infants "with major adverse criteria at birth were of normal intellectual development at 2–4 years of age, though all [had] severe physical handicaps and their life expectation [was] short." *Id.* at 300. Moreover, other researchers question the adequacy of Lorber's selection criteria. Ames and Shut, for example, in a report on unselected treatment cases of myelomeningocele find "it is not always possible to determine potential at birth," and report success with infants that Lorber would not have selected. *See* Ames & Schut, *supra* note 48, at 469–70.

[53] If this judgment is to be made, it is essential that the circumstances in which nontreatment may be said to be in a patient's best interests be specified beforehand by an authoritative body, and that procedures which assure that a particular case falls within such criteria be followed. *See* notes 104–109 *infra* and accompanying text.

essarily, and not to carry out multiple procedures and prolonged, expensive, acute hospitalization in an infant whose chance for acceptable growth and development is negligible.[54]

Such a frankly utilitarian argument raises problems. It assumes that because of the greatly curtailed orbit of his existence, the costs or suffering of others is greater than the benefit of life to the child. This judgment, however, requires a coherent way of measuring and comparing interpersonal utilities, a logical-practical problem that utilitarianism has never surmounted.[55] But even if such comparisons could reliably show a net loss from treatment, the fact remains that the child must sacrifice his life to benefit others. If the life of one individual, however useless, may be sacrificed for the benefit of any person, however useful, or for the benefit of any number of persons, then we have acknowledged the principle that rational utility may justify any outcome.[56] As many philosophers have demonstrated, utilitarianism can always permit the sacrifice of one life for other interests, given the appropriate arrangement of utilities on the balance sheet.[57] In the absence of principled grounds for such a decision, the social equation involved in mandating direct, involuntary euthanasia [58] becomes a difference of degree, not kind, and we reach the point where protection of life depends solely on social judgments of utility.

These objections may well be determinative.[59] But if we temporarily bracket them and examine the extent to which care of the defective infant subjects others to suffering, the claim that inordinate suffering outweighs the infant's interest in life is rarely plausible. In this regard we must examine the impact of caring for defective infants on the family, health professions, and society-at-large.

The family   The psychological impact and crisis created by birth of a defective infant is devastating.[60] Not only is the mother denied the normal tension release from the stresses of pregnancy,[61] but both parents feel a crushing blow to their dignity, self-esteem and self-confidence.[62] In a very

---

[54] Matson, *Surgical Treatment of Myelomeningocele,* 42 PEDIATRICS 225, 226 (1968).

[55] J. RAWLS, A THEORY OF JUSTICE 90–1 (1971).

[56] *Cf.* Silving, *Euthanasia: A Study in Comparative Criminal Law,* 103 U. PA. L. REV. 350, 356 (1954).

[57] *See, e.g.,* J. RAWLS, *supra* note 55, at 22–27.

[58] Alexander, *supra* note 28, at 39.

[59] The New Jersey Supreme Court, for example, would clearly reject a balancing test in such situations. *See* Gleitman v. Cosgrove, 49 N.J. 22, 227 A.2d 689 (1967).

[60] "The experience of learning that your child is defective immediately after birth can still be categorized among the most painful and stigmatizing experiences of modern people. It is as if the parents' raison d'etre were called into question before an imagined parental bar of justice and an ontological blow dealt to their hopes of continuing their identities." Fletcher, *supra* note 13, at 24.

[61] *See* Goodman, *supra* note 13. *See generally* Kennel & Klaus, *supra* note 43.

[62] Bentovim, *Emotional Disturbances of Handicapped Pre-School Children and Their Fami-*

short time, they feel grief for the loss of the normal expected child, anger at fate, numbness, disgust, waves of helplessness, and disbelief.[63] Most feel personal blame for the defect, or blame their spouse. Adding to the shock is fear that social position and mobility are permanently endangered.[64] The transformation of a "joyously awaited experience into one of catastrophe and profound psychological threat"[65] often will reactivate unresolved maturational conflicts. The chances for social pathology—divorce, somatic complaints, nervous and mental disorders—increase and hard-won adjustment patterns may be permanently damaged.[66]

The initial reactions of guilt, grief, anger, and loss, however, cannot be the true measure of family suffering caused by care of a defective infant, because these costs are present whether or not the parents choose treatment. Rather, the question is to what degree treatment imposes psychic and other costs greater than would occur if the child were not treated. The claim that care is more costly rests largely on the view that parents and family suffer inordinately from nurturing such a child.

Indeed, if the child is treated and accepted at home, difficult and demanding adjustments must be made. Parents must learn how to care for a disabled child, confront financial and psychological uncertainty, meet the needs of other siblings, and work through their own conflicted feelings. Mothering demands are greater than with a normal child, particularly if medical care and hospitalization are frequently required.[67] Counseling or professional support may be nonexistent or difficult to obtain.[68] Younger siblings may react with hostility and guilt, older with shame and anger.[69] Often the normal feedback of child growth that renders the turmoil of childrearing worthwhile develops mroe slowly or not at all. Family resources can be depleted (especially if medical care is needed), consumption patterns altered, or standards of living modified.[70] Housing may have to be found closer to a hospital, and plans for further children changed.[71] Finally,

---

lies—Attitudes to the Child, 3 BRIT. MED. J. 579, 580 (1972); Giannini & Goodman, Counseling Families During the Crisis Reaction to Mongolism, 67 AM. J. MENTAL DEFICIENCY 740, 740–41 (1962); Goodman, supra note 13; Mandelbaum & Wheeler, The Meaning of A Defective Child to Parents, 41 SOCIAL CASEWORK 360 (1960); Schild, Counselling with Parents of Retarded Children Living at Home, 9 SOCIAL WORK 86 (1964); Zachary, Ethical and Social Aspects of Treatment of Spina Bifida, THE LANCET, Aug. 3, 1968, at 274–75.

[63] See note 62 supra.

[64] See Giannini & Goodman, supra note 62, at 743.

[65] Goodman, supra note 13, at 92.

[66] Id. at 93.

[67] See Hunt, Implications of the Treatment of Myelomeningocele for the Child and his Family, THE LANCET, Dec. 8, 1973, at 1308, 1309–10; Zachary, supra note 62, at 275.

[68] Hunt, supra note 66, at 1310.

[69] Id. at 1309; Bentovim, supra note 62, at 581.

[70] Zachary, supra note 62, at 275.

[71] Hunt, supra note 67, at 1310.

the anxieties, guilt, and grief present at birth may threaten to recur or become chronic.[72]

Yet, although we must recognize the burdens and frustrations of raising a defective infant, it does not necessarily follow that these costs require nontreatment, or even institutionalization. Individual and group counseling can substantially alleviate anxiety, guilt, and frustration, and enable parents to cope with underlying conflicts triggered by the birth and the adaptations required.[73] Counseling also can reduce psychological pressures on siblings, who can be taught to recognize and accept their own possibly hostile feelings and the difficult position of their parents. They may even be taught to help their parents care for the child.[74]

The impact of increased financial costs also may vary.[75] In families with high income or adequate health insurance, the financial costs are man-

---

[72] "At each stage there may be a fresh feeling of loss: the precarious balance is once more shattered, rage, depression, rejecting feelings, fear of battering, strain, somatic aches and pains, may be the result. Problems such as financial difficulties, poor housing, marital strain, pressure from siblings can compound such problems. Social life can be severely restricted and the handicapped child then has to cope with the additional handicap of a withdrawn, preoccupied, depressed, angry and hopeless parent, as well as the effect of the handicap itself." Bentovim, *supra* note 62, at 581.

[73] *See, e.g.,* Cohen, *supra* note 13; Giannini & Goodman, *supra* note 62; Schild, *Supra* note 62, at 86.

[74] *See* citations in note 73 *supra.*

[75] The financial impact of caring for the defective child is difficult to estimate and varies with the seriousness of the defect, the resultant medical costs, health insurance coverage, and state assistance programs. For example, it may cost the parents of a child born with spina bifida from $5,000 to more than $40,000 to pay for the necessary operations, hospital care, medication, doctor's checkups, and braces. Interview with Peggy Miezio, Wis. Spina Bifida Ass'n, Aug. 24, 1974.

Since almost 180 million Americans in 1971 were covered by some form of health insurance, HEALTH INSURANCE INSTITUTE, 1972–73 SOURCE BOOK OF HEALTH INSURANCE DATA 19 (1972), many parents find that insurance covers at least some of the costs. Until recently many policies excluded coverage for disorders commencing before the age of 15 days, and thus did not cover such congenital disorders as spina bifida, Down's syndrome, or cystic fibrosis. *See, e.g.,* Kissel v. Beneficial Nat'l Life Ins., 64 N.J. 555, 319 A.2d 67 (1974). Recently, several states have passed legislation requiring health insurance policies to cover newborn children from the day of birth. *See, e.g.,* CAL. INS. CODE 10119 (West 1972). In addition, even if the policy lawfully excludes coverage of deformed newborns, indications are that in many cases, because of "social pressures," insurance companies cover newborn infants from the day of birth. Interview with Roy Anderson, Office of Comm'r of Ins., Madison, Wis., Aug. 22, 1974.

In addition to the availability of coverage, two other problems face parents of defective newborns. One is the limits of such coverage. If the medical expenses of the child are high, and the coverage limits of the policy low, parents may have to resort to use of savings or income, or seek state aid. Second, even if a parent were covered by a group policy, the coverage does not transfer if the primary insured leaves the business from which he obtained his policy. Availability of insurance coverage depends on "insurability," and as it is virtually impossible for a family to obtain new coverage for a handicapped child after birth, the families are, in effect, "locked into" their group policy, with a resulting decrease in mobility.

For families with inadequate or no insurance coverage and who lack the means to absorb high expenditures for care of a deformed newborn, the availability of state assistance becomes crucial. In general, fairly adequate state aid is available to parents who do not wish

ageable. In others, state assistance may be available.[76] If severe financial problems arise or pathological adjustments are likely, institutionalization, although undesirable for the child, remains an option.[77] Finally, in many

---

to institutionalize their child. In California, for example, the state Crippled Children Services offers extensive aid for families with deformed children. When a deformed child requires medical attention that the parents are unable to afford, the parents, hospital, or family doctor may contact the local health department, which will then determine if the child is "medically eligible" for the services of the Crippled Children Department. A diagnostic evaluation of the child's condition is performed and an estimate is made of the cost of care. The Crippled Children Services then determines if the family is financially eligible for aid. An allowable income level is set according to several factors, and below a certain level (presently $6,300 for a family of four), all expenses are paid by the state. Above this level, the families pay an amount not greater than one-half of the difference between their income and the cost-of-living allowance level. Hospital expenses, medication, braces, nursing care—all the needs of the deformed child—are provided, and the only limit on aid is the agency's budget. Telephone interview with Darleen Gibben, State Crippled Children Services, Sacramento, Cal., Aug. 22, 1974.

For retarded children without serious physical defects, state aid, whether the child is institutionalized or not, is available depending on parental income. Telephone interview with Robert Baldo, Regional Center for Developmentally Disabled, Sacramento, Cal., Aug. 22, 1974.

Similar systems of aid for both physical and mental handicaps, and special education needs, are available in Illinois, Telephone interview with Dr. Graham Blanton, Director of Developmental Disabilities, Dep't of Mental Health and Developmental Disabilities, Springfield, Ill., Aug. 22, 1974; and in Wisconsin, Telephone interview with Elie Asleson, Bureau of Handicapped Children, Dep't of Health and Social Services, Madison, Wis., Aug. 27, 1974; and presumably in other states, since much of the state budget for these services is federally funded.

Although the data is too incomplete to conclude that care of a defective newborn will never severely drain a family's financial resources, it seems clear that the impact can be cushioned or minimized by institutionalization of the child, health insurance, or state aid. Obviously, if legislative policy remains committed to the value of life, a strong argument may be made that the taxpayers as a whole rather than individual families or insurance holders should bear the cost of care.

I am indebted to Marsha Peckham for clarification of the financial issued involved in the care of the defective newborn.

[76] *See* note 75 *supra.*

[77] Moreover, parental rights and obligations can be terminated. Most states have some procedure by which parents may voluntarily divest themselves of legal rights to and legal obligations to provide for their children. Wisconsin and Delaware, for example, provide explicitly for a voluntary termination of all parental rights and obligations. 13 DEL. Code § § 1103–08 (Additional Supp. 1970); WIS. STAT. § 48.40 (West 1957). Other jurisdictions, such as Massachusetts, provide that upon application of a parent, the Department of Public Welfare "may accept a temporary delegation of certain rights and responsibilities regarding a child." MASS. LAWS ANN. ch. 119, § 23 (1973 Supp.). Other provisions of Massachusetts law suggest that a parent wishing to relinquish rights and responsibilities toward a child can successfully do so, although a formal right to termination is less clear. *See* MASS. LAWS ANN. ch. 119, § 23(B), (C), (E) (Additional Supp. 1973). Some states have statutes authorizing parents to apply to the Department of Welfare "for such care or custody of such child as the circumstances may require." N.J. STAT. 30:4C–11 (West 1964). Although most statutes speak only to the issue of involuntary termination, "this omission . . . has been criticized for the reasons, among others, that without the guidance of a statute and a judicial determination, the natural parent will be less likely to understand the implications of termination and secondly, the clarity and finality of a judicial determination will be absent." Gordon, *Terminal Placements of Children and*

cases, the experience of living through a crisis is a deepening and enriching one, accelerating personality maturation, and giving one a new sensitivity to the needs of spouse, siblings, and others. As one parent of a defective child states: "In the last months I have come closer to people and can understand them more. I have met them more deeply. I did not know there were so many people with troubles in the world."[78]

Thus, while social attitudes regard the handicapped child as an unmitigated disaster, in reality the problem may not be insurmountable, and often may not differ from life's other vicissitudes. Suffering there is, but seldom is it so overwhelming or so imminent that the only alternative is death of the child.[79]

Health professionals   Physicians and nurses also suffer when parents give birth to a defective child, although, of course, not to the degree of the parents. To the obstetrician or general practitioner the defective birth may be a blow to his professional identity. He has the difficult task of informing the parents of the defects, explaining their causes, and dealing with the parents' resulting emotional shock. Often he feels guilty for failing to produce a normal baby.[80] In addition, the parents may project anger or hostility on the physician, questioning his professional competence or seeking the services of other doctors.[81] The physician also may feel that his expertise and training are misused when employed to maintain the life of an infant whose chances for a productive existence are so diminished. By neglecting other patients, he may feel that he is prolonging rather than alleviating suffering.

Nurses, too, suffer role strain from care of the defective newborn. In-

---

Permanent Termination of Parental Rights: The New York Permanent Neglect Statute, 46 St. John's L. Rev. 215, 216 (1971). In practice, however, under any of the above or similar statutes, parents are generally able to divest themselves of parental rights and obligations, although parents with means may have to pay a reasonable sum toward the care of the child.

[78] *Quoted in* Johns, *Family Reactions to the Birth of a Child with a Congenital Abnormality,* 26 Obstet. & Gynecol. Survey 635, 637 (1971).

[79] Since parents and physicians now view treatment and acceptance of a defective child as discretionary with the parents, acceptance may be viewed as a gift on the part of the parents to the child. Because of the child's defects, however, the debt or obligation owed to the donor by the recipient of a gift cannot be repaid, and few substitutions for that debt seem available. Given the frequency with which families donate organs to ailing members, it may be that the defective infant situation is not structured to maximize the chance of parental giftgiving. *See* R. Fox & J. Swayze, The Courage To Fail: A Social View of Organ Transplants and Dialysis 20–27 (1974).

[80] Kennel & Klaus, *supra* note 209, at 946. This is particularly true if a physician identifies with the family and its values. "The physician may feel a sense of having failed the family with whom he has a relationship—and his own emotions and feelings come into play—seemingly to a greater extent than with lower class families. His recommendations may be influenced unconsciously by his discomfort with the situation and his strong desire to 'save' the family." Giannini & Goodman, *supra* note 62, at 744.

[81] Cohen, *supra* note 13, at 138.

tensive-care-unit nurses may work with only one or two babies at a time. They face the daily ordeals of care—the progress and relapses—and often must deal with anxious parents who are themselves grieving or ambivalent toward the child. The situation may trigger a nurse's own ambivalence about death and mothering, in a context in which she is actively working to keep alive a child whose life prospects seem minimal.[82]

Thus, the effects of care on physicians and nurses are not trivial, and must be intelligently confronted in medical education or in management of a pediatric unit. Yet to state them is to make clear that they can but weigh lightly in the decision of whether to treat a defective newborn. Compared with the situation of the parents, these burdens seem insignificant, are short term, and most likely do not evoke such profound emotions. In any case, these difficulties are hazards of the profession—caring for the sick and dying will always produce strain. Hence, on these grounds alone it is difficult to argue that a defective person may be denied the right to life.

Society   Care of the defective newborn also imposes societal costs, the utility of which is questioned when the infant's expected quality-of-life is so poor. Medical resources that can be used by infants with a better prognosis, or throughout the health-care system generally, are consumed in providing expensive surgical and intensive-care services to infants who may be severely retarded, never lead active lives, and die in a few months or years. Institutionalization imposes costs on taxpayers and reduces the resources available for those who might better benefit from it,[83] while reducing further the quality of life experienced by the institutionalized defective.

One answer to these concerns is to question the impact of the costs of caring for defective newborns. Precise data showing the costs to taxpayers or the trade-offs with health and other expenditures do not exist. Nor would ceasing to care for the defective necessarily lead to a reallocation within the health budget that would produce net savings in suffering or life;[84] in fact, the released resources might not be reallocated for health at all.[85] In any case, the trade-offs within the health budget may well be small. With advances in prenatal diagnosis of genetic disorders, many deformed infants

[82] Author's observations at conference concerning treatment of a defective newborn at St. Mary's Hospital, Madison, Wis., Apri. 15, 1974.

[83] "It may be true that further advances should improve the outlook for many, but unfortunately the basic defect is usually so severe that the children will always be severely handicapped in spite of any advances which can be foreseen today. Meanwhile it may be best to concentrate our therapeutic efforts on those who can truly benefit from treatment. If all the most severe cases are treated, the pressure of work will be such that adequate time cannot be devoted to the less severely affected who would benefit most." Lorber, *supra* note 45, at 300.

[84] For example, the resources instead might be used to increase physicians' salaries or the profits of drug or medical supply industries.

[85] Resources presently consumed in the care of the defective may have been appropriated for that purpose only, and if not so utilized, will be withdrawn.

who would formerly require care will be aborted beforehand.[86] Then, too, it is not clear that the most technical and expensive procedures always constitute the best treatment for certain malformations.[87] When compared with the almost seven percent of the GNP now spent on health,[88] the money in the defense budget, or tax revenues generally, the public resources required to keep defective newborns alive seem marginal, and arguably worth the commitment to life that such expenditures reinforce. Moreover, as the Supreme Court recently recognized,[89] conservation of the taxpayer's purse does not justify serious infringement of fundamental rights. Given legal and ethical norms against sacrificing the lives of nonconsenting others, and the imprecisions in diagnosis and prediction concerning the eventual outcomes of medical care,[90] the social-cost argument does not compel nontreatment of defective newborns.[91]

---

[86] For instance, amniocentesis carried out on pregnant women over 35—the most risky age for Down's syndrome—should reduce the incidence of mongolism and the attendant problems of care. *Cf.* Smith, *On Letting Some Babies Die,* HASTINGS CENTER STUDIES, Vol. 2, No. 2, at 37, 45 (1974).

[87] *See* Ames & Schut, *supra* note 48, at 467–70, which emphasizes the counseling and shunting of spina bifida babies rather than more elaborate and expensive intervention. *See also* C. FRIED, *supra* note 180, at 200–06.

[88] Mechanic, *Problems in the Future Organization of Medical Practice,* 35 LAW & CONTEMP. PROB. 233, 234 (1970).

[89] Memorial Hosp. v. Maricopa County, 415 U.S. 250 (1974).

[90] *See* note 52 *supra* and accompanying text.

[91] Moreover, although the case is unlikely to arise in medically developed nations, imagine, for example, that two myelomeningocele infants both need a shunt, orthopedic surgery, and other services, but resources are so limited that either complete care can be given to one and custodial care to the other, or both can be given only minimal care. Complete care for Baby *A* would lead to ambulation and normal intelligence, while complete care for Baby *B* would still leave him severely retarded and nonambulatory. Minimal care for both would leave both nonambulatory and retarded. Or suppose that resources would permit only one surgical procedure to correct duodenal atresia, but both a Down's syndrome and a normal baby need the operation. In either situation one may argue that physicians should be able to allocate scarce medical resources on the basis of their perception of which allocation will produce the most "good." Presumably, an outcome where the normal infant survives would be chosen. However, one may question whether, in situations of scarcity, distributive justice is satisfied by anything but a random or a first-come-first-served allocation, or an allocation system indifferent to the personal characteristics of each infant. To allocate health resources on the basis of prospective quality of life or social utility would raise in all but a few extreme cases the difficult task of (1) determining and measuring quality, and (2) specifying criteria for a nonarbitrary conclusion that quality *X* is better than quality *Y*. As David Smith observes: "Such an approach leads one to think that the ideal result is either a 'perfect' baby or a dead baby. And the root problems of this way of looking at the issue are that both the human rights of defectives and the imperfections of all babies are glossed over." Smith, *supra* note 86 at 46 (footnote omitted).

Thus, one may argue that even here qualitative or utilitarian judgments are out of place, for they depend on nonobjective, culturally relative standards of quality. The lot of some is improved by making others worse off, yet the reasons for preferring one group are not compelling on nonarbitrary grounds. Unless one were willing to accept the principle that medical decisionmakers may opt to maximize social utility when limited resources require a selection among patients, then the defective newborn could not be denied treatment because of his

C. The Decisionmaking Process

Assuming that the above arguments are rejected and we conclude that defective infants are either nonpersons, or persons from whom care justifiably can be withheld in certain cases, the question of procedure remains. Should parents and physicians have final discretion to determine whether a particular infant is treated, or should this power vest in a formally designated decisionmaking body? Should criteria and procedures for nonselection be promulgated? Should broad guidelines suffice? Since parents always may decide to treat and care for their child,[92] whatever its characteristics, the procedural question arises only when they have rejected treatment, and the attending physician concurs. The issue then posed is whether their decision should be determinative.

I. Who Should decide? *a. Final Authority with Parents and Physicians* Duff and Campbell present the argument for granting parents and physicians final discretion to decide whether a defective infant should be treated, and hence live or die:

> We believe the burdens of decisionmaking must be borne by families and their professional advisers because they are most familiar with the respective situations. Since families primarily must live with and are most affected by the decisions, it therefore appears that society and the health professions should provide only general guidelines for decisionmaking. Moreover, since variations between situations are so great, and the situations themselves so complex, it follows that much latitude in decisionmaking should be expected and tolerated.[93]

The logic of this argument, however, is unpersuasive. It rests on the assumption that parents have but two options—to withhold care or to be burdened with the care of the child throughout their lives. But a third option exists—termination of parental rights and obligations.[94] However, while parental discretion to terminate the parental relationship may be justified,[95] it does not follow that parents should also have the right to decide whether the child lives or dies. Clearly, discretion to terminate a relation-

---

defects alone. Fortunately, this dilemma, which arose frequently when hemodialysis resources were in short supply, does not yet seem to have arisen in the case of defective newborns. *See* C. FRIED, AN ANOTOMY OF VALUES 200–06 (1970); KATZ, *Process Design for Selection of Hemodialysis and Organ Transplant Recipients,* 22 BUFF. L. REV. 373 (1973).

[92] It is clear that parents have the right to retain and raise their offspring. Unless there exists a clear possibility that the offspring are or will be neglected, a statute depriving the parents of custody would be unconstitutional. *Cf.* Wisconsin v. Yoder, 406 U.S. 205 (1972); Pierce v. Society of Sisters, 268 U.S. 510 (1925); Meyer v. Nebraska, 262 U.S. 390 (1923).

[93] Duff & Campbell, *supra* note 3, at 894.

[94] In most states parents are empowered to terminate parental obligations, thereby leading to adoption or state custody. *See* note 77 *supra.*

[95] *See* notes 59–71 *supra* and accompanying text.

ship of dependency does not mandate that one have the power to impose death on the terminated party. Furthermore, a central element of procedural justice is impartial decisionmaking after full consideration of relevant information.[96] Yet, neither parents nor physicians are impartial or disinterested; both have a strong personal interest in the outcome of their decision. Parents face the decision with the guilt, grief, and damaged image that birth of a defective child brings.[97] They have a strong interest in maintaining previous life plans, and adjustment patterns, and in avoiding the psychic and financial costs of adjusting to care of a defective infant. Moreover, the treatment decision arises in highly emotional circumstances, when their rational faculties are weakest and full information concerning the defect and prognosis is wanting.[98] In addition, the physician's objectivity may be compromised. The obstetrician, for example, may feel guilt or responsibility for the defect, and prefer that the problem be eliminated as soon as possible.[99] He may think that the least he can do for the parents is to relieve them of a potential lifelong burden. Similarly, though less involved, the advice of a pediatrician or consultnt is likely to be influenced by his own values concerning care for defective infants. In short, since parents and physicians face the treatment decision with conflicting interests and the pressure of strong emotions, giving them final, unguided discretion to decide whether defective infants live will often lead to hasty, biased choices.

A glaring example of this danger is the 1971 Johns Hopkins case in which doctors did not operate on a Down's syndrome baby with duodenal atresia who died 15 days later of starvation.[100] The parents decided that they did not want to be burdened with a child who would be retarded and incapable of full human development, and rejected surgery. The physicians acquiesed in their decision, even though allowing the baby to starve to death created great consternation among the staff. The death of this child appears particularly unnecessary since mongols can interact, be trained, and lead a reasonably comfortable or happy existence. Moreover, the child

---

[96] Taylor v. Hayes, 94 S. Ct. 2697 (1974); Ward v. Village of Monroeville, 409 U.S. 57 (1972); Tumey v. Ohio, 273 U.S. 510 (1927).

[97] See notes 60–66 supra and accompanying text.

[98] Some physicians argue that patients or their guardians are incapable of rationally deciding for or against treatment in most circumstances, and some empirical evidence supports this view. See Fellner & Marshall, Kidney Donors—The Myth of Informed Consent, 126 AM. J. PSYCH. 79 (1970). Duff and Campbell claim, however, that if there is open sharing of information and decisionmaking with parents, a rational, informed choice will result. See note 18 supra and accompanying text. While the extent of their counseling is unclear (and hence we cannot assess to what degree the parents have worked through the emotional trauma of birth), the practices of Yale–New Haven Hospital's special nursery may be the exception rather than the rule. See also notes 61–72 supra and accompanying text.

[99] See note 80 supra and accompanying text.

[100] See Gustafson, Mongolism, Parental Desires, and the Right to Life, 16 PERSPECTIVES IN BIOL. & MED. 529, 529–33 (1973).

was otherwise healthy and would not have required constant medical care. The absence of a convincing case for death in this case illustrates the dangers of Duff's and Campbell's suggestion of having "only general guidelines." and allowing "much latitude" in this type of decisionmaking.[101]

However, arguably we can depend on the ethical commitments of the medical profession to prevent parental abuses. Physicians perhaps are better equipped than parents to consider these judgments and can intervene when parents misjudge the interests of society and child, thus operating as a check on parental decisionmaking. If the physician challenges the parental choice, as occurred recently in Maine, he can seek judicial protection for the child. There is some merit to this claim, but one cannot reliably base a rule on the contingency that physicians will intervene in particularly egregious cases. There is no guarantee that physicians can adequately strike the most socially desirable balance. While nearness to extreme situations often requires physicians to make such judgments, nothing in their training or background qualified them to identify, assess, and balance all interests involved—in short, to "play judge." [102] In addition, decisions by physicians are likely to reflect specific class, economic, ethical, and cultural biases or interests arising out of prior relationships with the parents. Perhaps the Johns Hopkins example is atypical of medical ethics, but that case and the now widespread practice of involuntary pediatric euthanasia hardly attest to physicians' ability to check questionable decisions of parents.

    b. A Decisionmaking Body An alternative that seeks to avoid the inherent bias of parents and attending physicians is the designation of a person or group of persons to decide whether a parental decision to terminate treatment, when acquiesced in by the attending physician, should be final. For example, such a decision could be made final only when approved by a judge, or a specially designated committee. In either case, the infant, through appointment of an advocate, could present evidence, confront witnesses, request a hearing, and seek review of the board's decision. Such a decisionmaker would be better equipped to examine and evaluate dispassionately all the interests involved, and reach a socially more desirable decision.

The main problems with this proposal are obvious: it adds another committee to a hospital setting already filled with committees; it is cumbersome and easily bureaucratized; it provides for a body that may be no better equipped to weigh social values than the ad hoc decisionmaking process of parents and physicians.[103] Moreover, a committee, while more

---

101 *See* note 93 *supra* and accompanying text.

102 Potter, *The Paradoxical Preservation of Principle,* 13 VILL. L. REV. 784, 788 (1968).

103 The unspectacular success of human experimentation committees is illustrative of these problems. *See* B. BARBER, J. LALLY, J. MAKARUSHKA & D. SULLIVAN, RESEARCH ON HUMAN SUBJECTS 166–67 (1973).

likely to achieve impartiality than physicians and parents, is vulnerable to pressures to accept the decisions of attending physicians. Thousands of such committees are unlikely to achieve uniform results or even implement equivalent criteria for nontreatment. Other problems may arise if the committees are judicialized with counsel, hearings, and appeals. This will extend the decisionmaking process and, accordingly, the agony of parents. Simply finding competent persons for such a committee in every hospital may be a tremendous task.

Beyond these practical concerns is the broader question of the wisdom of constituting citizen committees to mete out life or death. While society is fairly callous about saving lives when seen as statistics, to sanction directly the taking of identifiable lives on social-cost grounds is a step of a radically different order. We have, for example, very different attitudes toward a mining company's failure to install mine safety devices than toward its failure to undertake rescue of trapped miners. Calabresi observes:

> It should be clear that the foregoing does not mean that individual human life is not valued highly. Nor, certainly, does it suggest that we are indifferent to when and how society should choose to sacrifice lives. Quite the contrary; it indicates that there is a deep conflict between our fundamental need constantly to reaffirm our belief in the sanctity of life and our practical placing of some values (including future lives) above an individual life. That conflict suggests, at the very least, the need for a quite complex structuring to enable us *sometimes* to sacrifice lives, but hardly ever to do it blatantly and as a society, and above all to allow this sacrifice only under quite rigorous controls. . . .
> The consequence is that collective societal action seems always to be directed toward preserving the individual life rather than taking it, and our commitment is further strengthened.[104]

Hence, such a committee structure risks losing society's pervasive symbolic commitment to the value of individual life, as well as embarking on the slippery path of rational-utility assessments of personal worth.[105]

2. How should the decision be made?   *a. Criteria for Decisionmaking*
The difficulty of choosing an appropriate decisionmaker can be lessened by identifying the class of infants for whom treatment may lawfully be withheld and by specifying applicable clinical indicators. Any decisionmaking alternative runs the risk of leading to unfettered discretion, arbitrary unprincipled decisions, and unjustified deaths. But, just as authoritative and specific criteria have eased the physician's determination of when brain death has occurred,[106] the risks of delegating treatment discretion to par-

---

[104] Calabresi, *Reflections on Medical Experimentation in Humans,* 98 DAEDLUSA 387, 389–90 (1969).

[105] *See* notes 55–58 *supra* and accompanying text.

[106] *See* Capron & Kass, *A Statutory Definition of the Standards for Determining Human Death: An Appraisal and A Proposal,* 121 U. PA. L. REV. 87 (1972). But in practice such mecha-

ents, physicians, or committees can be similarly lessened if specific criteria are developed to describe defective characteristics and the familial or institutional situations in which treatment may be withheld from defective infants.

If recognized by the courts or legislature,[107] such criteria would represent a collective social judgment, rather than idiosyncratic choices of parents and committees, as to when social costs outweigh individual benefits. To achieve legislative consensus, the criteria for death necessarily should be narrow, reaching only the most extreme cases. Further protection can be gained by a procedure that assures that the required clinical findings are accurately assessed, for example, by certification by two nonattending physicians before treatment is withheld.

But can criteria that lend themselves to reliable identification of a justifiable nontreated class be articulated? Many thoughtful physicians and parents believe such a class exists, for on the basis of implicit or explicit standards, they approve withholding care in particular cases.[108] Hence, if considered thought produces a consensus that, for example, profoundly retarded, nonambulatory hydrocephalics who are blind and deaf or infants

---

nisms may not provide as much protection as desired because of the intrahospital familiarity and informal professional norms that often make fellow physicians reluctant to criticize or override the wishes of other physicians. *See* STAFF REPORT OF SENATE COMM. ON FINANCE, MEDICARE AND MEDICAID: PROBLEMS, ISSUES, AND ALTERNATIVES, 91st Cong., 1st Sess. 105–12 (1970).

[107] While explicit legislative approval of the criteria would be helpful, it would not be necessary for the legislature to draft or enact the criteria. A better solution might be to constitute formally a decisionmaking body with medical, community, and lay representation along the lines of the National Commission for the Protection of Human Subjects of Biomedical and Behavioral Research, created by the National Research Service Award Act of 1947, 42 U.S.C. § 2891, and delegate to it the development of the appropriate criteria and relevant clinical indicators. To prevent obsolescence in the criteria, and to monitor the extent of nontreatment and the effectiveness of developed standards, the body could be permanently constituted and perform similar functions with regard to other biomedical problems. Alternatively, the courts could give judicial recognition to criteria developed by authoritative medical or professional groups. In either case it is essential that the criteria be perceived as the expression of a community consensus concerning the limits of protecting human life.

[108] McCormick, in arguing for a definition of personhood based on a capacity for human relationships, also argues for explicit formulation of criteria for identifying defective newborns from whom treatment may justifiably be withheld: " 'Broad guidelines,' 'substantive standards.' There is the middle course, and it is the task of a community broader than the medical community. A guideline is not a slide rule that makes the decision. It is far less than that. But it is far more than the concrete decision of the parents and physicians, however seriously and conscientiously this is made. It is more like a light in a room, a light that allows the individual objects to be seen in the fullness of their context. Concretely, if there are certain infants that we agree ought to be saved in spite of illness or deformity, and if there are certain infants that we agree should be allowed to die, then there is a line to be drawn. And if there is a line to be drawn, there ought to be some criteria, even if very general, for doing this. Thus, if nearly every commentator has disagreed with the Hopkins decision, should we not be able to distill from such consensus some general wisdom that will inform and guide future decisions?" McCormick, *supra* note 40, at 172, 173. *See also* Carney, *Medical Standards for Deformed Newborns,* Wash. Post, Mar. 20, 1974, at A15, col. I.

who are unlikely to survive beyond a year are not owed ordinary treatment, a basis for developing criteria exists. Initially a common law approach might serve to identify certain categories of defects, with cases added or removed by their similarity to clear-cut categories. On the other hand, a common-law-like evolution may be less desirable than a forthright statement of the standards implicit in our considered judgments of clear-cut cases. The venture is risky, but considerable light may be shed by attempting to frame standards based on minimal capacity for social interaction, personality development, consciousness, and the like.

Perhaps acceptable criteria cannot be articulated, because factual variations are too many and justifiable ethical judgments cannot always be rationally explained. Nevertheless, the attempt should be made because the process of developing such criteria will at least reveal whether the judgments by which we presently decide to withhold care are principled or arbitrary, and thus whether they deserve to be honored at all.

b. Specified Procedures   If we grant the impossibility of articulating reliable and useful criteria for decisionmaking, the danger of arbitrary decisions by parents and physicians still may be reduced by mandating procedures that assure access to all relevant information and time for reflection. If decisionmaking could be structured so that all considerations enter into the calculus, the risk of arbitrariness by parents and physicians would lessen. Thus, if the postpartum hours are fraught with emotion, no treatment should be withheld for, say, 7 days. Alternatively, the parents' decision could be disregarded until they have one or more counseling sessions with a social worker or some other suitable adviser. Similar measures could assure exposure to the widest range of information relevant to their decision: for example, the parents expressly can be made aware of the benefits and costs of institutional care and the availability of state aid for home care.

Attending physicians also can be required to follow specified procedures before giving effect to parental choice. They can be required to state in writing their reasons for withholding treatment. A post hoc review, along the lines of a tissue committee or other forms of peer review, could be established. As we proliferate ideas for assuring impartial consideration of relevant factors, we move toward a committee structure. If we can achieve those advantages without undue bureaucracy, such an approach has appeal.

III. CONCLUSION

The pervasive practice of withholding ordinary medical care from defective newborns demonstrates that we have embarked on a widespread program of involuntary euthanasia. This practice has not resulted from a careful consideration of public policy alternatives, nor has it been arrived at by a public or collective decision. Formal public policy, in fact, condemns the practice, and until recently, the medical profession rarely acknowledged its existence. But now, as a result of new-found technological skills and perhaps changing attitudes toward social-utility assessments of human life, the practice has come to be accepted in the interstices of medical and legal practice. Given this situation, the crucial question is whether nontreatment of defective neonates is the opening wedge in expanding involuntary euthanasia, or whether its scope and impact can be limited. How we practice involuntary euthanasia thus becomes as important as the practice itself.

The problem of treating defective newborns may usefully be viewed as a problem of the proper limits of discretion, and is therefore amenable to traditional legal controls on discretion—rules, procedures, and review. Nonenforcement of existing criminal laws grants parents and physicians effective discretion to decide the fate of infants born with a range of defects. Their decisions inevitably reflect their perception of the child's, the family's, and perhaps society's interests. In short, they implicitly or explicitly constitute judgments as to when social costs outweigh the benefits of treatment. But these criteria are rarely articulated, and their judgments do not undergo the close scrutiny that decisions of such magnitude warrant. In nearly all cases in which the attending physician concurs in the parental decision to withhold care, neither parents nor physicians are required to justify their choice, nor is the decision reviewed by a disinterested party. The absence of due process for the infant is all the more striking given the emotional circumstances of the parental decision and the lack of publicly certified guidelines or criteria for withholding care. We thus have a situation in which interests other than the infants can dominate, and in which arbitrary and unjustified killings can and have occurred.

It is highly unlikely that full enforcement of present laws can correct the imbalances of the present situation. Some prosecutors might begin to enforce the law as the practice is more widely publicized. Yet if such enforcement occurs at all, it is likely to be scattered or sporadic. Although the law clothes the defective infant with a right to life, and a corresponding duty of care from those in certain relations with him, many people think that that right ends when it conflicts with the interests of parents, the medical profession, and the infant's own potential for full development. The law in action is likely to reflect this view, and, if the law in theory differs, this difference probably will be ignored.

If the nontreatment of defective newborns has become deeply engrained in medical practice, one can only hope that it will be confined to those cases in which the clearest and most indisputable grounds for withholding care exist. The attending physician is a partial check on parents who would unjustifiably deny treatment, even if the criminal law is not. But the peculiarities of his role, the risk of conflicting interests, and the lack of special ethical skill or training, make the physician an unreliable protector of the infant. In fact, granting the physician this authority may only foster present tendencies of the medical profession to assume decisionmaking authority over issues that are not theirs by law, training, or expertise to make. Unless physicians are to be final arbiters of all social policy and ethical issues with a medical component, they should not have such authority here.

By requiring that certain procedures be followed in deciding whether parents' nontreatment decision is to be final, the exercise of discretion can be structured to maximize the possibility of providing a disinterested decisionmaker who is equipped with relevant information and is sensitive to all interests. However, enforcing these procedures may present major problems, and even if administratively feasible, undoubtedly will require a relatively unfocused judgment as to whether care can be justifiably withheld.

Thus, in addition to procedures, the decisionmaking should be confined or limited by specific criteria, identifying the cases in which treatment can be justifiably withheld. Drafting criteria creates problems and difficult ethical choices, but these are no more significant than those that faced the Harvard Medical School committee that produced a definition of brain death. Rather, the problem will be in deciding whether rules such as "no anencephalics need be treated" or "no hydrocephalic can be denied treatment for this defect alone" provide justifiable differentiations in deciding the need for treatment.

The use of criteria thus confronts us with the question of whether there are classes of infants who may justifiably be allowed to die when parents so choose, and whether we can openly acknowledge the criteria which inform our decisionmaking. For while we may save lives and limit discretion by formalizing decisionmaking, we risk establishing a precedent that once loosed, is not easily cabined. Given the current acceptance of involuntary euthanasia of defective newborns, further danger from formalizing the precedent appears small. Indeed, subjecting the nontreatment decision to rules and procedures may demonstrate the solemn nature of a difficult situation. Since the power to cause the death of a defective newborn is an awesome one, it is essential that such decisions be carefully confined by law.

Index

Abdominal pain in vulnerable child syndrome, 187
  table, 185
Abortions: defined, 21
  dilemma faced by Supreme Court in abortion
      decision, 315
  prematurity and, 6, 10, 58
    table, 54
Abramson, J. H., 64
Abused children (see Child abuse)
Abusive families, 222–224
  assessed, in Infant Accident Study, 224
  characteristics of, 217, 222–223
  social class of, 224, 230
Abusive fathers, 217
  emotional problems of, 223
Abusive mothers, 229–234
  emotional problems of, 217–218, 223, 229
  expectations of, 233–234
  punishment meted out by, 232–233
  under stress, 230–232
Abusive parents, general characteristics of, 215
Academic failure: deficient communication skills and,
      262
  vulnerable child syndrome and school
      underachievement, 188
    tables, 185, 186
Accidental precipitating factors of crises, 91
Accidents (see Infant Accident Study)
Active accidents, defined, 228
Activity levels of abused children, 235

Acute emotional disorders, maternal reactions to
      prematurity as, 80–89
  data obtained in study, 81–84
  pathological deviations in, 86–88
  psychological tasks posed by prematurity, 84–86
    (See also Psychological tasks)
  theoretical basis of idea, 80
Adams, D. K., 136
Adaptive potential for pregnancy score, mean and
      standard deviation of, table, 70
Adolescents (see Teenage pregnancies)
Affectional bonding: mourning reaction as measure of,
      119
  (See also Mother-infant interactions)
Affective handling of crisis, mental health outcome
      and, 95, 96
Age: of abused children: developmental age, 234–235
  in Fifty Families Study, 216
  in Infant Accident Study, 223
  adoption, 126
  of failure-to-thrive infants, table, 205
  of siblings of failure-to-thrive infants, 206
  of teenagers in University Hospital study, 275
  (See also Gestational age; Maternal age)
Ainsworth, Mary D., 117, 136, 170
Alcoholism, prematurity and, 5
Alexander, Doris, 180, 203–213
Alexander, Frank, 10
American Academy of Pediatrics, 115
Anderson, Roy, 352n.

Anemia among pregnant teenagers, 278
Animal behavior (ethology), 159–160
Animals: effects of mother-infant separation on, 115–117
  gazing behavior among, 162
  object relations development among, 172–173
  stranger anxiety among, 167
Antibiotics to fight infections in low-birthweight infants, 247–248
Anticipatory grief, prematurity and, 85
  as psychological task facing premature mothers, 124
Anxiety: PKU Anxiety Syndrome, 197
  pregnancy outcome and, 64
  stranger, 167–169, 172
  vulnerable child syndrome and attacks of, table, 185
  (*See also* Separation anxiety; Stress)
Apgar scores, 19
Apneic attacks in low-birthweight infants, monitoring and managing, 246–247
Appeasement gesture, smiling as ritualized, 162
Approach-avoidance sequences: object-relational capacities and, 169
  in object relations development, 165–167
  (*See also* Avoidance behavior)
Armbruster, V. C., 262
Arthur Adaptation of the Leiter International Performance Scale (LIPS), 265, 266
Asleson, Elie, 353*n*.
Attachment in first year of life: as fundamental process, 160
  as learned phenomenon, 161–162
  maternal aspects of, 162–164
  need-fulfilling system separate from, 165
  object conservation concept and, 161
Attentiveness, maternal, 230–231
Aug, R. G., 32
Autopsies of low-birthweight infants, findings at, 253
Aversion to gazing, as avoidance behavior, 165
Avoidance behavior: basis for developing, 179
  stranger anxiety as, 167–169, 172
  syndromes of, 172
  (*See also* Approach-avoidance sequences)
Axelrod, S. J., 304
Aznar, Ramon, 279

Baldo, Robert, 353*n*.
Baldwin, A. L., 160
Baragwanath Hospital (Johannesburg, South Africa), 115
Barber, B., 359*n*.
Barbero, Giulio J., 180, 202–213
Barglow, P., 39, 45
Barnett, Clifford R., 120, 124, 136–150
Battaglia, F. C., 263
Battered child syndrome (*see* Child abuse)
Bauberger-Tell, L., 266
Bayley Mental Scales, 19, 237
Beck, J., 342*n*.
Beck, T., 342*n*.
Becker, H., 90
Beckwith, B., 181*n*.
Bedger, J. E., 16
Bell, Silvia, 161, 170
Benedek, Therese, 12, 30, 44, 77, 118
Benjamin, John, 167
Bennett, Alwyn E., 279
Bergman, A., 181
Berle, Beatrice B., 11, 63, 65
Bernstein, R., 41
"Best friend" pair phenomenon among pregnant teenagers, 35
Better Family Planning, Inc., 281
Bibring, G. L., 30, 77, 90, 105, 109, 118, 222

Bierman, P., 304
Biologic need-fulfilling, object-hungry infants and, 172
Biological incompetence, feelings of, in premature mothers, 137–138, 148
Biologically-determined maturational crisis, pregnancy as, 222
Birch, H. G., 16
Birdwhistell, M., 32
Birth rank: child abuse and, 222
  child development and, 19
  failure-to-thrive infants and, 206
  pregnancy outcome and, 17
Birth spacing: child abuse and, 222
  child development and, 19
  pregnancy outcome and, 17
  relationship between parity, maternal age, pregnancy outcome and, 24–26
  of siblings of failure-to-thrive infants, 206
Birth-to-three-months of age period, object relations development in, 164–165
Birthrate, predicted (1980), 302, 303
Birthweight: of children with failure-to-thrive syndrome, table, 205
  effects of, on maternal self-confidence, 147
  (*See also* Low-birthweight infants)
Blacks (*see* Race)
Blanton, Graham, 353*n*.
Blau, Abram, 12, 126
Blos, P., 35
Bodily overconcerns, vulnerable child syndrome and, 187–188
Body narcissism of premature mothers, 126
Body temperature, control of, in low-birthweight infants, 245
Boston, M., 136
Bottle feeding, cuddling and, 122–123
Bowlby, John, 136, 160, 169
Breast feeding, 114
  cuddling and, 122
  rooming-in and increase in, 119–120
Breath-holding spells in vulnerable child syndrome, table, 185
Brenner, R. F., 38
Bright, T. P., 32
British National Maternity Survey, 20
Brockington, C. F., 304
Bronson, Gordon W., 167–169
Burchinal, L. G., 39
Byrne, Garret, 339*n*.

Caffey, John, 220
Calderone, M. S., 33
California Death Index, 290
Campbell, A. G. M., 335, 336, 337*n*., 338, 339, 345*n*., 357*n*., 358*n*., 359
Cannon, W. B., 10
Caplan, Gerald, 30, 78, 79*n*., 89–107, 198
Carey, William B., 180, 195–202
Carpenter, Genevieve C., 164–166, 172
Case Western Reserve University, 120
Cassel, John, 62–75
Cerebral palsy among low-birthweight children, 254–255
Chance, Michael, 165
Charney, E., 179*n*.
Child abuse, 214–223, 238–242
  damages inflicted by, 1
  diagnosing, 238–239
  early mother-infant separation and, 178–179
  legal issues involved with, 239–240
  low-birthweight infants as victims of, 181, 220
  as mothering disorder, 124, 126
  prevention of, 240–242
  study of, 215–223

Child abuse: study of: case histories, 218–219
  characteristics of abusive families, 217, 222–223
    (*See also* Abusive families)
  characteristics of abusive mothers, 217–218
    (*See also* Abusive mothers)
  conditions of children: at time of admission, 221
    at time of study, 221-222
  findings on children, 219–221
  selection criteria used in, 215–216
Child care: effects of mother-infant separation on, 136, 137
  ability to care, 139–141
    study results, 146–147
      table, 146
    tables, 140, 141
  failure-to-thrive syndrome and disruption in, 208–209
  prematurity and: preparation for care, as psychological task, 85–86
    task accomplishment as prediction of, table, 101
    understanding needs of prematures, as psychological task, 98–99, 124
  received by abused children, 227–228
  (*See also* Infant feeding)
Child development: establishment of object constancy in, 110
  of high-risk infants: communication skills development in five-year-olds with high-risk neonatal histories, 262–269
    tables, 264, 268
  early indicators of, 316
  life-change events during pregnancy and, 64
  of low-birthweight infants, 20, 248–249
  maternal verbal responses and, 236
    mental development, 238
  mother-infant relationship and, 108, 110
    (*See also* Mother-infant interactions)
  pregnancy parameters, poverty and, 18–20
  (*See also* Language development; Mental development; Physical growth; Psychological development of low-birthweight infants)
Child neglect: accidents and, 225, 226
  activity levels of children, 235
  extent of, 1
Child Welfare Services (Penna.), 226
Childhood and Government Project (Boalt Hall School of Law; University of California), 315
Children's Bureau, 115, 239
Children's Hospital (Philadelphia, Penna.), 203, 210
Children's Hospital (Pittsburgh, Penna.), 214, 223
Children's Medical Center (Boston, Mass.), 203
Chomsky, C., 264
Christenson, W. N., 72
Chronic stress, child abuse and, 229–230
Churchill, Sir Winston, 199
City Health Centers (Philadelphia, Penna.), 284
Classical psychoanalytic theory, 158–159
Clifford, S. H., 300
Clinics: satellite, 305–306
  of University Hospital, 274–275
Coelho, G. V., 90
Cognitive handling of crises, mental health outcome and, 95, 96
Cognitive processes, development of, 161
Cohen, Marna, 316
Collaborative Perinatal Research Project (National Institutes of Health), 301
Collaborative Study of Cerebral Palsy and Other Neurological and Sensory Disorders of Infancy and Childhood, 263
Comatose, the basis for withholding treatment from, 344
  (*See also* Involuntary euthanasia)

Communication skills in five-year-olds with high-risk neonatal histories, 262–269
  tables, 264, 268
Community services: to deal with teenage pregnancies, 284
  patterns of involvement of, failure-to-thrive syndrome and, 210
  in prevention of child abuse, 241–242
Complications: child development and, 19–20
  defined, 64–65
  rate of, among pregnant teenagers, 278
  scoring, 66–67
    correlation of LCS and TAPPS with, table, 71
  social class and, 19
    age and, table, 71
  (*See also* Handicap(s); High-risk infants; Low-birthweight infants; Prematurity)
Conceptual ability, right to life and, 343–344
Confidentiality issues in child abuse cases, 239
Constanza, M., 179
Continuing Education Program (Philadelphia School Board), 278
Contraception, 26, 281–285
  (*See also* Family planning)
Convulsions in low-birthweight children, 255
Cooney, Martin, 114
Cooperative School study (*see* Teenage pregnancies, emotional crises in)
Coping methods, developing, to deal with teenage pregnancy, 36–41
Cornell Medical Index, 148
Costs of maintaining life in neonatal intensive care units, 316–317
  (*See also* Involuntary euthanasia, arguments in favor of)
Council of the California Medical Association, 290
Crane, Marian, 115
Crises: factors determining behavior during, 89–91
  (*See also* Early infancy health crises; Life-change events; Prematurity; Teenage pregnancies, emotional crises in)
"Critically ill," recommended cautious use of phrase, 193
Crosse, M., 115
Crume, E. P., 18
Crying behavior, sex differences in, 171
Cuddling, feeding and, 121–123

Daily, W. J., 266n.
David, L., 39
Deaths: of low-birthweight infants, causes of, 257, 259
  resulting from child abuse, 219
  (*See also* Fetal mortality; Infant mortality; Maternal mortality; Neonatal mortality; Perinatal mortality)
Defective newborns (*see* Involuntary euthanasia; Neonatal intensive care)
DeGoza, S., 90
Delivery: attitudes of premature and full-term mothers toward, 81–82
  levels of deprivation in normal, 124
  pregnant teenager's fear of, 42
Densen, P. M., 16
Depression, abusive mothers suffering from, 217–218
Deprivation: levels of, in normal deliveries, 124
  maternal privation differentiated from, 171
  (*See also* Failure-to-thrive syndrome; Mother-infant separation)
Deutsch, Helene, 11, 35, 77, 109, 118
Development (*see* Child development)
Developmental age of abused children, 234–235
Developmental psychology, 160–161
Developmental Quotient (DQ), 248, 254
Developmental Screening Inventory, 248

Developmental tasks of adolescence, 33
Diarrhea in response to stress, vulnerable child
    syndrome and, table, 186
Dickens, Helen O., 271, 273–287
Diet (*see* Nutrition)
Difficult infants, as reflection of parental inadequacy,
    171
Direction of effects problem, 160
Discipline: child abuse and, 217, 232–233
    vulnerable child syndrome and absence of, 186–187
    table, 186
Discussion groups to deal with teenage pregnancies,
    284–285
Disease: defined, 47
    general susceptibility to, psychosocial assets and,
    62–63
    as influenced by life-change events, 48
"Do no harm" principle, 321–322, 328–330
Doctors (*see* Physicians)
Donabedian, A., 304
Double effect doctrine, 330
Douglas, J. W. B., 20
DQ (Developmental Quotient), 248, 254
Drillien, C. M., 20, 181, 243
Drives (*see* Instinctual drives)
Drug addiction, prematurity and, 5
Duff, Raymond, 335, 336, 337*n*., 338, 339, 345*n*.,
    357*n*., 358*n*., 359
Duke Hospital, 119
Dunbar, F., 11
Dunbar, H. F., 10
Dunham, Ethel, 115
Dwyer, T. F., 77*n*.

Early Contact mothers, 120–122
Early infancy health crises: psychologic sequelae of,
    195–202
    excellent and deviant, 199
    mother's vulnerability and child's role in,
    197–198
    normal, 200
    overreactions and underreactions to minor crises
    and, 196–197
    reactions to major crises, 196
    (*See also* Failure-to-thrive syndrome; Vulnerable
    child syndrome)
Eastman, Nicholson J., 5
Economic Opportunity, Office of, 283
Economics, Department of (Swarthmore College), 316
Education: of abusive families, 217
    to deal with teenage pregnancies, 284–285
    family size and, 17
    maternal (*see* Maternal education)
    of parents with failure-to-thrive infants, 207
    of pregnant teenagers in University Hospital study,
    276–278
    to prevent child abuse, 240–241
    sex, 26
    (*See also* Schools)
Ego psychology, 158
Ego-relatedness: defined, 157
    experiences of: critical nature of, 159
    parental response failures and, 162
    factors accounting for harmonic or dissonant, 165
    object-hungry infants and, 172
    social and noninstinctual nature of, 173
    (*See also* Object relations development)
Ego-supportive values of special programs for pregnant
    teenagers, 33–36
Ehrlich, Carol H., 182, 262–269
Eibl-Eibesfeldt, I., 159, 174
Eight-month anxiety (stranger anxiety), 167–169, 172
Eliot, T. S., 174
Elliott, L., 262

Elmer, Elizabeth, 178, 179*n*., 180, 214–242
Emerson, P. E., 165
Emotional crises (*see* Teenage pregnancies, emotional
    crises in)
Emotional problems: of abused children, 221–222
    of abusive fathers, 223
    of abusive mothers, 217–218, 223, 229
    early object-relating and, 173
    habitual abortions and, 10–11
    prematurity and, 5, 126
    (*See also* Acute emotional disorders; Teenage
    pregnancies, emotional crises in)
Engel, L., 10, 300
Environment: child development and neonatal, 111
    failure-to-thrive syndrome and, 202
Erikson, Erik H., 33, 158
Ethical issues (*see* Involuntary euthanasia; Neonatal
    intensive care)
Ethology (animal behavior), 159–160
Europe: birthrates in, 302–303
    neonatal mortality in, 300–301
Euthanasia, 272
    basis for, 320
    ethical problems raised by, 314, 317–318
    table, 326–327
    (*See also* Involuntary euthanasia)
Exploratory behavior, development of, 123, 168
Extended families of children with failure-to-thrive
    syndrome, disruption in, 210
Eye-to-eye contact, importance of, 109, 119
    (*See also* Gazing)

Failure: academic, deficient communication skill and,
    262
    (*See also* School underachievement)
    acknowledgment of, by premature mothers, as
    psychological task, 98, 124
    to grow (*see* Failure-to-thrive syndrome)
Failure-to-thrive syndrome, 180, 202–213
    child abuse and, 221, 227, 238
    mother-infant separation and, 126
    (*See also* Mother-infant separation)
    study of: analysis of failure-to-thrive group,
    204–211
    tables, 205
    effects of hospitalization, table, 211
    follow up on, 211–212
    table, 212
    method of study, table, 203–204
Fairbairn, W. R., 158, 159
Falls, F. M., 279
Families: of defective children, sufferings of, 350–354
    of failure-to-thrive infants, 206–210
    disruption in, 208–210
    tables, 207
    of high-risk infants, intensive care and, 316
    nonabusive, characteristics of, 217, 222
    of pregnant teenagers: family living arrangements,
    37–38
    family relationships and occurrence of pregnancy,
    39–41
    telling the family about the pregnancy as first
    emotional crisis, 31–32
    (*See also* Abusive families; Fathers; Lower-class
    families; Middle-class families; Mothers;
    Upper-class families)
Family affair, child abuse as, 218
    (*See also* Child abuse)
Family income: of abusive families, 217
    failure-to-thrive syndrome and, 207
    mental development and, 237, 238
Family nurse practitioners, 304–307
    qualifications and functions of, 271–272, 306–307,
    310

Family nurse practitioners: in satellite clinics, 305–306
Family planning, 26
  preventing child abuse with, 222, 241
  in University Hospital study, 281–283
Family Planning Clinic, 280, 283
Family size, 17
  (*See also* Parity)
Fantz, Robert, 164
Fathers: abusive, 217
    emotional problems of, 223
  of children in communication skills study, occupations of, 264
  mental development of children in Infant Accident Study and presence of, 237–238
  of pregnant teenagers, 32
    occurrence of teenage pregnancy and relations with fathers, 40
  reactions of, to prematurity, 77–78
Feeding: problems of, vulnerable child syndrome and, 187
  tables, 185, 186
  (*See also* Infant feeding)
Feinmesser, M., 266
Fetal mortality: perinatal mortality and, 17
  poverty and, 22
  prenatal care, prematurity and, table, 295
Fifty Families Study (*see* Child abuse, study of)
Finck, G. H., 36
First year of life, object relations development in (*see* Object relations development)
Five-year-olds with high-risk neonatal histories, communication skills of, 262–269
  tables, 264, 268
Fixed action pattern, 161n.
Flavell, J. H., 161
Folsom, M. B., 303
Foster care, child abuse in, 223
Four-year-olds, assessing development of low-birthweight, 249
Fox, R., 354n.
Fraiberg, Selma, 161
Freedman, A., 181n.
Freedman, Daniel, 167
Freeman, H. E., 104
Freud, Anna, xx
Freud, Sigmund, 158, 159
Fried, C., 356n., 357n.
Frontier Nursing Service, 271, 289
Full-term mothers: attitudes of, toward labor and delivery, 81–82
  effects of prolonged postpartum separation on, 155
  responses of: to SRRS, 52, 54–57
    tables, 55–57
Fuller, M. L., 90
Functioning of abused children, 222
  activity levels, 235

Garcia, Cellso-Ramon, 273–287
Garland, M. J., 312–334
Gazing, 162–167
  approach-avoidance sequences in, 165–167
  aversion to, as avoidance behavior, 165
  maternal aspects of early attachment and, 163–164
  stranger anxiety and, 168
  visual interactions in, 162
Geisel, Paul, 214–242
General functioning of abused children (*see* Functioning of abused children)
Geographic differentials in pregnancy outcome, 16
Gestational age: low birthweight and, 2
  survival rate by, table, 251
Gewirtz, Jacob L., 161, 171
Gibben, Darleen, 353n.

Gibson, R. M., 179
Girdony, Bertram, 214–242
Goffman, E., 347n.
Goodall, Jane, 159
Goss, M. E., 90
Grayson, E. S., 39
Green, Mary Theresa, 275
Green, Morris, 126, 179, 183–195, 199, 200
Gregg, Grace, 180, 214–242
Gregory, I., 40
Grim, E., 67
Grinker, Roy, 10
Grobstein, R., 136
Group for Advancement of Psychology, 33
Growth failure (*see* Failure-to-thrive syndrome)
Guntrip, Harry, 158

Habitual abortions (*see* Abortions)
Haith, Marshall, 164
Hamburg, A., 90
Hamburg, D. A., 90
Hamovitch, M. D., 92
Handicap(s): defined, 253
  low birthweight and: causes of, 255–259
    relation of subsequent handling with presumed severe hypoxia and jaundice, table, 252
  summary of, at mean age of 5 years 2 months, table, 251
Hansen, E. W., 136
Hardy, J. B., 264
Hardy, Thomas, 199
Hare, P., 92
Harlow, Harry F., 116, 136, 165
Harlow, M. K., 136
Harvard Medical School, 364
Harvard School of Public Health Family Guidance Center, 81
Hassan, H. M., 279
Headaches in vulnerable child syndrome, 187, 188
  table, 185
Health: of abused children, 226–228
  of abusive mothers, 229
  of extended family members of failure-to-thrive infants, 210
  of parents of failure-to-thrive infants, 208
  of pregnant teenagers, 41–43
Health, Subcommittee on (Senate), 336
Health care services, 270–271
  in Madera County, changes in population and, 295–296
  pregnancy outcome and, 16, 25–26
  for pregnant teenagers (*see* Teenage pregnancies, University Hospital study of)
  present and future medical manpower needs and, 303–304
  present situation of, 300–302
  projected, 302–303
    table, 303
  proposal for (*see* Family nurse practitioners)
  quality of, as reflection of prevailing socioeconomic conditions, 299
  as rights, 308
  role of university-affiliated teaching hospitals in, 309
  (*See also* Prenatal care)
Health Department (Madera County, Calif.), 289
Health Department (Philadelphia, Penna.), 280
Healthy mental health outcome, crisis and, relationship between grappling patterns and, 94–96
Hearing: communication skill development and, 266, 267
  of low-birthweight children, 255
Height of failure-to-thrive children, follow up on, table, 212

Heiman, M., 38–40
Heinstein, M.·I., 67
Hellman, L. M., 288
Help, seeking, in crisis situations, mental health outcome and, 95–96
Hemostasis, problems of, in low-birthweight infants, 248
Hersey, John, 11
Hersher, L., 116
Herzog, E., 37, 41
Hess, E. H., 159
Hess, J., 114, 115
High-risk infants: communication skills of five-year-olds who were, 262–269
  tables, 264, 268
 development of, early indicators of, 316
 increased survival rate of, 3
 mortality and morbidity as related to, 4
  (See also Neonatal mortality; Perinatal mortality)
 socioeconomic conditions and, 2
  (See also Early infancy health crises; Low-birthweight infants; Prematurity)
High-risk mothers: characterized, 5
 pregnancy outcome vs., table, 24
High-risk pregnancy, determining factors in, 306
Hill, Reuben, 90, 231
Hinde, R. A., 159
Hinkle, L. E., Jr., 72
Holding positions, 151–154
 effects on prolonged postpartum separation on, 153–154
 importance of, 165
 tables, 151, 152
Holley, W. L., 19
Hollingshead, A. B., 69
Hollingshead Two-Factor Index, 229, 230
Holmes, M., 31
Holmes, Thomas H., 12, 47, 48, 56, 63, 65–66
Holt, K. S., 243
Homemaker services, 271
Horner, F., 181n.
Hospitalization: conditions of abused children at time of, 221
 of failure-to-thrive infants: age and diagnostic distribution of, table, 205
  tables, 203, 211
 failure-to-thrive syndrome following, 209
Hospitals, university-affiliated teaching, 309
Housing: of abusive families, 217
 quality of, and failure-to-thrive syndrome, 208
Howard, M., 33, 35
Hugo, Victor, 199
Human parentage, personhood and, 341, 342
Human Relations File, 117
Hunt, Jane, 316, 331n., 351n.
Huntington, D. S., 77n.
Huttner, Muriel, 262–269
Hydration of low-birthweight infants, 245–246
Hypocalcemia in low-birthweight infants, management of, 247
Hypoglycemia in low-birthweight infants, management of, 247
Hypoxia in low-birthweight infants, handicaps and, 255–256, 257–258
 relation of subsequent handicaps with, table, 252

Ideal mother, as viewed by abusive mothers, 234
Illegitimacy, failure-to-thrive syndrome and, 209
Illinois Test of Psycholinguistic Abilities (ITPA), 265
Income (see Family income)
Incompetence, feelings of biological, in premature mothers, 137–138, 148
Incongruity hypothesis, tenets of, 166
Indicators of high-risk infant development, 316

Infancy (less than three years of age) of low-birthweight infants, follow-up study on, 248
Infant Accident Study, 223–238
 accidents vs. abuse or neglect, 225–226
  initial findings on, 228–232
 age of children in, 223
 children in: final evaluation of, 237–238
  findings on, 234–235
  initial pediatric evaluation in, 227–228
 failure-to-thrive syndrome in, 227
 family assessed in, 224
 methods used in, 225–226
 modes of punishment, discipline, and teaching in, 232–233
 observation of mother-infant interactions in, 235–237
 values related to mothering in, 233–234
Infant effects, importance of, pathologic object relations development and, 171
Infant feeding: cuddling and bottle, 122–123
 of low-birthweight infants, 245–246
 as measure of mothering behavior, 121–122
Infant mortality: health care and, 271
 life crises, psychosocial assets and, 62
 1915–1969, 14
 1968, 4
 race and, 15, 16, 273
 social class and, 16
  (See also Neonatal mortality; Perinatal mortality)
Infantilization process, vulnerable child syndrome and, 187
Infants: born to pregnant teenagers: disposition of, 280–281
  table, 280
 sex of, maternal self-confidence and, in mothers of premature, 147
  (See also Failure-to-thrive syndrome; High-risk infants; Low-birthweight infants; Mother-infant separation; Prematurity; Vulnerable child syndrome)
Infections: in low-birthweight infants, antibiotics for, 247–248
 measures taken to prevent, in premature nurseries, 114–115
Ingraham, F., 336n.
Instinctual drives: in classical psychoanalytic theory, 158
 in psychoanalytic object relations theory, 159
Institute of Child Welfare, 264
Integrative ability at birth, 164
Intensive care (see Neonatal intensive care)
Intensive Care Nursery (University of California, San Francisco), 316
International Journal of Psychoanalysis, 158
Interview Guides, 94
Interviews in maternal self-confidence study, 145
Intrauterine devices (IUDs), 281–282, 285
Involuntary euthanasia, 335–364
 arguments in favor of, 340–356
  defective infants are not persons, 340–345
  no obligation to treat exists when costs of maintenance of life outweigh benefits, 345–356
  quality of defective infant's life and, 346–349
  suffering of others, 349–356
 conclusion on, 362–364
 decisionmaking process in, 357–362
  how should the decision be made? 360–362
  who should decide? 357–360
 emotional and ethical dilemmas facing parents and, 336–338
 evaluating the issue, 339–340
 gaining acceptance, 336
IQ (intelligence quotient): of five-year-olds, in communication skills study, 266

IQ (intelligence quotient): low-birthweight children and, 254
  pregnancy parameters and, 19, 20
Irving, Frederick C., 310
Israel, S. L., 41
ITPA (Illinois Test of Psycholinguistic Abilities), 265
IUDs (intrauterine devices), 281–282, 285

Jackson, Edith, 115
Jacobson, Howard N., 271, 299–311
Janis, I. L., 90
Jaundice in low-birthweight infants, handicaps and, 255–258
  management of, 247
  table, 252
Javert, Carl T., 10, 11
Jessner, L., 44
Johns Hopkins Hospital, 113, 227
Johnson, J. P., 266n.
Jonsen, A. R., 272, 312–334
Juvenile and Domestic Relations Courts (Philadelphia, Penna.), 210

Kahn, E., 115
Kaplan, Berton H., 62–75
Kaplan, David M., 78, 80–107, 124, 137, 148
Keith, R. W., 265
Kendall, Norman, 9, 14–26
Kennedy, John F., 5, 301
Kennedy, Patrick Bouvier, 5
Kennell, John H., 109, 113–135, 178, 200, 345n., 350n., 354n.
Khlentzos, M. T., 37
Kimball, Bud D., 262–269
Kirk, D., 302
Klaus, Marshall H., 108, 113–136, 163, 178, 345n., 350n., 354n.
Klerman, Lorraine V., 279
Klopfer, M. S., 136
Klopfer, P. H., 136
Knobloch, H., 19, 248, 254
Konopka, G., 38, 40
Koos, E. L., 90
Kramer, Marcia J., 316

LaBarre, Maureen, 12, 30–47
LaBarre, W., 30, 39
Labor: attitudes of full-term mothers toward, 81–82
  life crises and difficult, 64
  pregnant teenager's fear of, 42
Lally, J., 359n.
Language development: of abused children, 221
  gazing and, 162
Late Contact 1 mothers, behavior of, 120–122
Late Contact 2 mothers, behavior of, 120–122
LCS (see Life change score)
LCU (see Life-change units)
Learning theory, 161–162
Lebovitz, B. Z., 90
Legal aspects: of child abuse, 239–240
  of neonatal intensive care, 315–316
  (See also Involuntary euthanasia)
Legal personhood: of defective infants, 340–345
  withholding, from certain high-risk infants, 315
Lehrman, D. S., 136
Leiderman, P. Herbert, 136–150, 345n.
Leifer, A. D., 140
Lemperle, Herbert, 152
Lenneberg, E. H., 262
Lesser, A. J., 300
Levitt, E. G., 38–40
Levy, Barry S., 271, 288–298
Levy, D., 77n., 179
Levy, D. M., 89, 198

Life-change events (life crises), 47–75
  psychosocial assets and, 62–75
    discussion on, 71–73
      table, 71
    life change, defined, 63
    protective and deleterious assets, 64
    psychosocial assets, defined, 63, 65
    study method, 65–69
      tables, 65, 68–69
    study results, tables, 69–71
  relationship between prematurity and, 47–61
    implications of study and recommendations, 58–59
    method of study, 48–52
    results of study, 52–58
      tables, 53–58
  (See also Social Readjustment Scale)
Life change score (LCS), 66
  correlation of TAPPS score and complications, table, 71
  range, mean and standard deviations of, table, 70
Life-change units (LCU): life crises measured in, 47–48
  measuring adjustment to life crises with, 63
Life-supporting equipment, withdrawal of: ethical problems raised by, 314, 317–318
  table, 324–325
  recommendations on, 332–333
Lindemann, E., 90
LIPS (Arthur Adaptation of the Leiter International Performance Scale), 265, 266
Lipsitch, I., 179n.
Living arrangements of pregnant teenagers, 37–38, 276
Lorenz, Konrad, 159, 162
Low-birthweight infants (small-for-date infants; premature infants), 9
  development of, 20, 248–249
  gestational age and, 2
  poverty and, 22–24
  problems leading to, 18
  prognosis for, 243–263
    discussion on, 256–260
    increased survival rate of, 3
    study materials and methods used, 244–249
      follow-up on study, 248–249
    study results, 249–256
      tables, 250–252
  relationship between child abuse and, 181, 220
Lowell, E. L., 264
Lower-class families: abusive families as, 224, 230
  (See also Poverty)
Lower-class mothers: lack of attentiveness of, 230–231
  predisposed to complications, 19
  pregnancy outcome for, 21
  pregnancy outcome and reproduction patterns of, 17
  prematurity among, 18
    (See also Prematurity)
  (See also Poverty)
Lubchenco, L. O., 181, 263, 266

McBryde, A., 119
McCormick, Richard, 344n., 361n.
McDonald, R. L., 64, 67
McHenry, Thomas, 214–242
McNeill, D., 262, 264
Madera County NOA program study (see Nurse-midwives)
Mahler, Margaret, 109, 110
Makarushka, J., 359n.
Malachowsky, R. G., 266n.
Management: of apneic attacks, 246–247

Management: of hypoglycemia, jaundice and hypocalcemia, 247
of vulnerable child syndrome, 192–194
Mann, Edward C., 10
Mann-Whitney *U* test, 52, 56
tables, 54, 57
Marine, William M., 271, 288–298
Marital status of pregnant teenagers in University Hospital study, 276
Marital stress: child abuse and, 217
failure-to-thrive syndrome and, 209
Marks, F. Raymond, 315
Mason, Edward A., 78, 79*n.*, 89–107, 124, 137, 148
Maternal age: effects of, on child development, 19
failure-to-thrive infants and, 206–207
table, 207
perinatal mortality and, 17
prematurity and, 5
in psychosocial assets-life-change events study, table, 68
relationship between parity, birth spacing, pregnancy outcome and, 24–26
social class, complications and, table, 71
in Temple University study, 21
pregnancy outcome, table, 23
Maternal attentiveness, 230–231
Maternal deprivation (*see* Deprivation)
Maternal education: low birthweight and, 10
in psychosocial assets-life crises study, 68–69
table, 69
Maternal and Infant Care Program (Temple University), 21
Maternal mortality: health care and, 271
life-change events, psychosocial assets and, 62
1915–1967, 4, 14
race and, 273
Maternal reactions: to prematurity, as mourning reaction, 77
(*See also* Acute emotional disorders, maternal reactions to prematurity as)
(*See also* Early infancy health crises, psychologic sequelae of)
Maternal responses: child development and verbal, 236
mental development, 238
object relations development and response failures, 172, 173
Maternal role: adaptation to, by teenagers, 43–44
(*See also* Mothering behavior)
Maternal self-confidence (*see* Mother-infant separation, effects on maternal self-confidence of)
Matson, D., 336*n.*, 349, 350*n.*
Maturation, sex differences in, stranger anxiety and, 169
Maturational crisis, pregnancy as, 77
biologically-determined maturational crisis, 222
Mead, Margaret, 152
Mechanical ventilation for low-birthweight infants, 247
Medical care, ordinary, defined, 335*n.*
Medical manpower needs, health services and present and future, 303–304
(*See also* Physicians)
Medical schools, need for, to involve themselves in community health services, 309
Mellitis, E. D., 264
Mental development: of children in Infant Accident Study, 237–238
of low-birthweight children, 254
Mental health outcome, parental reactions to prematurity and, 89–90, 92, 102
exploratory study to determine psychological tasks facing mothers of premature babies and relationship of task accomplishment to, 98–100, 103–104

Mental health outcome, parental reactions to prematurity and, hypotheses on relationship between grappling patterns and, 94–96
predictive study to test hypotheses relating grappling patterns and mental health outcome, 96–98, 105–106
table, 97
testing hypotheses relating psychological task accomplishment to, 100–102
tables, 101, 102
Mental retardation: child abuse and, 221, 236, 237
in Infant Accident Study, 236
communication skills development and, 266
mother-infant relationship and, 224
Menyuk, P., 264
Merrill-Palmer Scale, 248
Middle-class families: pregnant teenagers in, family attitudes toward, 33
prematurity and, 5
Middle-class mothers: attentiveness of, 230–231
reproductive patterns of, 17
Middle-class teenagers in Cooperative School study, 31
Midwives (*see* Nurse-midwives)
Miezio, Peggy, 351*n.*
Miller, F., 115
Minnesota Occupational Scale, 264
Money Problem Checklist (Cooperative School), 38
Mood of abused children, 234–235
Moore, A. U., 116, 136
Moore, Henry, 152
Moral value of infants, 319
defined, 320
euthanasia and, 330
Morbidity: as related to high-risk infants, 4
(*See also* High-risk infants)
(*See also* Disease)
Mortality (*see* Fetal mortality; Infant mortality; Maternal mortality; Neonatal mortality; Perinatal mortality)
Moss, Howard A., 146, 163, 168, 171
Mother-daughter relationships: teenage pregnancy and, 39–40
teenager's adaptation to maternal role and, 43–44
teenager's emotional crises and, 31, 32
vulnerable child syndrome and, 186
Mother-infant interactions (mother-infant bonding): critical nature of postpartum period in establishing, 150–157
tables, 151, 152
effects of separation on, 108–112
(*See also* Mother-infant separation)
gazing and, 162
(*See also* Gazing)
in Infant Accident Study: assessed, 224, 229
observations on, 234–237
nature of infant's earliest social experiences in context of, 158
prediction of early, 97
prematurity and: mother's attitude and disordered relationship, 102–103
resumption of, as psychological task, 85, 98, 124
(*See also* Attachment; Child care; Object relations development)
Mother-infant separation, 113–150
animal studies in, 115–117
case problems of, 128–131
answers to, 129–131
child abuse and, 178–179
(*See also* Child abuse)
effects on maternal self-confidence of, 136–150
study methods, 138–141
tables, 140, 141

Mother-infant separation: effects on maternal self-confidence of, study results, 142–148
  tables, 143, 144, 146
  levels of deprivation and component variables in, 123–125
  tables, 123, 125
  maternal behavior of human mother and, 117–123
  table, 118
  in other cultures, 117
  practical considerations on, 126–128
  role and responsibilities of mothers in premature nurseries and, 113–115
  (*See also* Separation anxiety)
Mother-son relationships, vulnerable child syndrome and, table, 186
Mothering behavior: disorders of: child abuse as, 124, 126
  (*See also* Child abuse)
  mothering disability syndrome associated with Rh blood group incompatibility or prematurity, 192
  prematurity and, 77
  (*See also* Prematurity)
  sources of, 127
  types of, 124
  effects of mother-infant separation on, 115–123
  in animals, 115–116
  table, 118
  infant feeding as measure of, 121–122
  (*See also* Infant feeding)
  values related to, 233–234
  variables affecting, 160
  (*See also* Child care)
Mothers: high-risk, characterized, 5
  nonabusive, 217–218
  (*See also* Abusive mothers; Full-term mothers; Lower-class mothers; Middle-class mothers; Mother-infant interactions; Mother-infant separation; Mothering behavior; Premature mothers)
Motivation: ethologic conceptions of, 159–160
  in Piaget's developmental psychology, 161
Mourning reaction: maternal reaction to prematurity as, 77
  as measure of affectional bonding, 119
  psychological disequilibrium and, 90
  vulnerable child syndrome as pathological after-effect of disguised, 191
Mudd, Emily Hartshorne, 273–287
Murphey, E. B., 90
Murphy, L. B., 90

Nader, Laura, 318n.
Narcissism of premature mothers, 126
National Alliance Concerned with School-Age Parents, 31
National Bureau of Economic Research, Inc., 316
National Collaborative Perinatal Study, 17, 19, 20, 66, 67
National Institute of Neurological Disease and Blindness, 66
National Institutes of Health, 301
National Urban League, 301
Need-fulfilling system: attachment separated from, 165
  object-hungry infants and biologic, 172
Neglect (*see* Child neglect)
Neglectful families, characteristics of, 230
Neighborhood Health Center clinics (affiliated with Temple University), 21
Neonatal crisis syndrome (ominous infant phenomena), 181
Neonatal environment, child development and, 111
Neonatal intensive care, Sonoma Valley Conference on, 312

Neonatal intensive care, Sonoma Valley Conference on, case studies presented at, 313–314
  four clinical questions raised at, 317–318
  major considerations at, 315–317
  moral policy for, 318–333
    commentary on, 320–331
    ethical propositions in, 319–320
    procedural recommendations made at, 331–333
Neonatal mortality: poverty and, 301
  prematurity and, 291–292
    central-nervous-system deficits and, 300
    prematurity as major cause of mortality, 288
    prenatal care and, 294–295
    table, 295
    table, 292
  reducing: drop in last half of century, 6
    with nurse-midwives (*see* Nurse-midwives)
    with proper prenatal care, 271
  in Temple University experience, 22, 23
Neonatal mortality rate, urban (1950), 300
Neonatal period, prognosis for low-birthweight infants in, 250–253
  tables, 250–252
Neonatology, recommendations for research in, 332
Nervousness, vulnerable child syndrome and, table, 186
Neurosis, theory of traumatic, 80
Newborn Center (Children's Hospital, Denver), 263
Newton, M., 118
Newton, N., 118
Newton, Sir Isaac, 199
New York Hospital-Cornell Medical Center, 152, 153
NOAs (*see* Nurse-midwives)
Noirot, E., 136
Nonabusive families, characteristics of, 217, 222
Nonabusive mothers, characteristics of, 217–218
Noninstinctual nature of ego-relatedness, 173
Nonmother, stranger as, 167
Nonorgiastic interactions, infant-object, 159
Nonwhites (*see* Race)
Normal delivery, levels of deprivation in, 124
Nuckolls, Katherine B., 13, 62–75
Nurse-midwives (nurse obstetric assistants; NOAs), reducing neonatal mortality rate with, 271, 288–298
  general functions of nurse-midwives, 289–290
  study materials and methods, 290–291
  study results, 291–298
  tables, 292–295, 297
Nurseries, premature, role and responsibilities of mothers in, 113–115
Nursery and Children's Hospital, 113
Nurses: effects of birth of defective children on, 354–355
  (*See also* Famly nurse practitioners; Nurse-midwives)
Nursing Care Plan developed at University Hospital, 275
Nutrition: at Cooperative School, 41
  pregnancy outcome and, 24
  prematurity and poor, 5

Obesity in vulnerable child syndrome, table, 186
Object constancy concept (object conservation concept), 110, 161
  separation anxiety and, 169–171
Object-hungry infants, 172
Object permanence concept, 170
Object relations development, 157–177
  current theoretical models of, 158–162
    developmental psychology of Piaget as, 160–161
    ethology as, 159–160
    learning theory as, 161–162

Object relations development: current theoretical
    models of: psychoanalytic object relations
    theory as, 158–159
  manifestations of pathologic, 171–173
  normative studies of, 162–171
    approach-avoidance sequences, 165–167
    fear of strangers, 167–169
    infant object relating during the first three months,
        164–165
    maternal aspects of early attachment, 162–164
    separation and object constancy problems in,
        169–171
    visual interactions and gaze system in, 162
Object seeking, 159
Obstetrics and Gynecology, Department of (Temple
    University), 21
Obstetrics and Gynecology, Department of (University
    Hospital), 274, 283–286
Occupations held by parents of children with
    failure-to-thrive syndrome, 207–208
  table, 208
Ominous infant phenomena (neonatal crisis syndrome),
    181
Open-field accident infants, characteristics of,
    228–229
Oral contraceptives, 281–282, 285
Ordinary medical care, defined, 335n.
Osofsky, Howard J., 9, 14–26, 33, 41
Overprotectiveness, 179, 187, 198
Owens, C., 92
Oxygen therapy for low-birthweight infants, 246

Pagliaro, M. A., 37
Paired comparison questionnaires in maternal
    self-confidence study, 142
Pannor, R., 39
Parad, H. J., 30, 93
Parent-infant interactions: direction of effects problem
    in, 160
  (See also Mother-infant interactions)
Parentage, personhood and human, 341, 342
Parents: abusive, general characteristics of, 215
  of children with failure-to-thrive syndrome, health
      of, 208
  of defective newborns, involuntary euthanasia and:
      emotional and ethical dilemmas facing
      parents, 336–338
    final authority rests with parents, 357–359
    prosecution risks and, 339
  difficult infants as sign of parental inadequacy,
      171
  of high-risk infants, 332–333
    dilemma facing, 315–316
    responsibility of, 319–320
  in life-change events-prematurity study, 52–54
    tables, 53, 54
  of low-birthweight infants: intelligence assessment
      of parents, 249
    visiting by parents, 248
  (See also Fathers; Mothers; Prematurity, parental
      reactions to)
Parity: effects of, on child development, 19
  in premature mothers: and feelings of biological
      incompetence, 138
    maternal self-confidence and, 146, 148
  relationship between spacing of pregnancies,
      pregnancy outcome and, 24–26
  social class and, 17
Parmelee, A., 115
Pasamanick, B., 19, 20, 248
Pascal, Blaise, 199
Passive accidents, 228, 229
Pathologic object relational development, 171–173
Pavlova, Anna, 199

Peabody Picture Vocabulary Test (PPVT), 265
Pearling, L. I., 90
Peckham, Marsha, 353n.
Pedersen, Frank, 168, 169
Pediatrics (magazine), 315
Pediatrics, Department of (University of California,
    San Francisco), 316
Peer groups, pregnant teenagers' need to identify with,
    35–36
Perceptual ability at birth, 164
Perinatal mortality: 1935–1968, 14
  1967, 4
  prematurity as prime factor related to, 17–18
    (See also Prematurity)
  race and, 15
  social class and, 16
Perinatal period, prognosis for low-birthweight infants
    in, 250–253
  tables, 250–252
Perkins, R. F., 39
Personhood: of defective infants, 340–345
  withholding, from certain high-risk infants, 315
Phibbs, R. H., 312–334
Philadelphia-Camden Social Service Exchange, 210
Philadelphia School Board, 277, 278
Philadelphia Society to Protect Children, 210
Physical growth: of failure-to-thrive children,
    follow-up on, table, 212
  of low-birthweight children, 253–254
Physical punishment, child abuse and, 232–233
Physicians: duties of, 319–321
    defined, 320–321
  in early infancy health crises, 196, 198, 200
  effects of birth of defective children on, 354–355
  effects of shortage of, 288
  involuntary euthanasia and, final authority of
      physicians, 357–359, 363–364
Piaget, Jean, 158, 160–162, 166, 168, 170
Picasso, Pablo, 122, 199
PKU Anxiety Syndrome, 197
Plumb, N., 119
Population Council, Inc., 283
Postpartum period: activities of teenagers in, in
      University Hospital study, 279–280
    table, 280
  care given in, in Madera County study, 295
  critical nature of, in establishment of mother-infant
      relations, 150–157
    tables, 151, 152
Potter, 359n.
Poverty, 14–26, 271, 273
  chronic stress and, 230
  deficient health services and, 299
  elimination of, 310
  low birthweight and, 9
  pregnancy outcome and, 15–18
    experience at Temple University Health Service
        Center and, 20–24
      tables, 22–24
  pregnancy parameters, child development and,
      18–20
  pregnancy risk and, 24–25
  prematurity and, 4–5, 301
    (See also Prematurity)
  teenage pregnancies and, 31
PPVT (Peabody Picture Vocabulary Test), 265
Pregnancy: adaptive potential for pregnancy score,
    table, 70
  child abuse as phenomenon related to, 215
  failure-to-thrive syndrome and: attitudes toward
      pregnancy and, 209
    history of pregnancy and, 206
  high-risk, determining factors in, 306
  as maturational crisis, 77

Pregnancy: as maturational crisis: as biologically-determined maturational crisis, 222
  personality functioning affected by, 105
  poverty, child development and parameters of, 18–20
  prematurity and attitudes toward, 126, 148, 220
  as stress, abusive mothers and, 231
  (See also Teenage pregnancies)
Pregnancy outcome: anxiety and, 64
  health care services and, 16, 25–26
  poverty and, 15–18
    experience at Temple University Health Service Center, 20–24
    tables, 22–24
  psychosocial assets, life-change events and (see Life-change events, psychosocial assets and)
  stress and, 11
Premature mothers, 3–4
  attitudes toward delivery among, 81–82
  (See also Mother-infant separation; Prematurity; Psychological tasks facing premature mothers)
Premature nurseries, role and responsibilities of mothers in, 113–115
Prematurity: attitudes toward pregnancy and, 126, 148, 220
  child abuse and, 220–221
  child development and, 20
  as crisis, 76–79
  defined, 153
  elimination of, through prevention, 308
  factors favoring, 5–6
  mortality and morbidity as related to, 4
    (See also Neonatal mortality, prematurity and)
  mother-infant interactions and: mother's attitude and disordered interactions, 102–103
    resumption of, as psychological task, 85, 98, 124
  mothering disability syndrome associated with, 192
  parental reactions to, 89–101
    data collection, 92–94
    (See also Mental health outcome, parental reactions to prematurity and)
  percentage of, 105
  as prime factor related to perinatal mortality, 17–18
    (See also Perinatal mortality)
  socioeconomic factors of, 4–5, 301–302
    (See also specific socioeconomic factors)
  stress and, 11
  among teenagers, 41, 271, 278
    table, 279
  vulnerable child syndrome and, 189
  (See also Acute emotional disorders, maternal reactions to prematurity as; High-risk infants; Life-change events, relationship between prematurity and)
Prenatal care, 21
  low birthweight and lack of, 23–24
  in Madera County study: live births related to, table, 295
    table, 293–295
  reducing prematurity and neonatal mortality rate with proper, 271, 288
  in University Hospital study, 276–278
    table, 277
Prenatal Clinic (University Hospital), 274–283, 286
President's Manpower Report, 302
President's Panel Report, 301, 303
Primary anxiety, separation anxiety as, 169–170
Privation: deprivation differentiated from, 171
  experienced by object-hungry infants, 172
Prognosis: for high-risk infants: resource allocation and, 320
  value of life-saving intervention and, 319

Prognosis: (See also Low-birthweight infants, prognosis for; Survival rate)
Prolonged postpartum separation, defined, 153, 155
Prosecution, involuntary euthanasia and risks of, 338, 339
Proximity-seeking behavior, survival value of, 160
Prugh, Dane, 78
Psychoanalytic object relations theory, 158–159
Psychological development of low-birthweight infants, assessed, 249
Psychological disequilibrium, acute crises as periods of, 89–92
Psychological life, development of, 110–111
Psychological sequelae of early infancy health crises (see Early infancy health crises, psychologic sequelae of; Failure-to-thrive syndrome; Vulnerable child syndrome)
Psychological tasks facing premature mothers, 84–86, 98–102
  listed, 124
  relationship of task accomplishment to mental health outcome, 98–100
  testing hypotheses relating mental health outcome to, 100–102
    table, 101
Psychology: developmental, 160–161
  ego, 158
Psychosocial assets (see Life-change events, psychosocial assets and)
Psychosomatic problems related to early infancy health crises, 199
Psychotherapy for habitual abortions, 10–11
Public Assistance, Department of (Philadelphia, Penna.), 210
Public Health Nursing (Philadelphia, Penna.), 210
Public Health Service (U.S.), 303
Public Welfare, Department of (Philadelphia, Penna.), 210
Punishment, child abuse and physical, 232–233

Quality of life of defective infants, involuntary euthanasia and, 346–349

Race: of abused children: in Fifty Family Study, 216
  in Infant Accident Study, 224, 237
  of abusive mothers, 230, 232
  birthweight and, 220
  in Cooperative School study, 31
  failure-to-thrive syndrome and, 206
  and family attitudes toward pregnant teenagers, 33
  family size and, 17
  infant mortality and, 15, 16, 273
  low birthweight and (1967), 18
  pregnancy outcome and, 15–16
    in Temple University experience, 21–23
    table, 23
  of pregnant teenagers in University Hospital study, 276
  prematurity and, 5
Rahe, Richard H., 12, 47–48, 54, 66
Rapoport, Rhona, 91, 103
Rawls, J., 350n.
Ray, G., 181n.
Reed, L., 181n.
Reid, Duncan E., 271, 299–311
Reiner, B. S., 38, 40
Reinhart, John B., 180, 214–242
Religion of pregnant teenagers in University Hospital study, 276
Relocation Bureau (Philadelphia, Penna.), 210
Repeat pregnancies, rate of, among teenagers, 280–283, 286
  table, 280

Reproduction patterns: fetal and neonatal mortality and, 21
   pregnancy outcome and, 17
Resource allocation in neonatal intensive care, 317–318, 320
   medicomoral rule of triage and, 330–331
   table, 328–329
Response expectancies of infants, 161–162
   approach-avoidance sequences and, 166
Response failures: maternal, object relations development and, 172, 173
   parental, approach-avoidance sequences and, 166
Resuscitation: of low-birthweight infants at birth, 244–245
   recommendations for establishing criteria of, 332
Retarded abused children, maternal verbal responses to, in Infant Accident Study, 236
Revised Stanford-Binet Intelligence Scale, 248
Reynolds, E. O. R., 181, 243–262
Rh blood group incompatibility, mothering disability syndrome associated with, 192
Richards, Martin, 165
Richmond, J., 116
Rider, R. V., 18
Right to life of defective newborns, 337
   conceptual capability and, 343–344
Robbins, F. C., 192
Robertson, John A., 272, 335–364
Robey, A., 40
Robinson, D., 39
Robson, Kenneth S., 109, 119, 157–177
Rockefeller Panel Report, 303
Rolnick, A. R., 119, 200
Rooming-in, 113, 115
   breast feeding increased with, 119–120
Rose, J. A., 192, 199, 200
Rosenberg, M., 90
Rosenberg, P. P., 90
Rosenblatt, J. S., 136
Rosenbluth, D., 136
Rosenwaike, Ira, 10
Rousseau, Jean-Jacques, 199
Rubenstein, Judith, 123
Rubin, R., 119
Rubinstein, E., 39
Rubinstein, J., 168
Russell, J. K., 19
Rutter, Michael, 169

Sackett, Gene P., 167, 173
Salk, Lee, 109, 150–157
Salkovitz, Lisa, 315
Sample population: in communication skills study, 263–264
   table, 264
   of life-change events-prematurity study, parental screening interviews of, 52–54
   tables, 53, 54
   in low-birthweight infant study, 244
   in parental reactions-to-prematurity study, 94
   in psychosocial assets-life-change events study, 67–69
     distribution of subjects by duration of pregnancy at clinic admission, table, 69
     tables, 68–69
   in study of relationship between life-change events and prematurity, 49–50
   in teenage pregnancy study, 275–276
   in Temple University experience, 21
Sarah Morris Hospital, 114
Sarrel, Phillip M., 41, 274, 279
Satellite clinics, family nurse practitioners in, 305–306
Sauber, M., 39
Schaffer, H. R., 165

Schaller, G., 159
Schedule of Recent Experiences (SRE), 63, 66, 68
Schema, defined, 161
School phobia, vulnerable child syndrome and, 184
   table, 185
Schools: medical, involvement in community health services, 309
   pregnant teenagers' rejection from, as emotional crisis, 33–36
   (*See also* Academic failure)
Schwartz, Jane Linker, 47–61
Schweitzer, Albert, 199
Scott, R. B., 18
Screening Inventory, 254
Seashore, Marjorie J., 109, 136–150
Seay, B., 172
Segal, Julius, 214*n.*
Self, sense of, capacity for having, legal personhood and, 342–343
Self-concepts of abused children, 221
Self-confidence, maternal (*see* Mother-infant separation, effects on maternal self-confidence)
Selye, Hans, 10
Separation (*see* Mother-infant separation)
Separation anxiety: object constancy problem and, 169–171
   in object-hungry infants, 172
   vulnerable child syndrome and, 184, 186–188
Sex: of abused children in Fifty Family Study, 216
   of children: in communication skills study, 264
     study results, 266
     in Infant Accident Study, 224
   mood distribution of abused children by, 234–235
Sex differences: in child abuse, 222
   in crying behavior, 171
   effects on maternal self-confidence of, 147
   in failure-to-thrive syndrome, 206
   in imposition of punishments, 233
   in stranger anxiety, 168, 169
Sex education, 26
Shaheen, Eleanor, 180, 202–213
Shakhashiri, Zekin A., 66*n.*
Shapiro, Esther, 182, 262–269
Shapiro, S., 16, 25
Sherard, E. S., 248
Shereshefsky, P. M., 42
Sheridan, M. D., 248, 254
Shorr, Dorothy, 152
Siblings of failure-to-thrive infants: age and spacing of, 206
   health of, 208
   illegitimacy and, 209
Silber, E., 90
Simmons, O. G., 104
Sleeplessness in vulnerable child syndrome, 184–187
   tables, 185, 186
Slyter, H., 119
Smiling behavior: approach-avoidance sequences and, 166–167
   effects of, on mother-infant interactions, 234
   maternal aspects of early attachment and, 163–164
   of object-hungry infants, 172
   as ritualized appeasement gesture, 162
Smith, Clement, 315, 332*n.*
Smith, David, 356*n.*
Smith, Nora, 76*n.*
Smoking, prematurity and, 5
Social behavior, stranger anxiety and development of, 168, 169
Social class: child abuse and, 230–231
   child development and, 20
   complications, age and, table, 71
   discipline and, 233
   parity and, 17

Social class: of patients in psychosocial assets-life-change events study, 68–69
  table, 68
  pregnancy outcome and, 15–16, 18
  (*See also* Lower-class families; Lower-class mothers; Middle-class families; Middle-class mothers; Middle-class teenagers; Upper-class families; Upper-class mothers)
Social nature of ego-relatedness, 173
Social policy, advocated at Sonoma Valley Conference, 315–316
Social Readjustment Rating Scale (SRRS), 11, 47–59
  administration of, 50–51
  analyzing data obtained on, 51–52, 54–58
  table, 55–57
  responses to, by full-term mothers, 52–54, 57
  tables, 55–57
  table, 49
  usefulness of, 58–59
Social Security Administration, 271, 273
Society: costs to, of defective newborns, 355–356
  interest of: defined, 321
  well-being of infants and, 319
Socioeconomic status: birthweight and, 220
  of children in communication skills study, 264
  chronic stress and, 230
  of failure-to-thrive infants, 206–211
  tables, 207, 208
  pregnancy outcome and, 16–18
  of pregnant teenagers in University Hospital study, 275–276
  (*See also* specific socioeconomic factors)
Solnit, Albert J., 77*n.*, 126, 179, 183–195, 199, 200
Sonoma Valley Conference (*see* Neonatal intensive care)
Species-specific stimuli, 160
Speigel, John, 10
Spitz, Rene A., 109–111, 136, 167
Spontaneous abortions (*see* Abortions)
Squier, R., 11
SRE (Schedule of Recent Experiences), 63, 66, 68
SRRS (*see* Social Readjustment Rating Scale)
Stanford-Binet test, 19, 20
Stark, M. H., 77
State, the (*see* Society)
Stern, Daniel, 166
Stern, L., 178, 179*n.*
Stewart, Ann L., 181, 243–262
Stimuli, species-specific, in animal behavior, 160
Stranger anxiety (eight-month anxiety), 167–169
Stress: child abuse and, 231–232
  chronic, child abuse and, 229–230
  defined, 80*n.*
  diarrhea as response to, in vulnerable child syndrome, table, 186
  familial, in Infant Accident Study, 224
  life-change events and, 62–64
  menopause, puberty and pregnancy as periods of, 77
  spontaneous abortions and, 10–12
  (*See also* Anxiety; Crises; Marital stress)
Sullivan, D., 359*n.*
Sunshine, P., 266*n.*
Supreme Court, 315, 356
Survival rate: by gestational age, table, 251
  of high-risk infants, 3
  of low-birthweight infants, 250–253, 256
  tables, 250–252
  of prematures, 77
Susceptibility to disease, concept of generalized, 72
Swayze, J., 354*n.*
Symptomatology of vulnerable child syndrome, 184–187
  table, 185–186

Tactile contact, 116, 163
Talis, H. P., 265
Tanner, J. M., 253
TAPPS index score (psychological asset score), 65, 67, 69–71
  correlation of LCS and, with complications, table, 71
Tartaglia, J., 265
Tawney, R. H., 308
Teaching, 232–233
  child abuse and lack of discrimination between punishment and, 233
Teen Obstetrical Clinic (University Hospital), 274–285
Teen pregnancies: annual number of, 271
  emotional crises and, 30–47
    adaptation to maternal role, 43–44
    data used in study of, 30–31
    dynamic factors and development of methods to cope with, 36–41
    health crises and, 41–43
    rejection from school as, 33–36
    telling the family as first emotional crisis, 31–32
  prematurity among, 5
  University Hospital study of, 273–287
    clinics described, 274–275
    depressing cycle set in motion by, 274
    family planning in, 281–283
    medical findings in, 278–279
    table, 279
    postpartum activities in, 279–280
    table, 280
    prenatal contacts made, 276–278
    table, 277
Temple University Health Service Center, study made at, 20–24
  tables, 23–24
Templin-Darley Articulation Screening Test, 265
Tervoort, B., 262
Tests used in communication skills study, 264–266
Therapeutic abortions (*see* Abortions)
Thomson, A. M., 18
Three-year-olds, follow-up study on low-birthweight, 248
Tinbergen, N., 164
"To Play Your Family" (film), 279
Tomar, Karen, 273–287
Tooley, Michael, 341*n.*, 343–344
Tooley, W. H., 312–324
Toxemia among pregnant teenagers, 278, 279
Traumatic neurosis, theory of, 80
Triage, medicomoral rule of, 330–331
Trumbo, R., 336*n.*
Truskowski, Marie, 180
Twin births, failure-to-thrive syndrome and, 206
Two Factor Index of Social Class, 69
Tyhurst, J. S., 90

Unhealthy mental health outcome of crisis, relationship between grappling patterns and, 94–96
Unintegrated organisms, infants as, 158
United States: estimates of population of (1980), 302
  neonatal mortality rate in, 288, 300
University-affiliated teaching hospitals, 309
University College Hospital (UCH; London, England), 181, 244, 251
University Hospital study (University of Pennsylvania) (*see* Teenage pregnancies, University Hospital study of)
Upper-class families, prematurity in, 5
Upper-class mothers, reproductive patterns of, 17

Valenstein, A. F., 77*n.*
Van den Berg, B. J., 181

Ventura, S. J., 40
Verbal responses, maternal: child development and, 236
    mental development, 238
Vincent, D. E., 36
Vision of five-year-olds in communication skills study, 267
Visiting patterns: mental health outcome and, 101
    table, 102
    of parents of low-birthweight infants, 248
    to premature nurseries, 115
Visotsky, H., 90
Visual behavior: in first three months of life, 164
    of low-birthweight children, 255
    (See also Gazing)
Vital statistics, Bureau of, 290, 291
Vocalizations, 164, 167
    maternal responses to, 236
    pathological object relations development and, 172
Voltaire (François Arouet), 199
Von der Ahe, G. V., 32
Vulnerable child syndrome, 179–180, 183–195
    clinical features of, 184
    factors predisposing to, and determinants of, 189–191
    management of, 192–194
    as pathological after-effect of mourning reaction, 191
    pediatric interviews dealing with, 188–189
    symptomatology of, 184–188
        table, 185–186
"Vulnerable Children Revisited, The," 195

Waldrop, M. F., 197
Wall, The (Hersey), 11
Warnaby, J., 344n.–345n.
Washington, University of, 47
Wechsler Adult Intelligence Scale, 249
Wechsler Intelligence Scale for Children (WISC), 20
Wechsler Preschool and Primary Intelligence Scale (WPPSI), 249, 265, 266

Weight: changes in, of failure-to-thrive infants, tables, 211, 212
    excessive gain among pregnant teenagers, 278
    obesity in vulnerable child syndrome, table, 186
    (See also Birthweight; Low-birthweight infants)
Welcher, D. W., 264, 267
Werner, E., 198
Wesley, 199
Wheeler, 337n., 351n.
White House Conference on Children (1971), 1
Whitehouse, R. H., 253
Wilcoxon Rank Sum Test, 52
Wilkinson, Frederick S., 271, 288–298
Williams, G., 336n., 340
Williams, J. A., 140
Windle, W. F., 19
Winnicott, D. W., 158, 159
WISC (Wechsler Intelligence Scale for Children), 20
Wittenberg, Clarissa, 214–242
Wolff, P. H., 161
Women: estimated increase in number of, between 20 and 25 years of age (by 1980), 302
    table, 303
    (See also Mothers)
World Health Organization (WHO), 305
Wortis, Helen, 78, 79n., 99, 181
Woutersz, T., 41
WPPSI (Wechsler Preschool and Primary Intelligence Scale), 249, 265, 266
Wright, Byron, 180, 214–242
Wright, David, 273–287
Wuthering Heights (Brontë), 11

Yale-New Haven Hospital, 335
Yerby, A. S., 16
Yernshalmy, J., 181
Young, L., 38
Young, Whitney, Jr., 301

Zuehlke, S., 119